JUSTICE LEAGUE of AMERICA

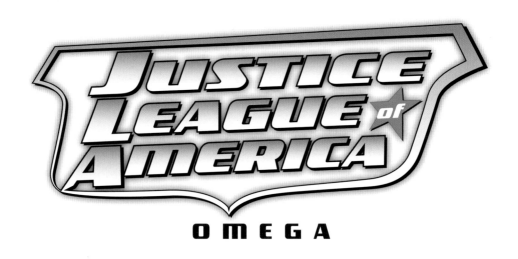

OMEGA

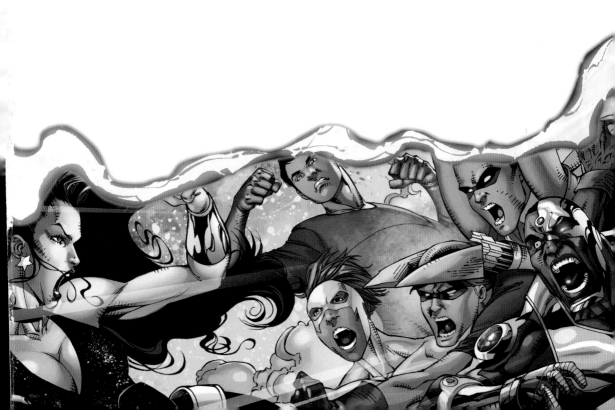

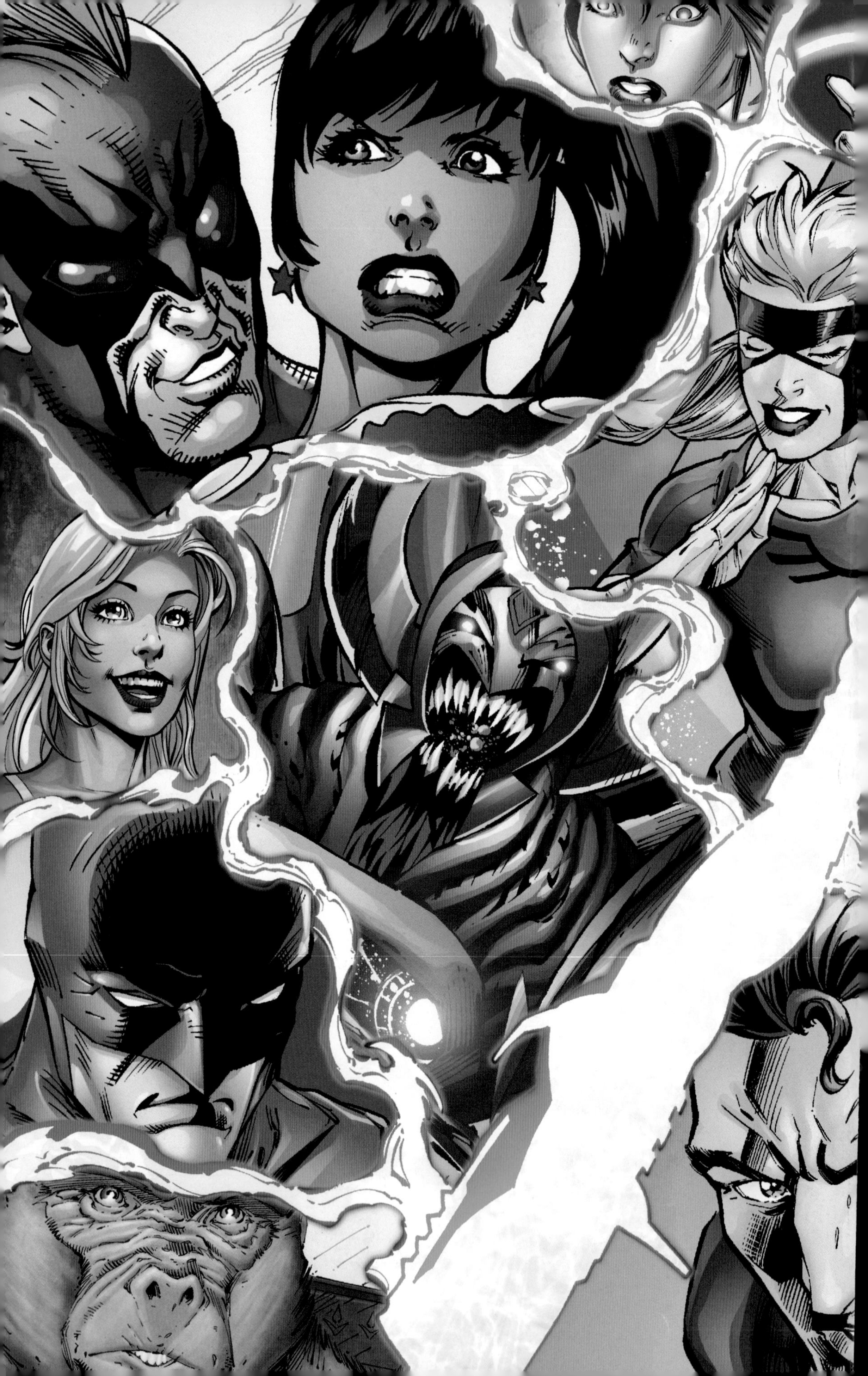

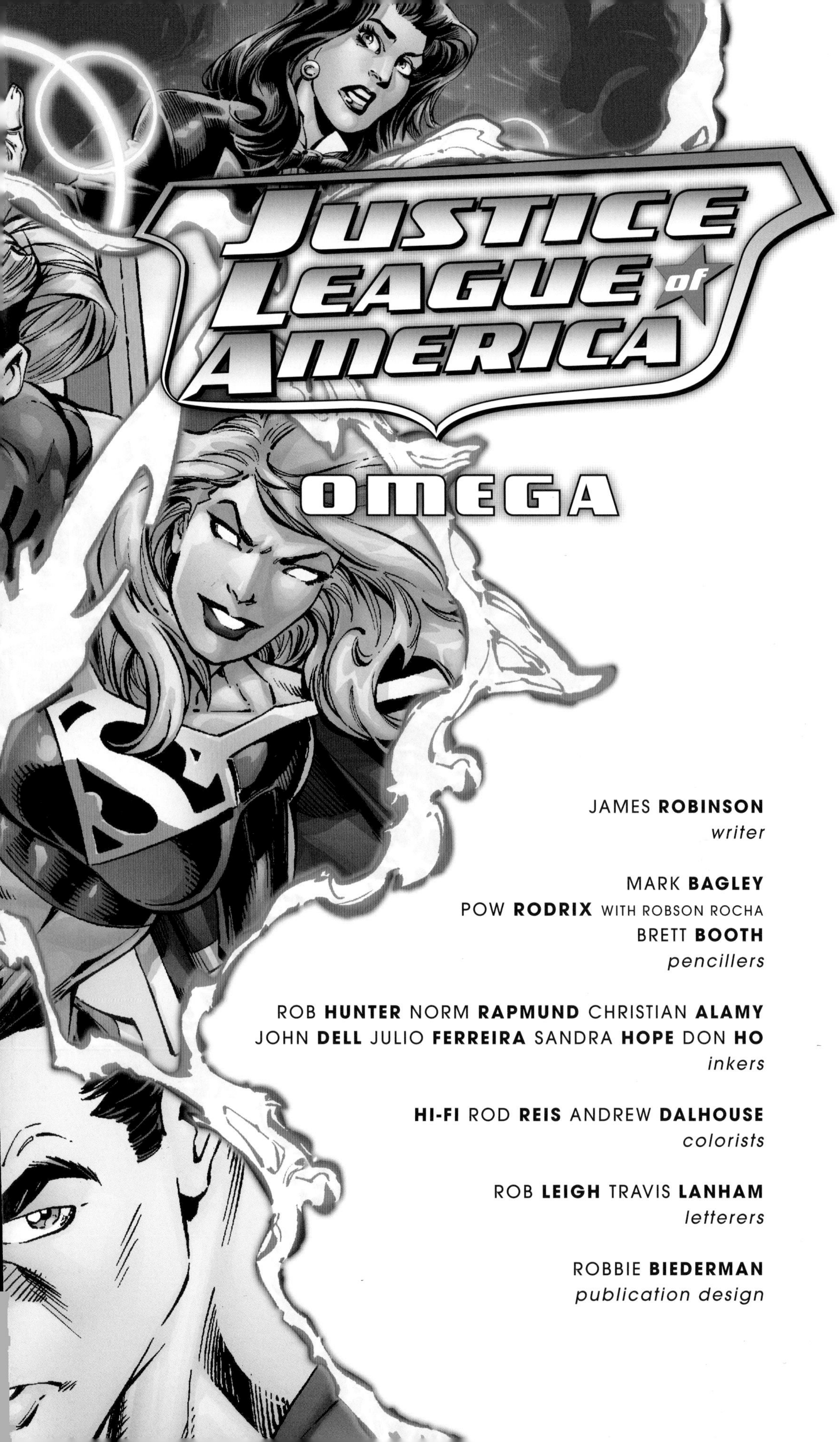

JUSTICE LEAGUE of AMERICA

OMEGA

JAMES **ROBINSON**
writer

MARK **BAGLEY**
POW **RODRIX** WITH ROBSON ROCHA
BRETT **BOOTH**
pencillers

ROB **HUNTER** NORM **RAPMUND** CHRISTIAN **ALAMY**
JOHN **DELL** JULIO **FERREIRA** SANDRA **HOPE** DON **HO**
inkers

HI-FI ROD **REIS** ANDREW **DALHOUSE**
colorists

ROB **LEIGH** TRAVIS **LANHAM**
letterers

ROBBIE **BIEDERMAN**
publication design

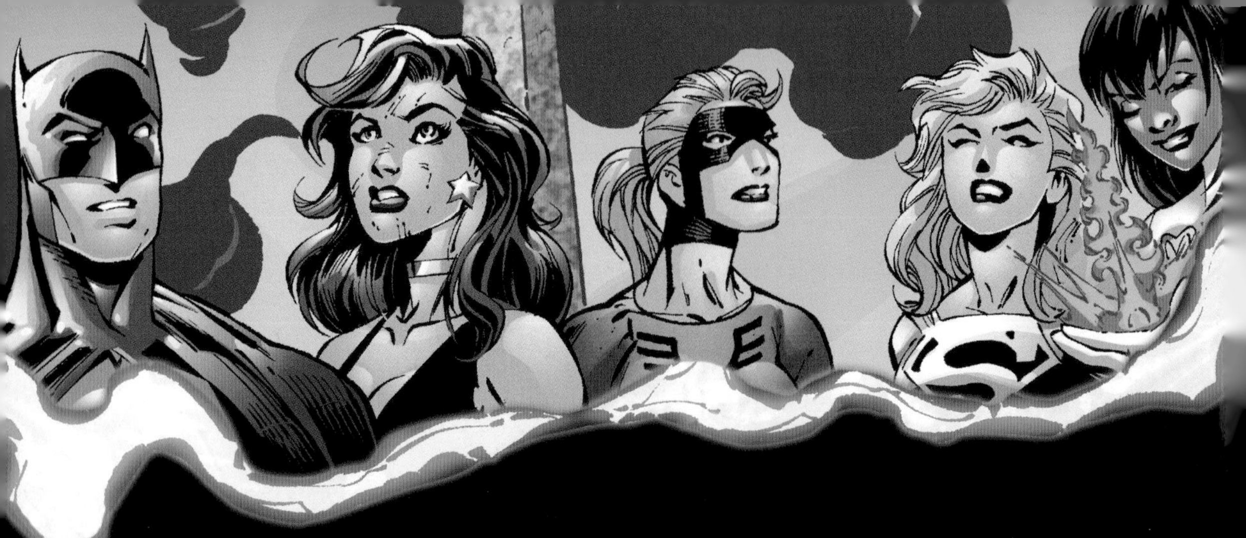

Eddie Berganza Adam Schlagman Editors - Original Series
Rex Ogle Associate Editor - Original Series
Ian Sattler Director Editorial, Special Projects and Archival Editions
Robbin Brosterman Design Director - Books
Eddie Berganza Executive Editor
Bob Harras VP - Editor in Chief

Diane Nelson President
Dan DiDio and Jim Lee Co-Publishers
Geoff Johns Chief Creative Officer
John Rood Executive VP - Sales, Marketing and Business Development
Amy Genkins Senior VP - Business and Legal Affairs
Nairi Gardiner Senior VP - Finance
Jeff Boison VP - Publishing Operations
Mark Chiarello VP - Art Direction and Design
John Cunningham VP - Marketing
Terri Cunningham VP - Talent Relations and Services
Alison Gill Senior VP - Manufacturing and Operations
David Hyde VP - Publicity
Hank Kanalz Senior VP - Digital
Jay Kogan VP - Business and Legal Affairs, Publishing
Jack Mahan VP - Business Affairs, Talent
Nick Napolitano VP - Manufacturing Administration
Ron Perazza VP - Online
Sue Pohja VP - Book Sales
Courtney Simmons Senior VP - Publicity
Bob Wayne Senior VP - Sales

JUSTICE LEAGUE OF AMERICA: OMEGA

DC Comics, 1700 Broadway, New York, NY 10019
A Warner Bros. Entertainment Company
Printed by RR Donnelly, Roanoke, VA, USA. 8/19/11.
HC ISBN: 978-1-4012-3243-6 SC ISBN: 978-1-4012-3356-3

SUSTAINABLE FORESTRY INITIATIVE
Certified Chain of Custody
Promoting Sustainable Forest Management
www.sfiprogram.org

Fiber used in this product line meets the sourcing requirements of the SFI program.
www.sfiprogram.org SGS-SFI/COC-US10/81072

JUSTICE LEAGUE OF AMERICA 49
cover by Mark Bagley, Rob Hunter & Ulises Arreola

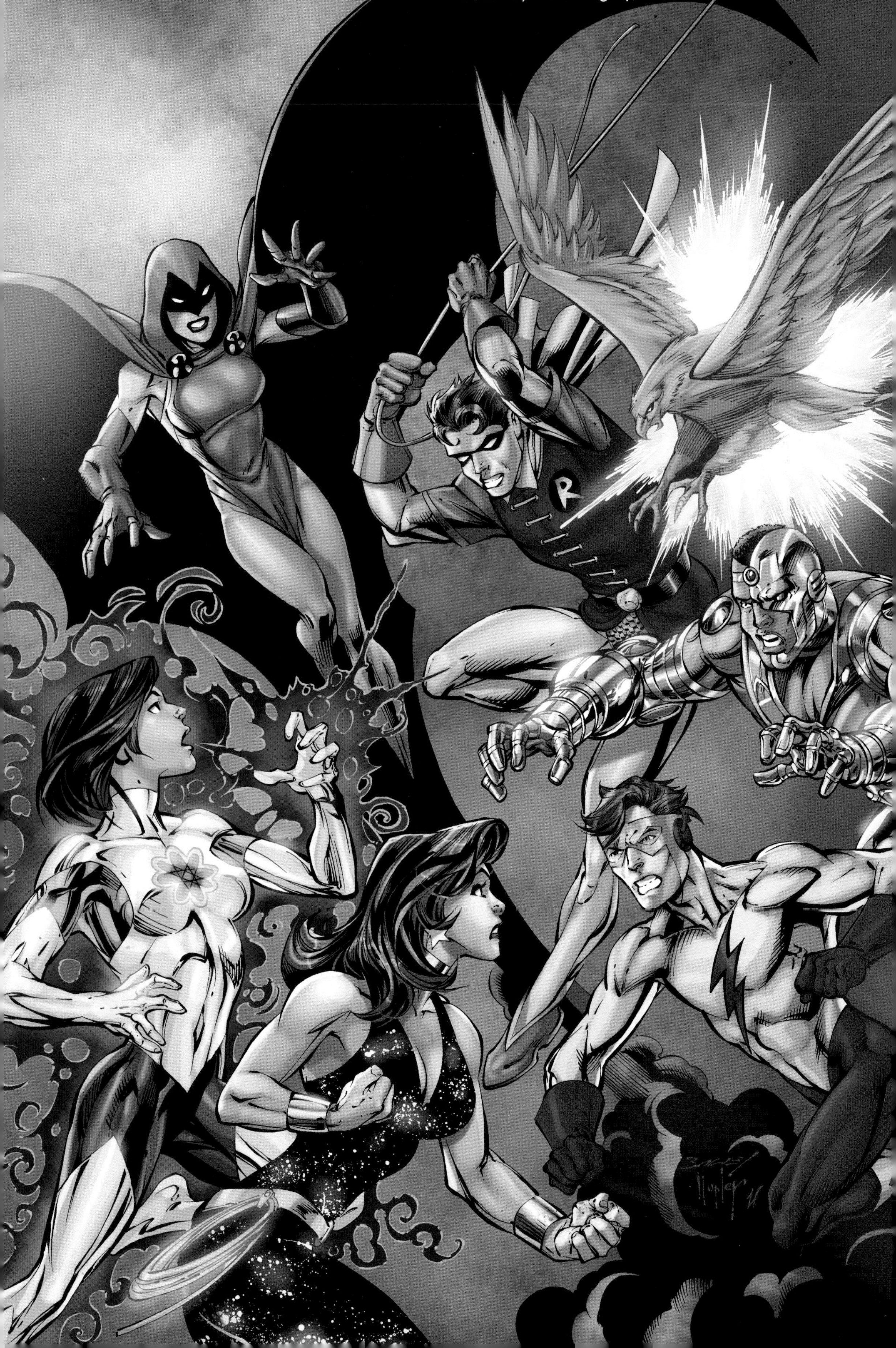

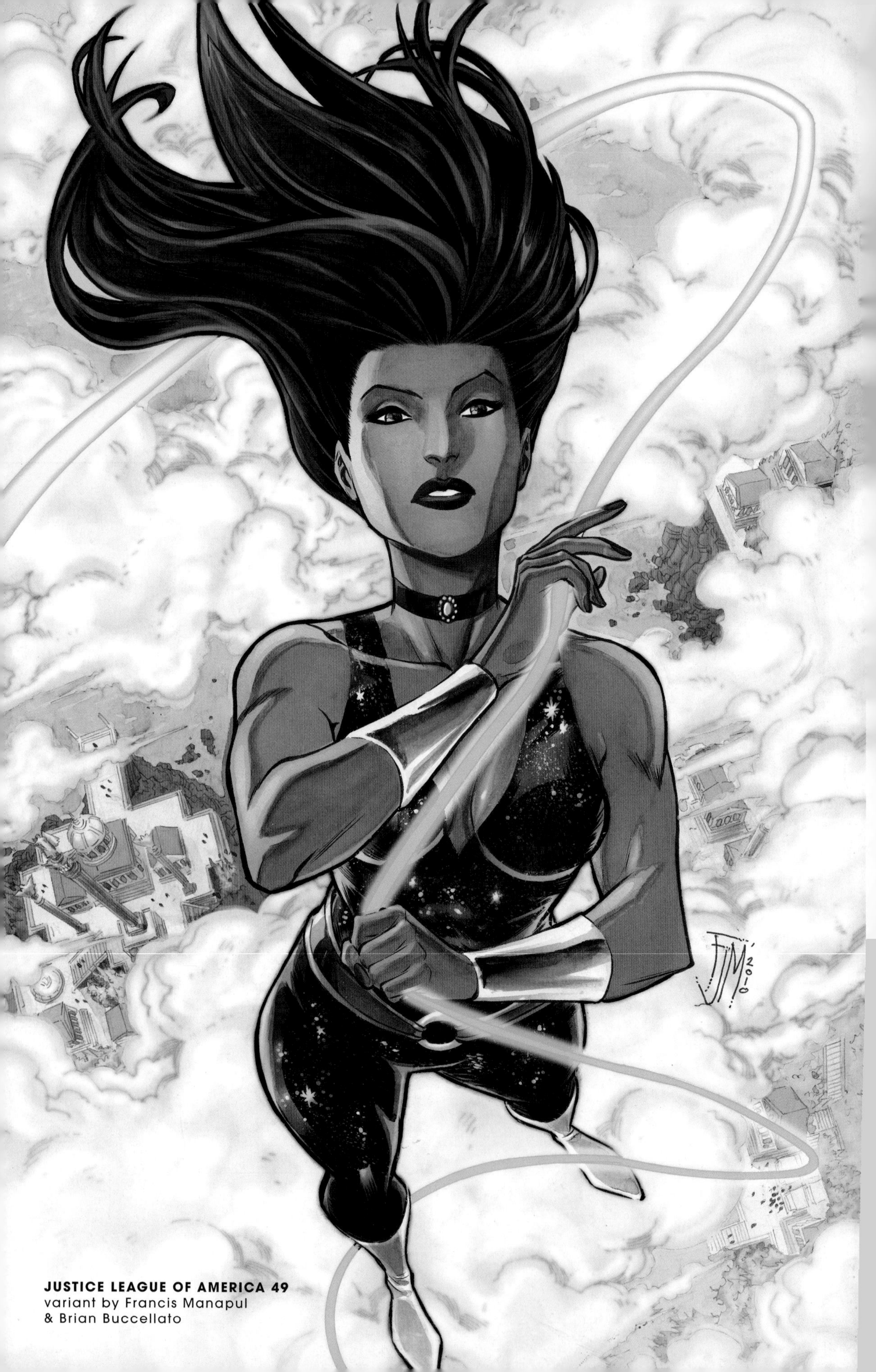

JUSTICE LEAGUE OF AMERICA 49
variant by Francis Manapul
& Brian Buccellato

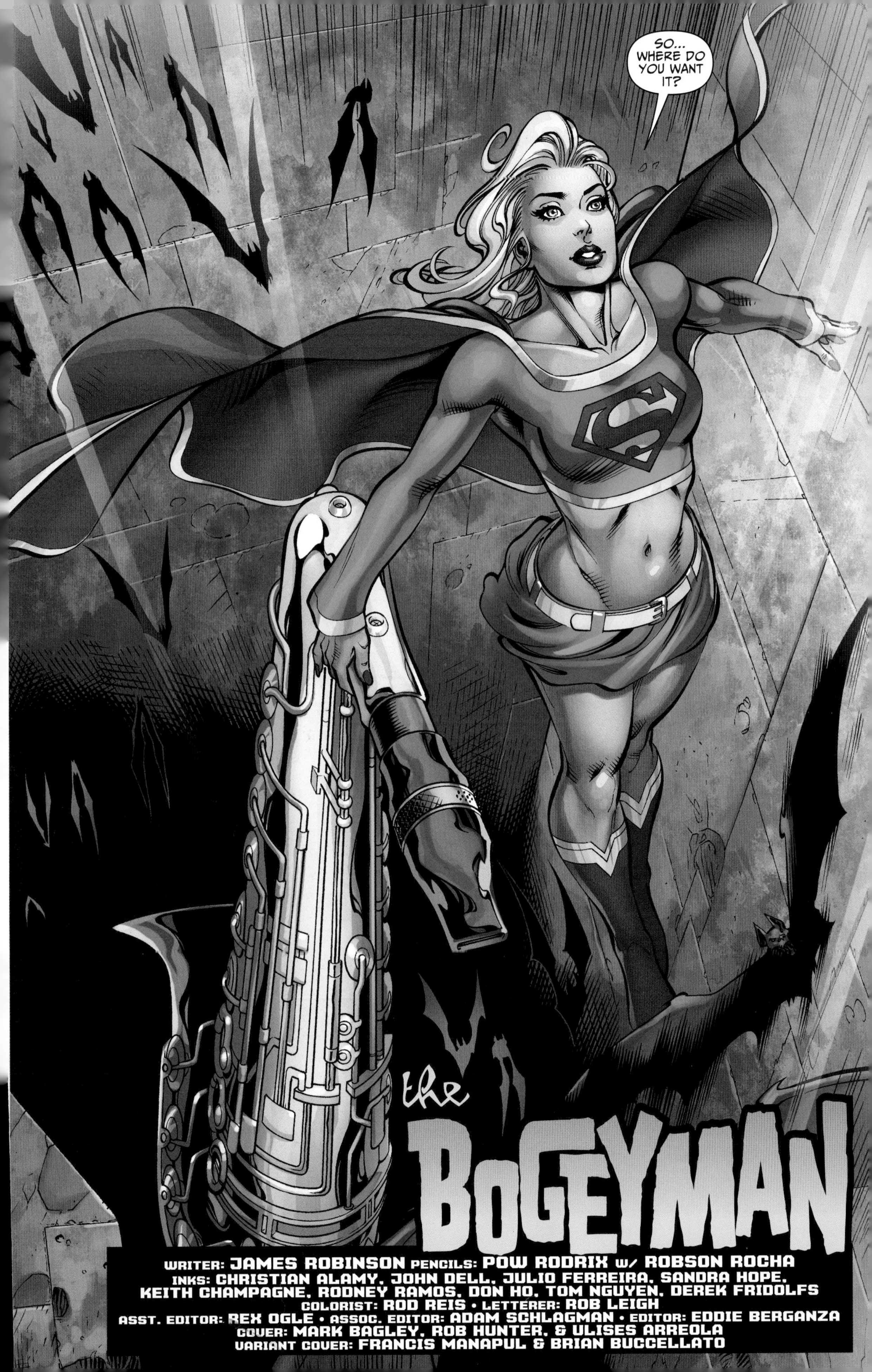

SO... WHERE DO YOU WANT IT?
the BOGEYMAN
WRITER: JAMES ROBINSON PENCILS: POW RODRIX W/ ROBSON ROCHA
INKS: CHRISTIAN ALAMY, JOHN DELL, JULIO FERREIRA, SANDRA HOPE, KEITH CHAMPAGNE, RODNEY RAMOS, DON HO, TOM NGUYEN, DEREK FRIDOLFS
COLORIST: ROD REIS • LETTERER: ROB LEIGH
ASST. EDITOR: REX OGLE • ASSOC. EDITOR: ADAM SCHLAGMAN • EDITOR: EDDIE BERGANZA
COVER: MARK BAGLEY, ROB HUNTER, & ULISES ARREOLA
VARIANT COVER: FRANCIS MANAPUL & BRIAN BUCCELLATO

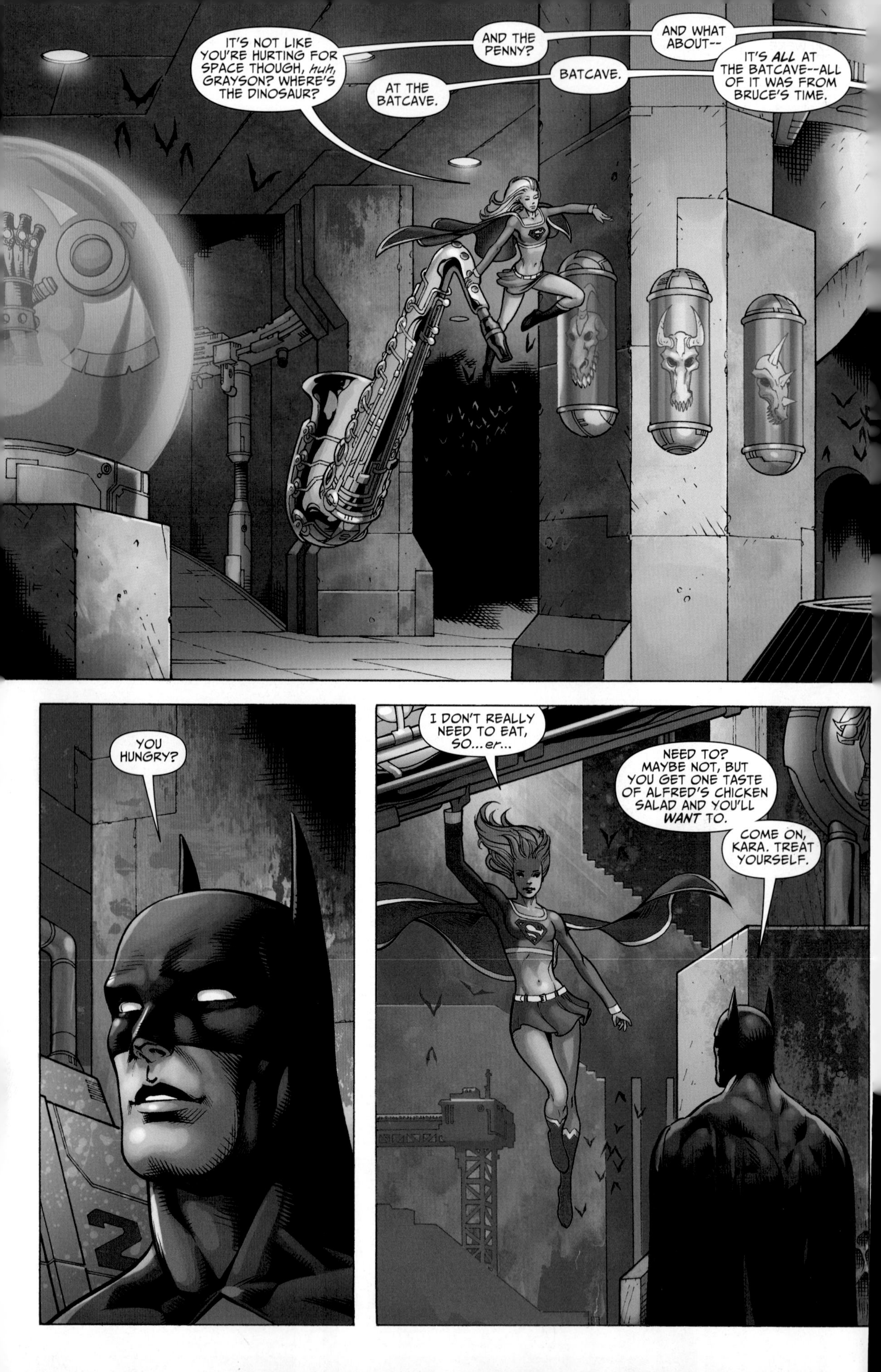
IT'S NOT LIKE YOU'RE HURTING FOR SPACE THOUGH, *huh*, GRAYSON? WHERE'S THE DINOSAUR?
AT THE BATCAVE.
AND THE PENNY?
BATCAVE.
AND WHAT ABOUT--
IT'S *ALL* AT THE BATCAVE--ALL OF IT WAS FROM BRUCE'S TIME.
YOU HUNGRY?
I DON'T REALLY NEED TO EAT, SO... *er*...
NEED TO? MAYBE NOT, BUT YOU GET ONE TASTE OF ALFRED'S CHICKEN SALAD AND YOU'LL *WANT* TO.
COME ON, KARA. TREAT YOURSELF.

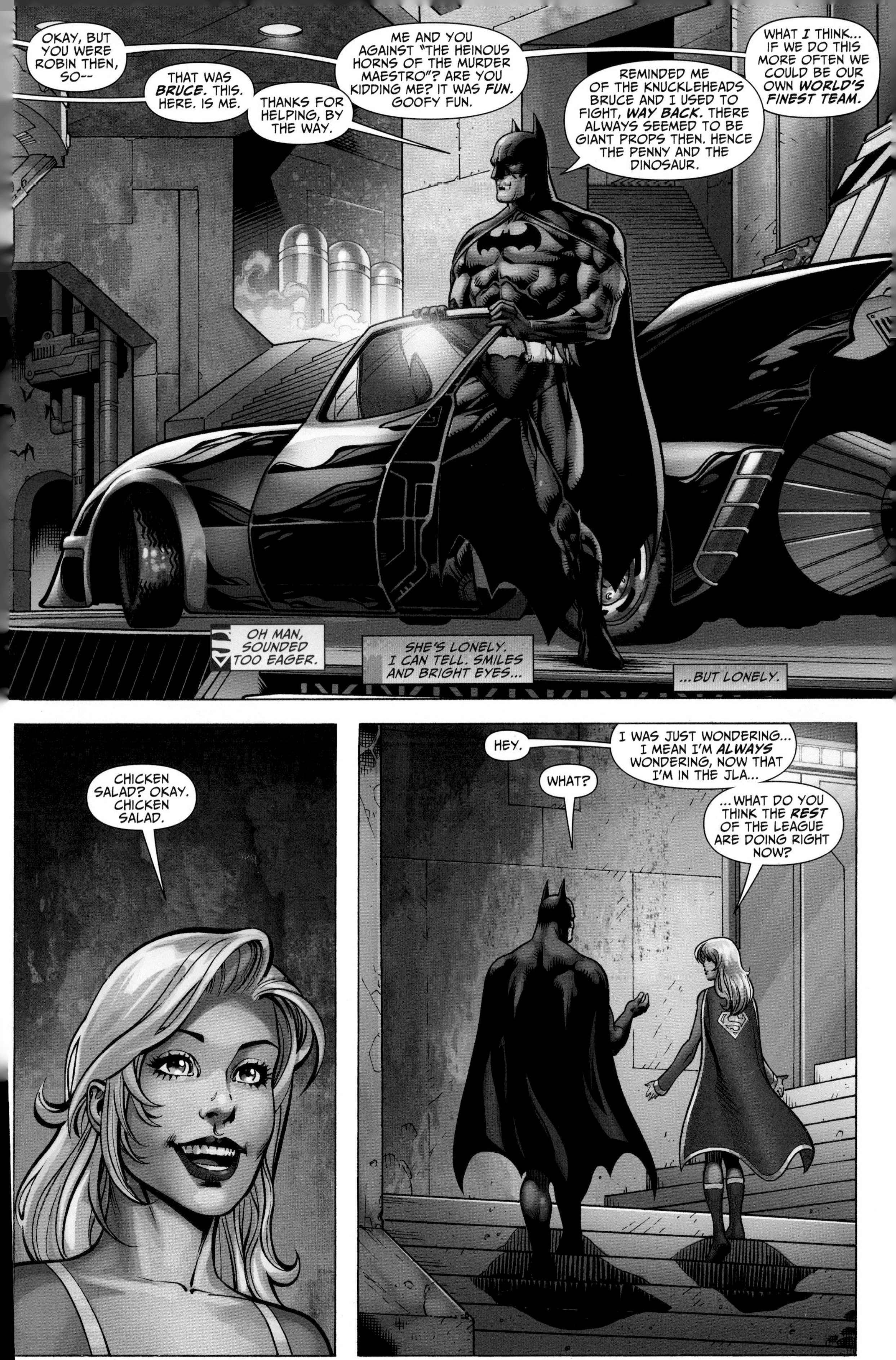

THANKS FOR HELPING, BY THE WAY.
ME AND YOU AGAINST "THE HEINOUS HORNS OF THE MURDER MAESTRO"? ARE YOU KIDDING ME? IT WAS *FUN.* GOOFY FUN.
REMINDED ME OF THE KNUCKLEHEADS BRUCE AND I USED TO FIGHT, *WAY BACK.* THERE ALWAYS SEEMED TO BE GIANT PROPS THEN. HENCE THE PENNY AND THE DINOSAUR.
OKAY, BUT YOU WERE ROBIN THEN, SO--
THAT WAS *BRUCE.* THIS. HERE. IS ME.
WHAT *I* THINK... IF WE DO THIS MORE OFTEN WE COULD BE OUR OWN *WORLD'S FINEST TEAM.*
OH MAN, SOUNDED TOO EAGER.
SHE'S LONELY. I CAN TELL. SMILES AND BRIGHT EYES...
...BUT LONELY.
CHICKEN SALAD? OKAY. CHICKEN SALAD.
HEY.
WHAT?
I WAS JUST WONDERING... I MEAN I'M *ALWAYS* WONDERING, NOW THAT I'M IN THE JLA...
...WHAT DO YOU THINK THE *REST* OF THE LEAGUE ARE DOING RIGHT NOW?

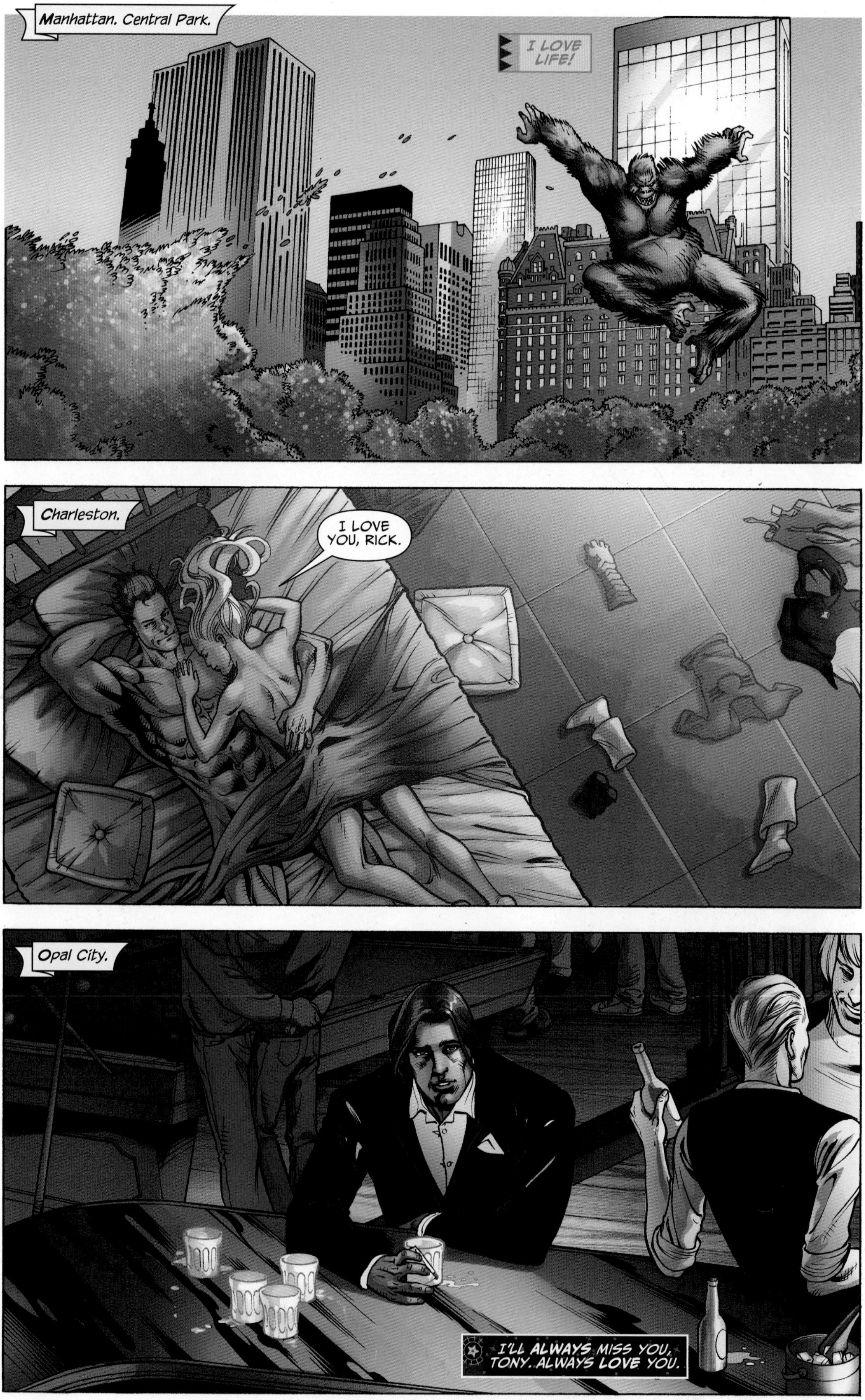
Manhattan. Central Park.
I LOVE LIFE!
Charleston.
I LOVE YOU, RICK.
Opal City.
I'LL ALWAYS MISS YOU, TONY. ALWAYS LOVE YOU.

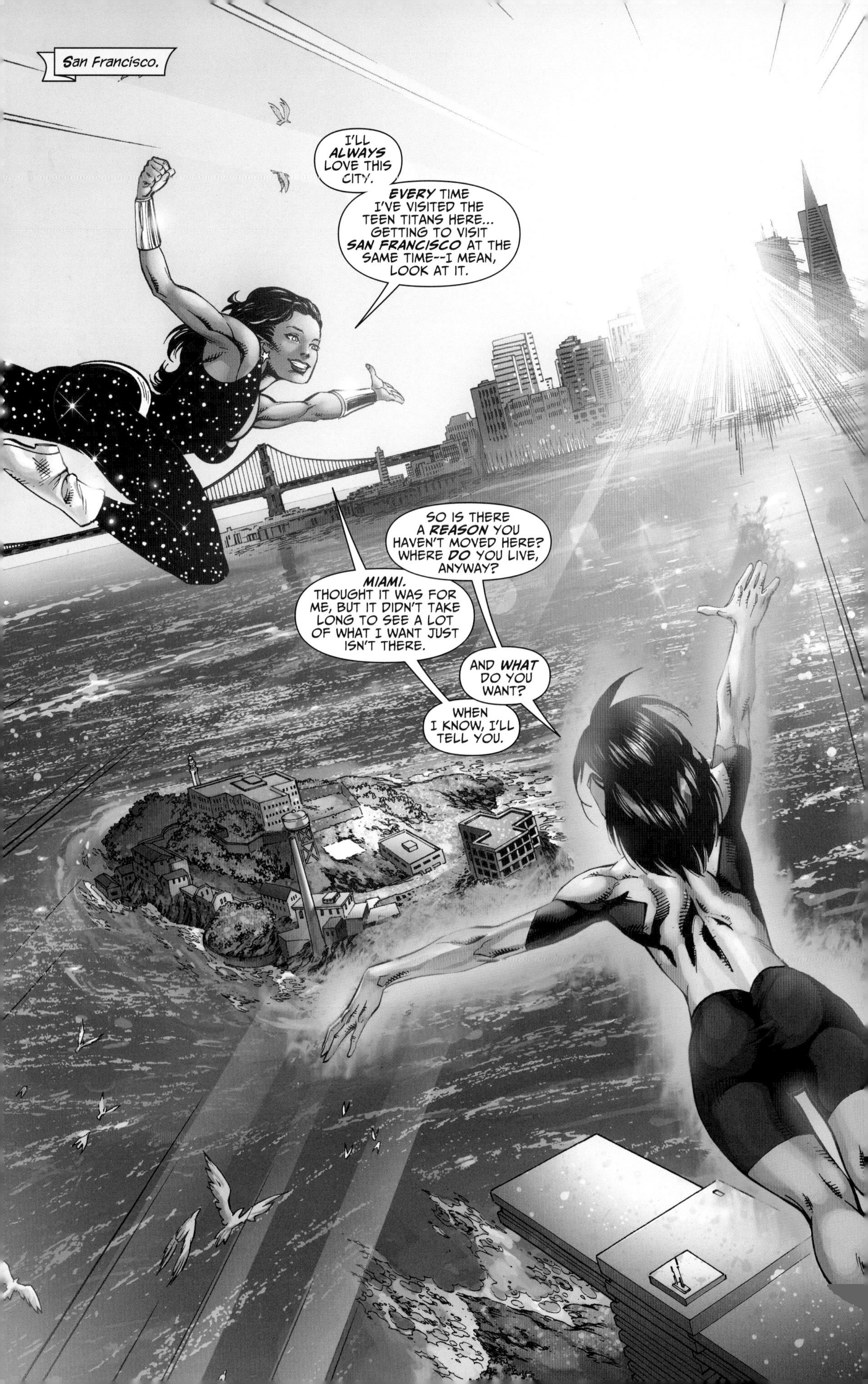
San Francisco.
I'LL ALWAYS LOVE THIS CITY.
EVERY TIME I'VE VISITED THE TEEN TITANS HERE... GETTING TO VISIT SAN FRANCISCO AT THE SAME TIME--I MEAN, LOOK AT IT.
SO IS THERE A REASON YOU HAVEN'T MOVED HERE? WHERE DO YOU LIVE, ANYWAY?
MIAMI. THOUGHT IT WAS FOR ME, BUT IT DIDN'T TAKE LONG TO SEE A LOT OF WHAT I WANT JUST ISN'T THERE.
AND WHAT DO YOU WANT?
WHEN I KNOW, I'LL TELL YOU.

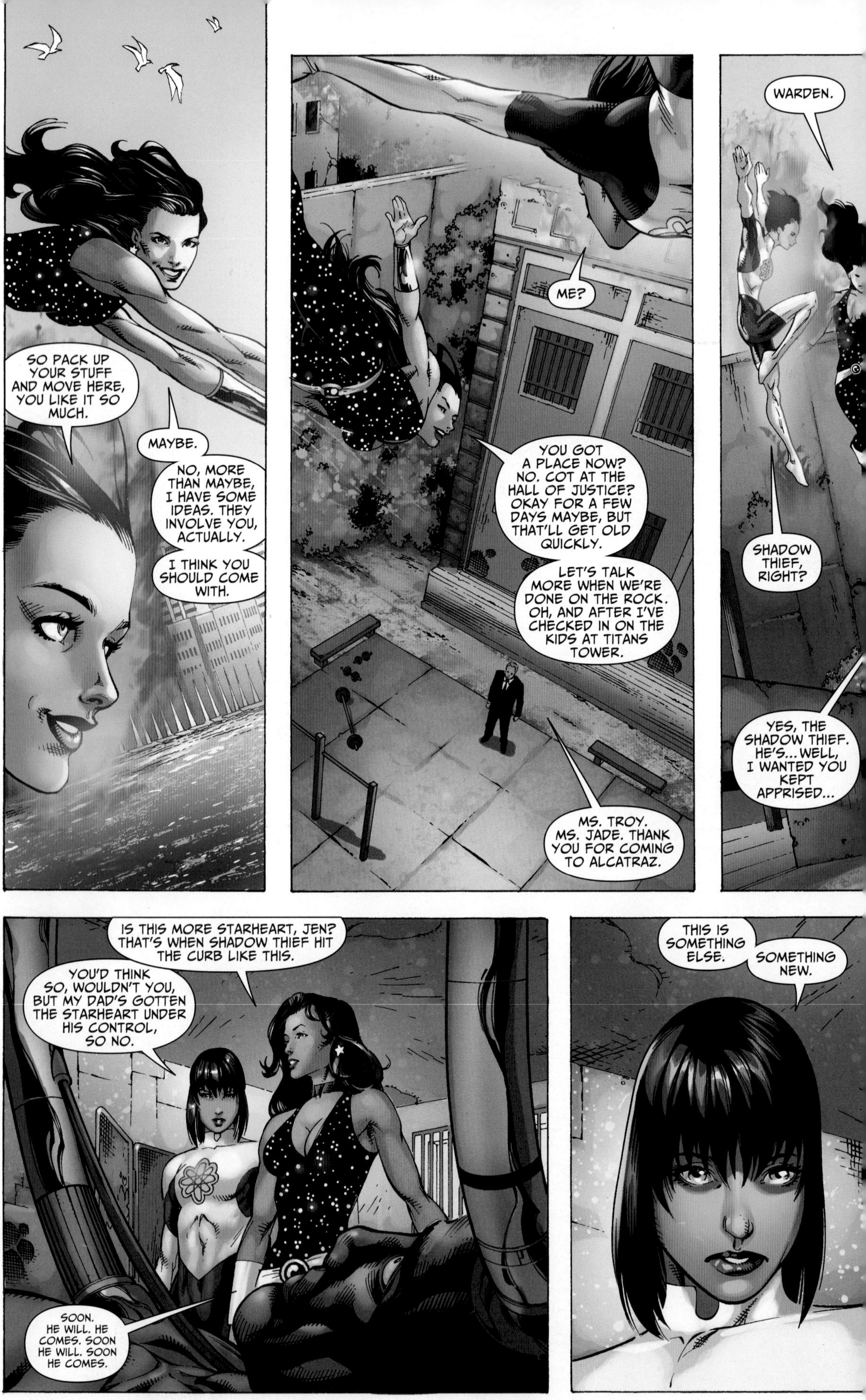
SO PACK UP YOUR STUFF AND MOVE HERE, YOU LIKE IT SO MUCH.
MAYBE.
NO, MORE THAN MAYBE, I HAVE SOME IDEAS. THEY INVOLVE YOU, ACTUALLY.
I THINK YOU SHOULD COME WITH.
ME?
YOU GOT A PLACE NOW? NO. COT AT THE HALL OF JUSTICE? OKAY FOR A FEW DAYS MAYBE, BUT THAT'LL GET OLD QUICKLY.
LET'S TALK MORE WHEN WE'RE DONE ON THE ROCK. OH, AND AFTER I'VE CHECKED IN ON THE KIDS AT TITANS TOWER.
MS. TROY. MS. JADE. THANK YOU FOR COMING TO ALCATRAZ.
WARDEN.
SHADOW THIEF, RIGHT?
YES, THE SHADOW THIEF. HE'S...WELL, I WANTED YOU KEPT APPRISED...
IS THIS MORE STARHEART, JEN? THAT'S WHEN SHADOW THIEF HIT THE CURB LIKE THIS.
YOU'D THINK SO, WOULDN'T YOU, BUT MY DAD'S GOTTEN THE STARHEART UNDER HIS CONTROL, SO NO.
SOON. HE WILL. HE COMES. SOON HE WILL. SOON HE COMES.
THIS IS SOMETHING ELSE.
SOMETHING NEW.

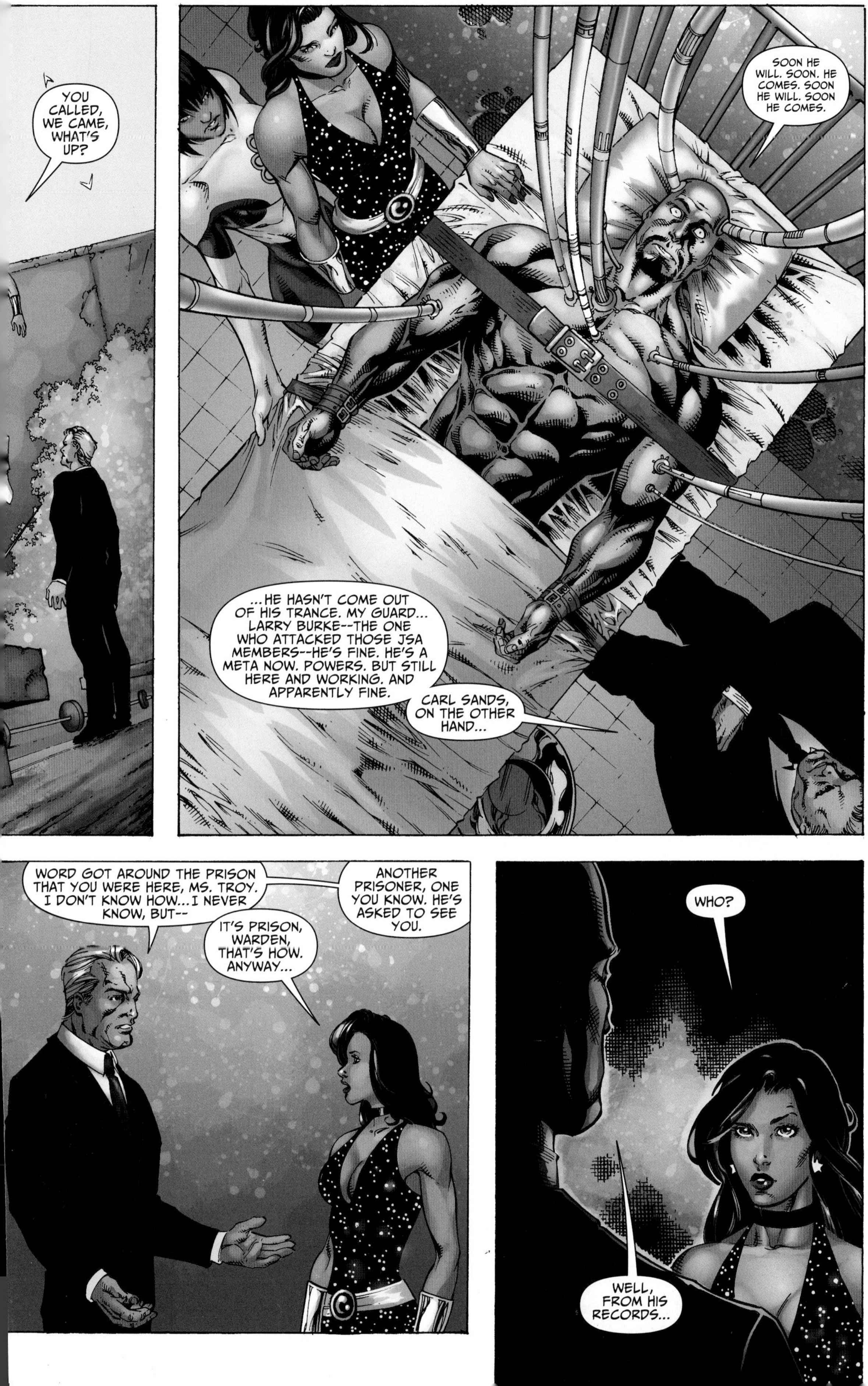
YOU CALLED, WE CAME, WHAT'S UP?
SOON HE WILL. SOON. HE COMES. SOON HE WILL. SOON HE COMES.
...HE HASN'T COME OUT OF HIS TRANCE. MY GUARD... LARRY BURKE--THE ONE WHO ATTACKED THOSE JSA MEMBERS--HE'S FINE. HE'S A META NOW. POWERS. BUT STILL HERE AND WORKING. AND APPARENTLY FINE.
CARL SANDS, ON THE OTHER HAND...
WORD GOT AROUND THE PRISON THAT YOU WERE HERE, MS. TROY. I DON'T KNOW HOW...I NEVER KNOW, BUT--
IT'S PRISON, WARDEN, THAT'S HOW. ANYWAY...
ANOTHER PRISONER, ONE YOU KNOW. HE'S ASKED TO SEE YOU.
WHO?
WELL, FROM HIS RECORDS...

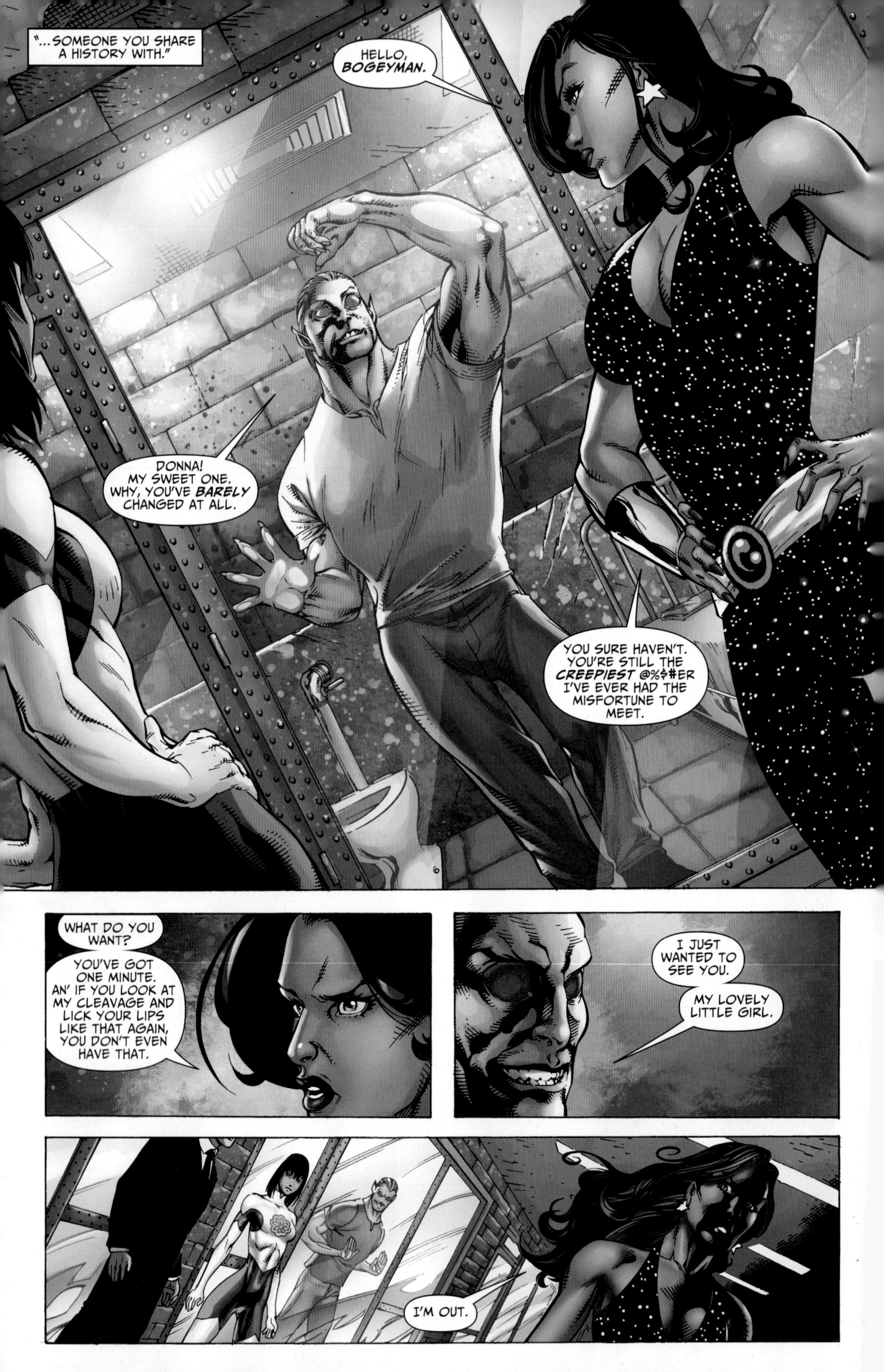
"...SOMEONE YOU SHARE A HISTORY WITH."
HELLO, BOGEYMAN.
DONNA! MY SWEET ONE. WHY, YOU'VE BARELY CHANGED AT ALL.
YOU SURE HAVEN'T. YOU'RE STILL THE CREEPIEST @%$#ER I'VE EVER HAD THE MISFORTUNE TO MEET.
WHAT DO YOU WANT?
YOU'VE GOT ONE MINUTE. AN' IF YOU LOOK AT MY CLEAVAGE AND LICK YOUR LIPS LIKE THAT AGAIN, YOU DON'T EVEN HAVE THAT.
I JUST WANTED TO SEE YOU.
MY LOVELY LITTLE GIRL.
I'M OUT.

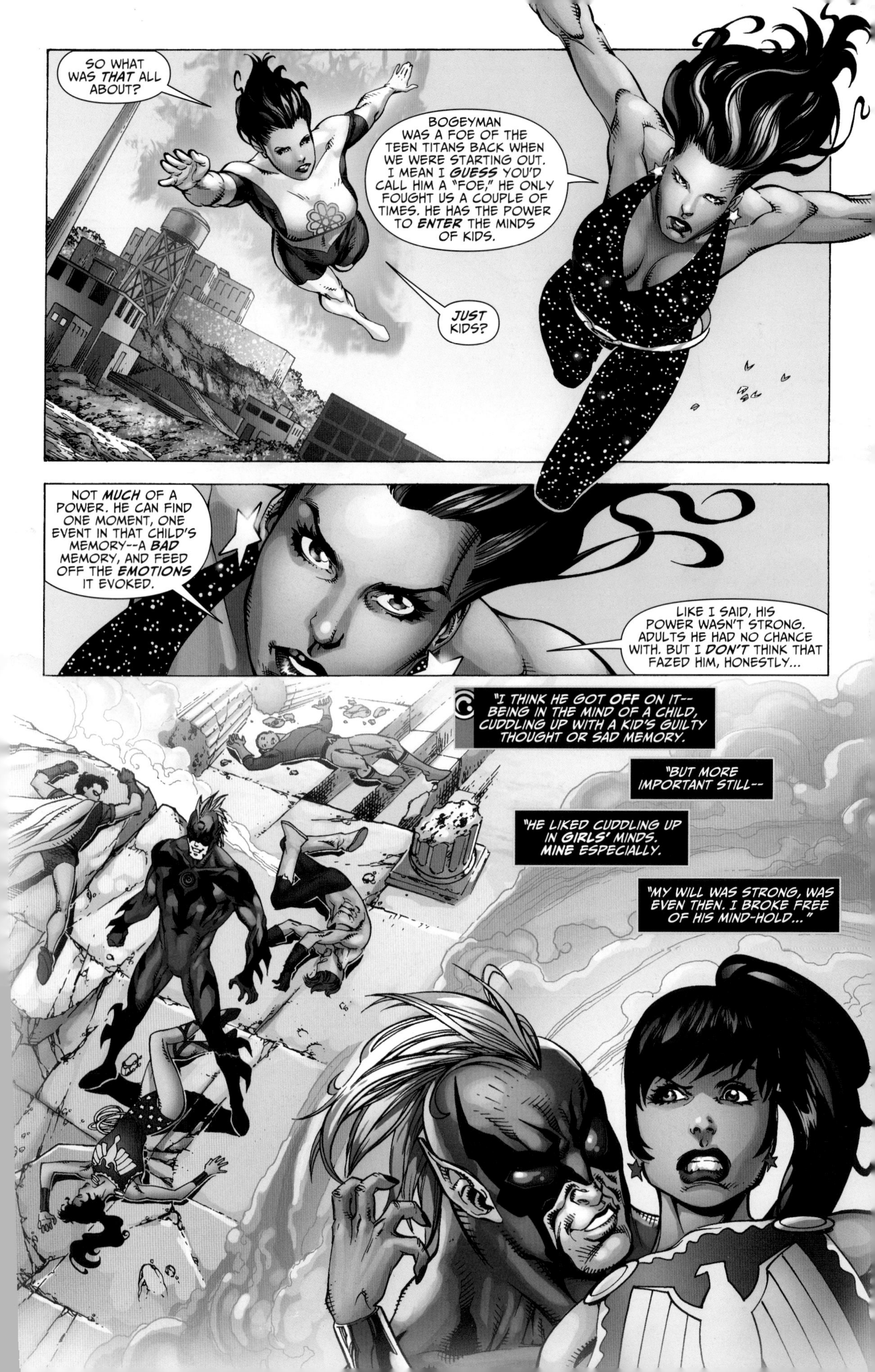
SO WHAT WAS THAT ALL ABOUT?
BOGEYMAN WAS A FOE OF THE TEEN TITANS BACK WHEN WE WERE STARTING OUT. I MEAN I GUESS YOU'D CALL HIM A "FOE," HE ONLY FOUGHT US A COUPLE OF TIMES. HE HAS THE POWER TO ENTER THE MINDS OF KIDS.
JUST KIDS?
NOT MUCH OF A POWER. HE CAN FIND ONE MOMENT, ONE EVENT IN THAT CHILD'S MEMORY--A BAD MEMORY, AND FEED OFF THE EMOTIONS IT EVOKED.
LIKE I SAID, HIS POWER WASN'T STRONG. ADULTS HE HAD NO CHANCE WITH. BUT I DON'T THINK THAT FAZED HIM, HONESTLY...
"I THINK HE GOT OFF ON IT-- BEING IN THE MIND OF A CHILD, CUDDLING UP WITH A KID'S GUILTY THOUGHT OR SAD MEMORY.
"BUT MORE IMPORTANT STILL--
"HE LIKED CUDDLING UP IN GIRLS' MINDS. MINE ESPECIALLY.
"MY WILL WAS STRONG, WAS EVEN THEN. I BROKE FREE OF HIS MIND-HOLD..."

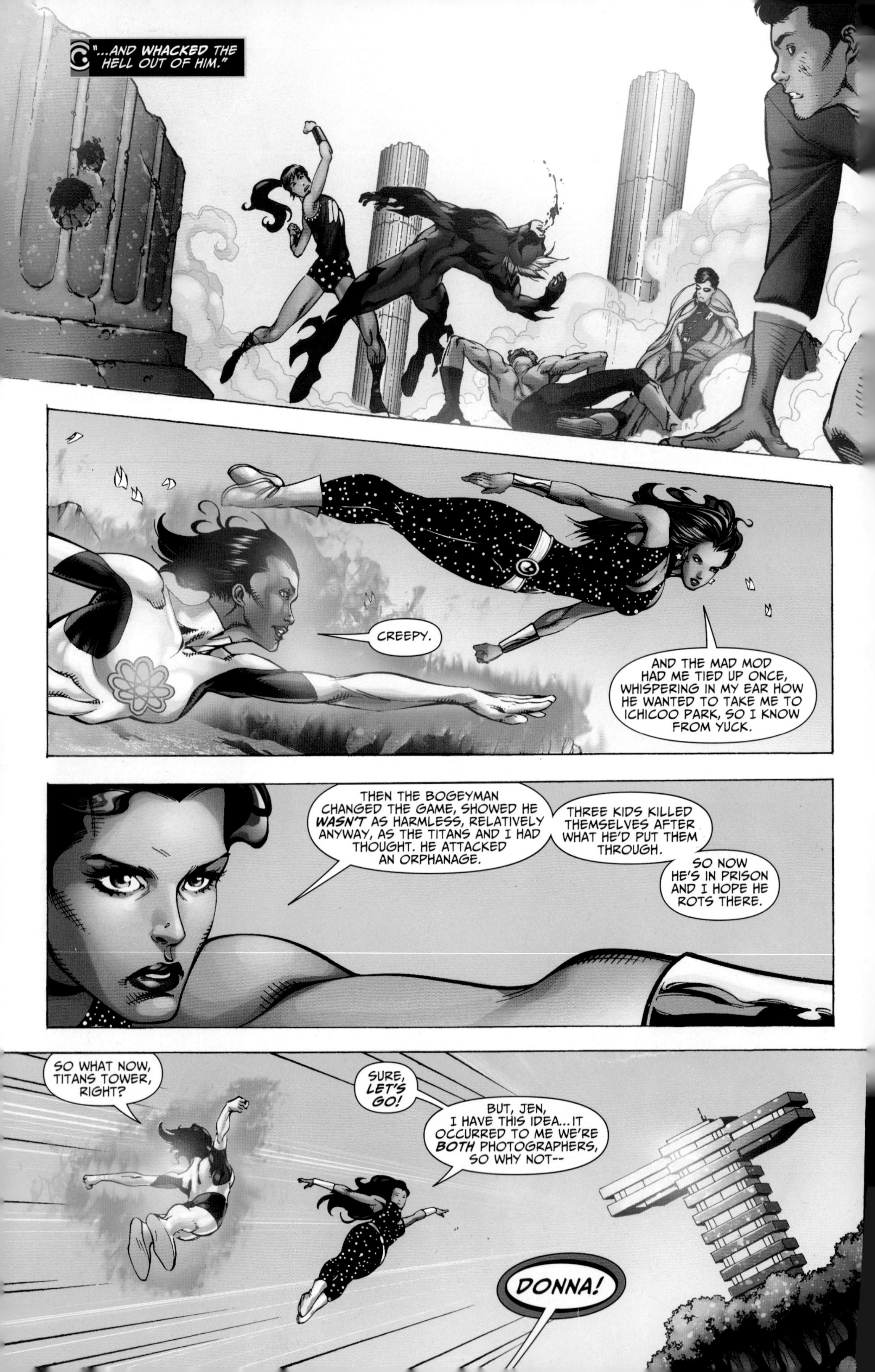
"...AND WHACKED THE HELL OUT OF HIM."
CREEPY.
AND THE MAD MOD HAD ME TIED UP ONCE, WHISPERING IN MY EAR HOW HE WANTED TO TAKE ME TO ICHICOO PARK, SO I KNOW FROM YUCK.
THEN THE BOGEYMAN CHANGED THE GAME, SHOWED HE WASN'T AS HARMLESS, RELATIVELY ANYWAY, AS THE TITANS AND I HAD THOUGHT. HE ATTACKED AN ORPHANAGE.
THREE KIDS KILLED THEMSELVES AFTER WHAT HE'D PUT THEM THROUGH.
SO NOW HE'S IN PRISON AND I HOPE HE ROTS THERE.
SO WHAT NOW, TITANS TOWER, RIGHT?
SURE, LET'S GO!
BUT, JEN, I HAVE THIS IDEA...IT OCCURRED TO ME WE'RE BOTH PHOTOGRAPHERS, SO WHY NOT--
DONNA!

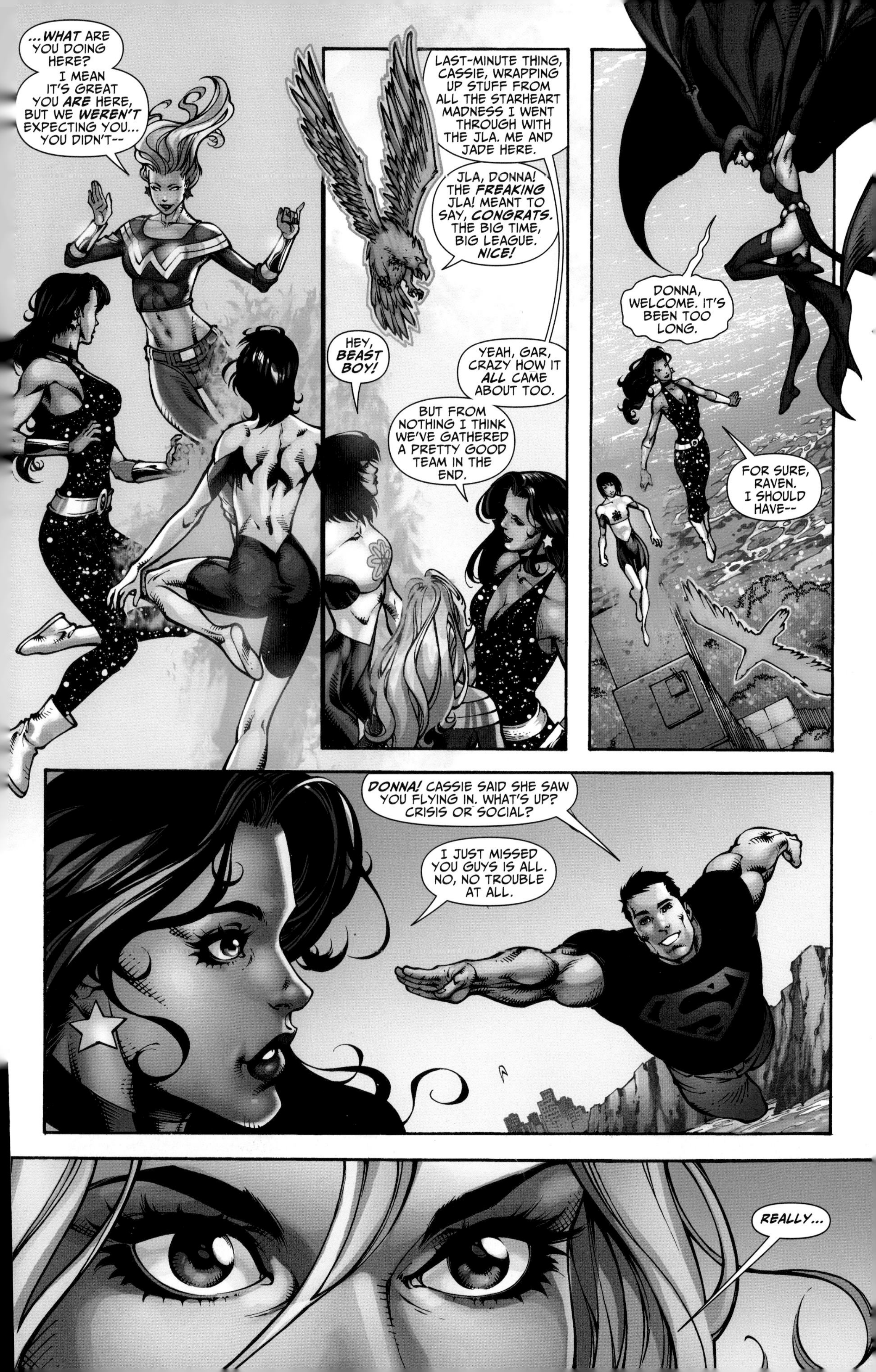
...WHAT ARE YOU DOING HERE? I MEAN IT'S GREAT YOU ARE HERE, BUT WE WEREN'T EXPECTING YOU... YOU DIDN'T--
LAST-MINUTE THING, CASSIE, WRAPPING UP STUFF FROM ALL THE STARHEART MADNESS I WENT THROUGH WITH THE JLA. ME AND JADE HERE.
JLA, DONNA! THE FREAKING JLA! MEANT TO SAY, CONGRATS. THE BIG TIME, BIG LEAGUE. NICE!
HEY, BEAST BOY!
YEAH, GAR, CRAZY HOW IT ALL CAME ABOUT TOO.
BUT FROM NOTHING I THINK WE'VE GATHERED A PRETTY GOOD TEAM IN THE END.
DONNA, WELCOME. IT'S BEEN TOO LONG.
FOR SURE, RAVEN. I SHOULD HAVE--
DONNA! CASSIE SAID SHE SAW YOU FLYING IN. WHAT'S UP? CRISIS OR SOCIAL?
I JUST MISSED YOU GUYS IS ALL. NO, NO TROUBLE AT ALL.
REALLY...

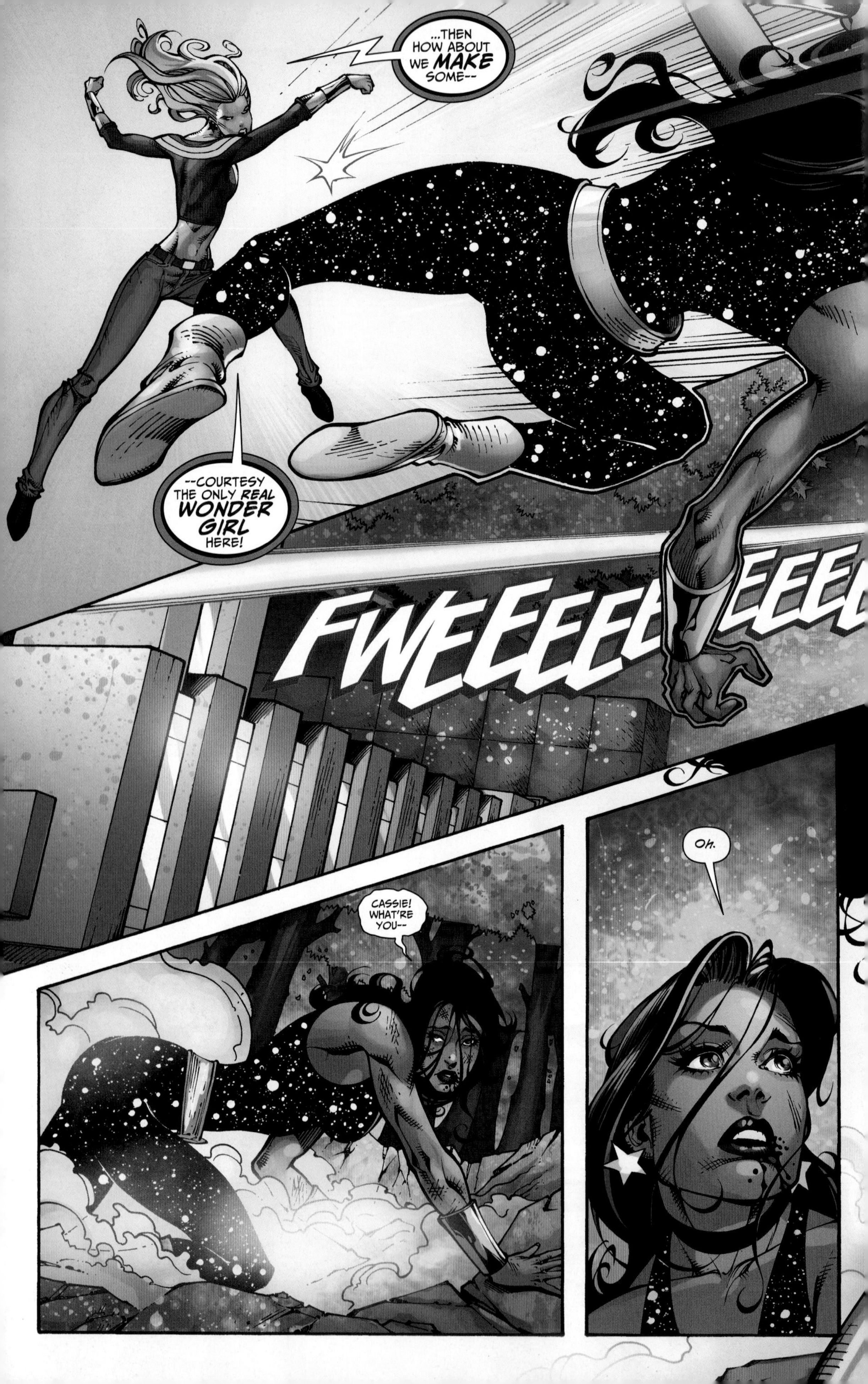
...THEN HOW ABOUT WE MAKE SOME--
--COURTESY THE ONLY REAL WONDER GIRL HERE!
FWEEEEEEEEEE
CASSIE! WHAT'RE YOU--
Oh.

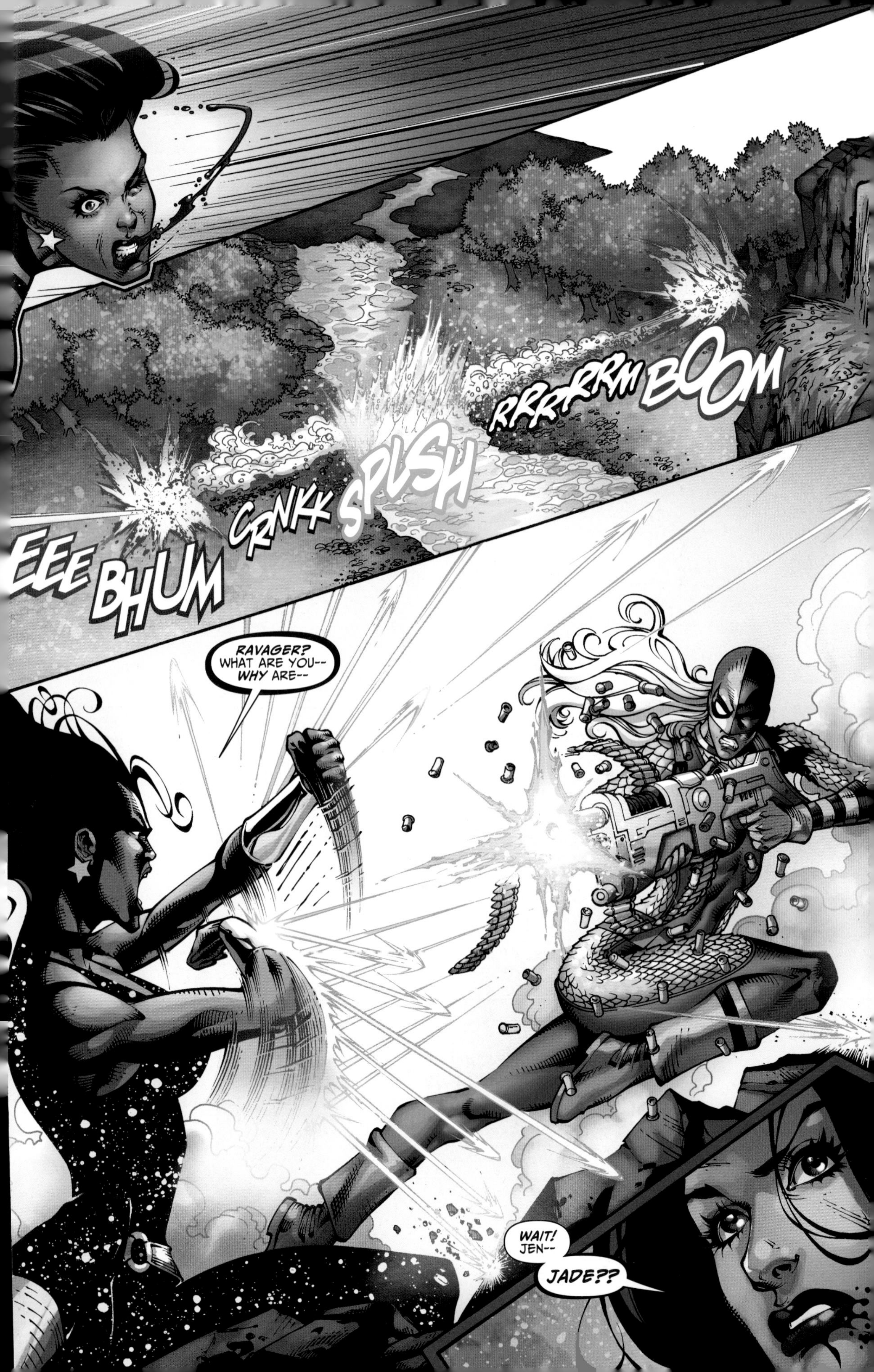
EEE BHUM
CRNKK SPLSH
RRRRRRM BOOM
RAVAGER? WHAT ARE YOU-- WHY ARE--
WAIT! JEN--
JADE??

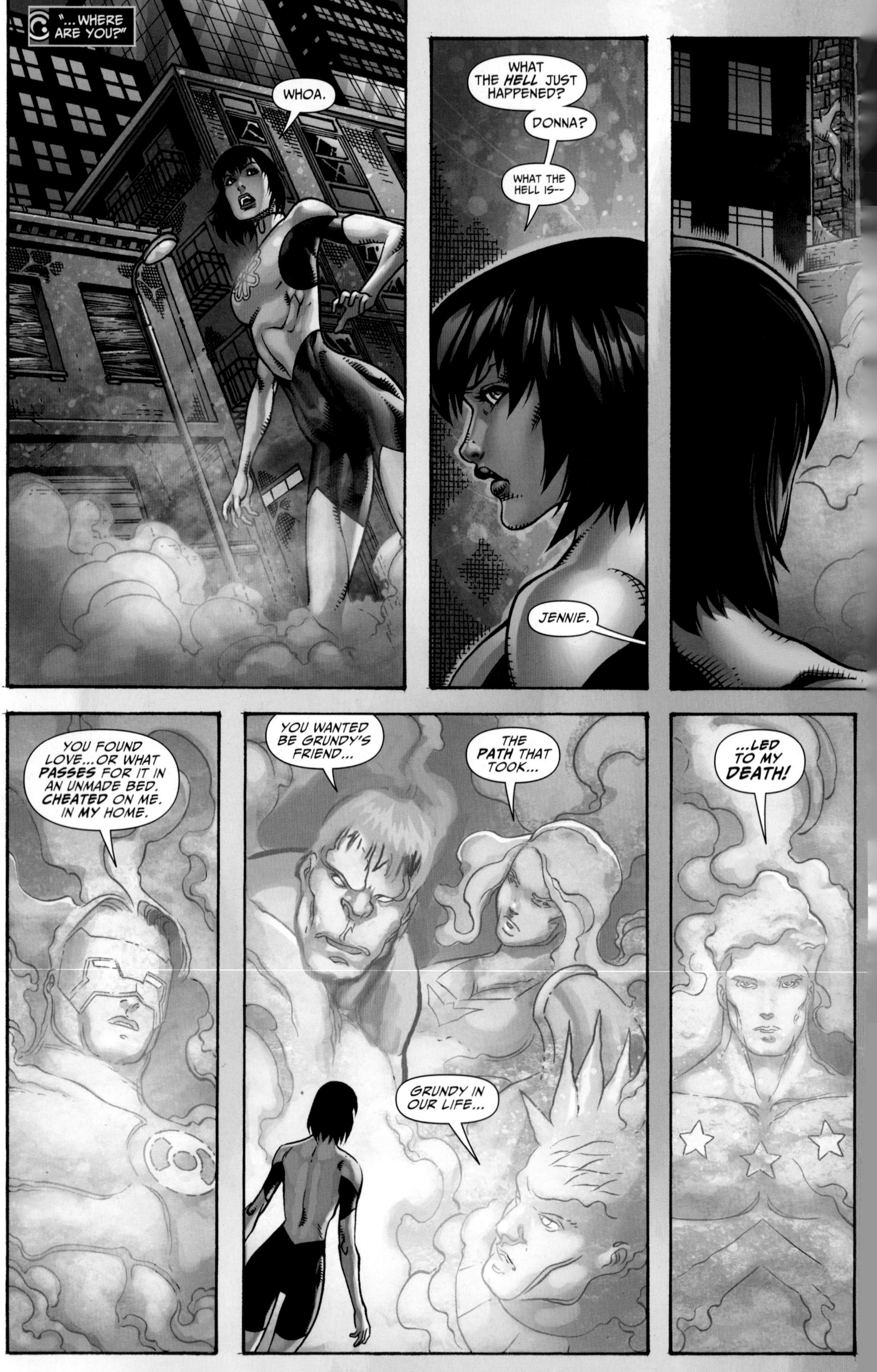
"...WHERE ARE YOU?"
WHOA.
WHAT THE HELL JUST HAPPENED?
DONNA?
WHAT THE HELL IS--
JENNIE.
YOU FOUND LOVE...OR WHAT PASSES FOR IT IN AN UNMADE BED. CHEATED ON ME. IN MY HOME.
YOU WANTED BE GRUNDY'S FRIEND...
THE PATH THAT TOOK...
GRUNDY IN OUR LIFE...
...LED TO MY DEATH!

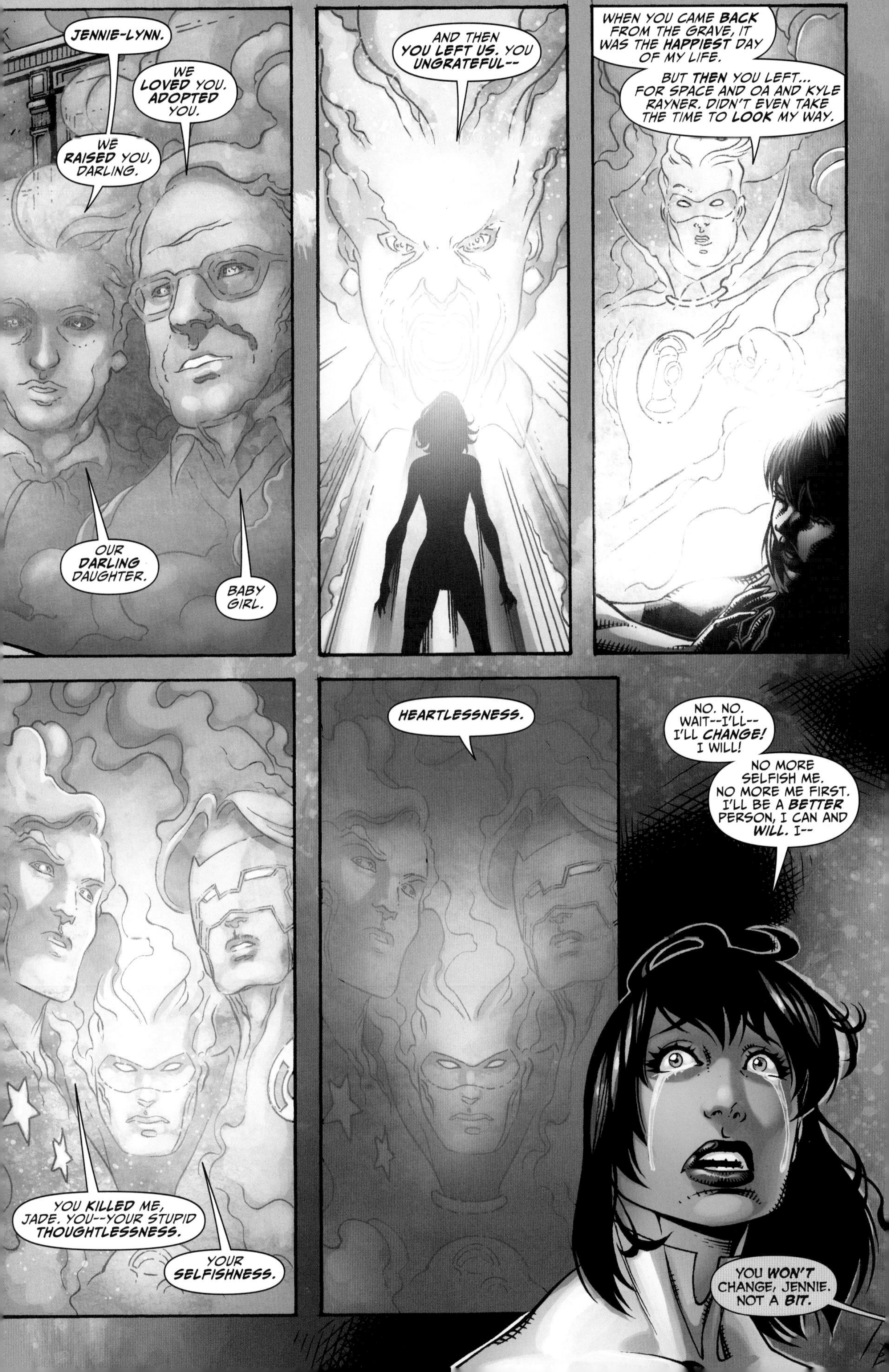
JENNIE-LYNN.
WE LOVED YOU. ADOPTED YOU.
WE RAISED YOU, DARLING.
OUR DARLING DAUGHTER.
BABY GIRL.
AND THEN YOU LEFT US. YOU UNGRATEFUL--
WHEN YOU CAME BACK FROM THE GRAVE, IT WAS THE HAPPIEST DAY OF MY LIFE.
BUT THEN YOU LEFT... FOR SPACE AND OA AND KYLE RAYNER. DIDN'T EVEN TAKE THE TIME TO LOOK MY WAY.
YOU KILLED ME, JADE. YOU--YOUR STUPID THOUGHTLESSNESS.
YOUR SELFISHNESS.
HEARTLESSNESS.
NO. NO. WAIT--I'LL--I'LL CHANGE! I WILL!
NO MORE SELFISH ME. NO MORE ME FIRST. I'LL BE A BETTER PERSON, I CAN AND WILL. I--
YOU WON'T CHANGE, JENNIE. NOT A BIT.

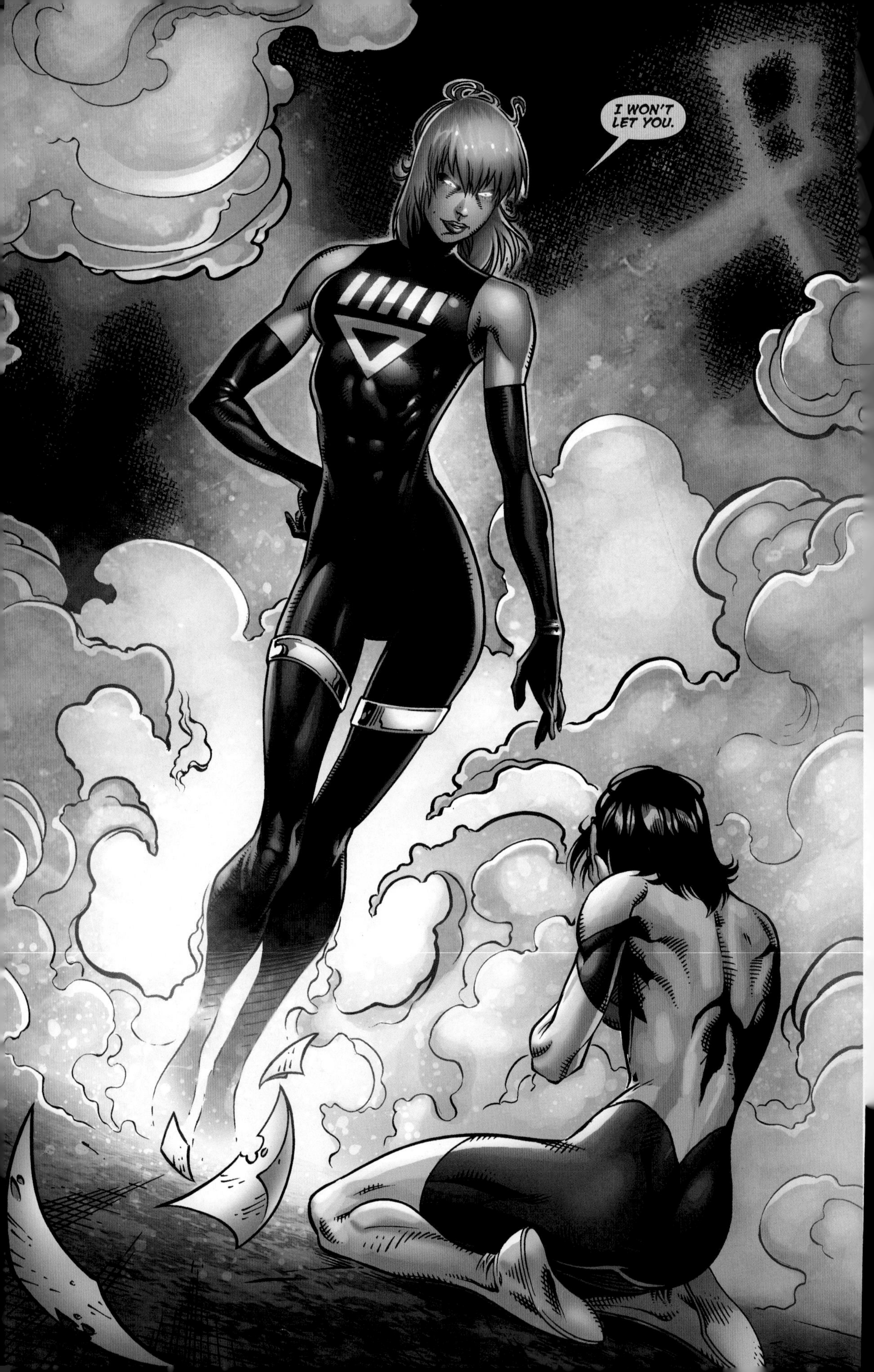
I WON'T LET YOU.

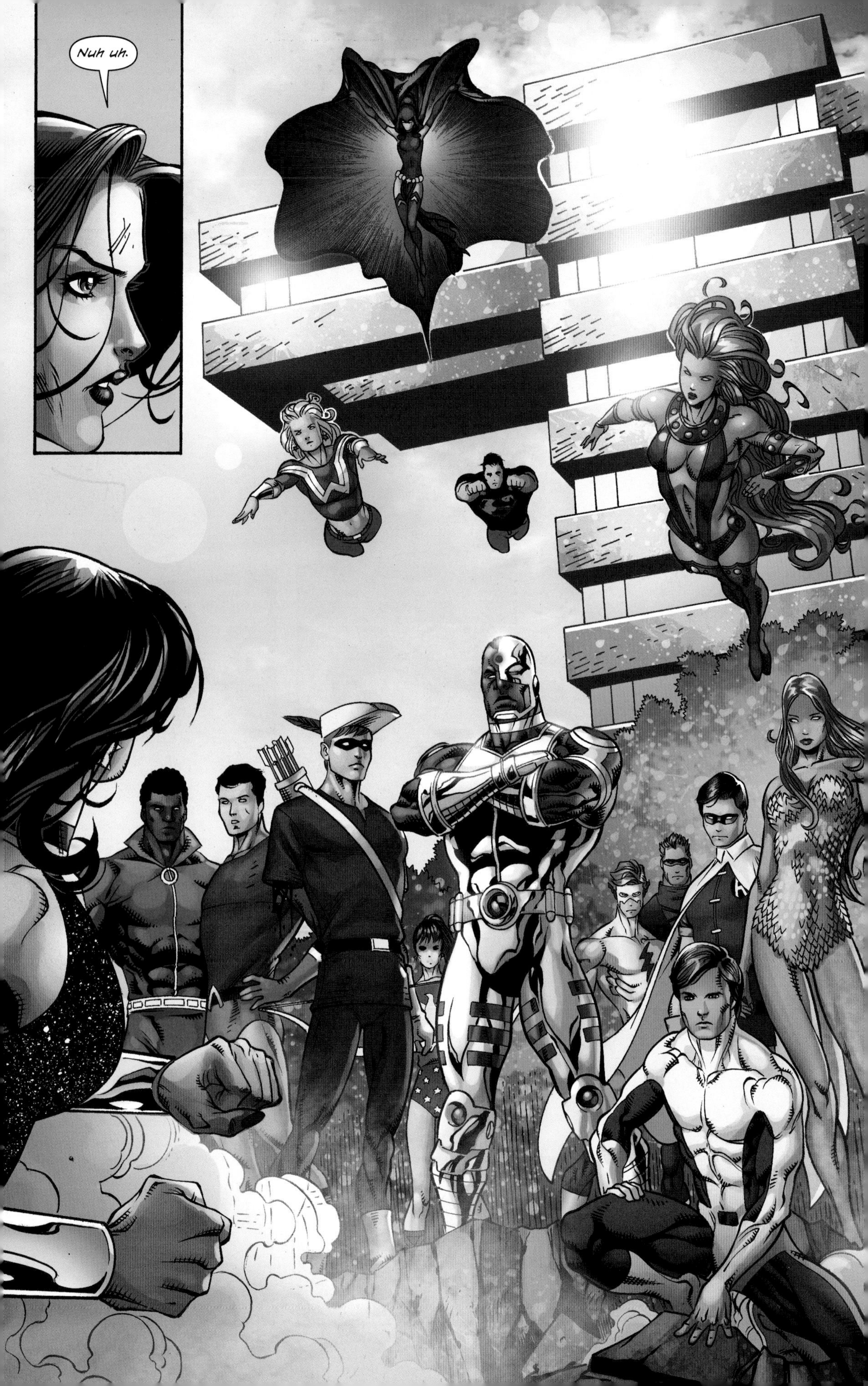
Nuh uh.

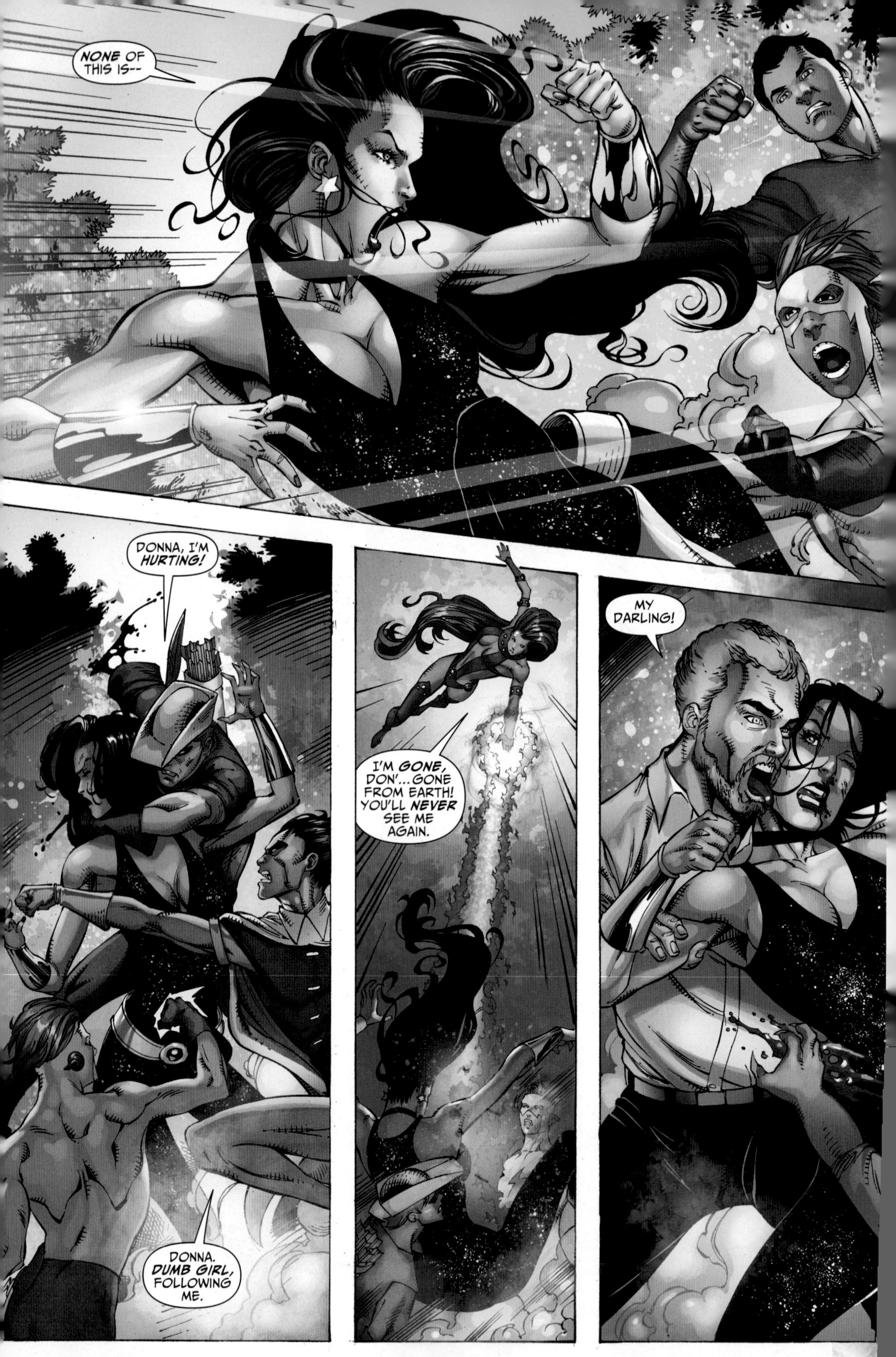
NONE OF THIS IS--
DONNA, I'M HURTING!
DONNA. DUMB GIRL, FOLLOWING ME.
I'M GONE, DON'...GONE FROM EARTH! YOU'LL NEVER SEE ME AGAIN.
MY DARLING!

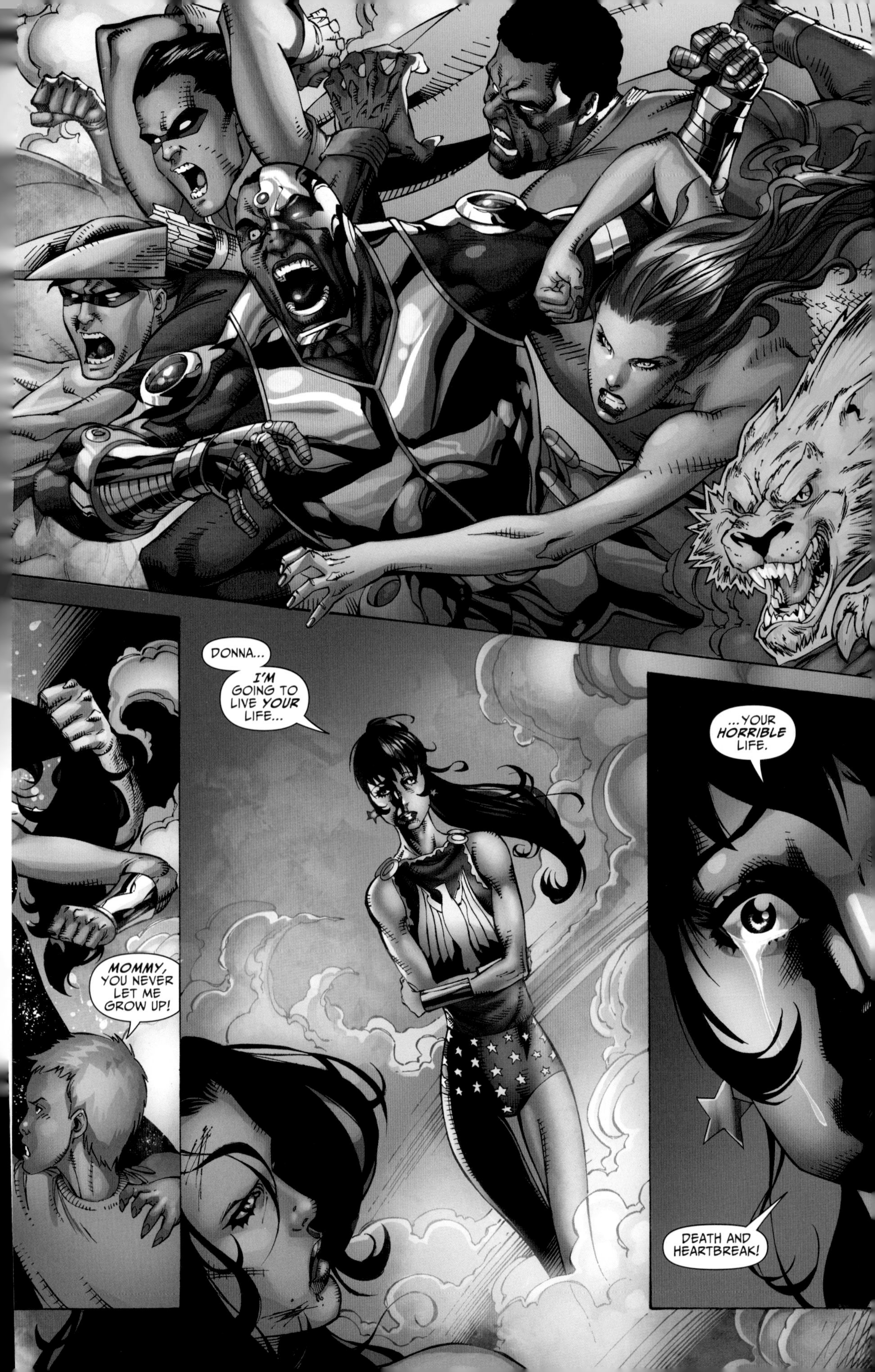
DONNA...
I'M GOING TO LIVE YOUR LIFE...
...YOUR HORRIBLE LIFE.
MOMMY, YOU NEVER LET ME GROW UP!
DEATH AND HEARTBREAK!

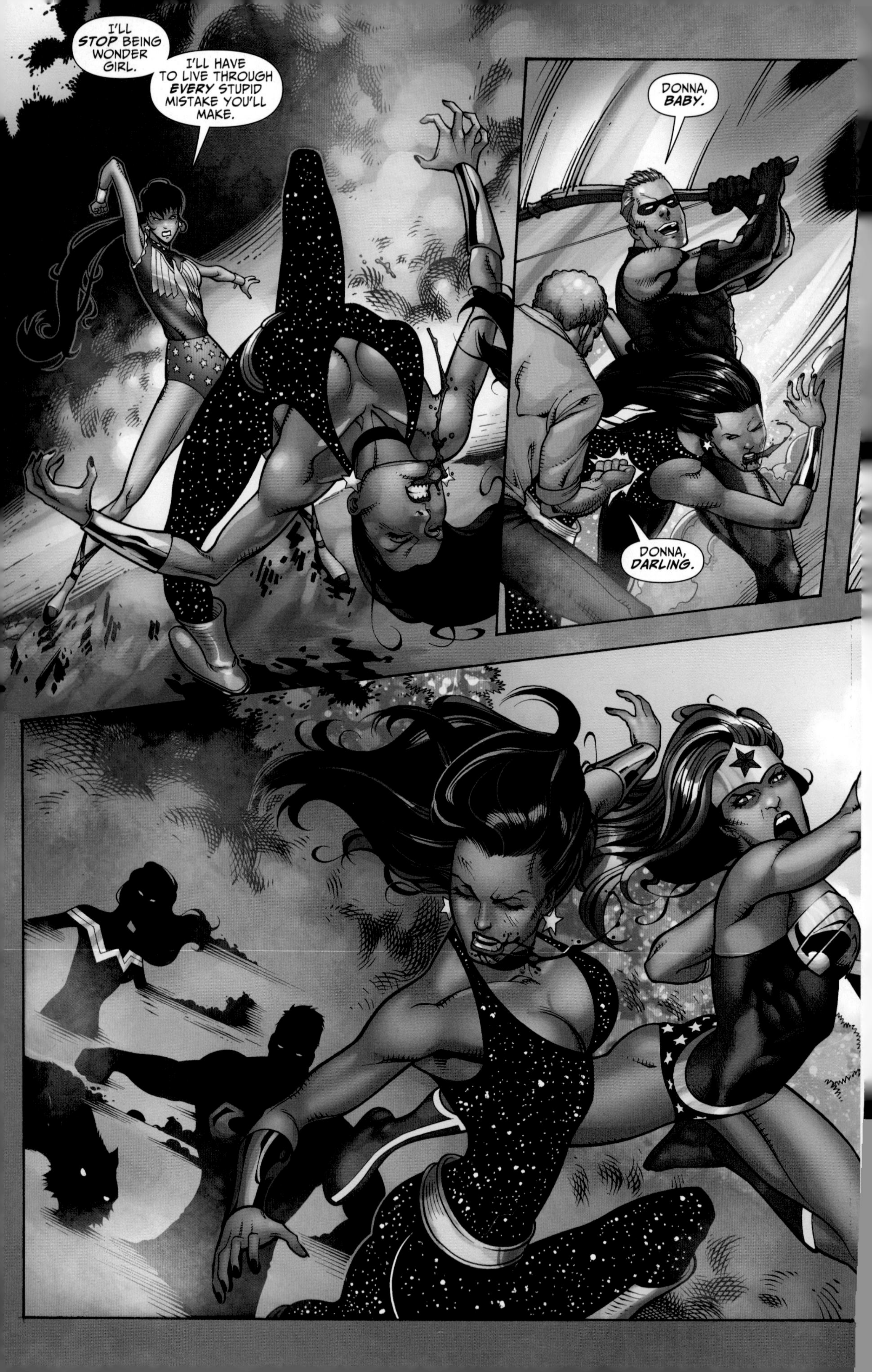
I'LL STOP BEING WONDER GIRL.
I'LL HAVE TO LIVE THROUGH EVERY STUPID MISTAKE YOU'LL MAKE.
DONNA, BABY.
DONNA, DARLING.

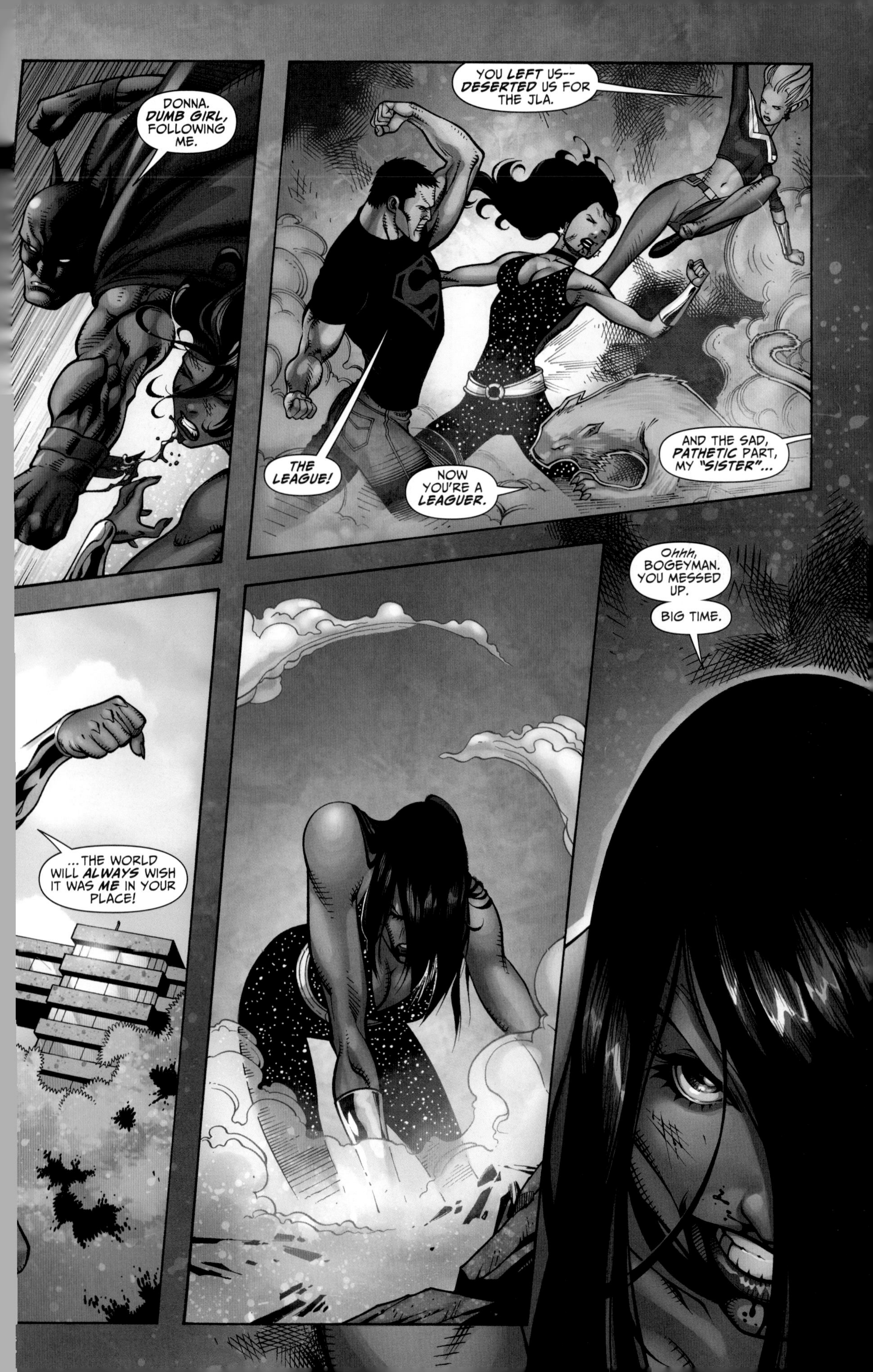
DONNA. DUMB GIRL, FOLLOWING ME.
YOU LEFT US-- DESERTED US FOR THE JLA.
THE LEAGUE!
NOW YOU'RE A LEAGUER.
AND THE SAD, PATHETIC PART, MY "SISTER"...
...THE WORLD WILL ALWAYS WISH IT WAS ME IN YOUR PLACE!
Ohhh, BOGEYMAN. YOU MESSED UP.
BIG TIME.

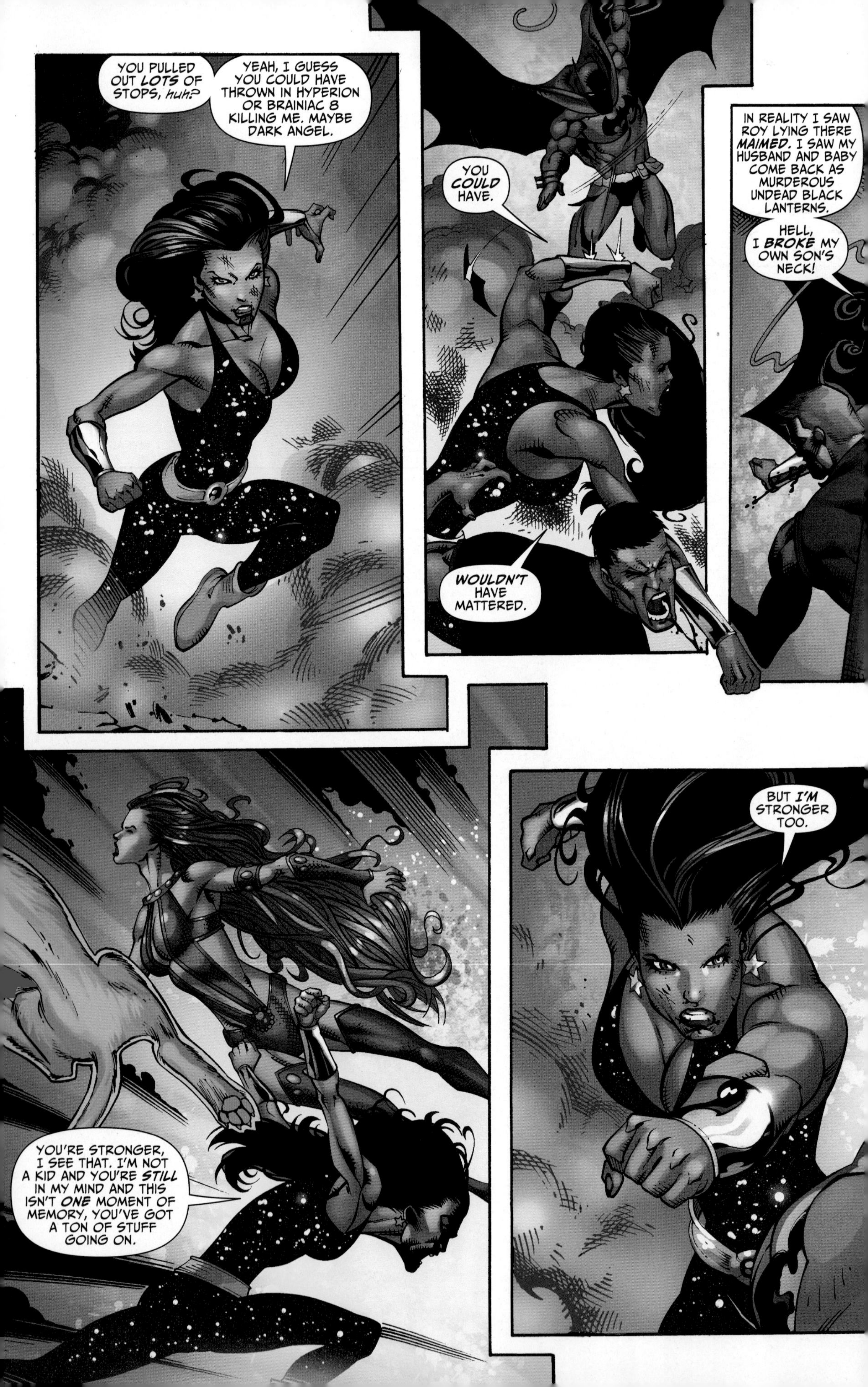
YOU PULLED OUT *LOTS* OF STOPS, *huh?*
YEAH, I GUESS YOU COULD HAVE THROWN IN HYPERION OR BRAINIAC 8 KILLING ME. MAYBE DARK ANGEL.
YOU *COULD* HAVE.
WOULDN'T HAVE MATTERED.
IN REALITY I SAW ROY LYING THERE *MAIMED.* I SAW MY HUSBAND AND BABY COME BACK AS MURDEROUS UNDEAD BLACK LANTERNS.
HELL, I *BROKE* MY OWN SON'S NECK!
YOU'RE STRONGER, I SEE THAT. I'M NOT A KID AND YOU'RE *STILL* IN MY MIND AND THIS ISN'T *ONE* MOMENT OF MEMORY, YOU'VE GOT A TON OF STUFF GOING ON.
BUT *I'M* STRONGER TOO.

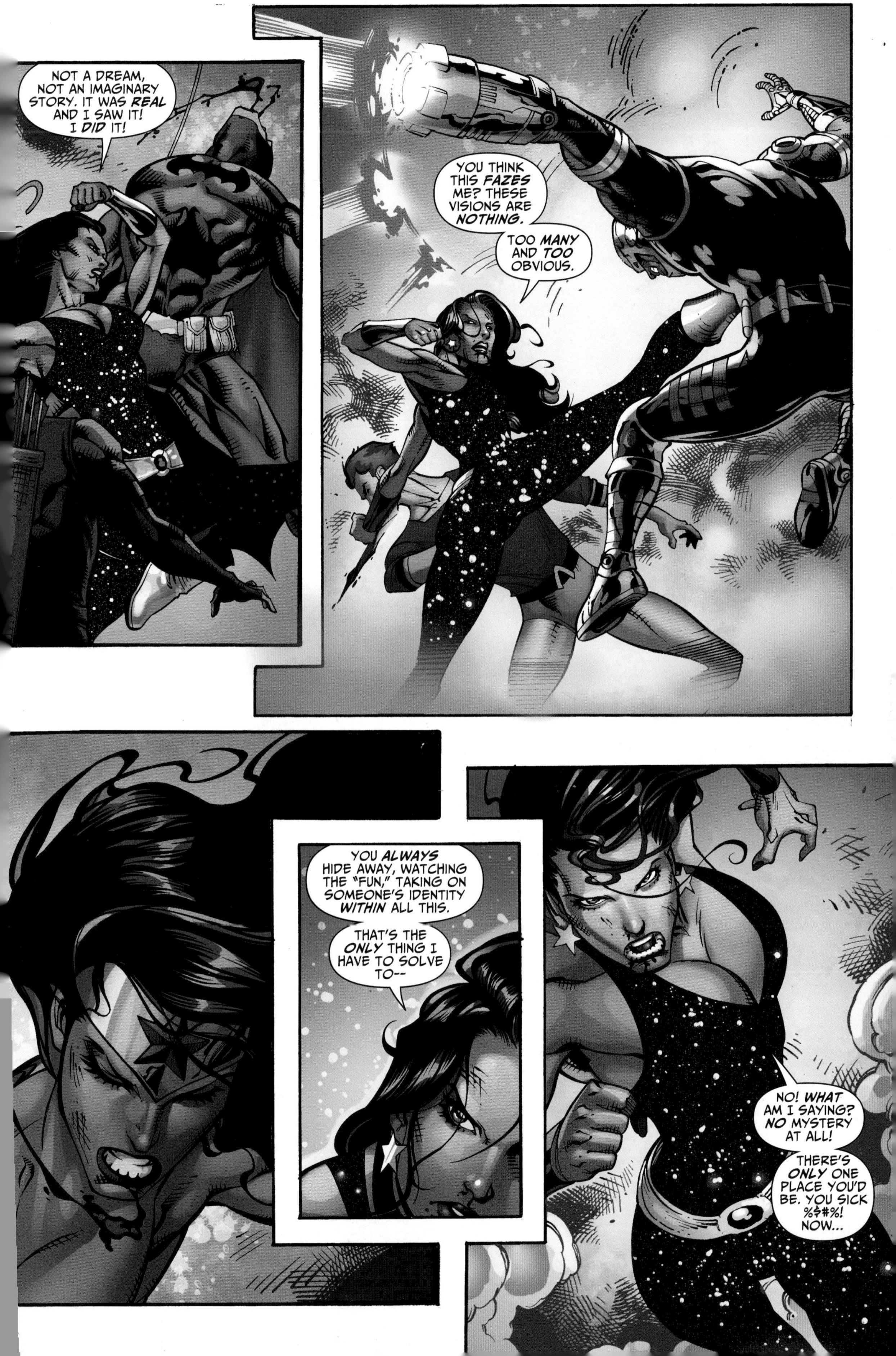
NOT A DREAM, NOT AN IMAGINARY STORY. IT WAS REAL AND I SAW IT! I DID IT!
YOU THINK THIS FAZES ME? THESE VISIONS ARE NOTHING.
TOO MANY AND TOO OBVIOUS.
YOU ALWAYS HIDE AWAY, WATCHING THE "FUN," TAKING ON SOMEONE'S IDENTITY WITHIN ALL THIS.
THAT'S THE ONLY THING I HAVE TO SOLVE TO--
NO! WHAT AM I SAYING? NO MYSTERY AT ALL!
THERE'S ONLY ONE PLACE YOU'D BE. YOU SICK %$#%! NOW...

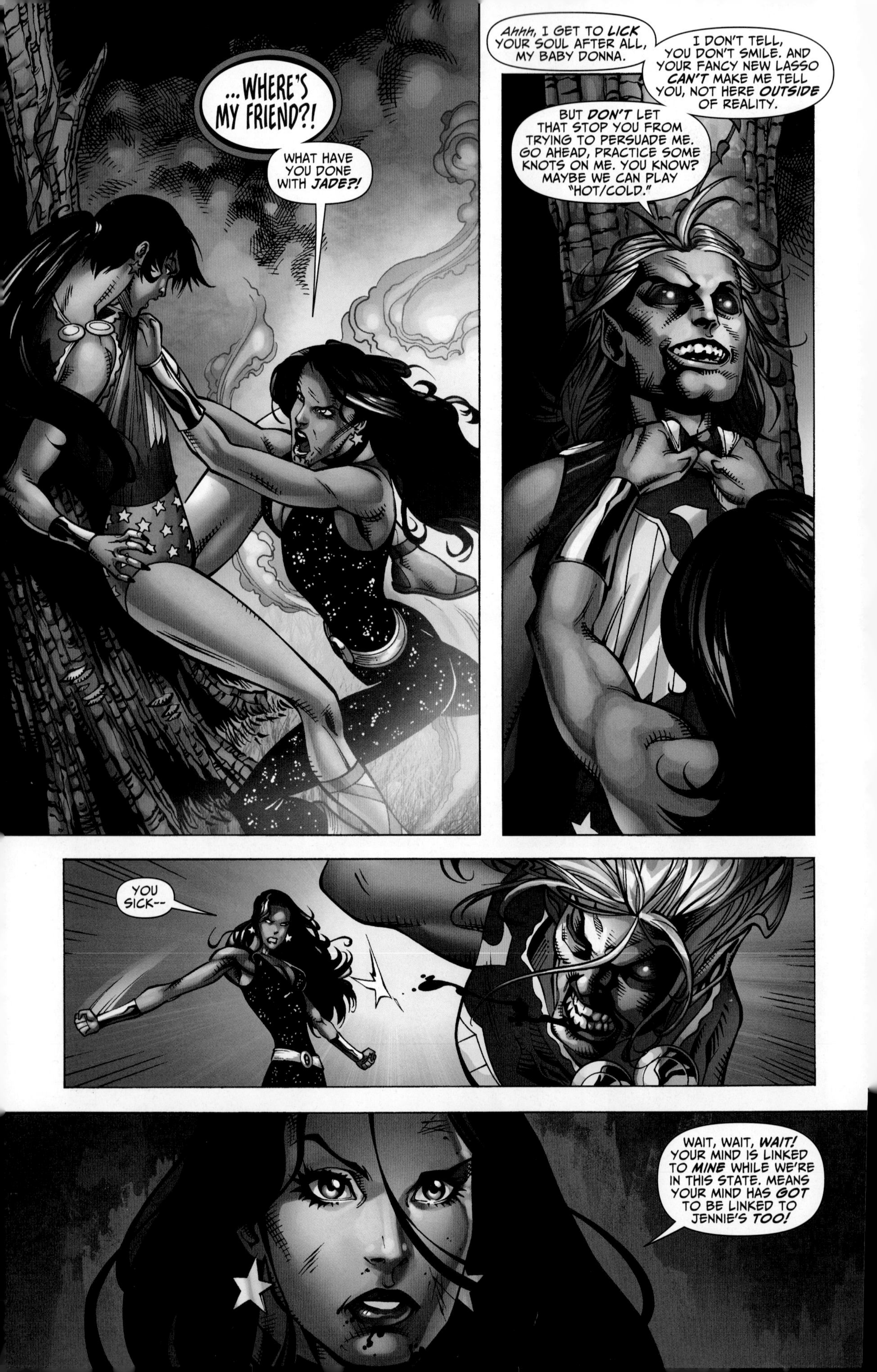
...WHERE'S MY FRIEND?!
WHAT HAVE YOU DONE WITH JADE?!
Ahhh, I GET TO LICK YOUR SOUL AFTER ALL, MY BABY DONNA.
I DON'T TELL, YOU DON'T SMILE. AND YOUR FANCY NEW LASSO CAN'T MAKE ME TELL YOU, NOT HERE OUTSIDE OF REALITY.
BUT DON'T LET THAT STOP YOU FROM TRYING TO PERSUADE ME. GO AHEAD, PRACTICE SOME KNOTS ON ME. YOU KNOW? MAYBE WE CAN PLAY "HOT/COLD."
YOU SICK--
WAIT, WAIT, WAIT! YOUR MIND IS LINKED TO MINE WHILE WE'RE IN THIS STATE. MEANS YOUR MIND HAS GOT TO BE LINKED TO JENNIE'S TOO!

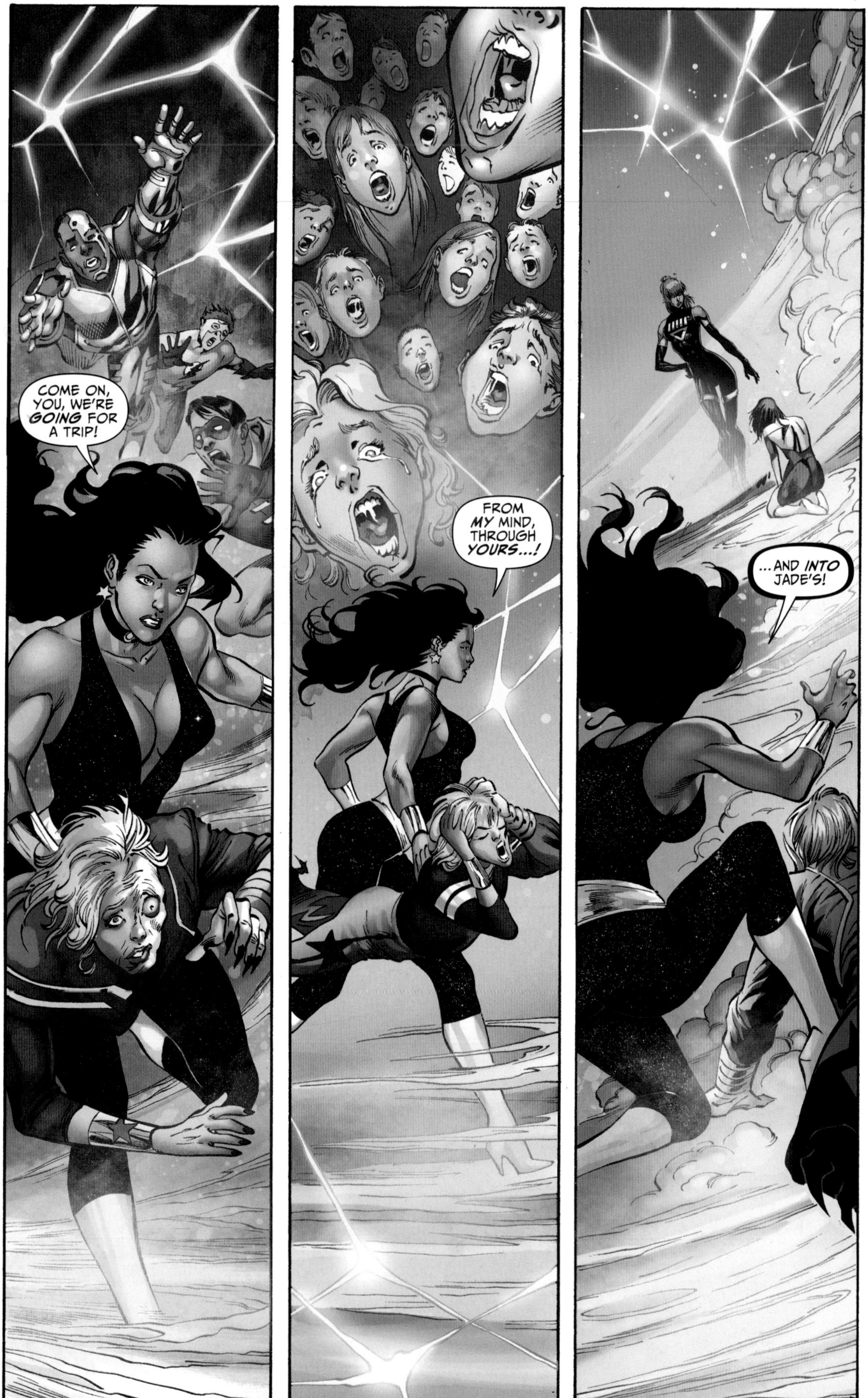

COME ON, YOU, WE'RE GOING FOR A TRIP!
FROM MY MIND, THROUGH YOURS...!
...AND INTO JADE'S!

HEY, BABE. HOW YOU HOLDING UP?

OH, DONNA...

...DONNA...

I'LL *NEVER* CHANGE. I *CAN'T* CHANGE. I WANT TO BE A BETTER PERSON... *BETTER*, BUT--

THE DARKNESS WITHIN THE STARHEART IS STILL PART OF ME.

LOOK...

LISTEN TO ME, JENNIE. THIS *ISN'T* REAL, NONE OF THIS! THE BOGEYMAN'S DOING IT. HE'S--

NO, MY POWER... HAVE YOU NOTICED?...THERE'S A *DARKNESS* WITHIN MY LIGHT NOW FROM WHEN I SAVED MY DAD. I *ABSORBED*--

WHEN I... WE WERE ON THE MOON, I BECAME THE WHITE LANTERN FOR A MOMENT. I'D HOPED IT WAS A *SIGN* THAT-- I'D HOPED...

...THAT I WAS *FREE* FROM BOTH THE BLACK LANTERN AND THE STARHEART DARKNESS.

OF *ME?* NEVER, JENNIE. NOT EVER.

EVERYONE HAS THAT ONE, DARK, DIRTY SECRET LURKING WITHIN THEM. I'M *YOURS.*

WHY, LOOK AT THE *POWER* WE HAVE, JENNIE, YOU AND I.

WHAT? *WHAT?* DON'T LISTEN TO *ANY* OF THE %$?!&$#@ THIS THING IS TELLING YOU.

JADE. JENNIE. *DON'T* DO THIS...DON'T LET IT EAT YOUR SOUL. YOU'RE *BETTER* THAN THAT.

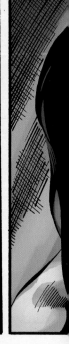

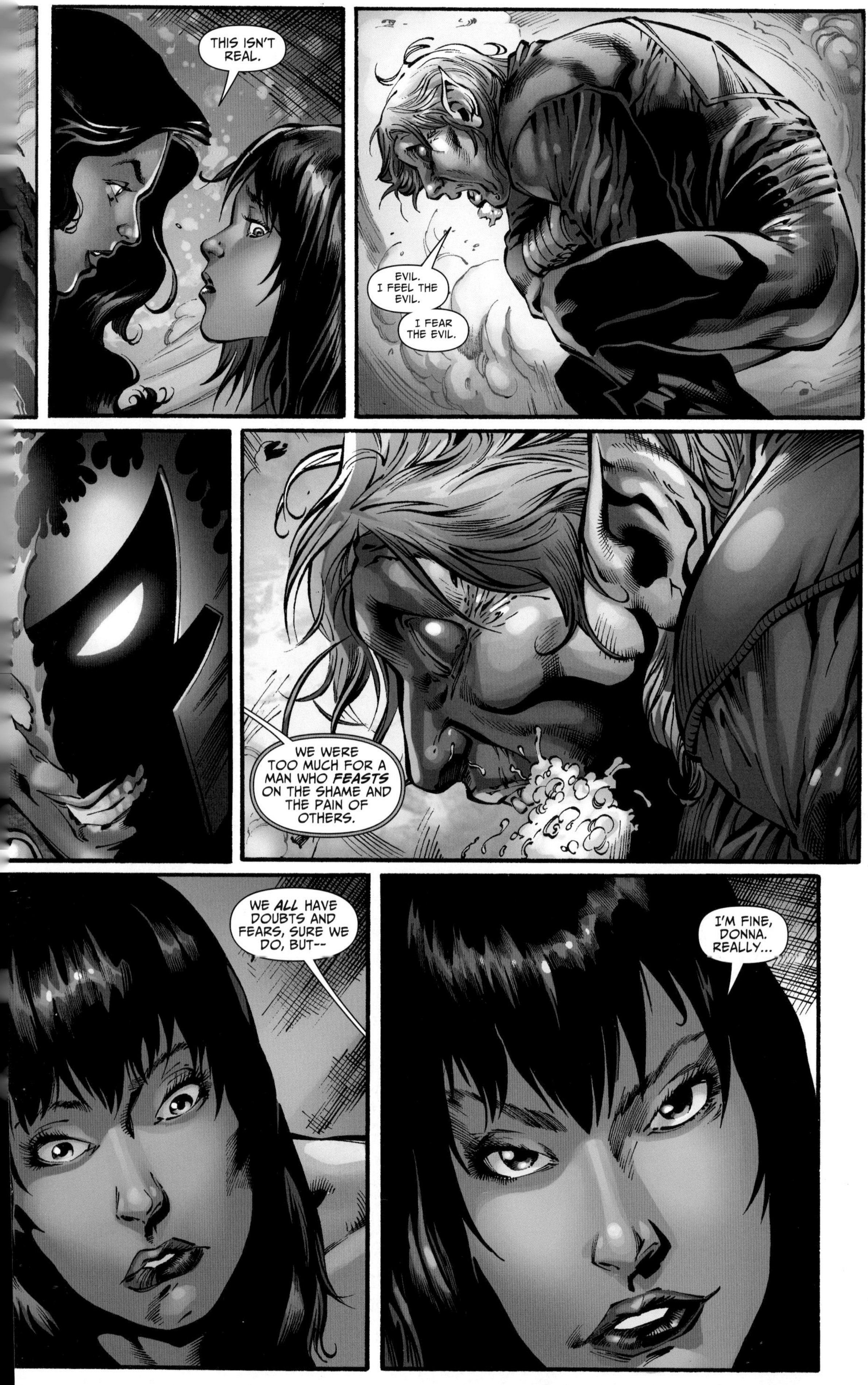
THIS ISN'T REAL.
EVIL. I FEEL THE EVIL.
I FEAR THE EVIL.
WE WERE TOO MUCH FOR A MAN WHO FEASTS ON THE SHAME AND THE PAIN OF OTHERS.
WE ALL HAVE DOUBTS AND FEARS, SURE WE DO, BUT--
I'M FINE, DONNA. REALLY...

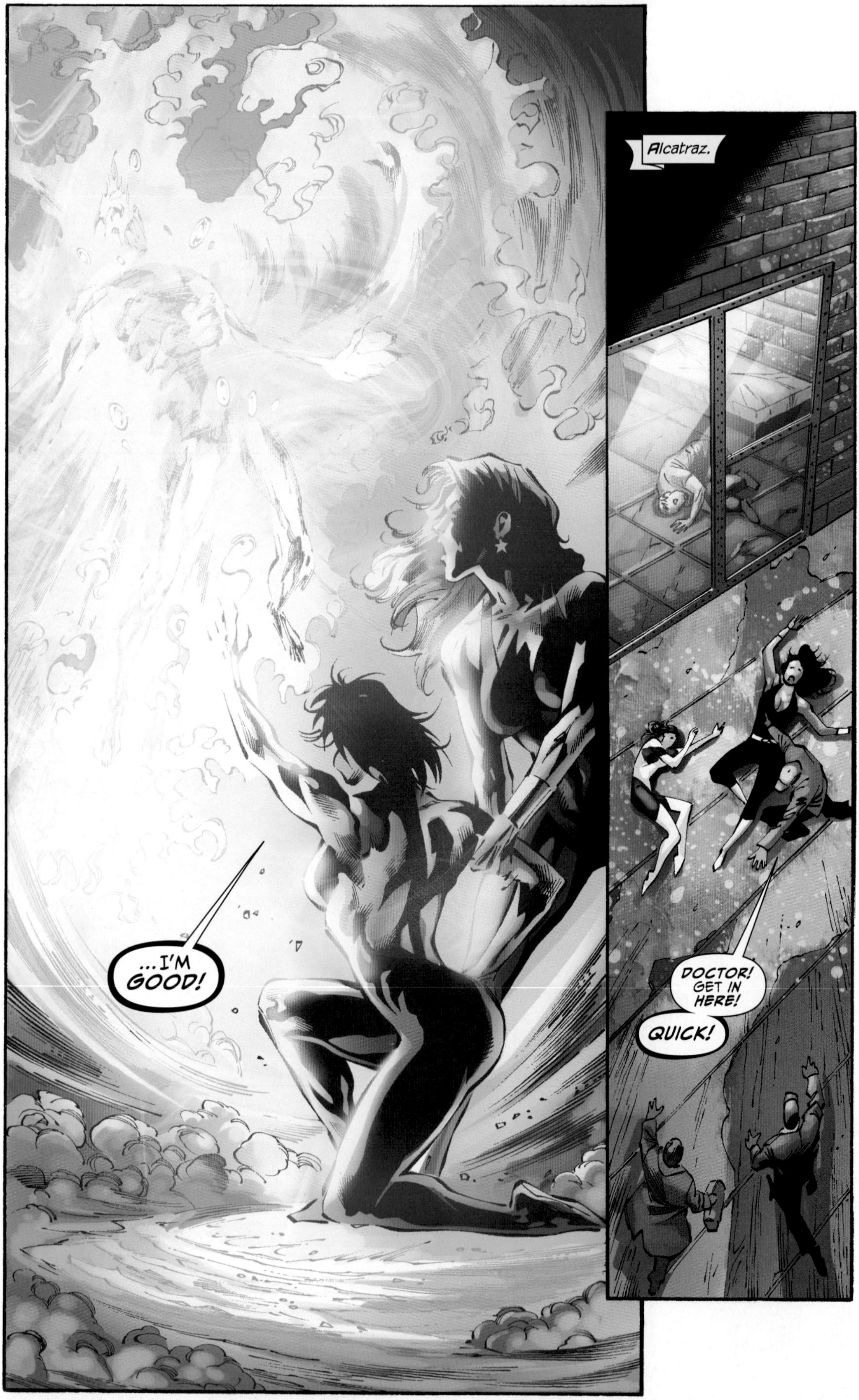
...I'M GOOD!
Alcatraz.
DOCTOR! GET IN HERE!
QUICK!

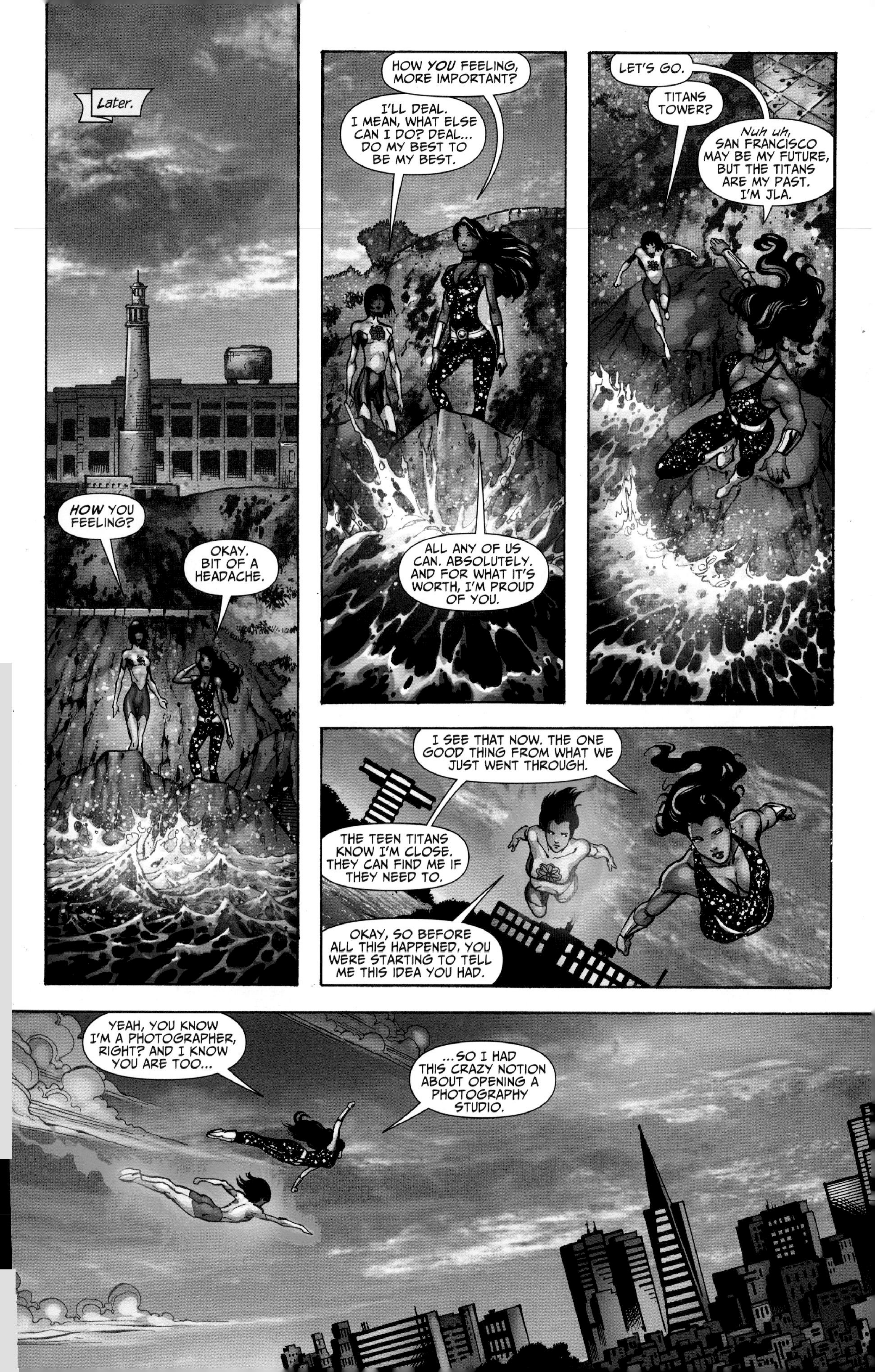
Later.
HOW YOU FEELING?
OKAY. BIT OF A HEADACHE.
HOW YOU FEELING, MORE IMPORTANT?
I'LL DEAL. I MEAN, WHAT ELSE CAN I DO? DEAL... DO MY BEST TO BE MY BEST.
ALL ANY OF US CAN. ABSOLUTELY. AND FOR WHAT IT'S WORTH, I'M PROUD OF YOU.
LET'S GO.
TITANS TOWER?
Nuh uh, SAN FRANCISCO MAY BE MY FUTURE, BUT THE TITANS ARE MY PAST. I'M JLA.
I SEE THAT NOW. THE ONE GOOD THING FROM WHAT WE JUST WENT THROUGH.
THE TEEN TITANS KNOW I'M CLOSE. THEY CAN FIND ME IF THEY NEED TO.
OKAY, SO BEFORE ALL THIS HAPPENED, YOU WERE STARTING TO TELL ME THIS IDEA YOU HAD.
YEAH, YOU KNOW I'M A PHOTOGRAPHER, RIGHT? AND I KNOW YOU ARE TOO...
...SO I HAD THIS CRAZY NOTION ABOUT OPENING A PHOTOGRAPHY STUDIO.

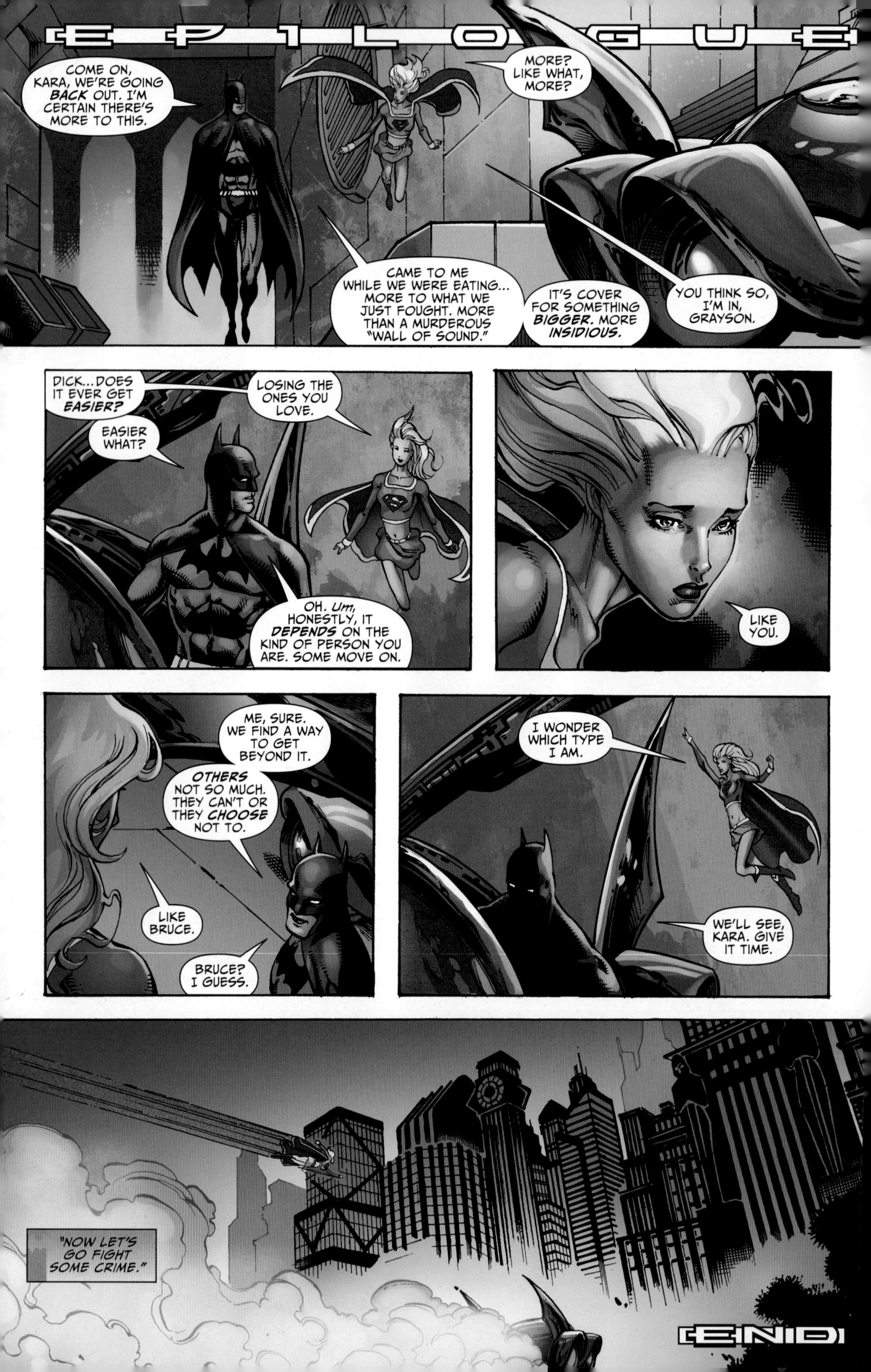
EPILOGUE
COME ON, KARA, WE'RE GOING BACK OUT. I'M CERTAIN THERE'S MORE TO THIS.
MORE? LIKE WHAT, MORE?
CAME TO ME WHILE WE WERE EATING... MORE TO WHAT WE JUST FOUGHT. MORE THAN A MURDEROUS "WALL OF SOUND."
IT'S COVER FOR SOMETHING BIGGER. MORE INSIDIOUS.
YOU THINK SO, I'M IN, GRAYSON.
DICK...DOES IT EVER GET EASIER?
EASIER WHAT?
LOSING THE ONES YOU LOVE.
OH. Um, HONESTLY, IT DEPENDS ON THE KIND OF PERSON YOU ARE. SOME MOVE ON.
LIKE YOU.
ME, SURE. WE FIND A WAY TO GET BEYOND IT.
OTHERS NOT SO MUCH. THEY CAN'T OR THEY CHOOSE NOT TO.
LIKE BRUCE.
BRUCE? I GUESS.
I WONDER WHICH TYPE I AM.
WE'LL SEE, KARA. GIVE IT TIME.
"NOW LET'S GO FIGHT SOME CRIME."
END

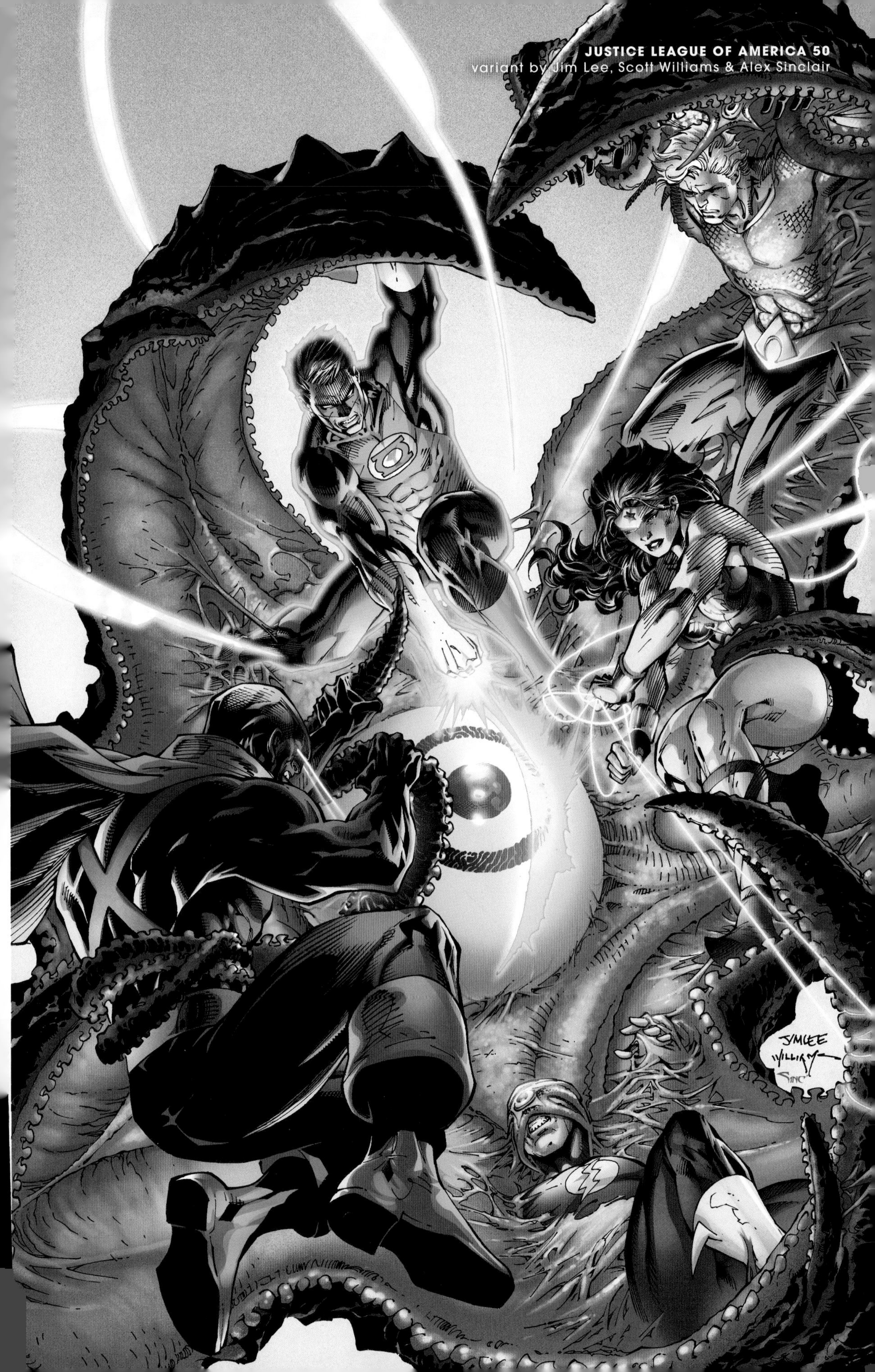

JUSTICE LEAGUE OF AMERICA 50
variant by Jim Lee, Scott Williams & Alex Sinclair

JUSTICE LEAGUE OF AMERICA 50
variant by Mark Bagley, Rob Hunter & Hi-Fi after Frank Quitely

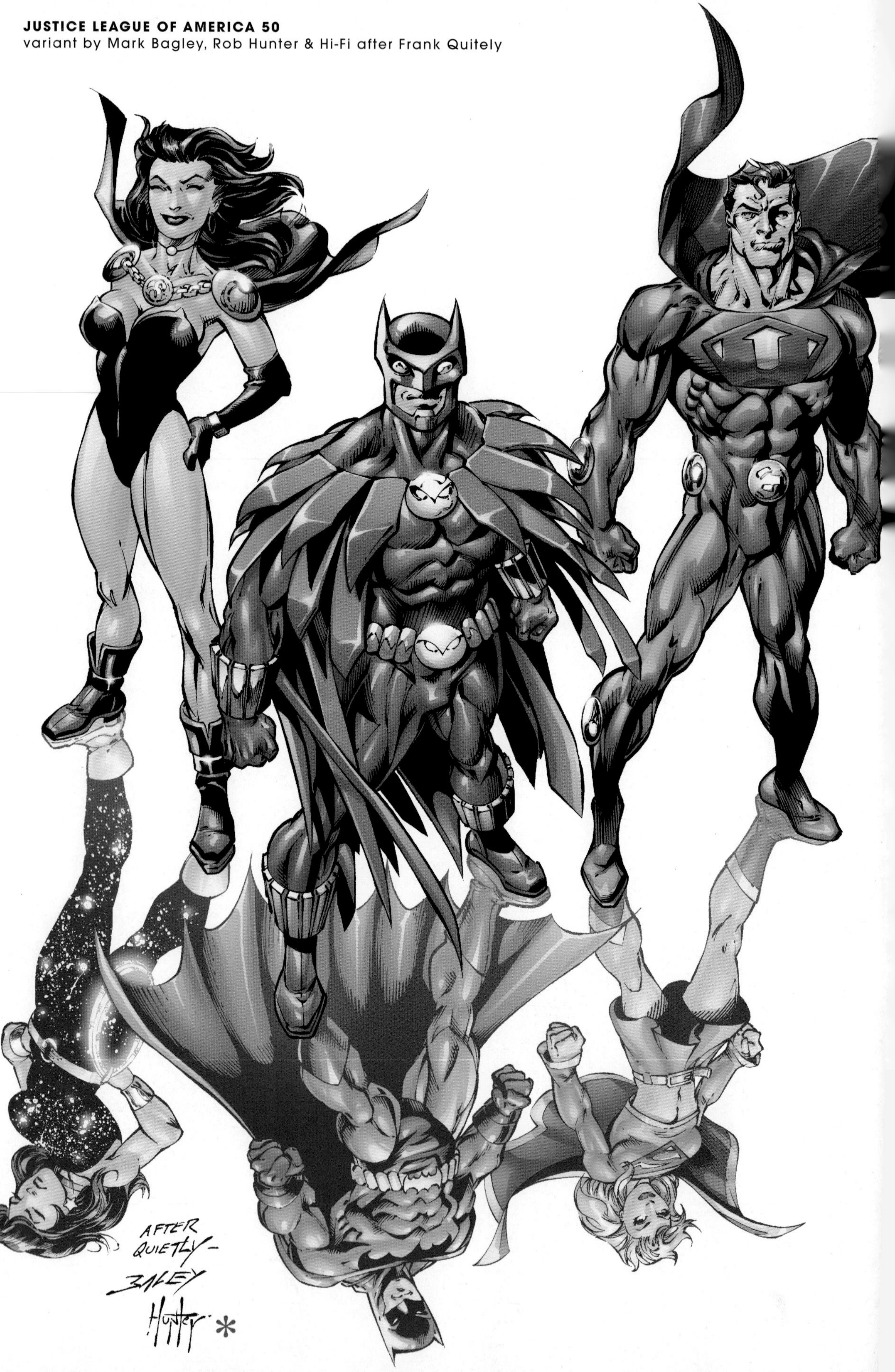
AFTER QUIETLY-
BAGLEY
Hunter

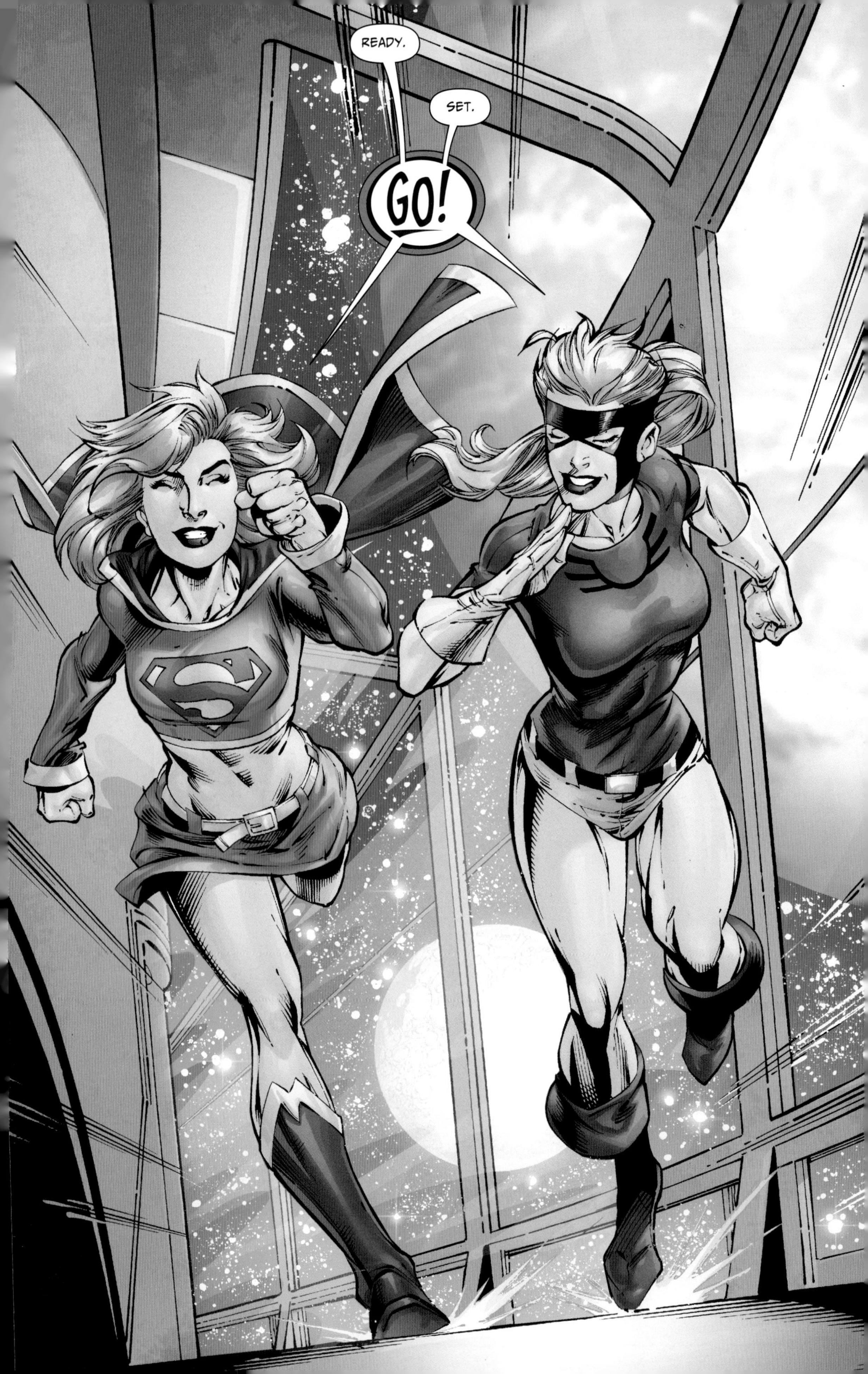
READY.
SET.
GO!

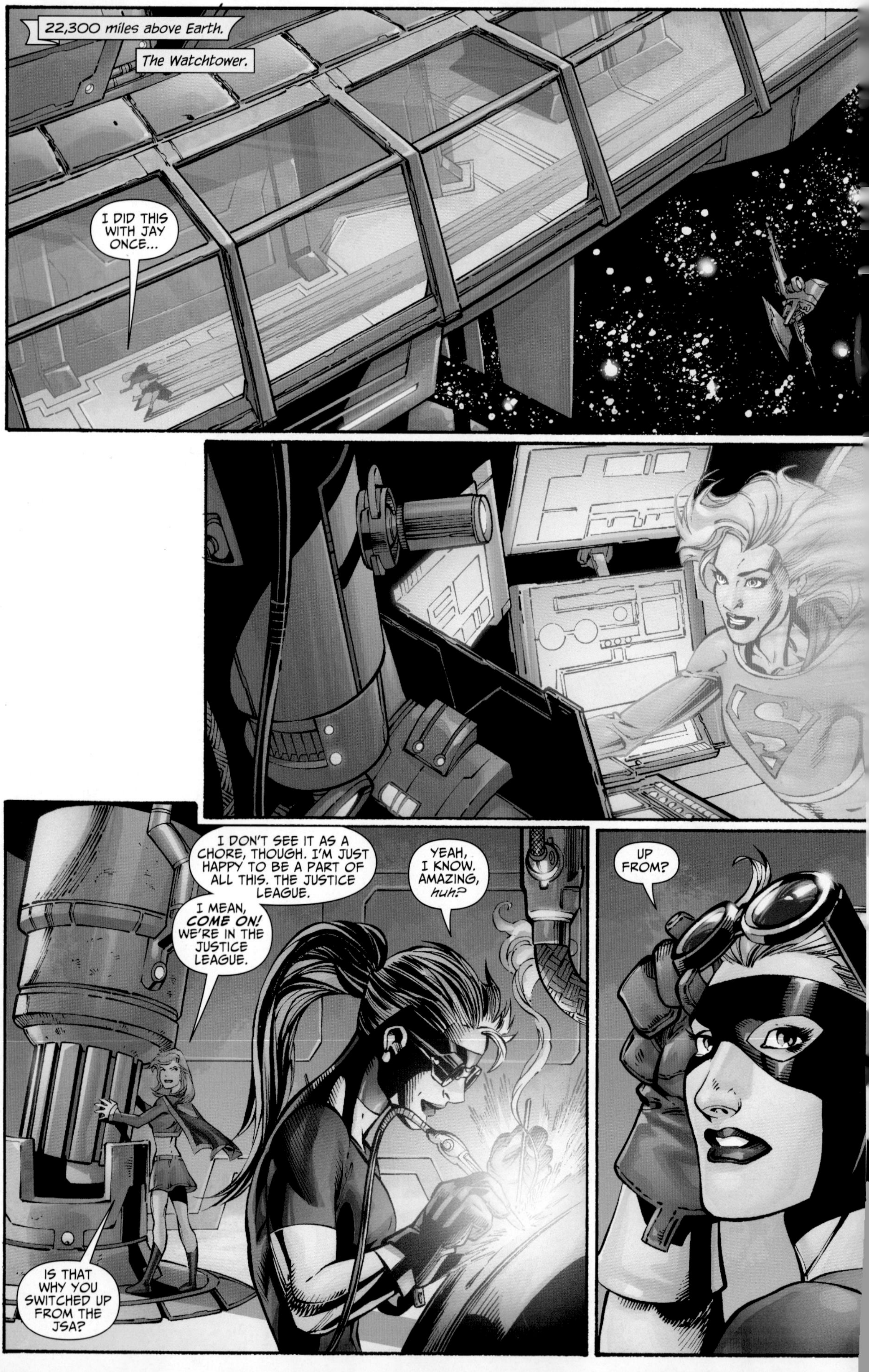
22,300 miles above Earth.
The Watchtower.
I DID THIS WITH JAY ONCE...
I DON'T SEE IT AS A CHORE, THOUGH. I'M JUST HAPPY TO BE A PART OF ALL THIS. THE JUSTICE LEAGUE.
I MEAN, COME ON! WE'RE IN THE JUSTICE LEAGUE.
YEAH, I KNOW. AMAZING, huh?
IS THAT WHY YOU SWITCHED UP FROM THE JSA?
UP FROM?

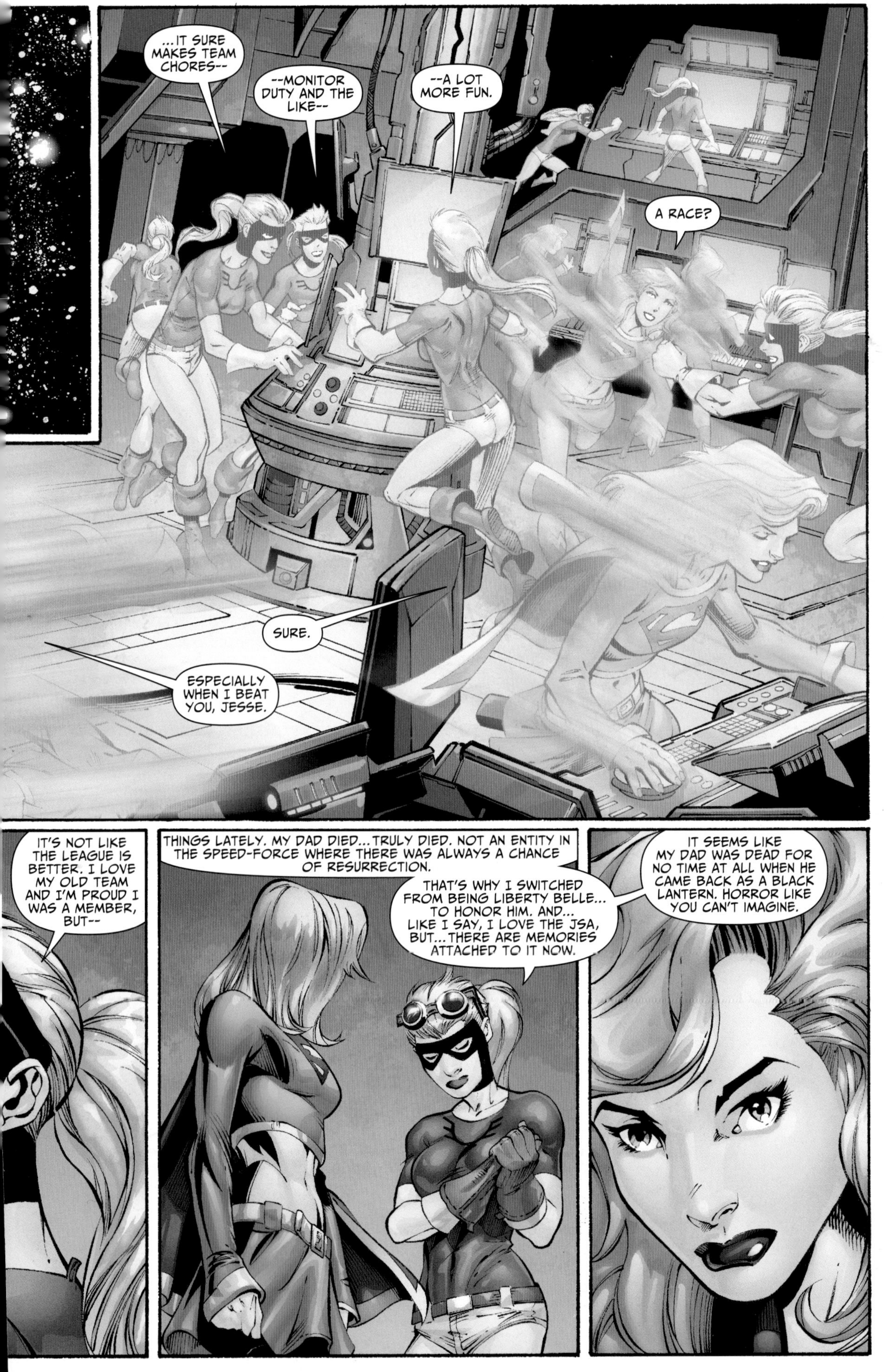
...IT SURE MAKES TEAM CHORES--
--MONITOR DUTY AND THE LIKE--
--A LOT MORE FUN.
A RACE?
SURE.
ESPECIALLY WHEN I BEAT YOU, JESSE.
IT'S NOT LIKE THE LEAGUE IS BETTER. I LOVE MY OLD TEAM AND I'M PROUD I WAS A MEMBER, BUT--
THINGS LATELY. MY DAD DIED...TRULY DIED. NOT AN ENTITY IN THE SPEED-FORCE WHERE THERE WAS ALWAYS A CHANCE OF RESURRECTION.
THAT'S WHY I SWITCHED FROM BEING LIBERTY BELLE... TO HONOR HIM. AND... LIKE I SAY, I LOVE THE JSA, BUT...THERE ARE MEMORIES ATTACHED TO IT NOW.
IT SEEMS LIKE MY DAD WAS DEAD FOR NO TIME AT ALL WHEN HE CAME BACK AS A BLACK LANTERN. HORROR LIKE YOU CAN'T IMAGINE.

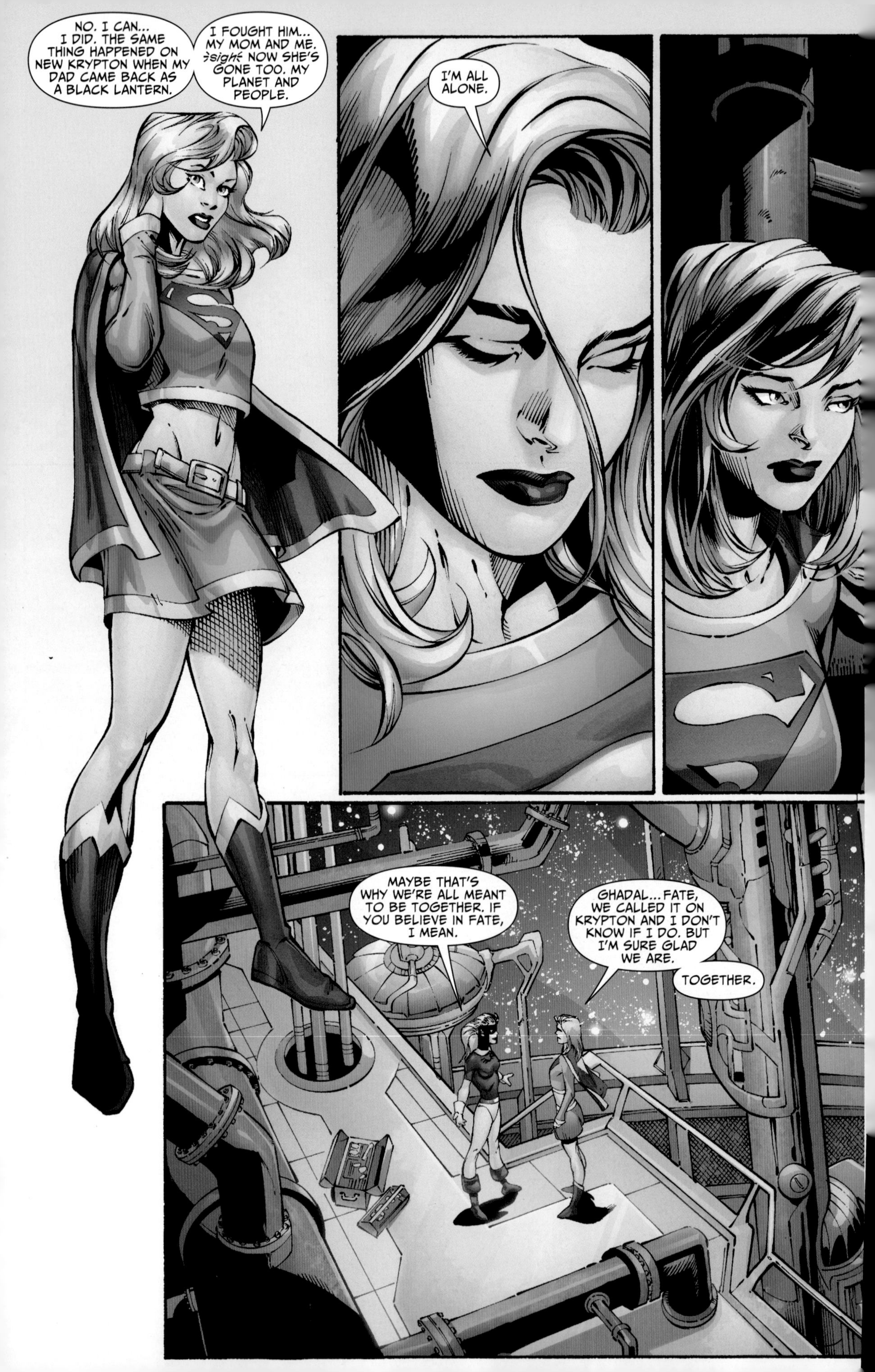
NO. I CAN... I DID. THE SAME THING HAPPENED ON NEW KRYPTON WHEN MY DAD CAME BACK AS A BLACK LANTERN.
I FOUGHT HIM... MY MOM AND ME. *sigh* NOW SHE'S GONE TOO. MY PLANET AND PEOPLE.
I'M ALL ALONE.
MAYBE THAT'S WHY WE'RE ALL MEANT TO BE TOGETHER. IF YOU BELIEVE IN FATE, I MEAN.
GHADAL... FATE, WE CALLED IT ON KRYPTON AND I DON'T KNOW IF I DO. BUT I'M SURE GLAD WE ARE.
TOGETHER.

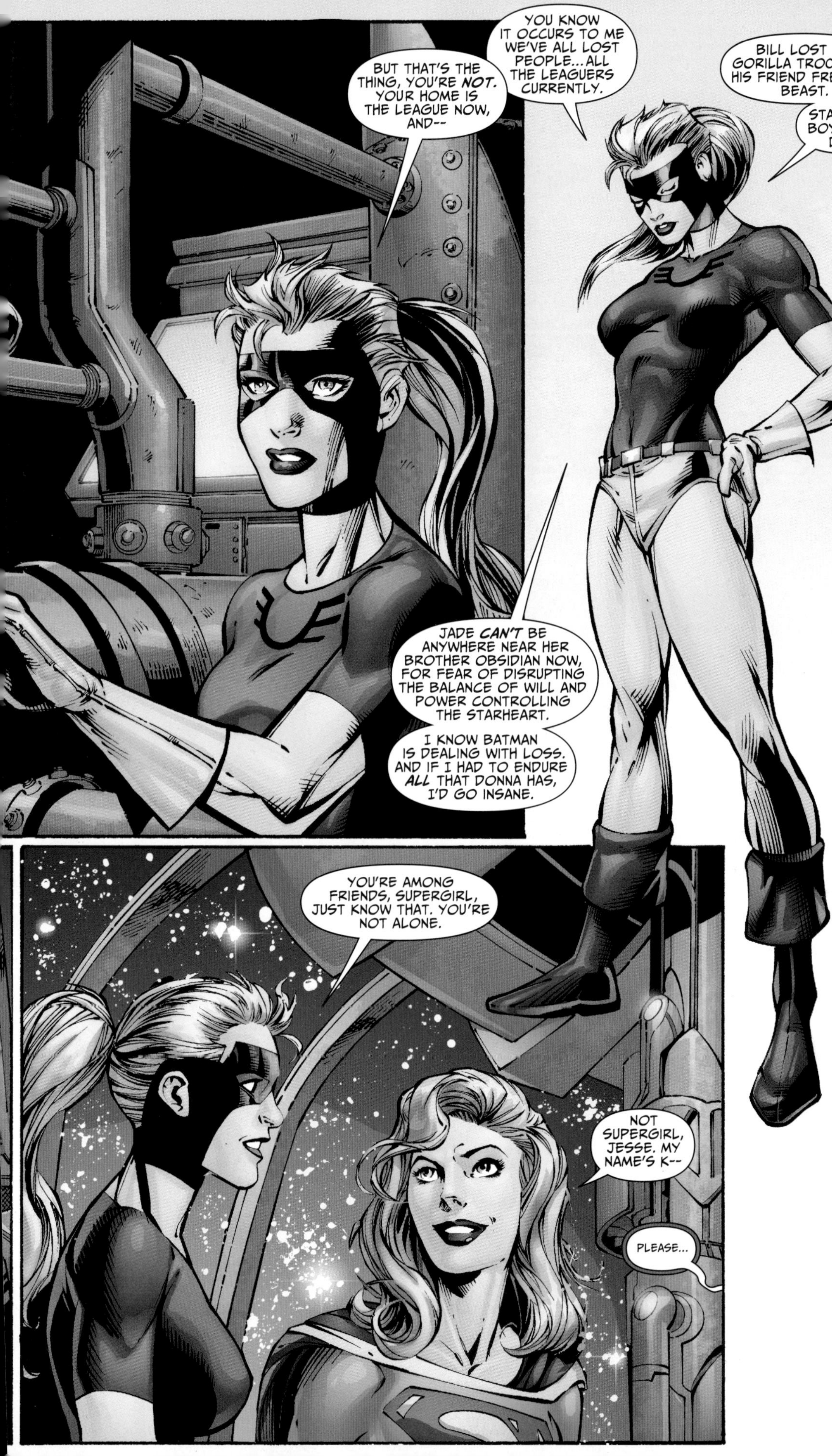

BUT THAT'S THE THING, YOU'RE NOT. YOUR HOME IS THE LEAGUE NOW, AND--
YOU KNOW IT OCCURS TO ME WE'VE ALL LOST PEOPLE...ALL THE LEAGUERS CURRENTLY.
BILL LOST HIS GORILLA TROOP AND HIS FRIEND FREEDOM BEAST.
STARMAN'S BOYFRIEND DIED.
JADE CAN'T BE ANYWHERE NEAR HER BROTHER OBSIDIAN NOW, FOR FEAR OF DISRUPTING THE BALANCE OF WILL AND POWER CONTROLLING THE STARHEART.
I KNOW BATMAN IS DEALING WITH LOSS. AND IF I HAD TO ENDURE ALL THAT DONNA HAS, I'D GO INSANE.
YOU'RE AMONG FRIENDS, SUPERGIRL, JUST KNOW THAT. YOU'RE NOT ALONE.
NOT SUPERGIRL, JESSE. MY NAME'S K--
PLEASE...

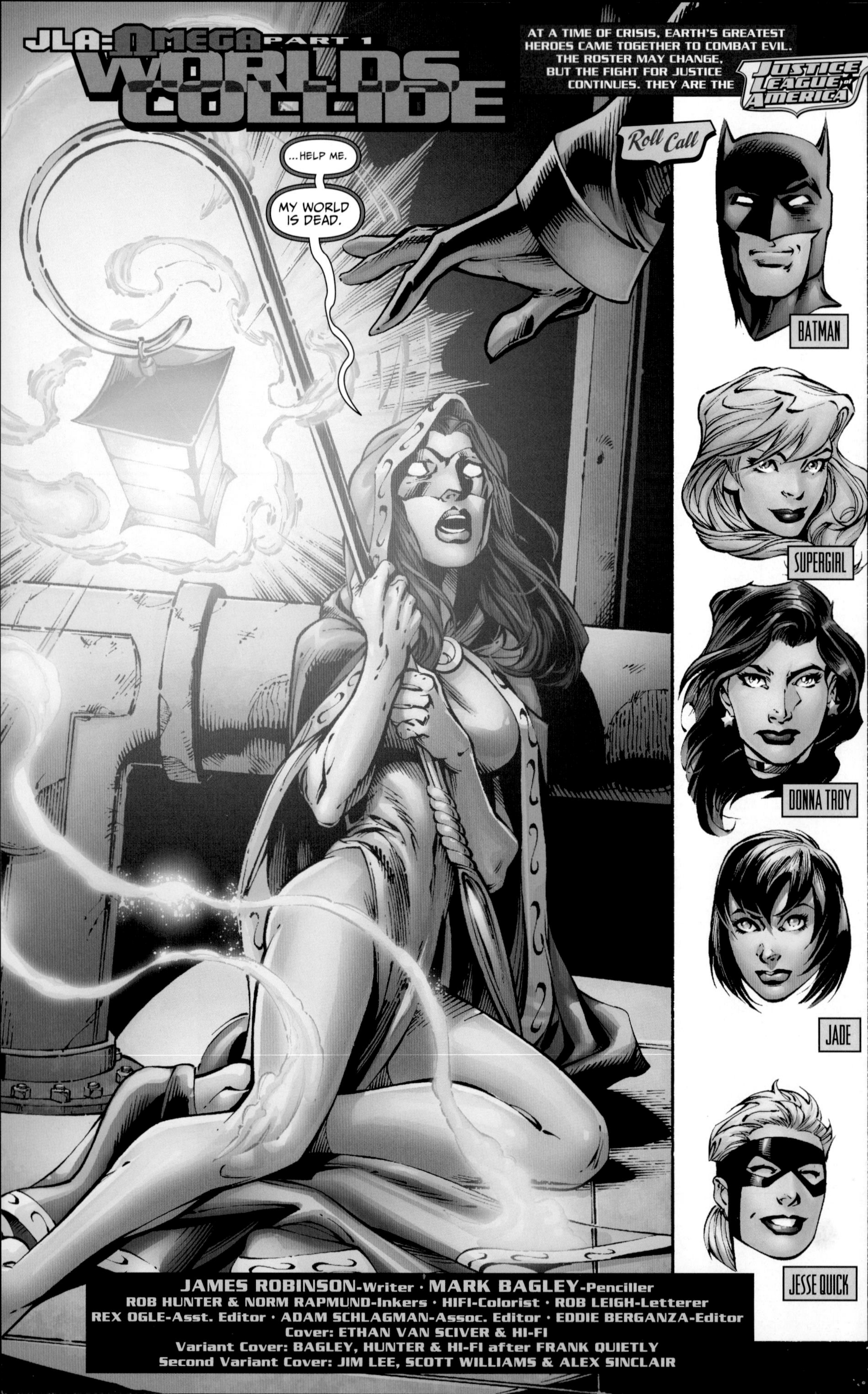
JLA: OMEGA PART 1
WORLDS COLLIDE
AT A TIME OF CRISIS, EARTH'S GREATEST HEROES CAME TOGETHER TO COMBAT EVIL. THE ROSTER MAY CHANGE, BUT THE FIGHT FOR JUSTICE CONTINUES. THEY ARE THE JUSTICE LEAGUE of AMERICA
Roll Call
...HELP ME.
MY WORLD IS DEAD.
BATMAN
SUPERGIRL
DONNA TROY
JADE
JESSE QUICK
JAMES ROBINSON-Writer · MARK BAGLEY-Penciller
ROB HUNTER & NORM RAPMUND-Inkers · HIFI-Colorist · ROB LEIGH-Letterer
REX OGLE-Asst. Editor · ADAM SCHLAGMAN-Assoc. Editor · EDDIE BERGANZA-Editor
Cover: ETHAN VAN SCIVER & HI-FI
Variant Cover: BAGLEY, HUNTER & HI-FI after FRANK QUIETLY
Second Variant Cover: JIM LEE, SCOTT WILLIAMS & ALEX SINCLAIR

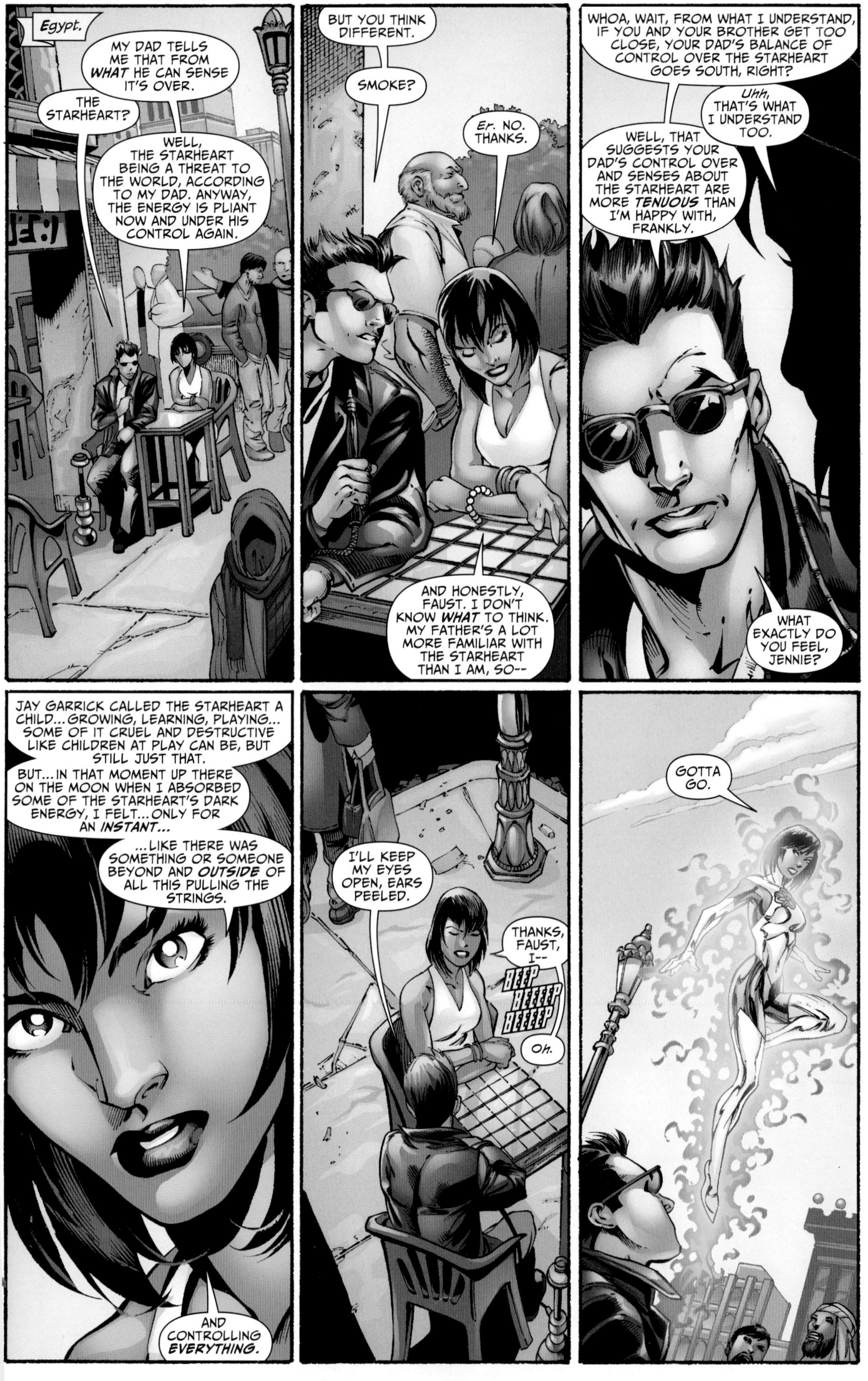
Egypt.
MY DAD TELLS ME THAT FROM WHAT HE CAN SENSE IT'S OVER.
THE STARHEART?
WELL, THE STARHEART BEING A THREAT TO THE WORLD, ACCORDING TO MY DAD. ANYWAY, THE ENERGY IS PLIANT NOW AND UNDER HIS CONTROL AGAIN.
BUT YOU THINK DIFFERENT.
SMOKE?
Er. NO. THANKS.
AND HONESTLY, FAUST. I DON'T KNOW WHAT TO THINK. MY FATHER'S A LOT MORE FAMILIAR WITH THE STARHEART THAN I AM, SO--
WHOA, WAIT, FROM WHAT I UNDERSTAND, IF YOU AND YOUR BROTHER GET TOO CLOSE, YOUR DAD'S BALANCE OF CONTROL OVER THE STARHEART GOES SOUTH, RIGHT?
Uhh, THAT'S WHAT I UNDERSTAND TOO.
WELL, THAT SUGGESTS YOUR DAD'S CONTROL OVER AND SENSES ABOUT THE STARHEART ARE MORE TENUOUS THAN I'M HAPPY WITH, FRANKLY.
WHAT EXACTLY DO YOU FEEL, JENNIE?
JAY GARRICK CALLED THE STARHEART A CHILD...GROWING, LEARNING, PLAYING... SOME OF IT CRUEL AND DESTRUCTIVE LIKE CHILDREN AT PLAY CAN BE, BUT STILL JUST THAT.
BUT...IN THAT MOMENT UP THERE ON THE MOON WHEN I ABSORBED SOME OF THE STARHEART'S DARK ENERGY, I FELT...ONLY FOR AN INSTANT...
...LIKE THERE WAS SOMETHING OR SOMEONE BEYOND AND OUTSIDE OF ALL THIS PULLING THE STRINGS.
AND CONTROLLING EVERYTHING.
I'LL KEEP MY EYES OPEN, EARS PEELED.
THANKS, FAUST, I--
BEEP BEEEEP BEEEEP
Oh.
GOTTA GO.

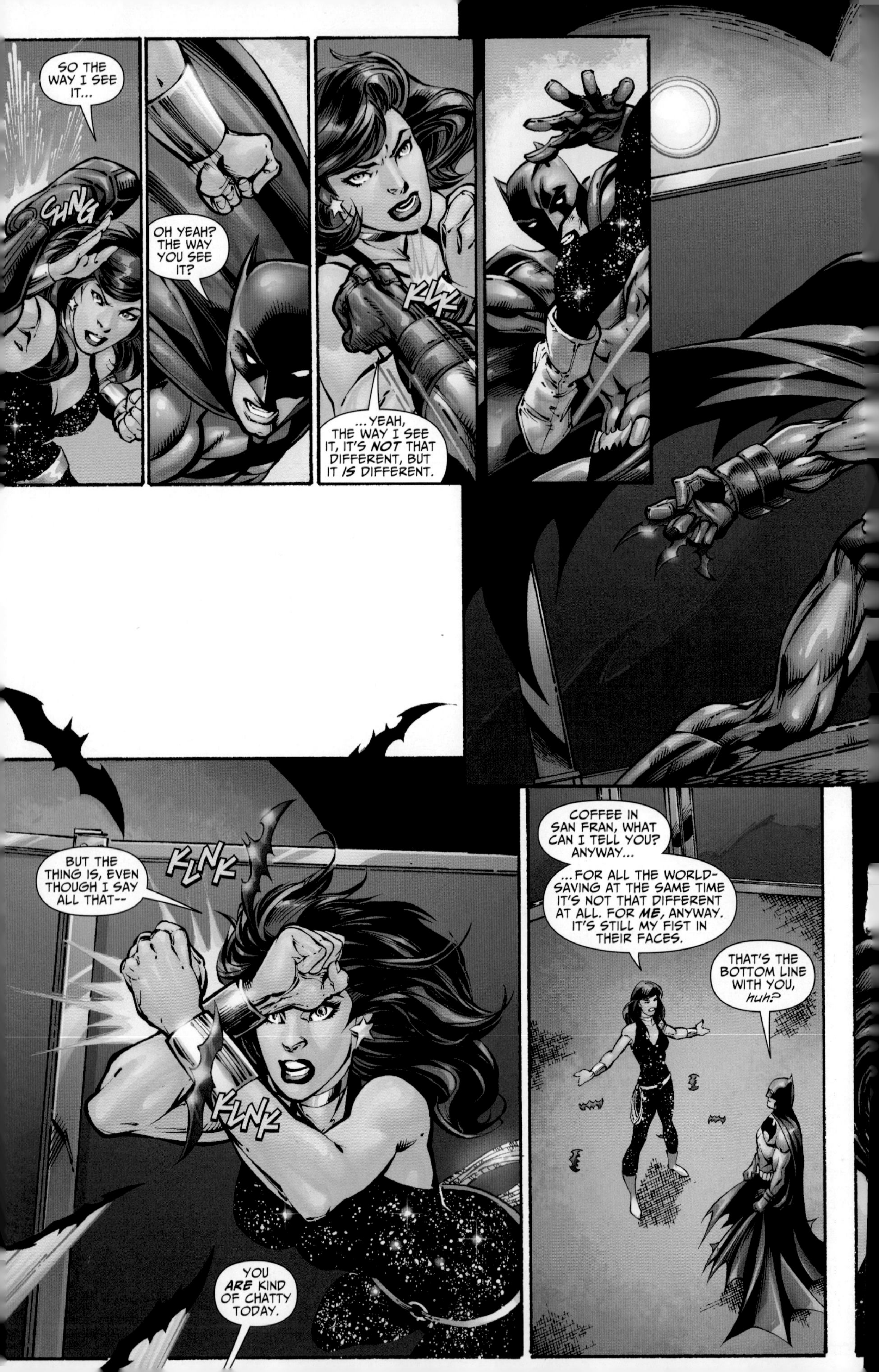
SO THE WAY I SEE IT...
CHING
OH YEAH? THE WAY YOU SEE IT?
KLNK
...YEAH, THE WAY I SEE IT, IT'S NOT THAT DIFFERENT, BUT IT IS DIFFERENT.
BUT THE THING IS, EVEN THOUGH I SAY ALL THAT--
KLNK
KLNK
YOU ARE KIND OF CHATTY TODAY.
COFFEE IN SAN FRAN, WHAT CAN I TELL YOU? ANYWAY...
...FOR ALL THE WORLD-SAVING AT THE SAME TIME IT'S NOT THAT DIFFERENT AT ALL. FOR ME, ANYWAY. IT'S STILL MY FIST IN THEIR FACES.
THAT'S THE BOTTOM LINE WITH YOU, huh?

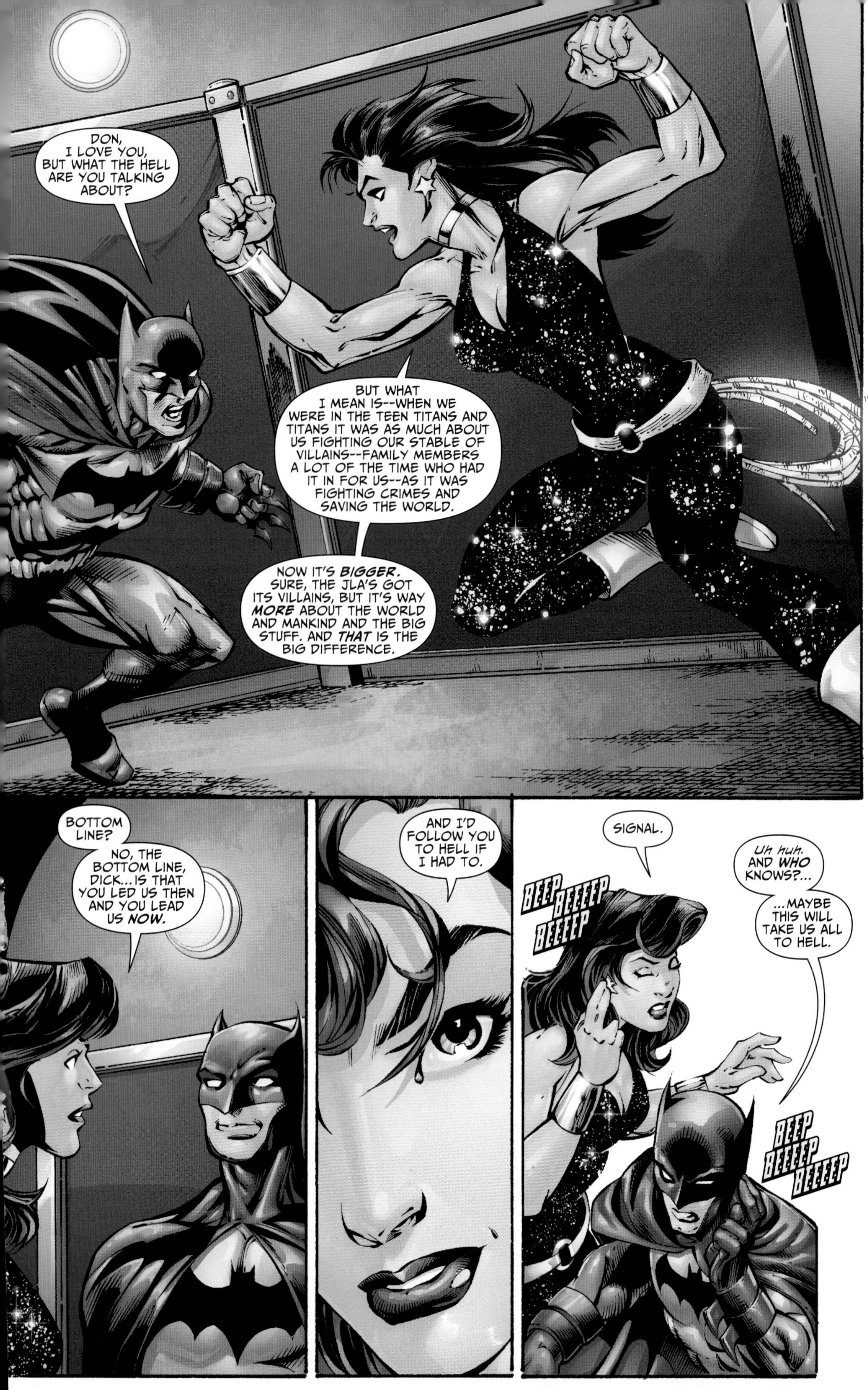

DON, I LOVE YOU, BUT WHAT THE HELL ARE YOU TALKING ABOUT?
BUT WHAT I MEAN IS--WHEN WE WERE IN THE TEEN TITANS AND TITANS IT WAS AS MUCH ABOUT US FIGHTING OUR STABLE OF VILLAINS--FAMILY MEMBERS A LOT OF THE TIME WHO HAD IT IN FOR US--AS IT WAS FIGHTING CRIMES AND SAVING THE WORLD.
NOW IT'S **BIGGER.** SURE, THE JLA'S GOT ITS VILLAINS, BUT IT'S WAY ***MORE*** ABOUT THE WORLD AND MANKIND AND THE BIG STUFF. AND ***THAT*** IS THE BIG DIFFERENCE.
BOTTOM LINE?
NO, THE BOTTOM LINE, DICK...IS THAT YOU LED US THEN AND YOU LEAD US ***NOW.***
AND I'D FOLLOW YOU TO HELL IF I HAD TO.
SIGNAL.
BEEP BEEEEP BEEEEP
Uh huh. AND ***WHO*** KNOWS?...
...MAYBE THIS WILL TAKE US ALL TO HELL.
BEEP BEEEEP BEEEEP

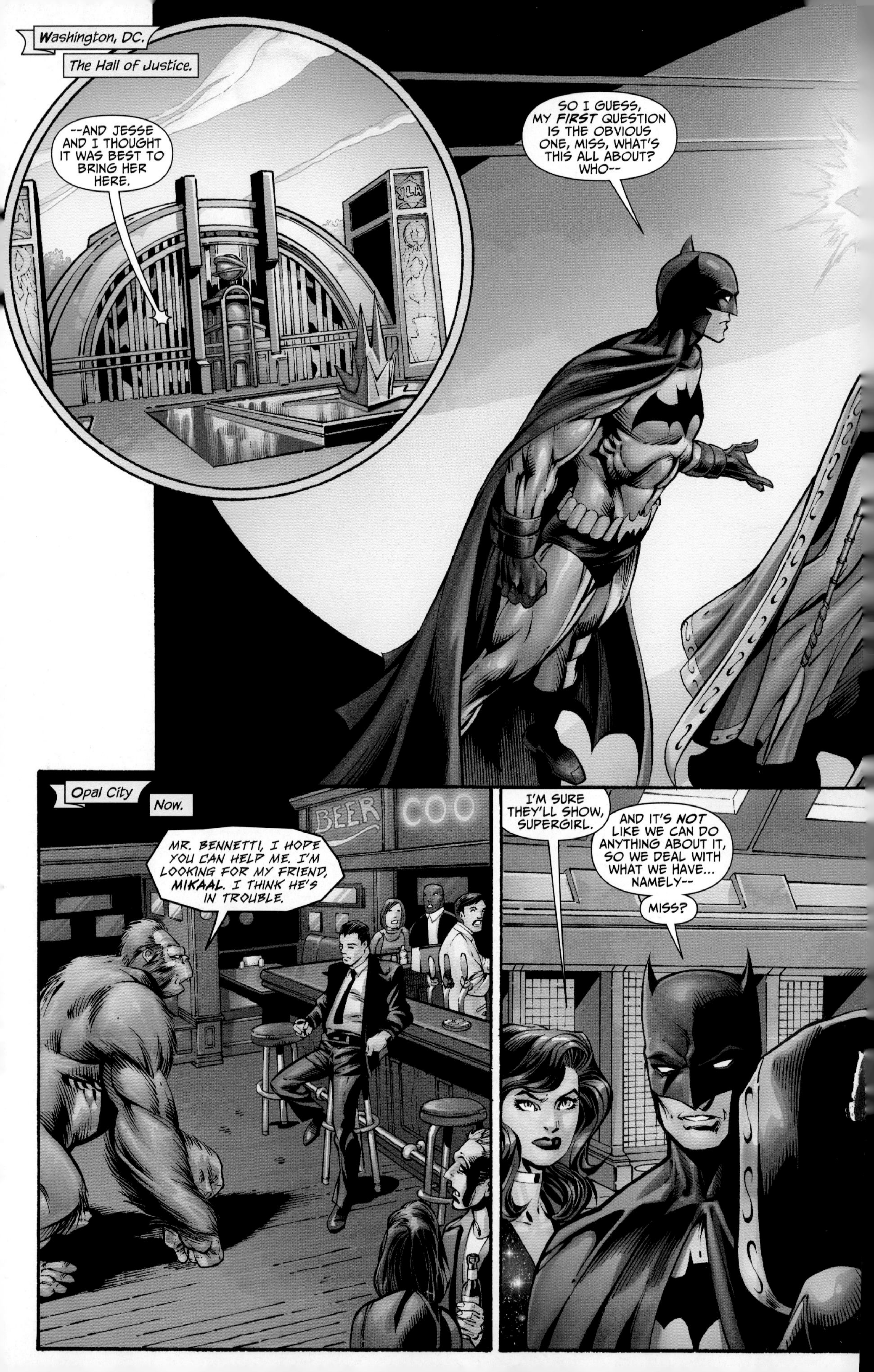
Washington, DC.
The Hall of Justice.
--AND JESSE AND I THOUGHT IT WAS BEST TO BRING HER HERE.
SO I GUESS, MY FIRST QUESTION IS THE OBVIOUS ONE, MISS, WHAT'S THIS ALL ABOUT? WHO--
Opal City
Now.
BEER
COO
MR. BENNETTI, I HOPE YOU CAN HELP ME. I'M LOOKING FOR MY FRIEND, MIKAAL. I THINK HE'S IN TROUBLE.
I'M SURE THEY'LL SHOW, SUPERGIRL.
AND IT'S NOT LIKE WE CAN DO ANYTHING ABOUT IT, SO WE DEAL WITH WHAT WE HAVE... NAMELY--
MISS?

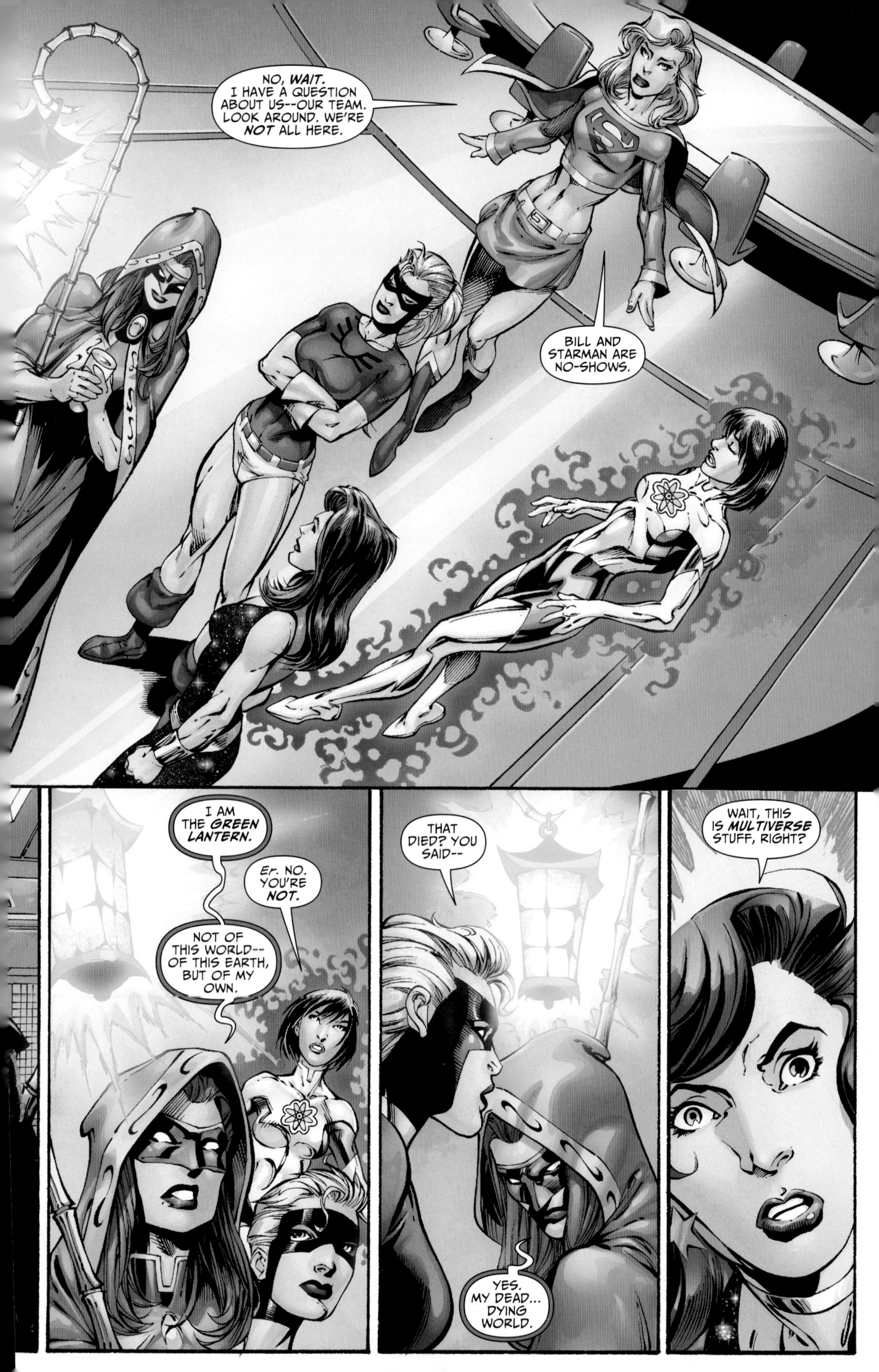
NO, WAIT. I HAVE A QUESTION ABOUT US--OUR TEAM. LOOK AROUND. WE'RE NOT ALL HERE.
BILL AND STARMAN ARE NO-SHOWS.
I AM THE GREEN LANTERN.
Er. NO. YOU'RE NOT.
NOT OF THIS WORLD-- OF THIS EARTH, BUT OF MY OWN.
THAT DIED? YOU SAID--
YES. MY DEAD... DYING WORLD.
WAIT, THIS IS MULTIVERSE STUFF, RIGHT?

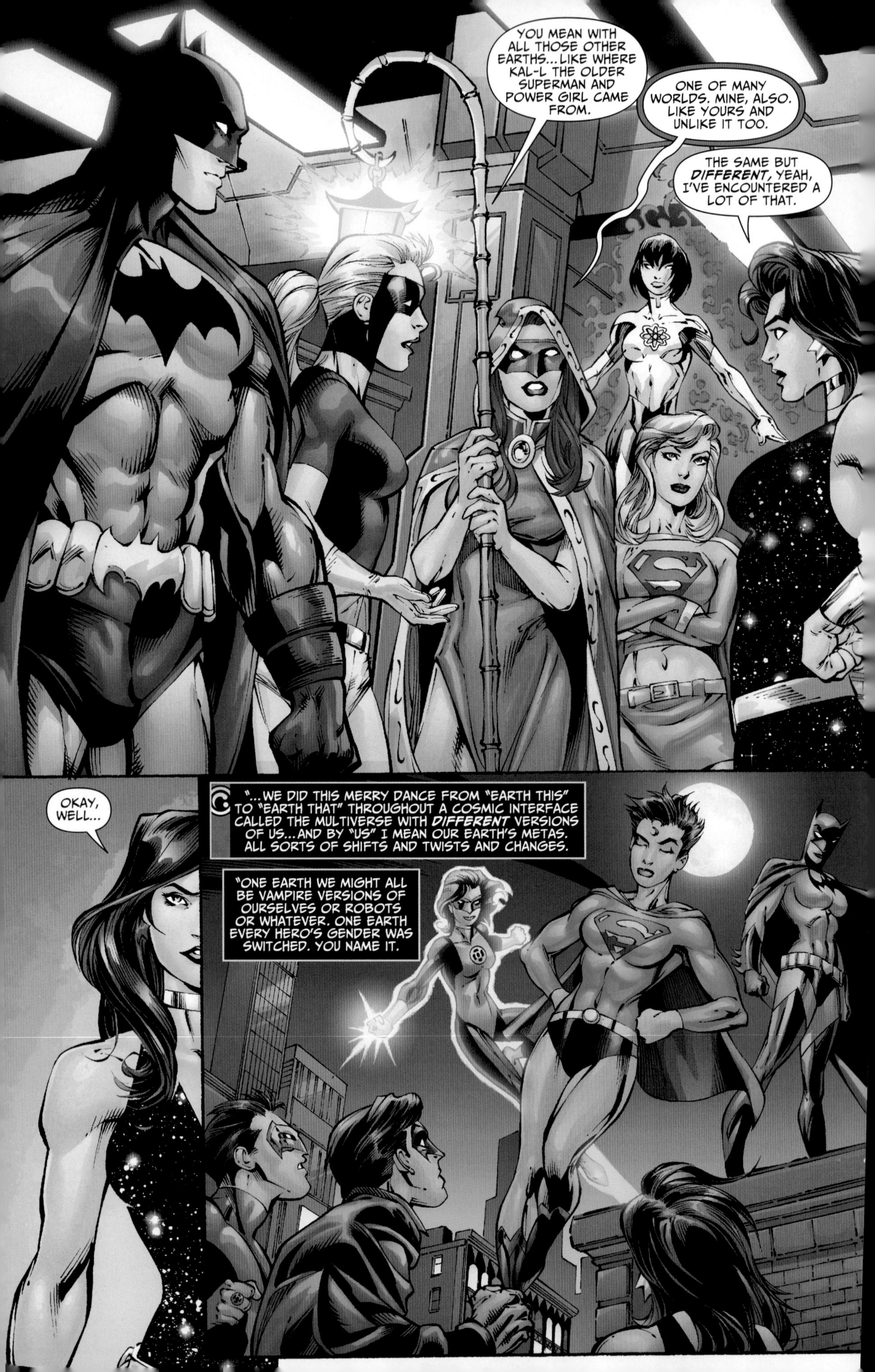
YOU MEAN WITH ALL THOSE OTHER EARTHS...LIKE WHERE KAL-L THE OLDER SUPERMAN AND POWER GIRL CAME FROM.
ONE OF MANY WORLDS. MINE, ALSO. LIKE YOURS AND UNLIKE IT TOO.
THE SAME BUT DIFFERENT, YEAH, I'VE ENCOUNTERED A LOT OF THAT.
OKAY, WELL...
"...WE DID THIS MERRY DANCE FROM "EARTH THIS" TO "EARTH THAT" THROUGHOUT A COSMIC INTERFACE CALLED THE MULTIVERSE WITH DIFFERENT VERSIONS OF US...AND BY "US" I MEAN OUR EARTH'S METAS. ALL SORTS OF SHIFTS AND TWISTS AND CHANGES.
"ONE EARTH WE MIGHT ALL BE VAMPIRE VERSIONS OF OURSELVES OR ROBOTS OR WHATEVER. ONE EARTH EVERY HERO'S GENDER WAS SWITCHED. YOU NAME IT.

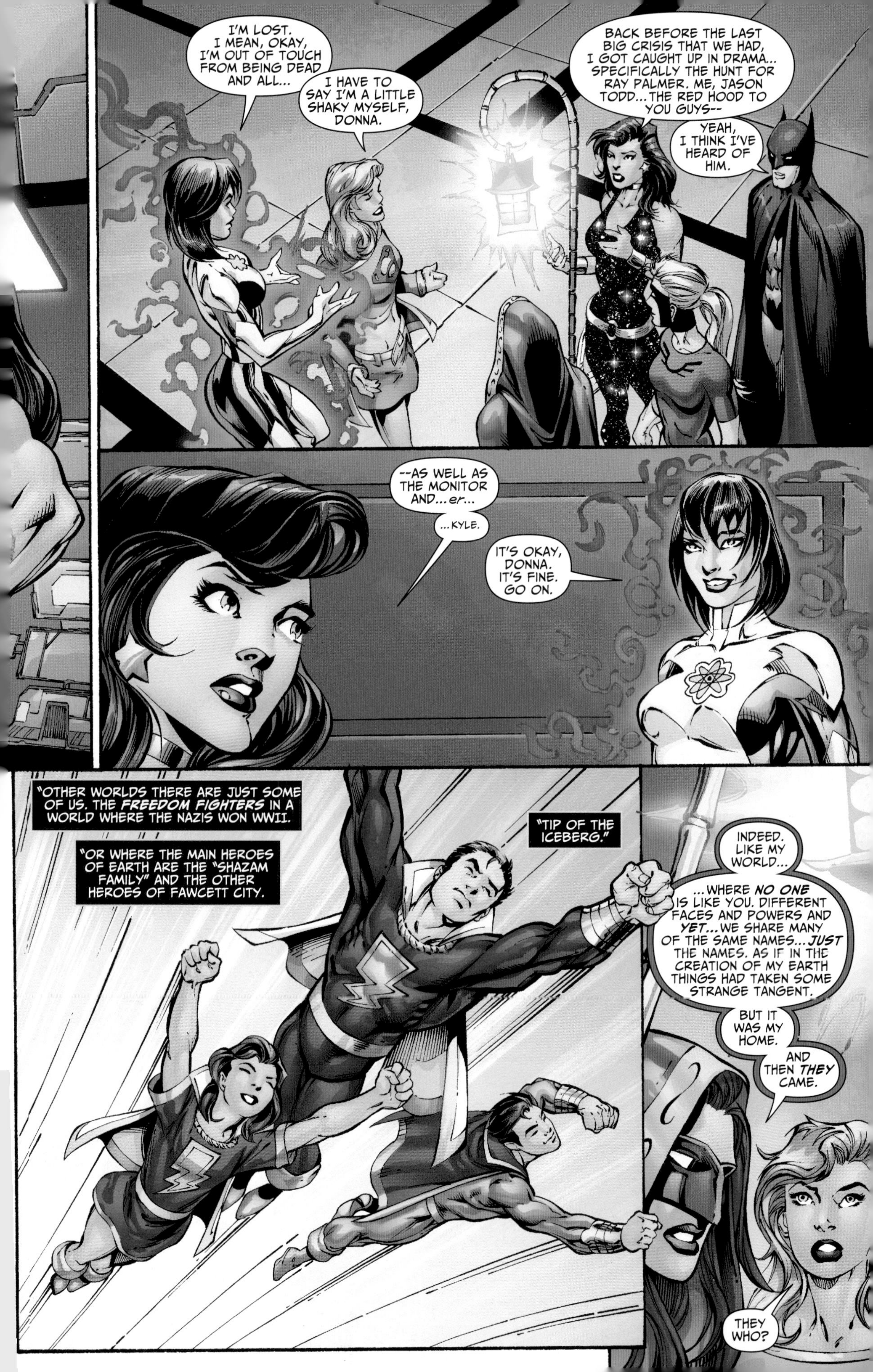
I'M LOST. I MEAN, OKAY, I'M OUT OF TOUCH FROM BEING DEAD AND ALL...
I HAVE TO SAY I'M A LITTLE SHAKY MYSELF, DONNA.
BACK BEFORE THE LAST BIG CRISIS THAT WE HAD, I GOT CAUGHT UP IN DRAMA... SPECIFICALLY THE HUNT FOR RAY PALMER. ME, JASON TODD... THE RED HOOD TO YOU GUYS--
YEAH, I THINK I'VE HEARD OF HIM.
--AS WELL AS THE MONITOR AND... er...
...KYLE.
IT'S OKAY, DONNA. IT'S FINE. GO ON.
"OTHER WORLDS THERE ARE JUST SOME OF US. THE FREEDOM FIGHTERS IN A WORLD WHERE THE NAZIS WON WWII.
"OR WHERE THE MAIN HEROES OF EARTH ARE THE "SHAZAM FAMILY" AND THE OTHER HEROES OF FAWCETT CITY.
"TIP OF THE ICEBERG."
INDEED. LIKE MY WORLD...
...WHERE NO ONE IS LIKE YOU. DIFFERENT FACES AND POWERS AND YET... WE SHARE MANY OF THE SAME NAMES... JUST THE NAMES. AS IF IN THE CREATION OF MY EARTH THINGS HAD TAKEN SOME STRANGE TANGENT.
BUT IT WAS MY HOME.
AND THEN THEY CAME.
THEY WHO?

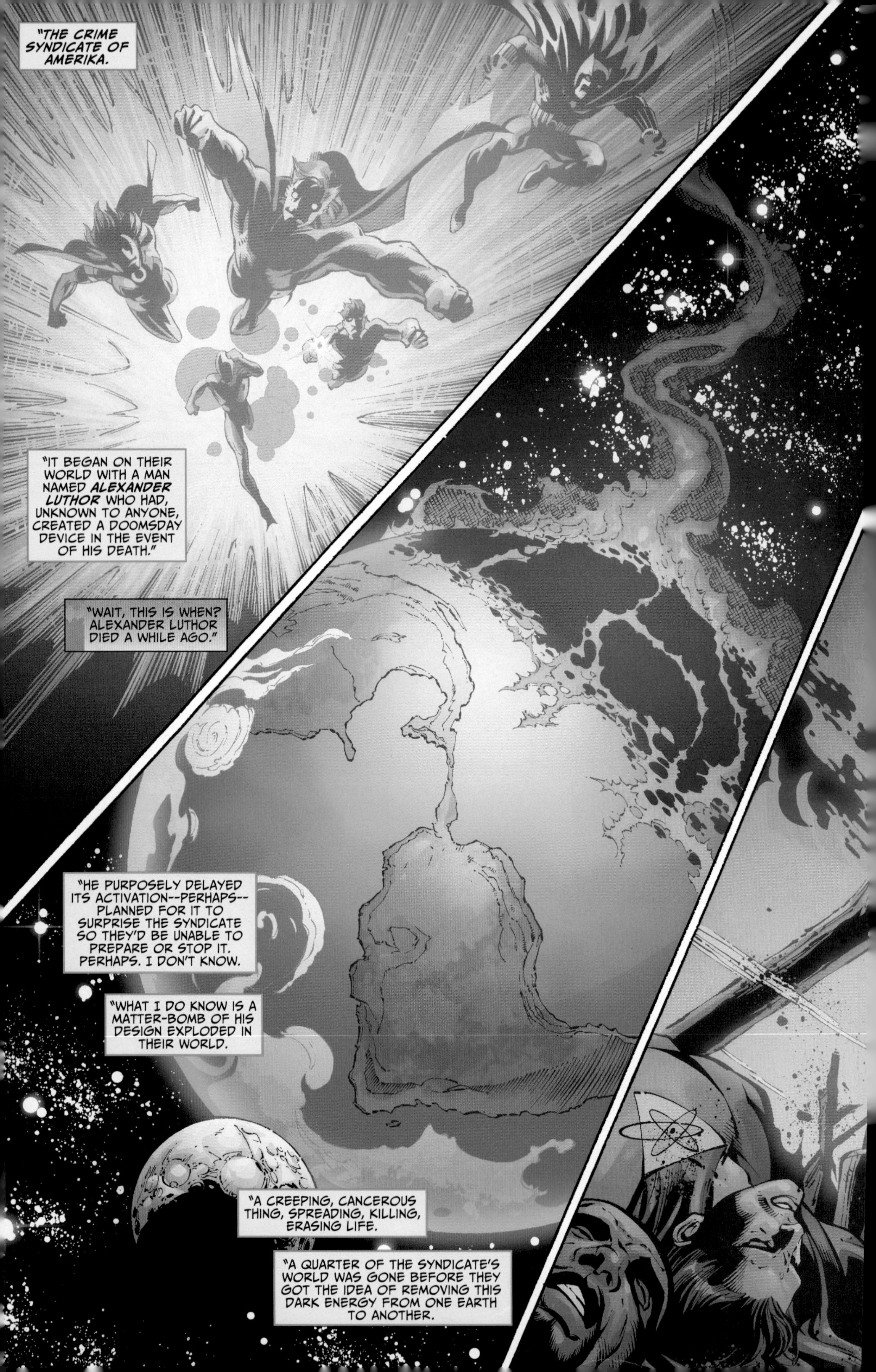
"THE CRIME SYNDICATE OF AMERIKA.
"IT BEGAN ON THEIR WORLD WITH A MAN NAMED ***ALEXANDER LUTHOR*** WHO HAD, UNKNOWN TO ANYONE, CREATED A DOOMSDAY DEVICE IN THE EVENT OF HIS DEATH."
"WAIT, THIS IS WHEN? ALEXANDER LUTHOR DIED A WHILE AGO."
"HE PURPOSELY DELAYED ITS ACTIVATION--PERHAPS--PLANNED FOR IT TO SURPRISE THE SYNDICATE SO THEY'D BE UNABLE TO PREPARE OR STOP IT. PERHAPS. I DON'T KNOW.
"WHAT I DO KNOW IS A MATTER-BOMB OF HIS DESIGN EXPLODED IN THEIR WORLD.
"A CREEPING, CANCEROUS THING, SPREADING, KILLING, ERASING LIFE.
"A QUARTER OF THE SYNDICATE'S WORLD WAS GONE BEFORE THEY GOT THE IDEA OF REMOVING THIS DARK ENERGY FROM ONE EARTH TO ANOTHER.

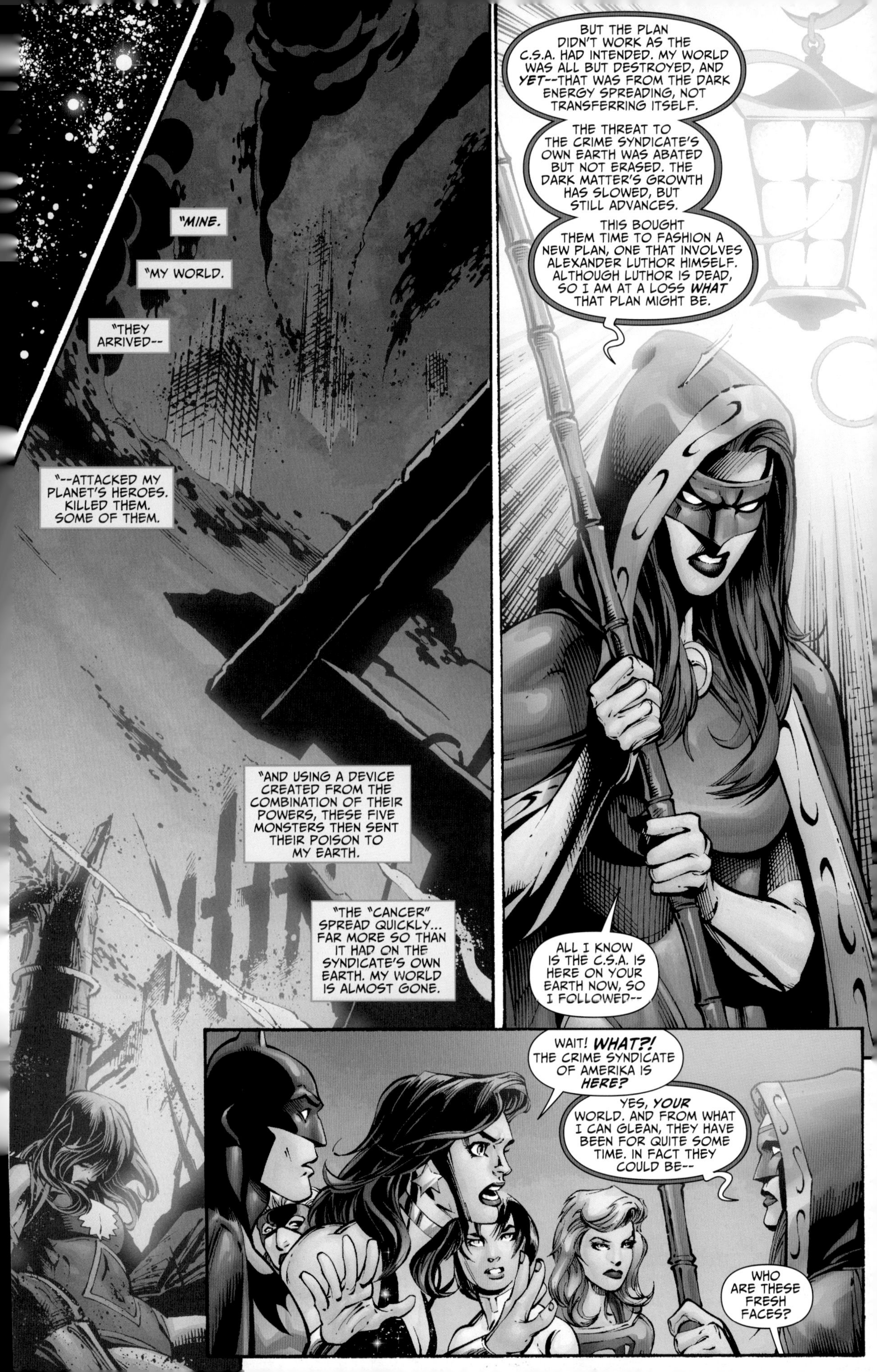
"MINE.
"MY WORLD.
"THEY ARRIVED--
"--ATTACKED MY PLANET'S HEROES. KILLED THEM. SOME OF THEM.
"AND USING A DEVICE CREATED FROM THE COMBINATION OF THEIR POWERS, THESE FIVE MONSTERS THEN SENT THEIR POISON TO MY EARTH.
"THE "CANCER" SPREAD QUICKLY... FAR MORE SO THAN IT HAD ON THE SYNDICATE'S OWN EARTH. MY WORLD IS ALMOST GONE.
BUT THE PLAN DIDN'T WORK AS THE C.S.A. HAD INTENDED. MY WORLD WAS ALL BUT DESTROYED, AND YET--THAT WAS FROM THE DARK ENERGY SPREADING, NOT TRANSFERRING ITSELF.
THE THREAT TO THE CRIME SYNDICATE'S OWN EARTH WAS ABATED BUT NOT ERASED. THE DARK MATTER'S GROWTH HAS SLOWED, BUT STILL ADVANCES.
THIS BOUGHT THEM TIME TO FASHION A NEW PLAN, ONE THAT INVOLVES ALEXANDER LUTHOR HIMSELF. ALTHOUGH LUTHOR IS DEAD, SO I AM AT A LOSS WHAT THAT PLAN MIGHT BE.
ALL I KNOW IS THE C.S.A. IS HERE ON YOUR EARTH NOW, SO I FOLLOWED--
WAIT! WHAT?! THE CRIME SYNDICATE OF AMERIKA IS HERE?
YES, YOUR WORLD. AND FROM WHAT I CAN GLEAN, THEY HAVE BEEN FOR QUITE SOME TIME. IN FACT THEY COULD BE--
WHO ARE THESE FRESH FACES?

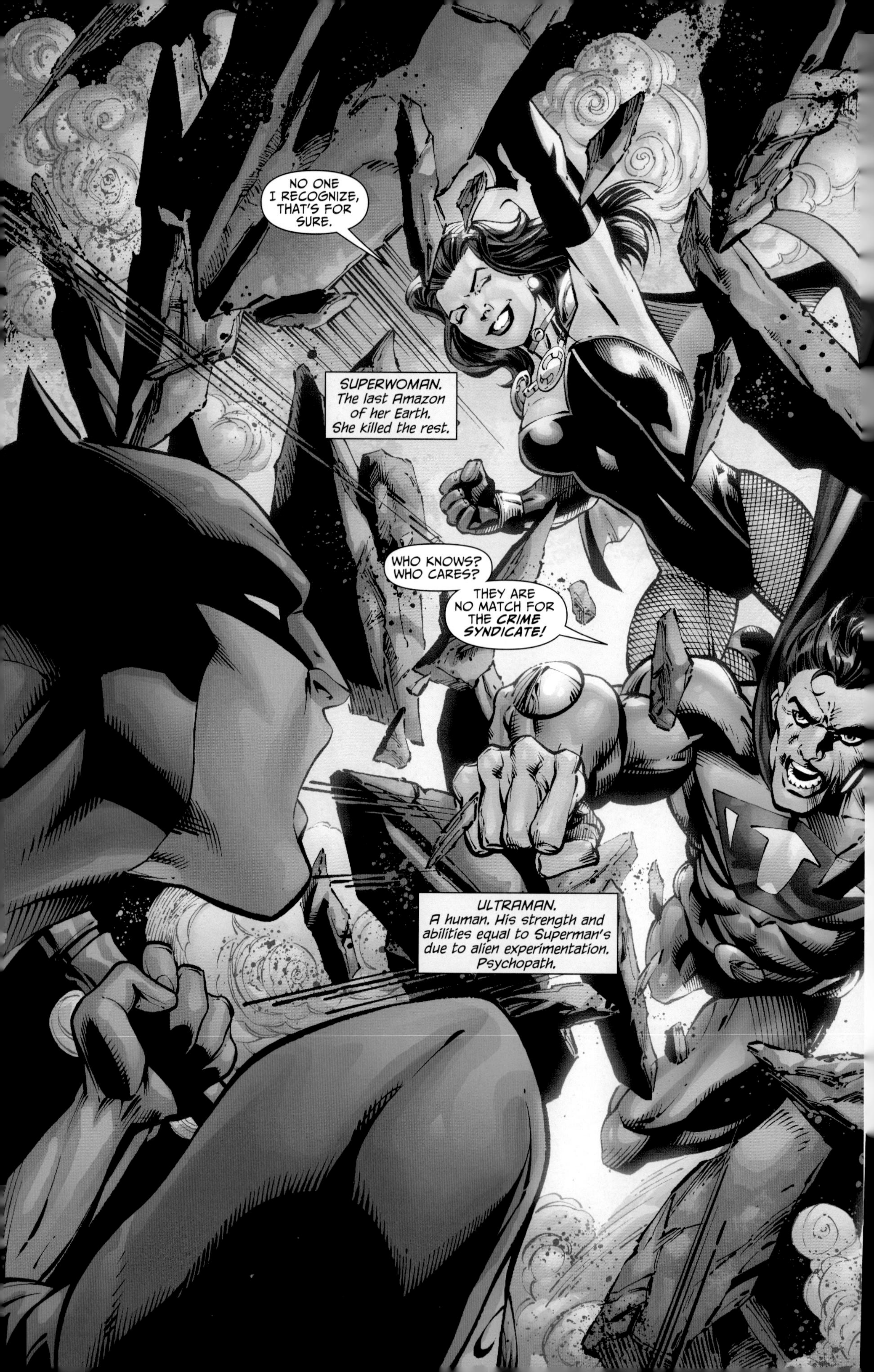
NO ONE I RECOGNIZE, THAT'S FOR SURE.
SUPERWOMAN. The last Amazon of her Earth. She killed the rest.
WHO KNOWS? WHO CARES?
THEY ARE NO MATCH FOR THE CRIME SYNDICATE!
ULTRAMAN. A human. His strength and abilities equal to Superman's due to alien experimentation. Psychopath.

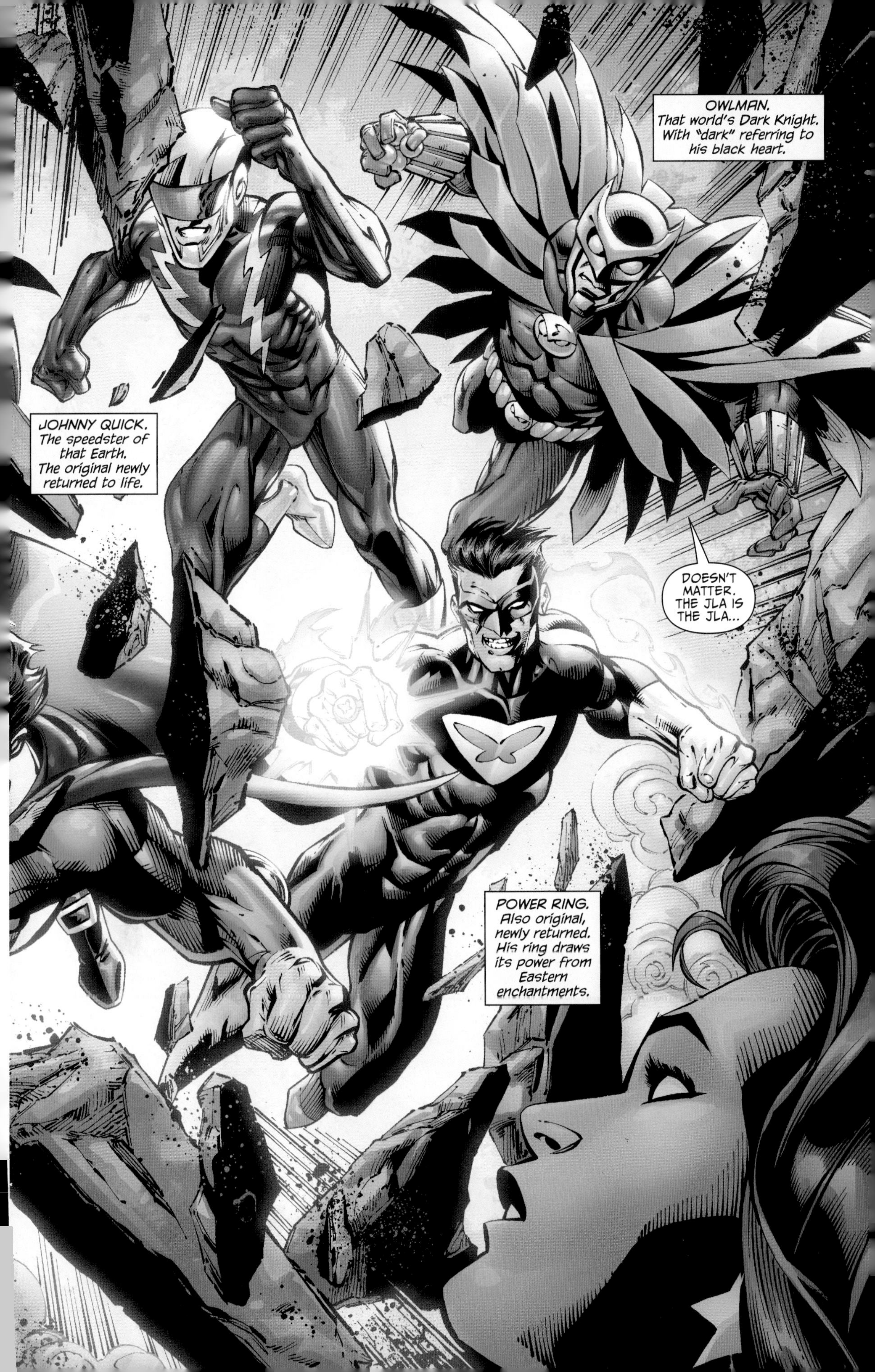
OWLMAN. That world's Dark Knight. With "dark" referring to his black heart.
JOHNNY QUICK. The speedster of that Earth. The original newly returned to life.
DOESN'T MATTER. THE JLA IS THE JLA...
POWER RING. Also original, newly returned. His ring draws its power from Eastern enchantments.

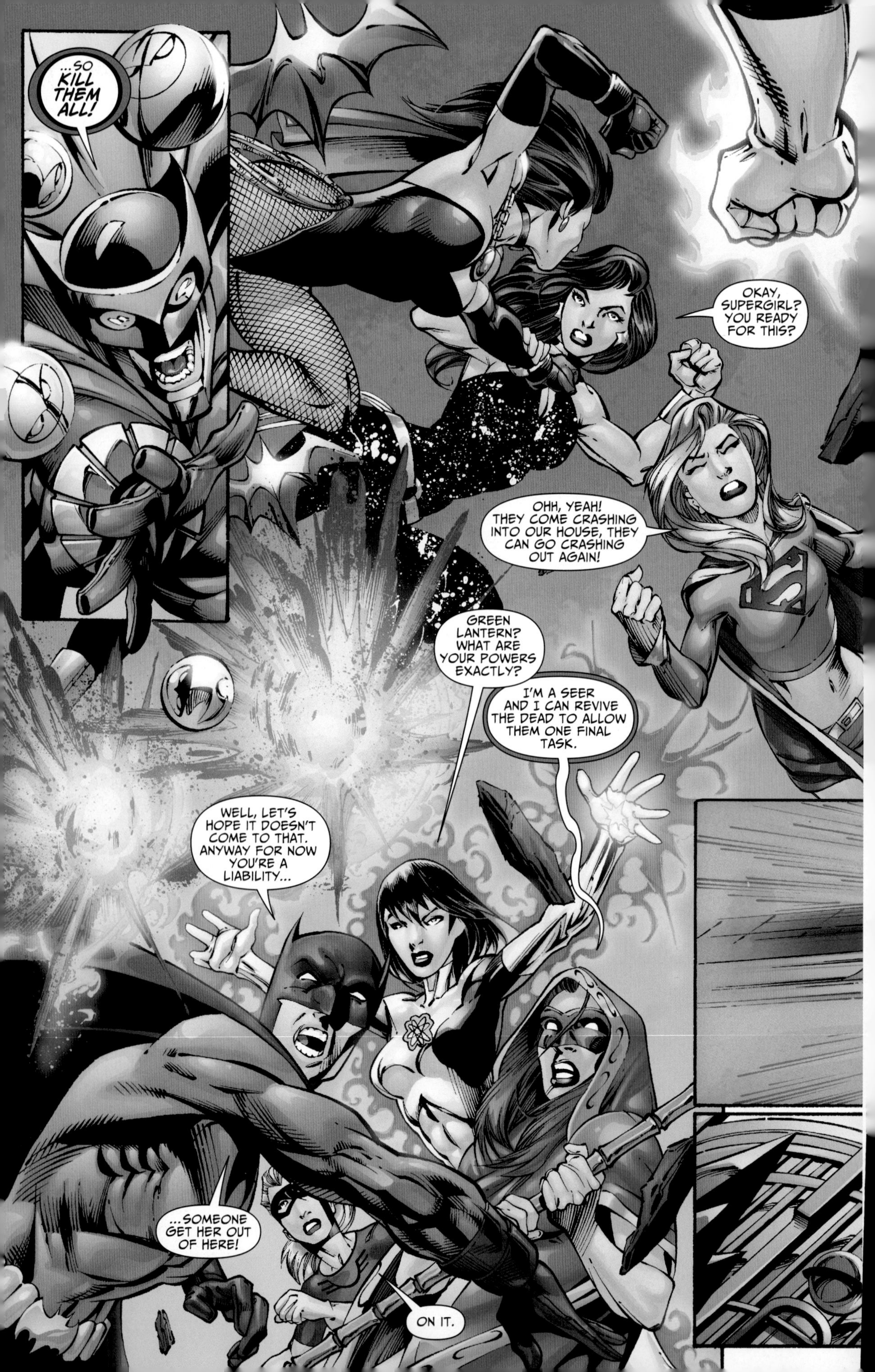
...SO KILL THEM ALL!
OKAY, SUPERGIRL? YOU READY FOR THIS?
OHH, YEAH! THEY COME CRASHING INTO OUR HOUSE, THEY CAN GO CRASHING OUT AGAIN!
GREEN LANTERN? WHAT ARE YOUR POWERS EXACTLY?
I'M A SEER AND I CAN REVIVE THE DEAD TO ALLOW THEM ONE FINAL TASK.
WELL, LET'S HOPE IT DOESN'T COME TO THAT. ANYWAY FOR NOW YOU'RE A LIABILITY...
...SOMEONE GET HER OUT OF HERE!
ON IT.

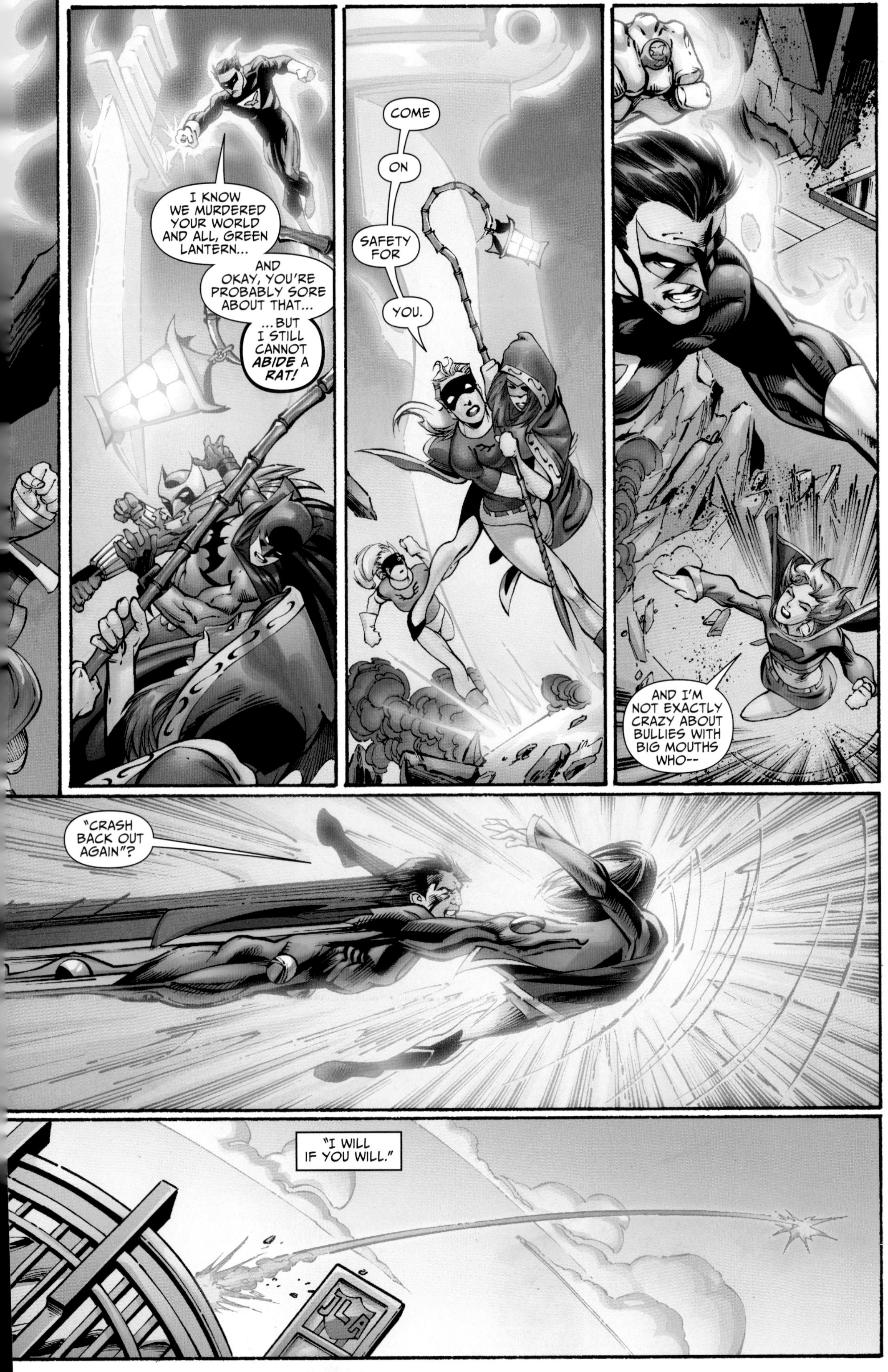
I KNOW WE MURDERED YOUR WORLD AND ALL, GREEN LANTERN...
AND OKAY, YOU'RE PROBABLY SORE ABOUT THAT...
...BUT I STILL CANNOT *ABIDE* A *RAT!*
COME
ON
SAFETY FOR
YOU.
AND I'M NOT EXACTLY CRAZY ABOUT BULLIES WITH BIG MOUTHS WHO--
"CRASH BACK OUT AGAIN"?
"I WILL IF YOU WILL."
JLA

NOSAFETY DEATHFORBOTH OFYOU.

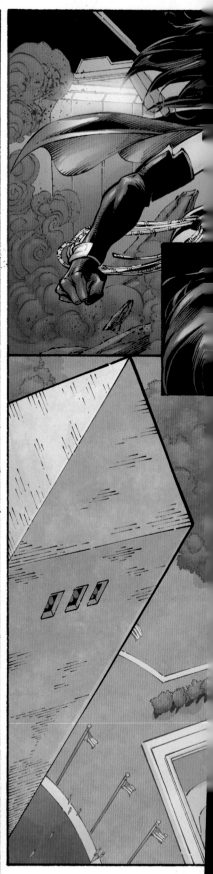

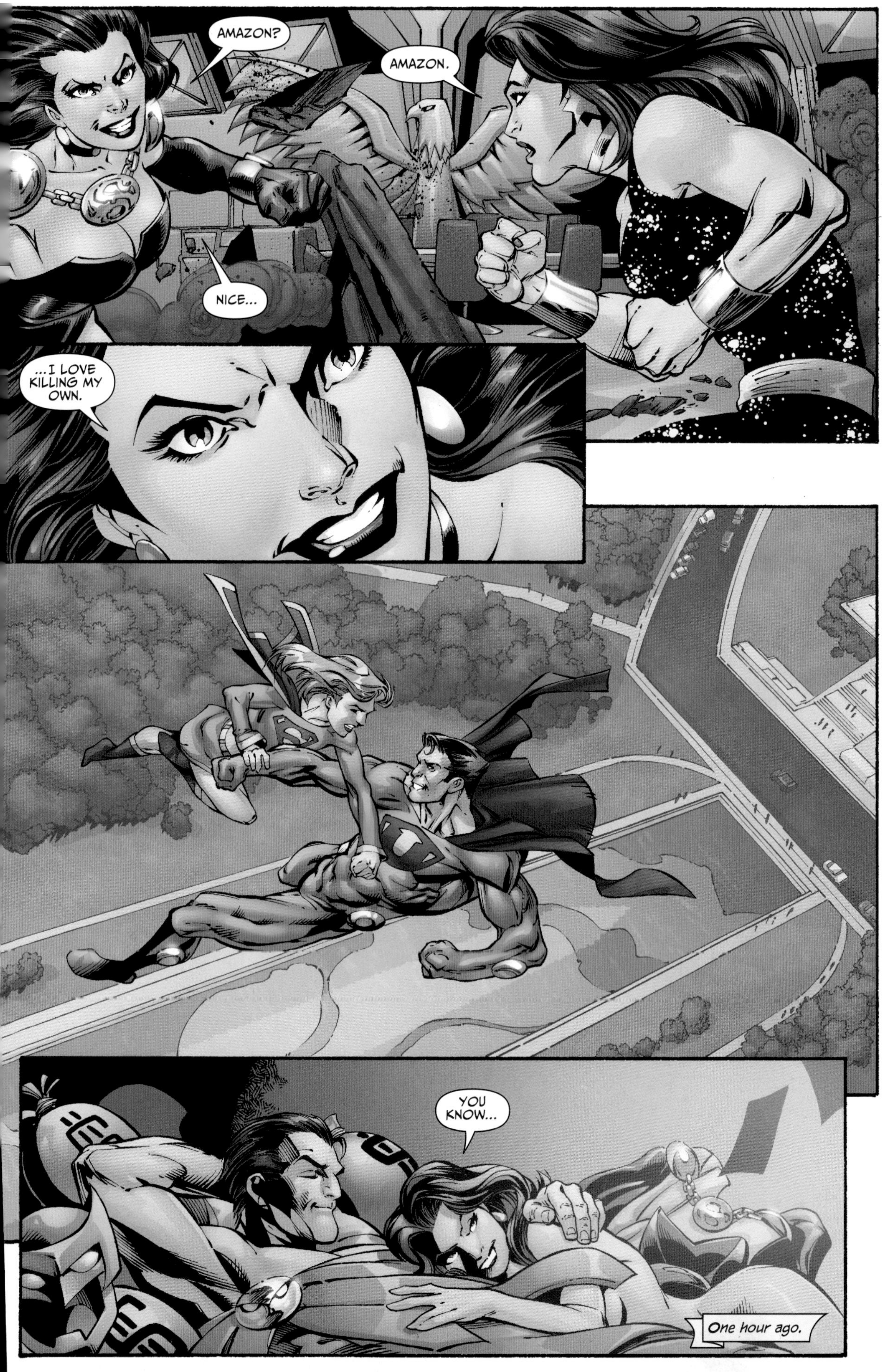
AMAZON?
AMAZON.
NICE...
...I LOVE KILLING MY OWN.
YOU KNOW...
One hour ago.

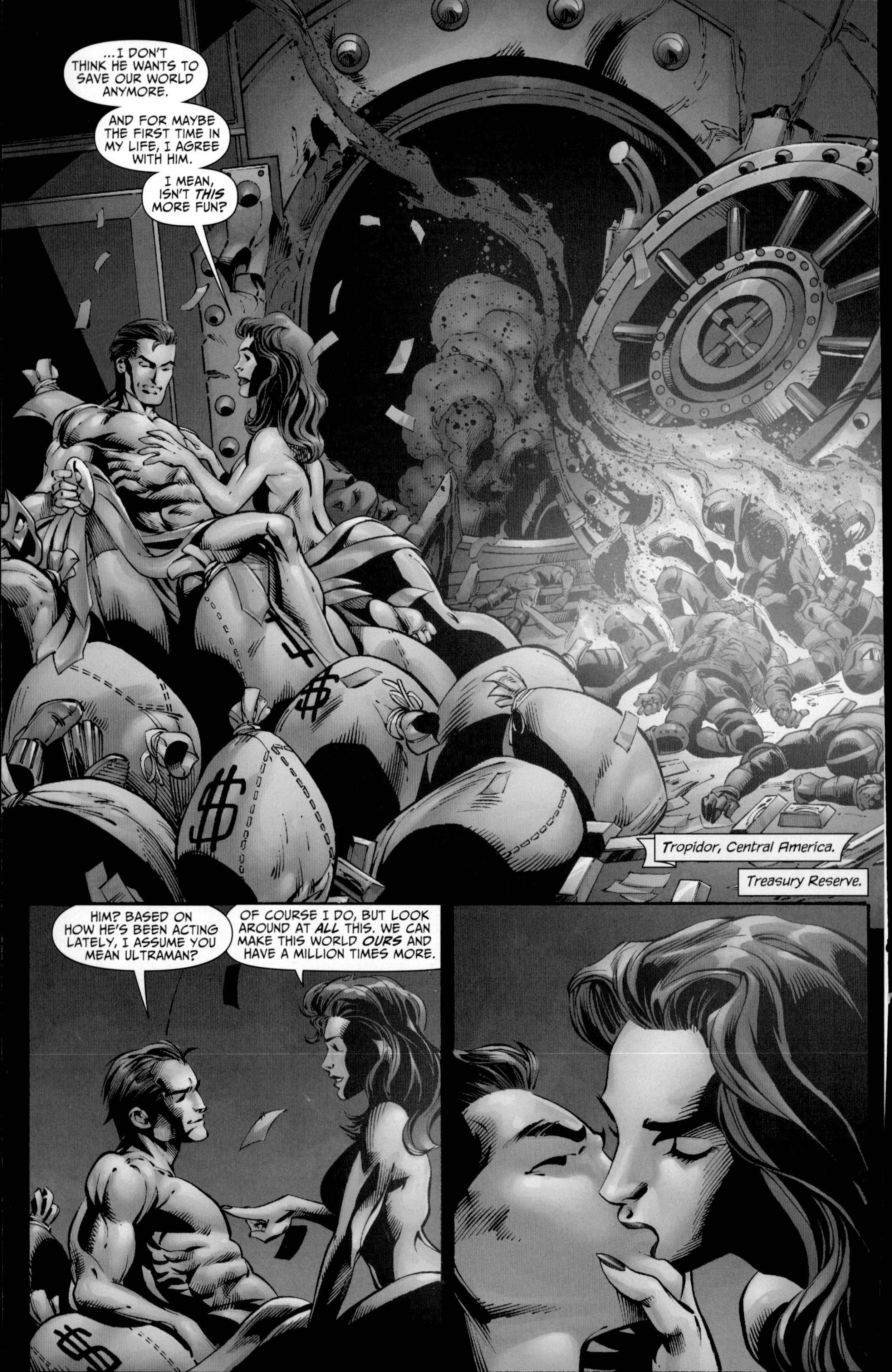
...I DON'T THINK HE WANTS TO SAVE OUR WORLD ANYMORE.
AND FOR MAYBE THE FIRST TIME IN MY LIFE, I AGREE WITH HIM.
I MEAN, ISN'T *THIS* MORE FUN?
Tropidor, Central America.
Treasury Reserve.
HIM? BASED ON HOW HE'S BEEN ACTING LATELY, I ASSUME YOU MEAN ULTRAMAN?
OF COURSE I DO, BUT LOOK AROUND AT *ALL* THIS. WE CAN MAKE THIS WORLD *OURS* AND HAVE A MILLION TIMES MORE.

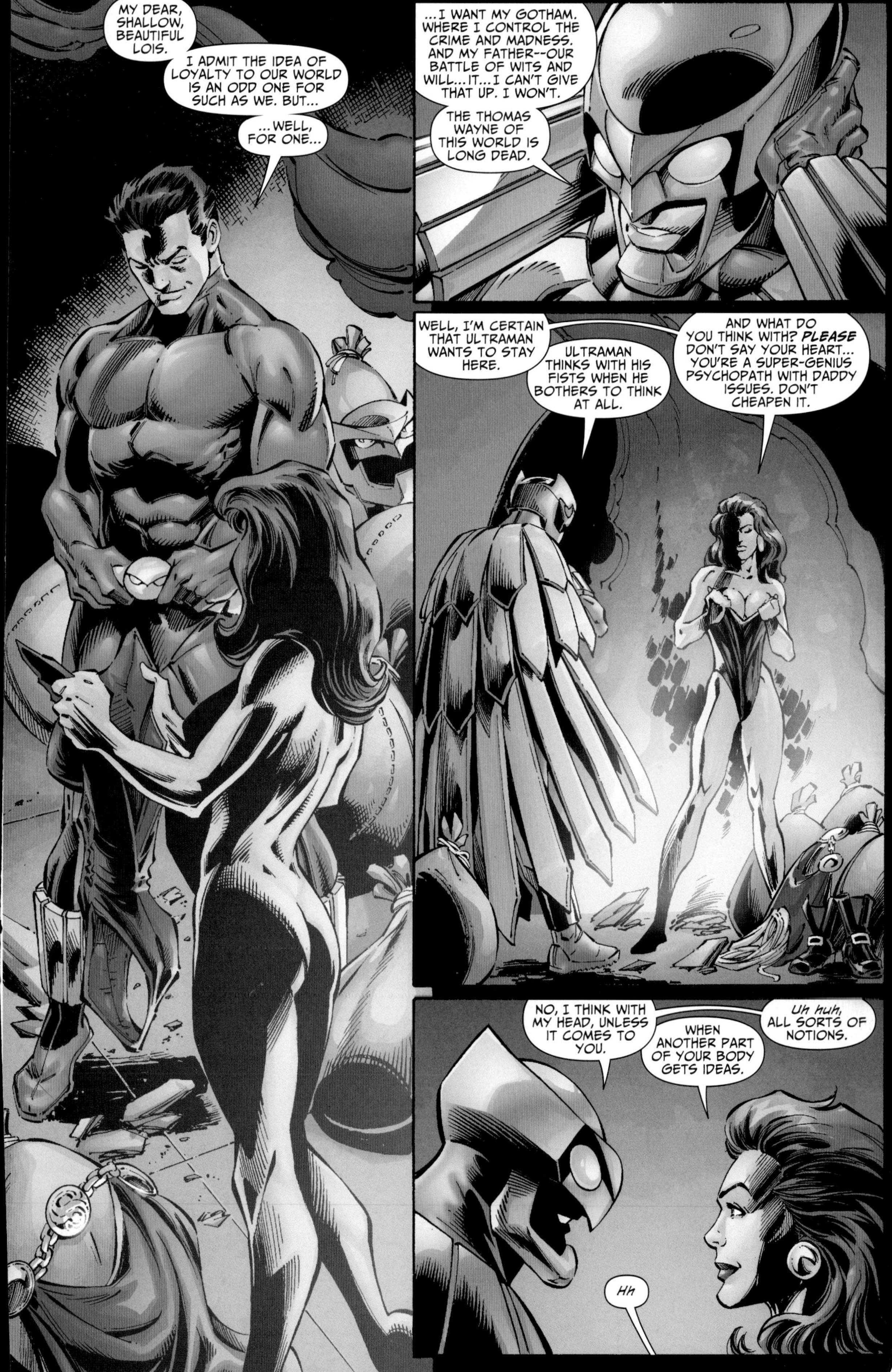
MY DEAR, SHALLOW, BEAUTIFUL LOIS.
I ADMIT THE IDEA OF LOYALTY TO OUR WORLD IS AN ODD ONE FOR SUCH AS WE. BUT...
...WELL, FOR ONE...
...I WANT MY GOTHAM. WHERE I CONTROL THE CRIME AND MADNESS. AND MY FATHER--OUR BATTLE OF WITS AND WILL...IT...I CAN'T GIVE THAT UP. I WON'T.
THE THOMAS WAYNE OF THIS WORLD IS LONG DEAD.
WELL, I'M CERTAIN THAT ULTRAMAN WANTS TO STAY HERE.
ULTRAMAN THINKS WITH HIS FISTS WHEN HE BOTHERS TO THINK AT ALL.
AND WHAT DO YOU THINK WITH? *PLEASE* DON'T SAY YOUR HEART... YOU'RE A SUPER-GENIUS PSYCHOPATH WITH DADDY ISSUES. DON'T CHEAPEN IT.
NO, I THINK WITH MY HEAD, UNLESS IT COMES TO YOU.
WHEN ANOTHER PART OF YOUR BODY GETS IDEAS.
Uh huh, ALL SORTS OF NOTIONS.
Hh

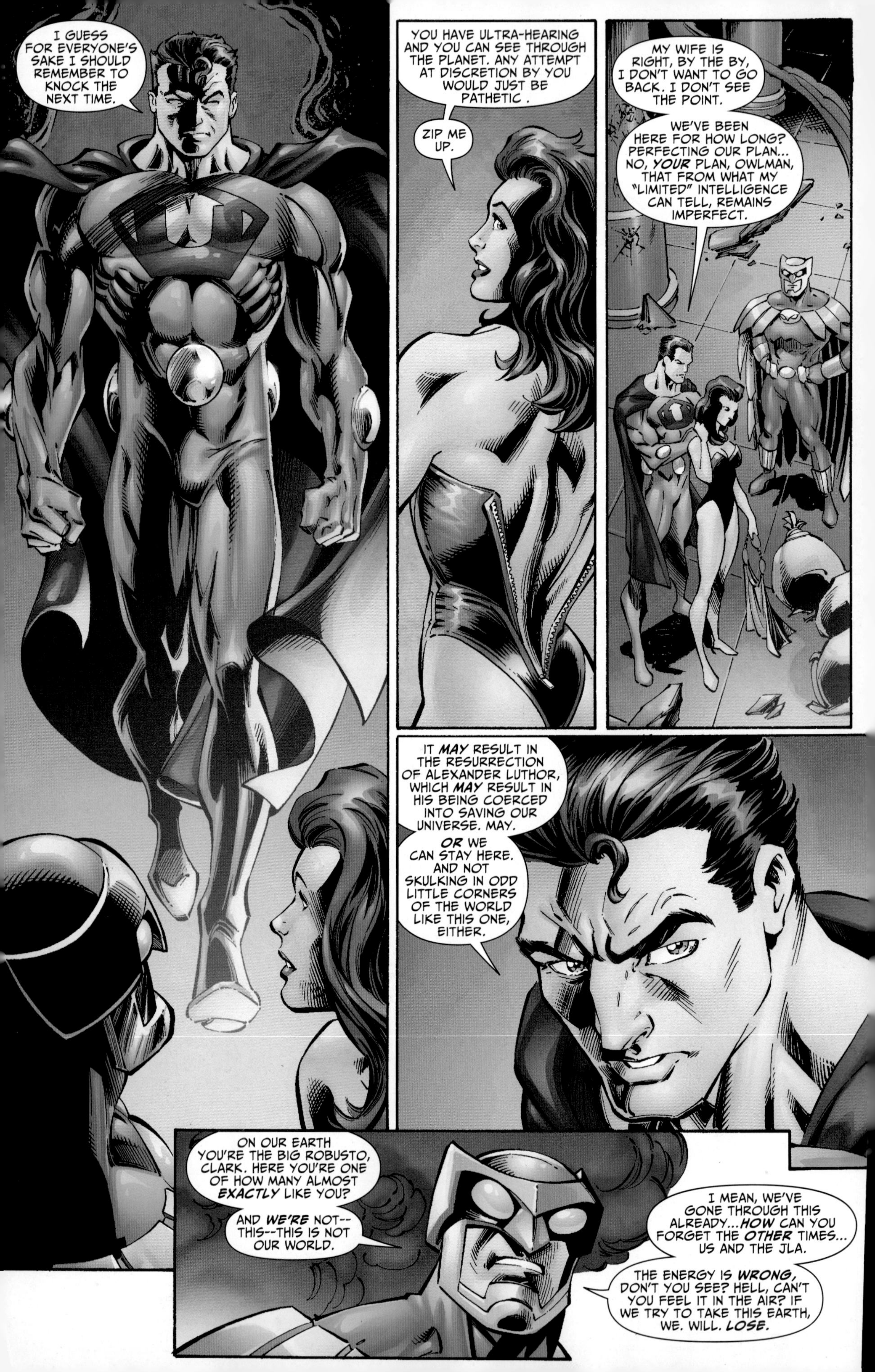
I GUESS FOR EVERYONE'S SAKE I SHOULD REMEMBER TO KNOCK THE NEXT TIME.
YOU HAVE ULTRA-HEARING AND YOU CAN SEE THROUGH THE PLANET. ANY ATTEMPT AT DISCRETION BY YOU WOULD JUST BE PATHETIC .
ZIP ME UP.
MY WIFE IS RIGHT, BY THE BY, I DON'T WANT TO GO BACK. I DON'T SEE THE POINT.
WE'VE BEEN HERE FOR HOW LONG? PERFECTING OUR PLAN... NO, *YOUR* PLAN, OWLMAN, THAT FROM WHAT MY "LIMITED" INTELLIGENCE CAN TELL, REMAINS IMPERFECT.
IT *MAY* RESULT IN THE RESURRECTION OF ALEXANDER LUTHOR, WHICH *MAY* RESULT IN HIS BEING COERCED INTO SAVING OUR UNIVERSE. MAY.
OR WE CAN STAY HERE. AND NOT SKULKING IN ODD LITTLE CORNERS OF THE WORLD LIKE THIS ONE, EITHER.
ON OUR EARTH YOU'RE THE BIG ROBUSTO, CLARK. HERE YOU'RE ONE OF HOW MANY ALMOST *EXACTLY* LIKE YOU?
AND *WE'RE* NOT-- THIS--THIS IS NOT OUR WORLD.
I MEAN, WE'VE GONE THROUGH THIS ALREADY...*HOW* CAN YOU FORGET THE *OTHER* TIMES... US AND THE JLA.
THE ENERGY IS *WRONG,* DON'T YOU SEE? HELL, CAN'T YOU FEEL IT IN THE AIR? IF WE TRY TO TAKE THIS EARTH, WE. WILL. *LOSE.*

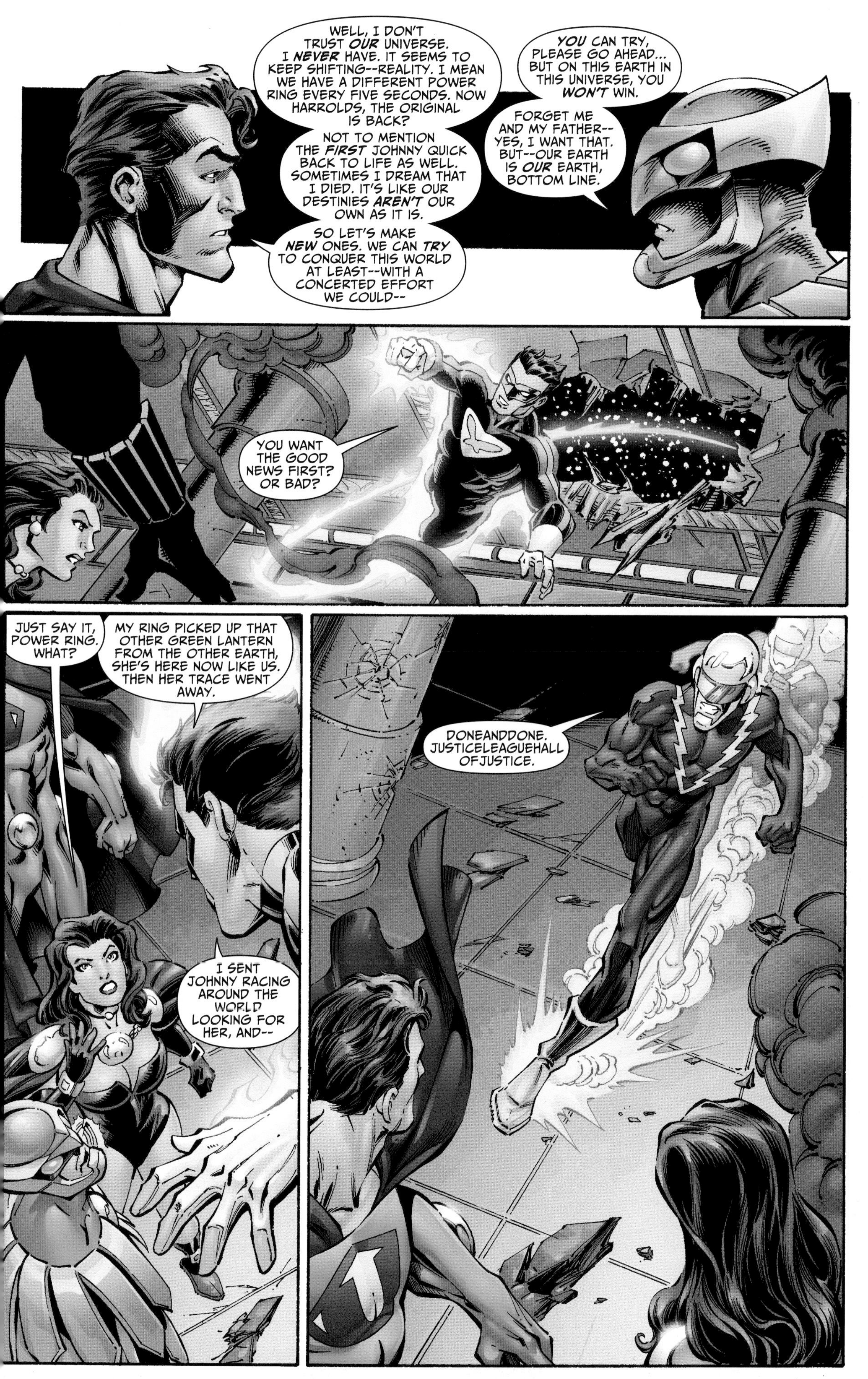
WELL, I DON'T TRUST OUR UNIVERSE. I NEVER HAVE. IT SEEMS TO KEEP SHIFTING--REALITY. I MEAN WE HAVE A DIFFERENT POWER RING EVERY FIVE SECONDS. NOW HARROLDS, THE ORIGINAL IS BACK?
NOT TO MENTION THE FIRST JOHNNY QUICK BACK TO LIFE AS WELL. SOMETIMES I DREAM THAT I DIED. IT'S LIKE OUR DESTINIES AREN'T OUR OWN AS IT IS.
SO LET'S MAKE NEW ONES. WE CAN TRY TO CONQUER THIS WORLD AT LEAST--WITH A CONCERTED EFFORT WE COULD--
YOU CAN TRY, PLEASE GO AHEAD... BUT ON THIS EARTH IN THIS UNIVERSE, YOU WON'T WIN.
FORGET ME AND MY FATHER-- YES, I WANT THAT. BUT--OUR EARTH IS OUR EARTH, BOTTOM LINE.
YOU WANT THE GOOD NEWS FIRST? OR BAD?
JUST SAY IT, POWER RING. WHAT?
MY RING PICKED UP THAT OTHER GREEN LANTERN FROM THE OTHER EARTH, SHE'S HERE NOW LIKE US. THEN HER TRACE WENT AWAY.
I SENT JOHNNY RACING AROUND THE WORLD LOOKING FOR HER, AND--
DONEANDDONE. JUSTICELEAGUEHALL OFJUSTICE.

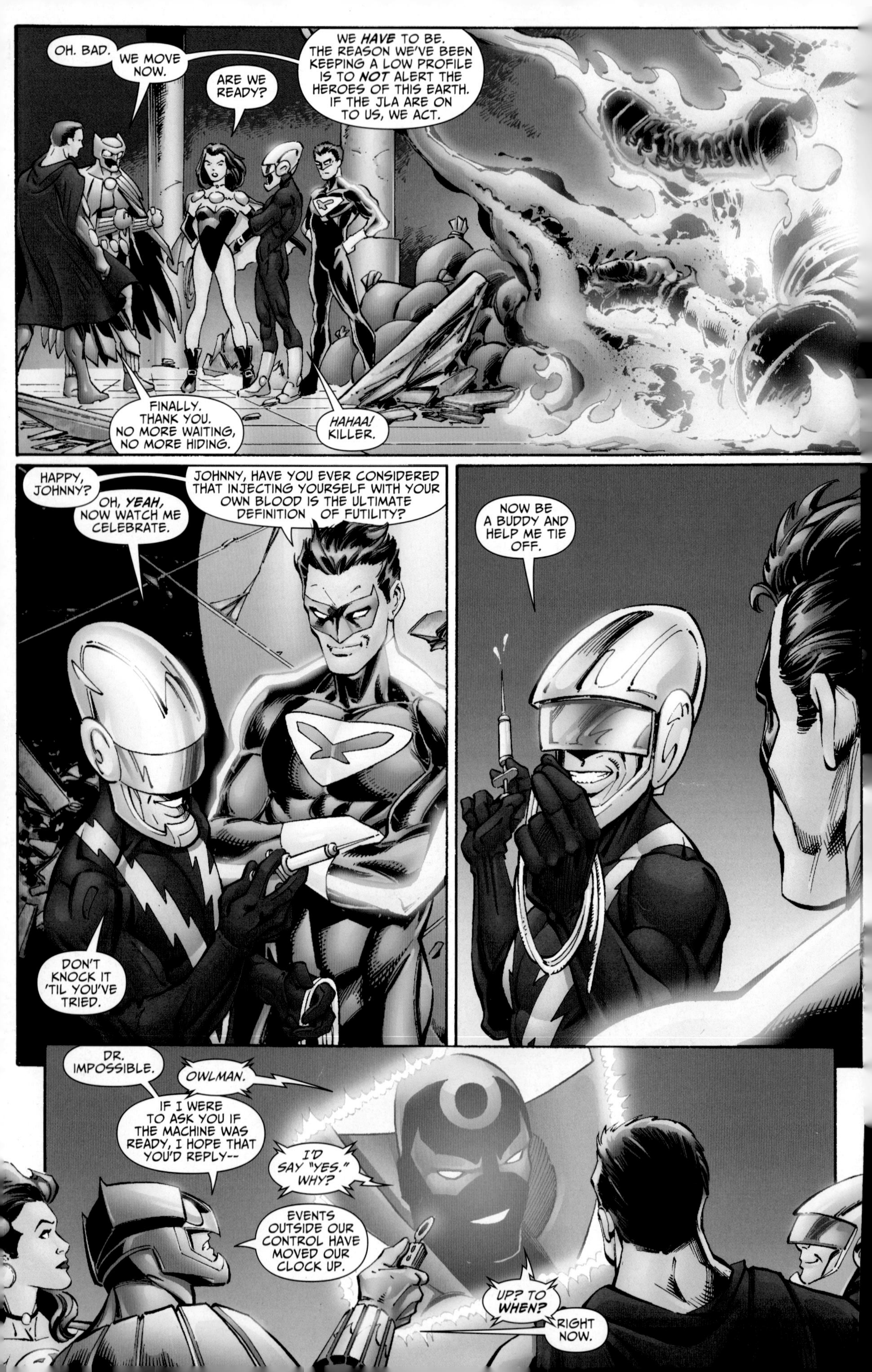
OH. BAD.
WE MOVE NOW.
ARE WE READY?
WE HAVE TO BE. THE REASON WE'VE BEEN KEEPING A LOW PROFILE IS TO NOT ALERT THE HEROES OF THIS EARTH. IF THE JLA ARE ON TO US, WE ACT.
FINALLY. THANK YOU. NO MORE WAITING, NO MORE HIDING.
HAHAA! KILLER.
HAPPY, JOHNNY?
OH, YEAH, NOW WATCH ME CELEBRATE.
JOHNNY, HAVE YOU EVER CONSIDERED THAT INJECTING YOURSELF WITH YOUR OWN BLOOD IS THE ULTIMATE DEFINITION OF FUTILITY?
DON'T KNOCK IT 'TIL YOU'VE TRIED.
NOW BE A BUDDY AND HELP ME TIE OFF.
DR. IMPOSSIBLE.
OWLMAN.
IF I WERE TO ASK YOU IF THE MACHINE WAS READY, I HOPE THAT YOU'D REPLY--
I'D SAY "YES." WHY?
EVENTS OUTSIDE OUR CONTROL HAVE MOVED OUR CLOCK UP.
UP? TO WHEN?
RIGHT NOW.

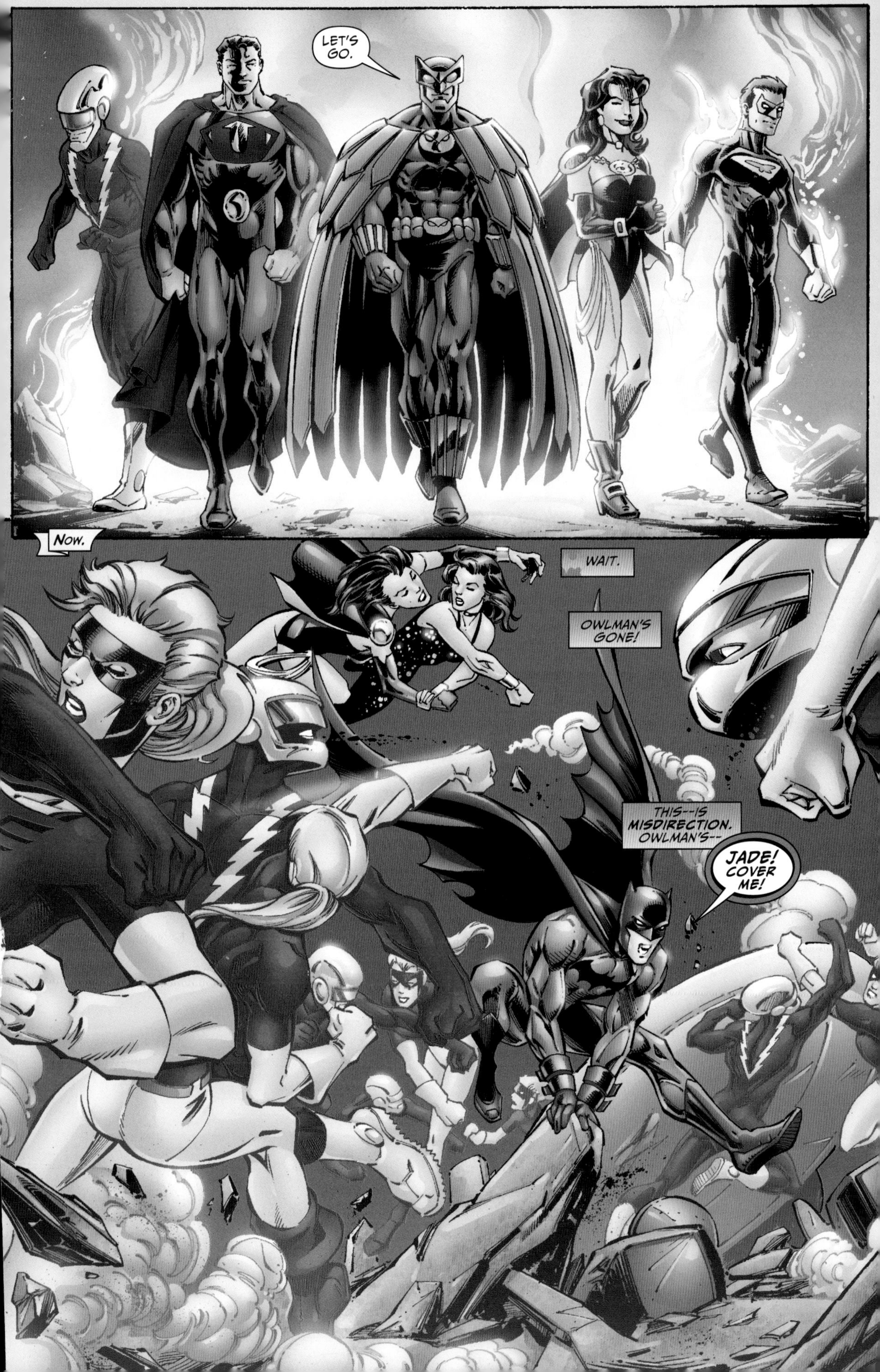
LET'S GO.
NOW.
WAIT.
OWLMAN'S GONE!
THIS--IS MISDIRECTION. OWLMAN'S--
JADE! COVER ME!

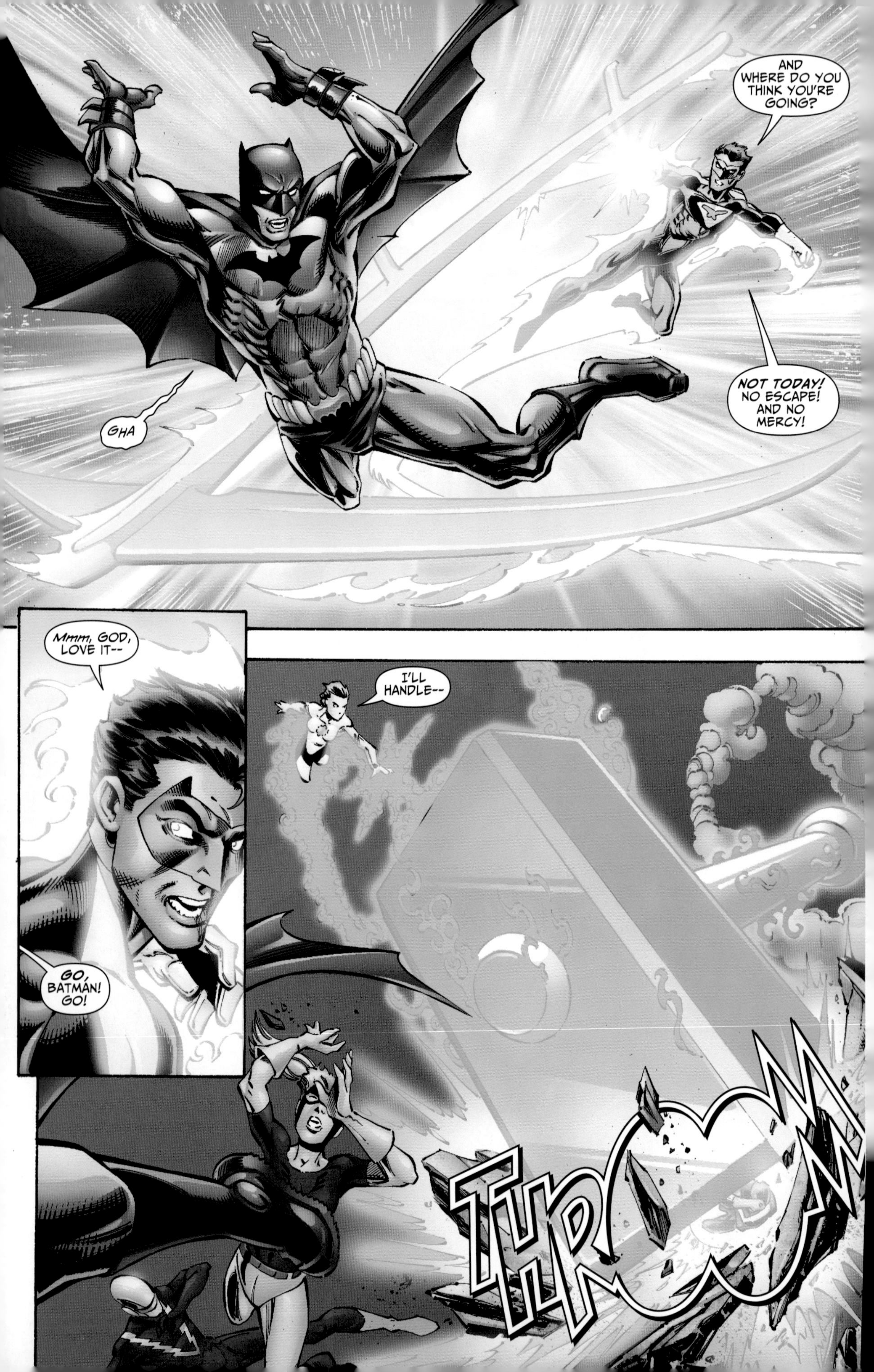
AND WHERE DO YOU THINK YOU'RE GOING?
GHA
NOT TODAY! NO ESCAPE! AND NO MERCY!
Mmm, GOD, LOVE IT--
GO, BATMAN! GO!
I'LL HANDLE--
THROOM

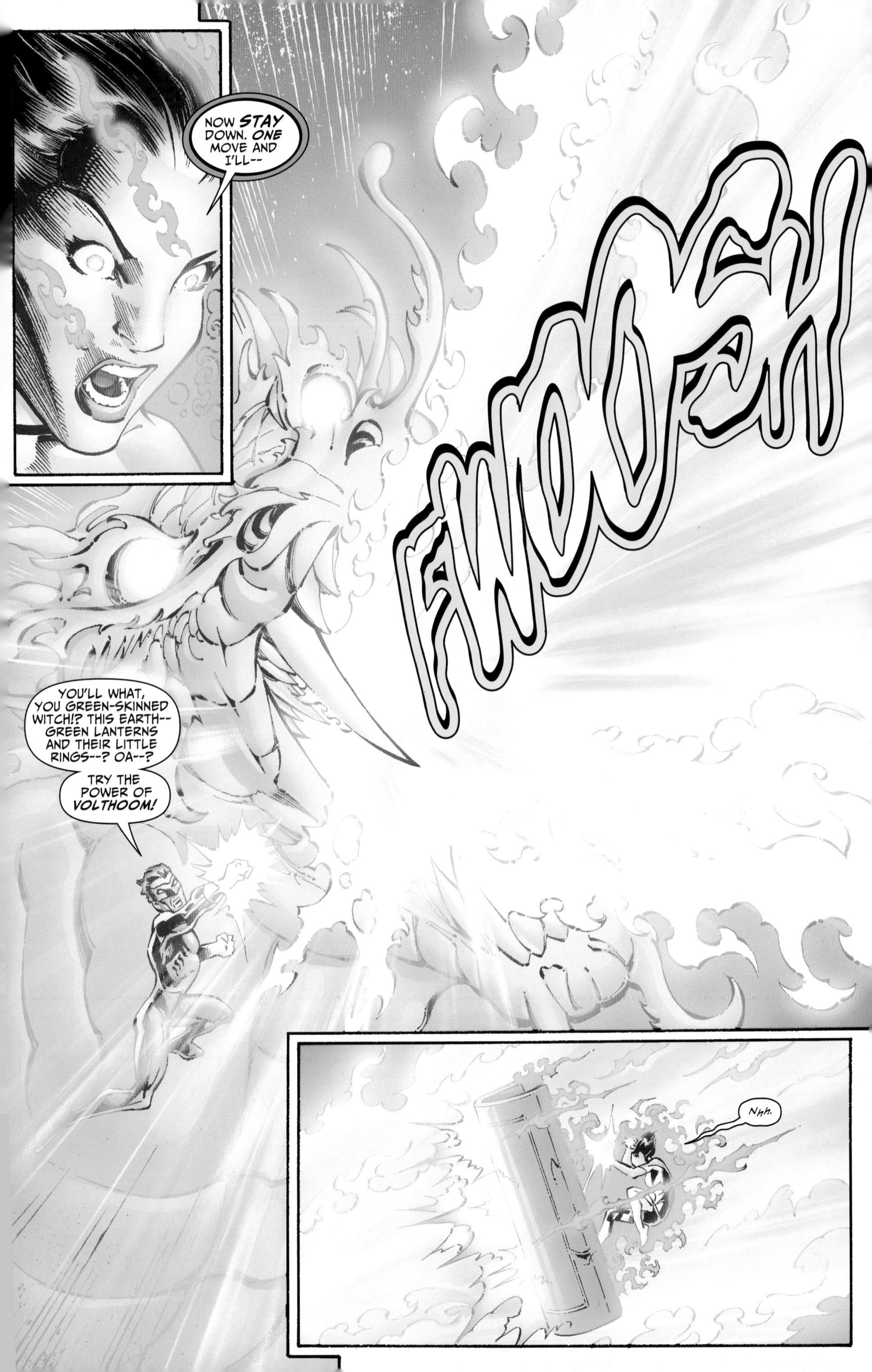
NOW STAY DOWN. ONE MOVE AND I'LL--
FWOOSH
YOU'LL WHAT, YOU GREEN-SKINNED WITCH!? THIS EARTH--GREEN LANTERNS AND THEIR LITTLE RINGS--? OA--?
TRY THE POWER OF VOLTHOOM!
Nhh.

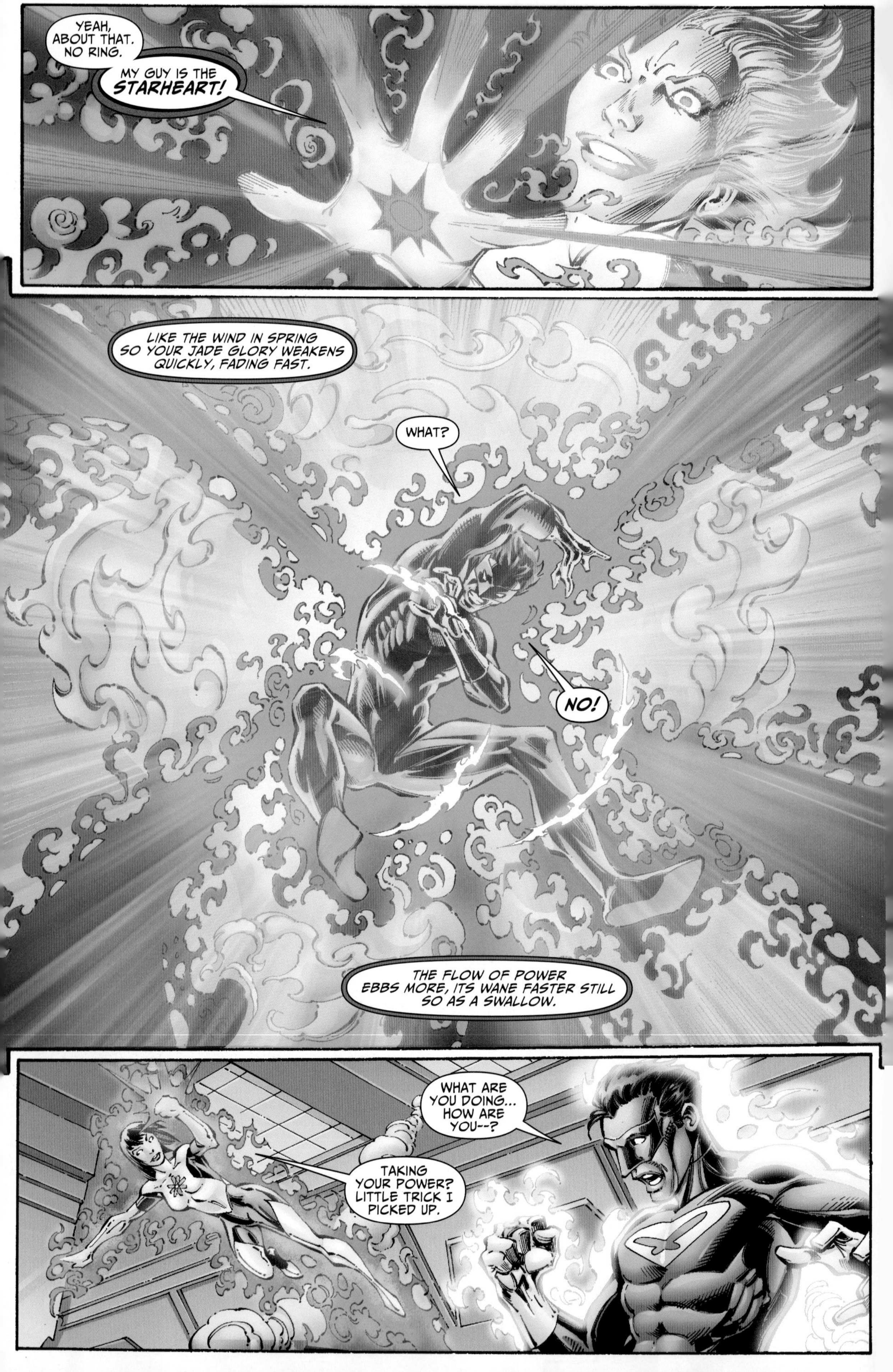
YEAH, ABOUT THAT. NO RING.
MY GUY IS THE STARHEART!
LIKE THE WIND IN SPRING SO YOUR JADE GLORY WEAKENS QUICKLY, FADING FAST.
WHAT?
NO!
THE FLOW OF POWER EBBS MORE, ITS WANE FASTER STILL SO AS A SWALLOW.
WHAT ARE YOU DOING... HOW ARE YOU--?
TAKING YOUR POWER? LITTLE TRICK I PICKED UP.

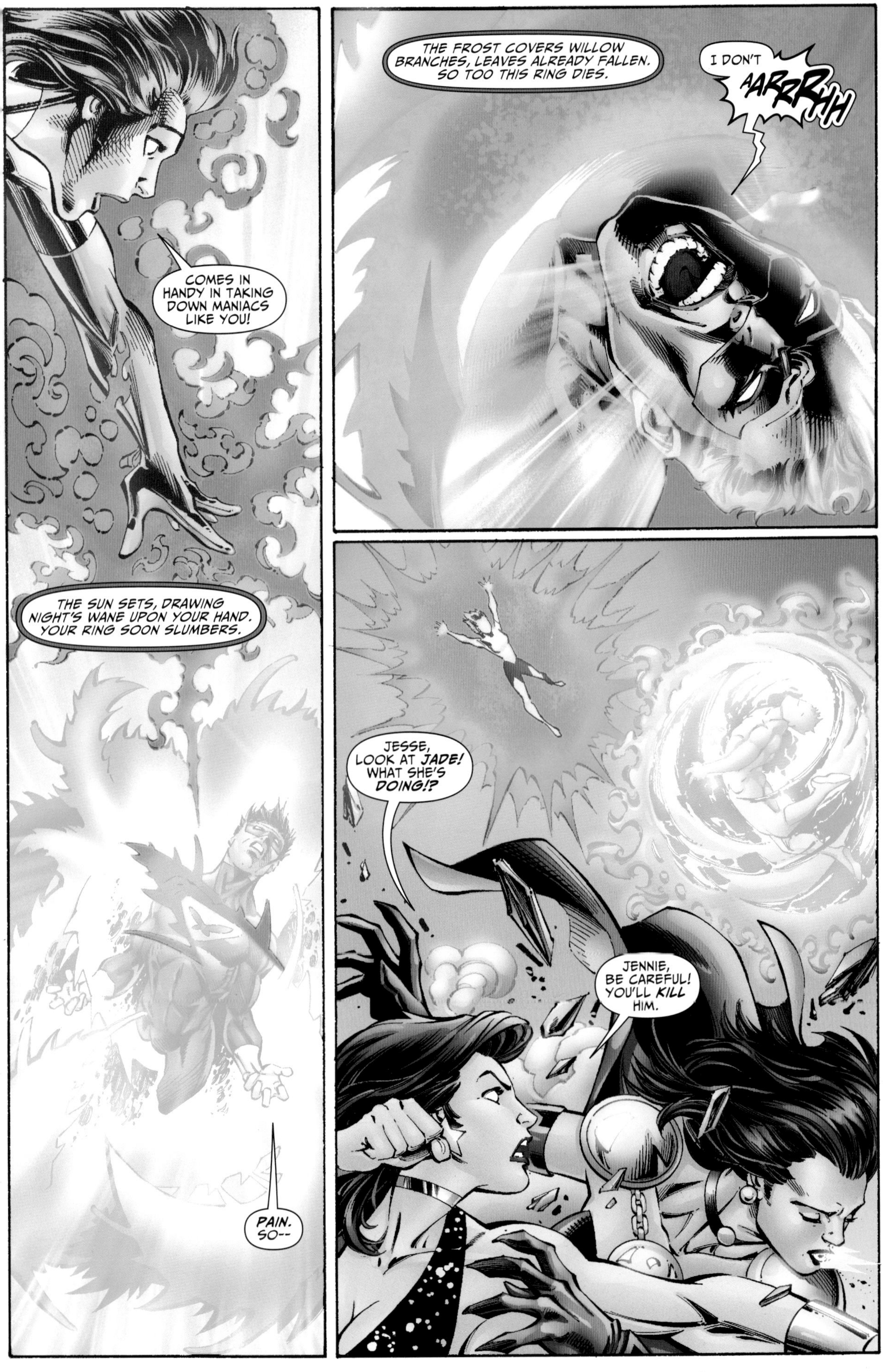
COMES IN HANDY IN TAKING DOWN MANIACS LIKE YOU!
THE FROST COVERS WILLOW BRANCHES, LEAVES ALREADY FALLEN. SO TOO THIS RING DIES.
I DON'T
AARRRHH
THE SUN SETS, DRAWING NIGHT'S WANE UPON YOUR HAND. YOUR RING SOON SLUMBERS.
PAIN. SO--
JESSE, LOOK AT JADE! WHAT SHE'S DOING!?
JENNIE, BE CAREFUL! YOU'LL KILL HIM.

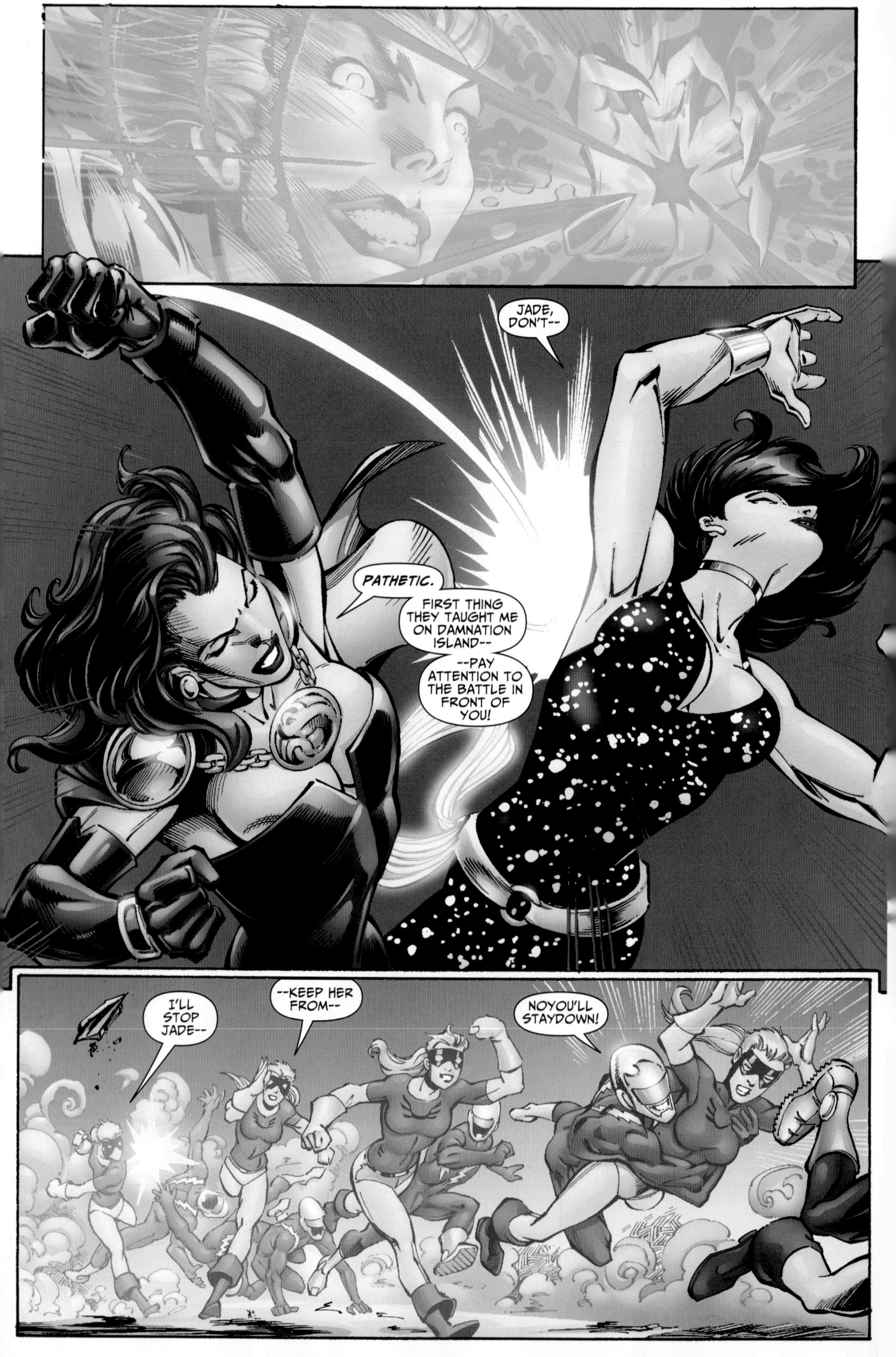
JADE, DON'T--
PATHETIC.
FIRST THING THEY TAUGHT ME ON DAMNATION ISLAND--
--PAY ATTENTION TO THE BATTLE IN FRONT OF YOU!
I'LL STOP JADE--
--KEEP HER FROM--
NOYOU'LL STAYDOWN!

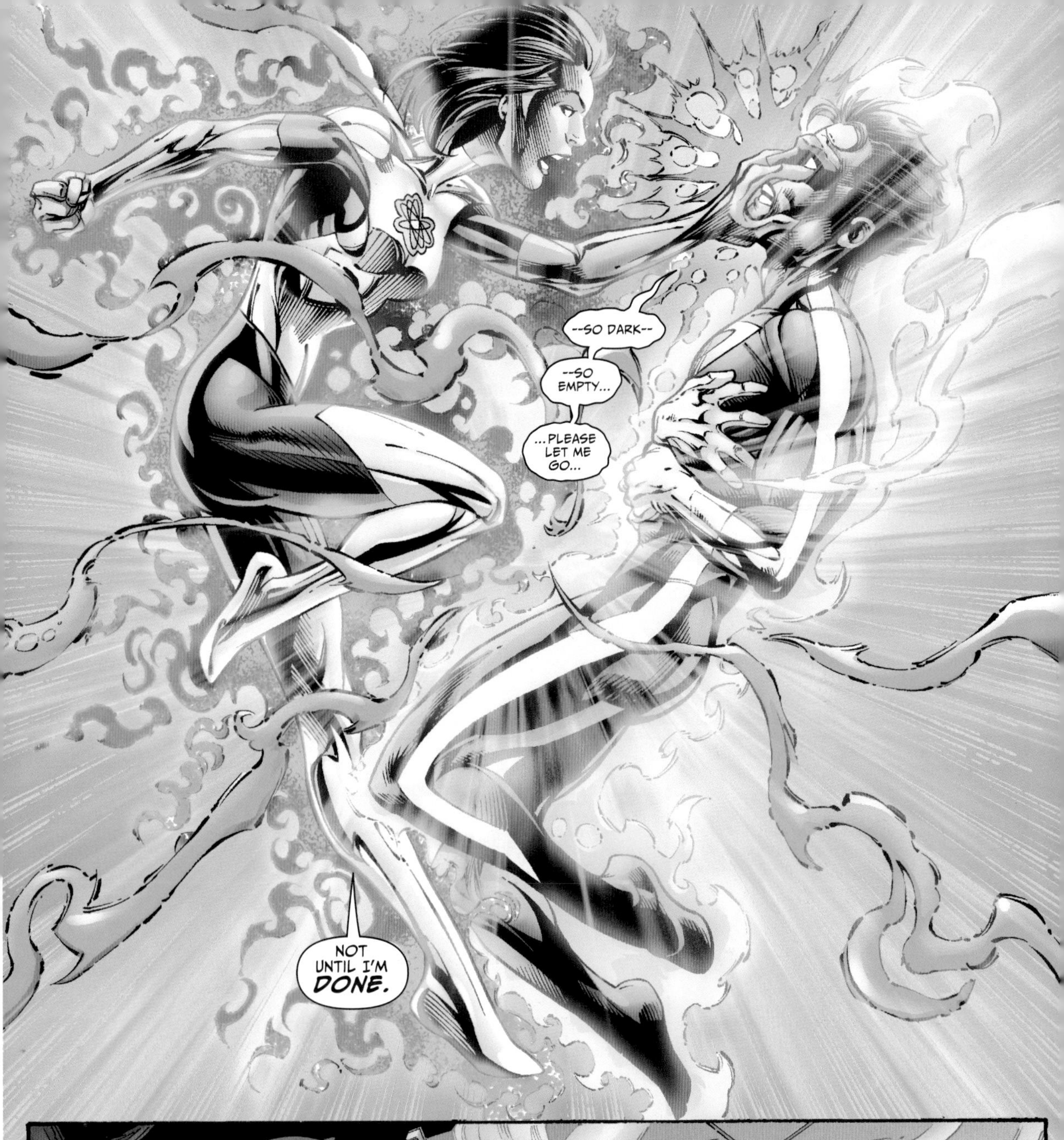
--SO DARK--
--SO EMPTY...
...PLEASE LET ME GO...
NOT UNTIL I'M DONE.

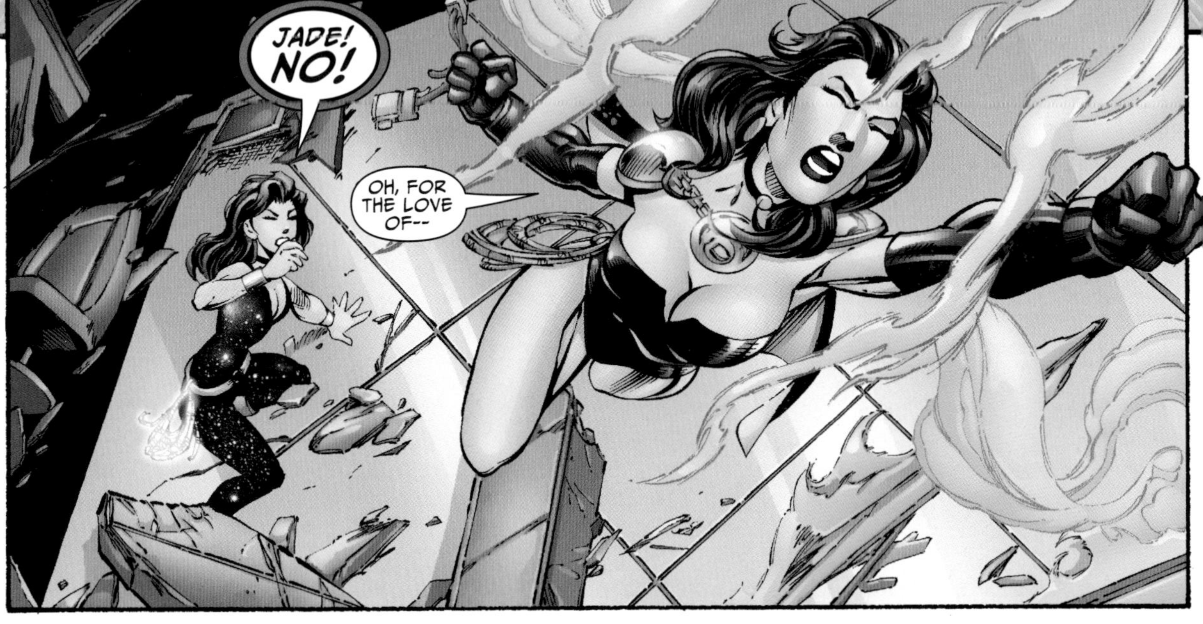
JADE! NO!
OH, FOR THE LOVE OF--

One hour ago.

EVENTS OUTSIDE OUR CONTROL HAVE MOVED OUR CLOCK UP.

UP? TO WHEN?

RIGHT NOW.

YOU CAN BE OF USE TO A GREATER CAUSE, EARL.

BUT, DEAR SIR, I AM SO GOOD AT DOING NOTHING MUCH AT ALL.

DON'T YOU SEE? YOU'RE A BANA-MIGHDALL--NOT EVEN RECOGNIZED AS A TRUE AMAZON. ABANDONED BY YOUR GODS--

--SO WHY NOT BECOME A GOD YOURSELF?

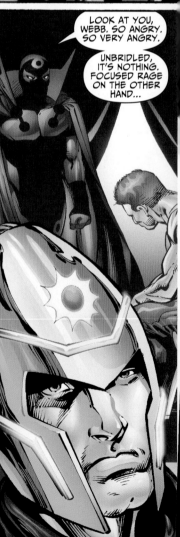

LOOK AT YOU, WEBB. SO ANGRY. SO VERY ANGRY.

UNBRIDLED, IT'S NOTHING. FOCUSED RAGE ON THE OTHER HAND...

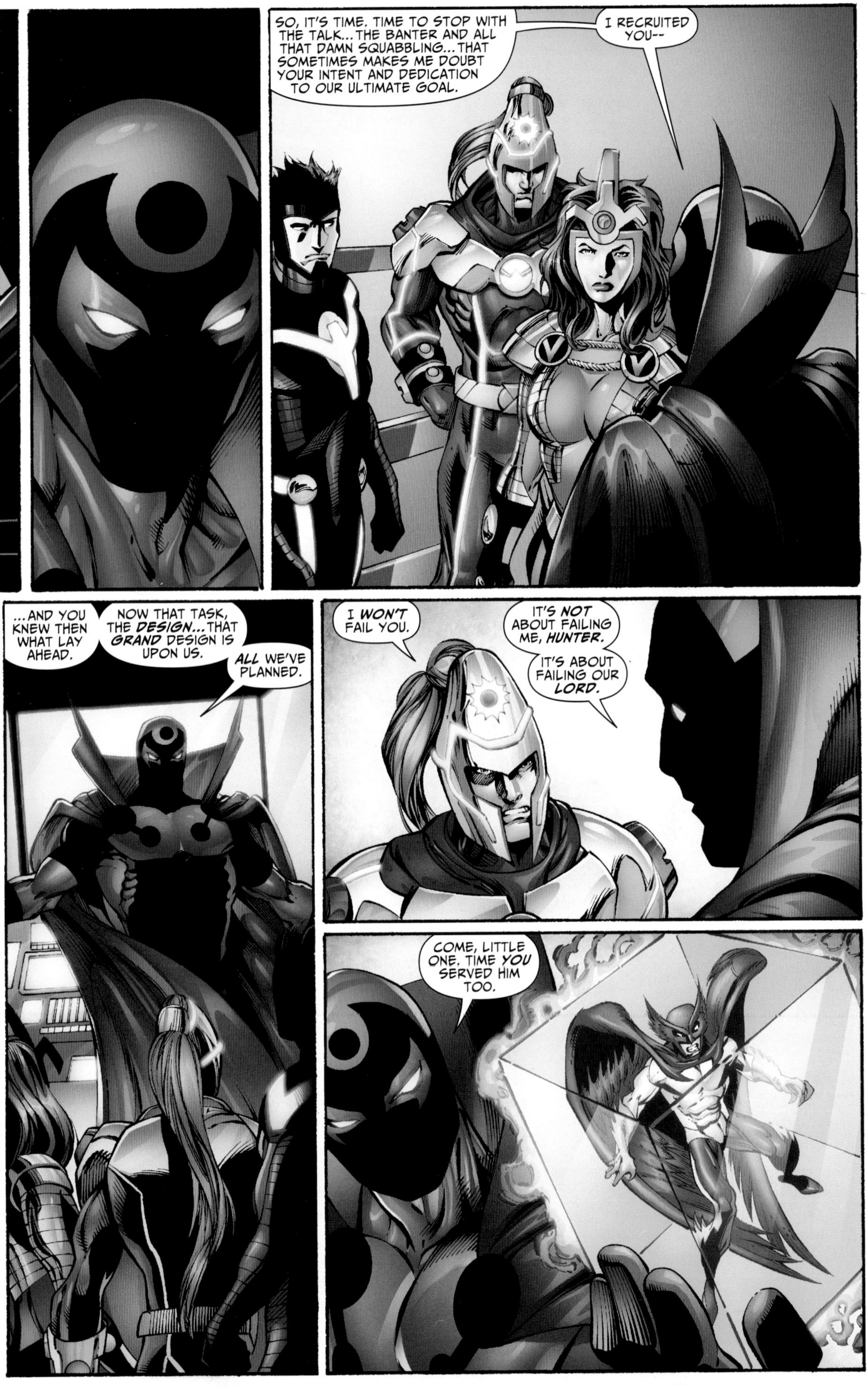
SO, IT'S TIME. TIME TO STOP WITH THE TALK... THE BANTER AND ALL THAT DAMN SQUABBLING... THAT SOMETIMES MAKES ME DOUBT YOUR INTENT AND DEDICATION TO OUR ULTIMATE GOAL.
I RECRUITED YOU--
...AND YOU KNEW THEN WHAT LAY AHEAD.
NOW THAT TASK, THE DESIGN... THAT GRAND DESIGN IS UPON US.
ALL WE'VE PLANNED.
I WON'T FAIL YOU.
IT'S NOT ABOUT FAILING ME, HUNTER.
IT'S ABOUT FAILING OUR LORD.
COME, LITTLE ONE. TIME YOU SERVED HIM TOO.

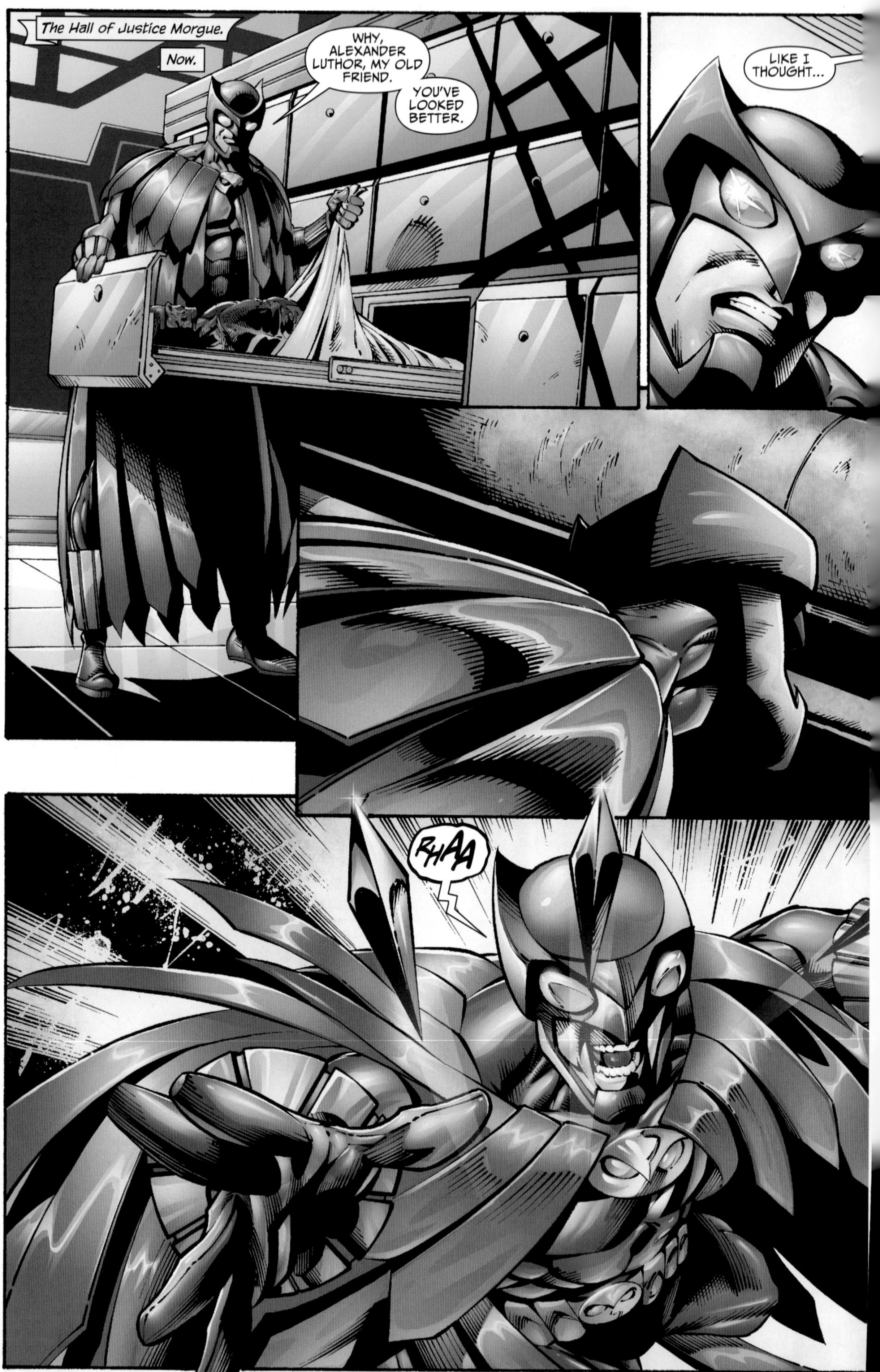
The Hall of Justice Morgue.
Now.
WHY, ALEXANDER LUTHOR, MY OLD FRIEND.
YOU'VE LOOKED BETTER.
LIKE I THOUGHT...
RHAA

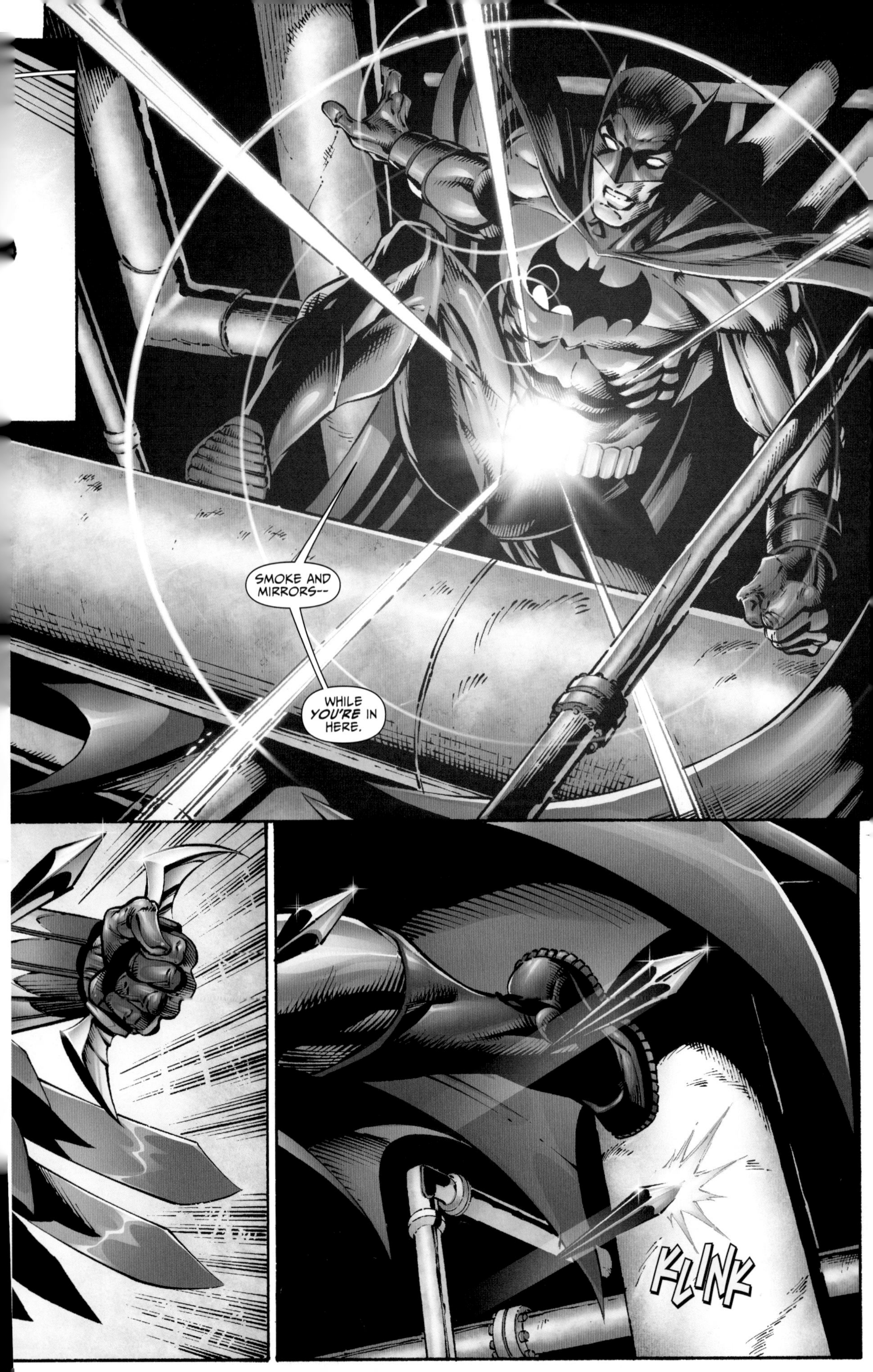
SMOKE AND MIRRORS--
WHILE YOU'RE IN HERE.
KLINK

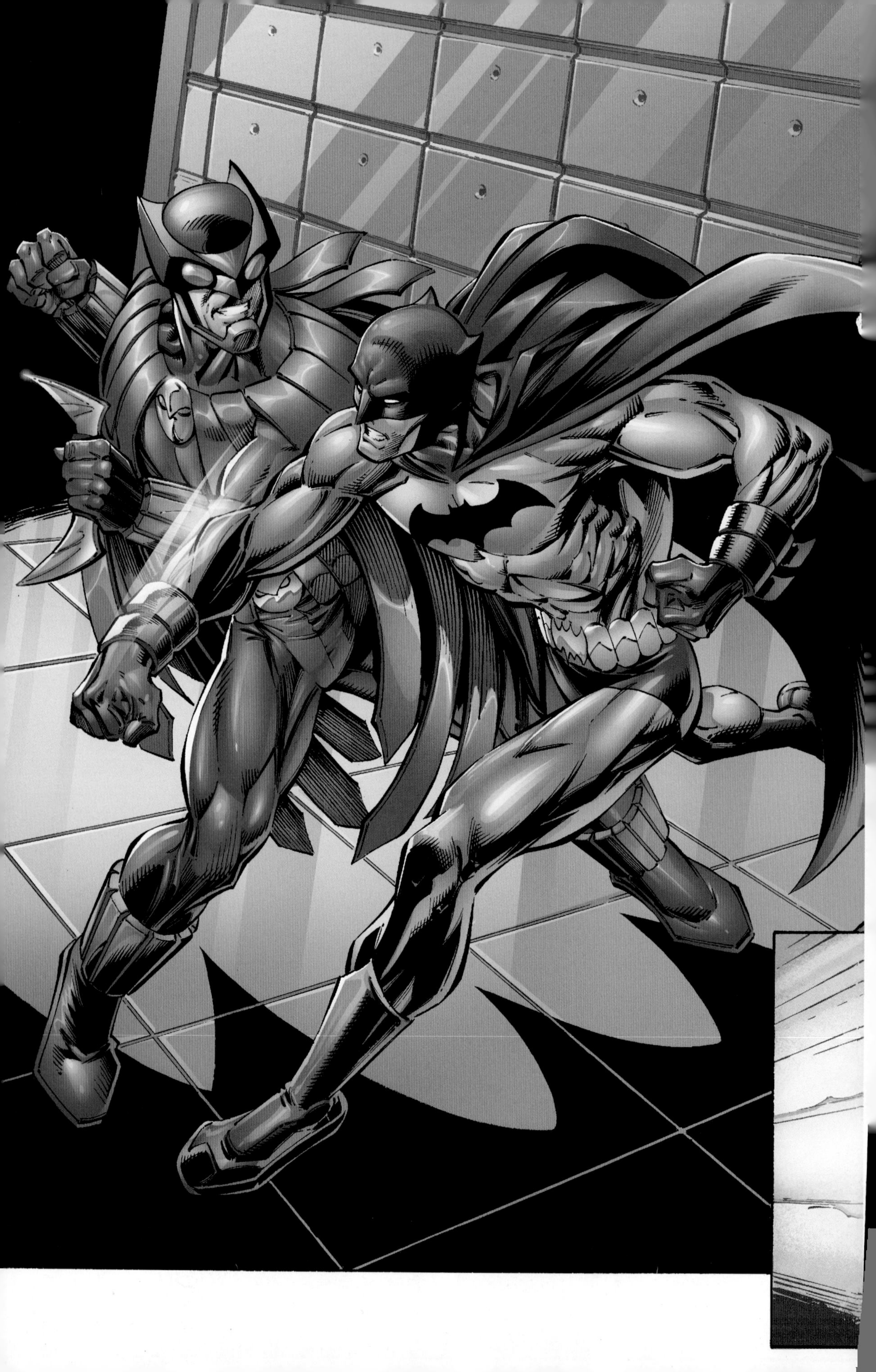

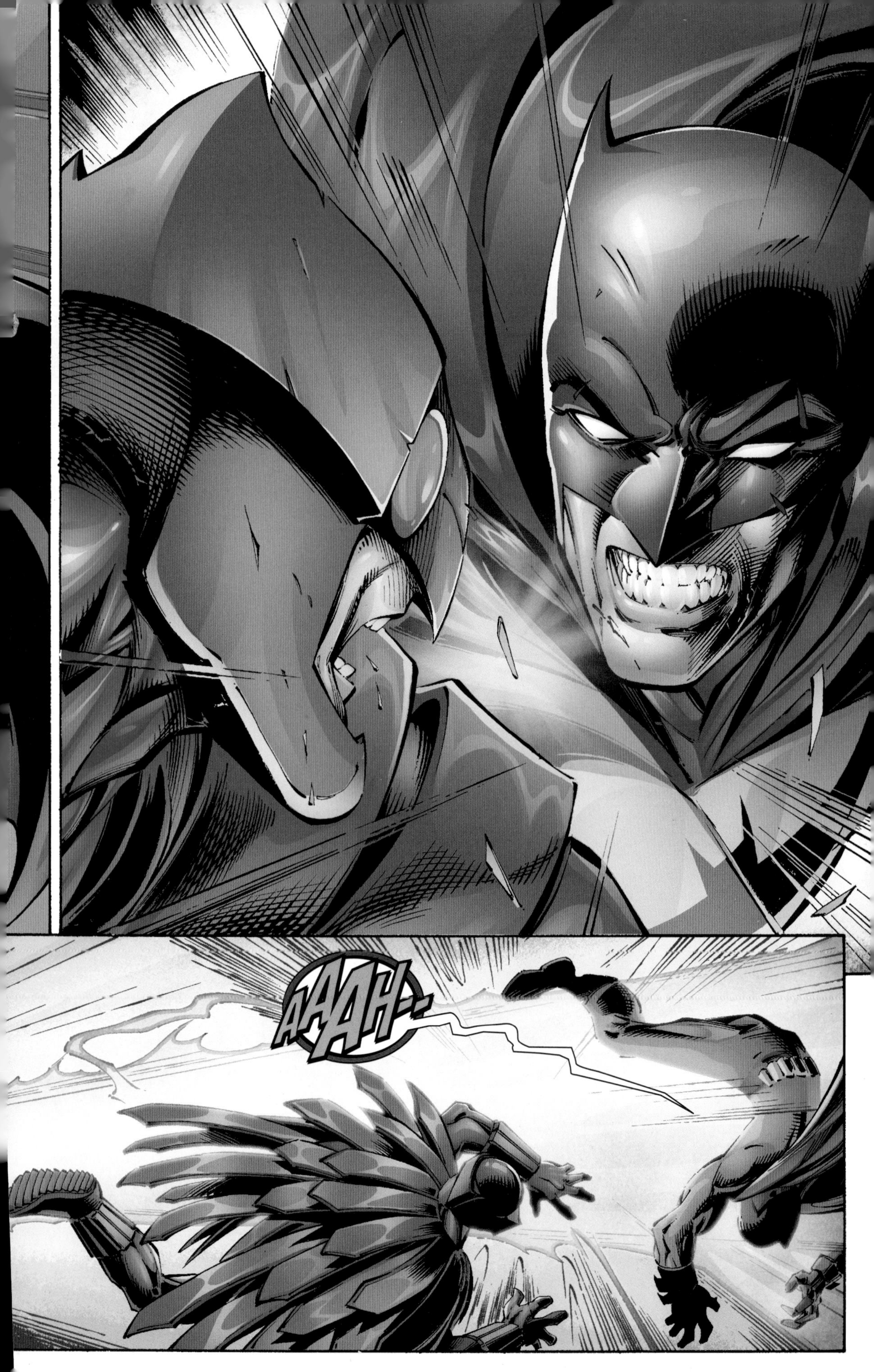
AAAH--

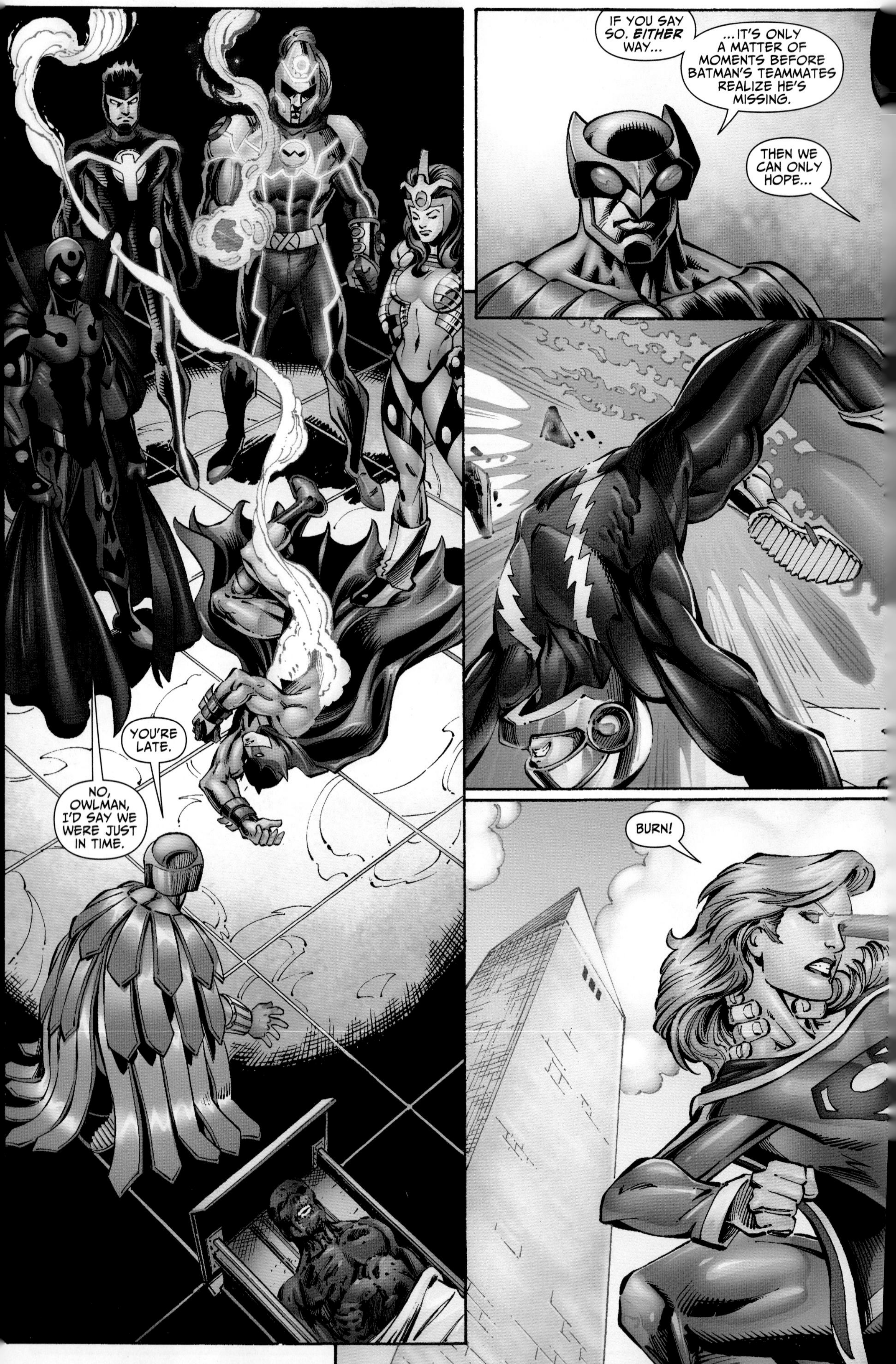
YOU'RE LATE.
NO, OWLMAN, I'D SAY WE WERE JUST IN TIME.
IF YOU SAY SO. *EITHER* WAY...
...IT'S ONLY A MATTER OF MOMENTS BEFORE BATMAN'S TEAMMATES REALIZE HE'S MISSING.
THEN WE CAN ONLY HOPE...
BURN!

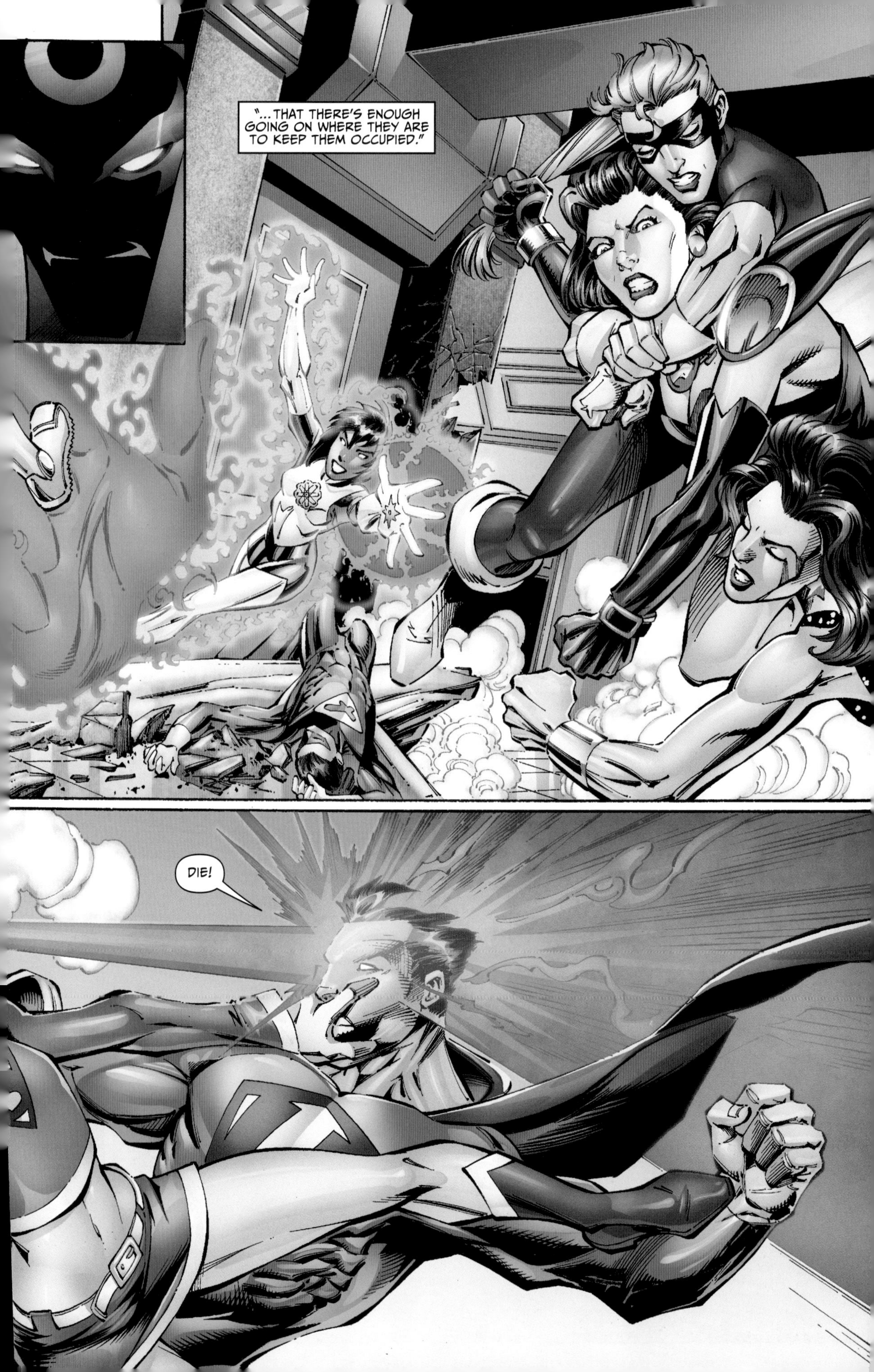
"...THAT THERE'S ENOUGH GOING ON WHERE THEY ARE TO KEEP THEM OCCUPIED."
DIE!

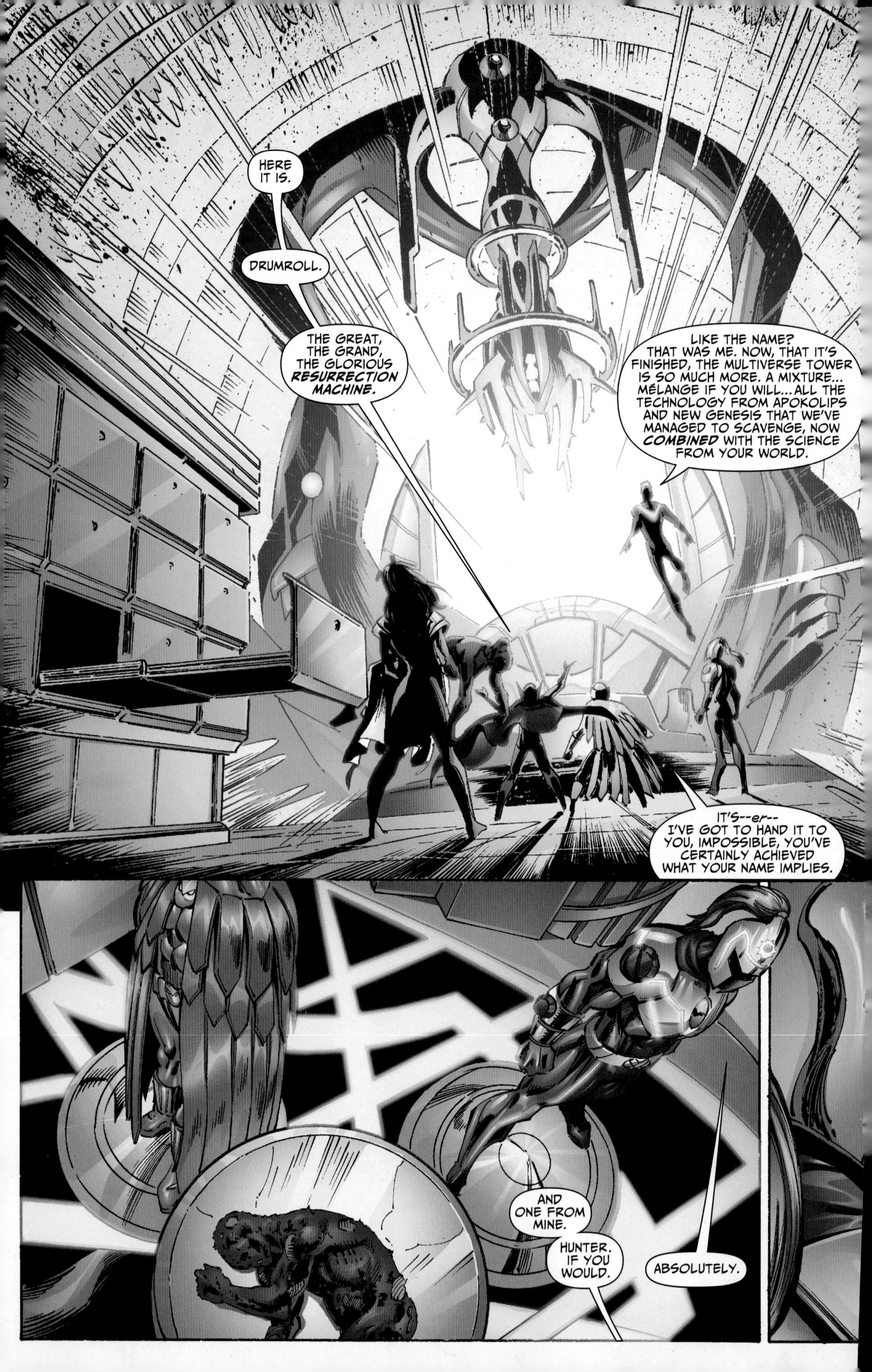
HERE IT IS.
DRUMROLL.
THE GREAT, THE GRAND, THE GLORIOUS *RESURRECTION MACHINE.*
LIKE THE NAME? THAT WAS ME. NOW, THAT IT'S FINISHED, THE MULTIVERSE TOWER IS SO MUCH MORE. A MIXTURE... MÉLANGE IF YOU WILL... ALL THE TECHNOLOGY FROM APOKOLIPS AND NEW GENESIS THAT WE'VE MANAGED TO SCAVENGE, NOW *COMBINED* WITH THE SCIENCE FROM YOUR WORLD.
IT'S--*er*-- I'VE GOT TO HAND IT TO YOU, IMPOSSIBLE, YOU'VE CERTAINLY ACHIEVED WHAT YOUR NAME IMPLIES.
AND ONE FROM MINE.
HUNTER. IF YOU WOULD.
ABSOLUTELY.

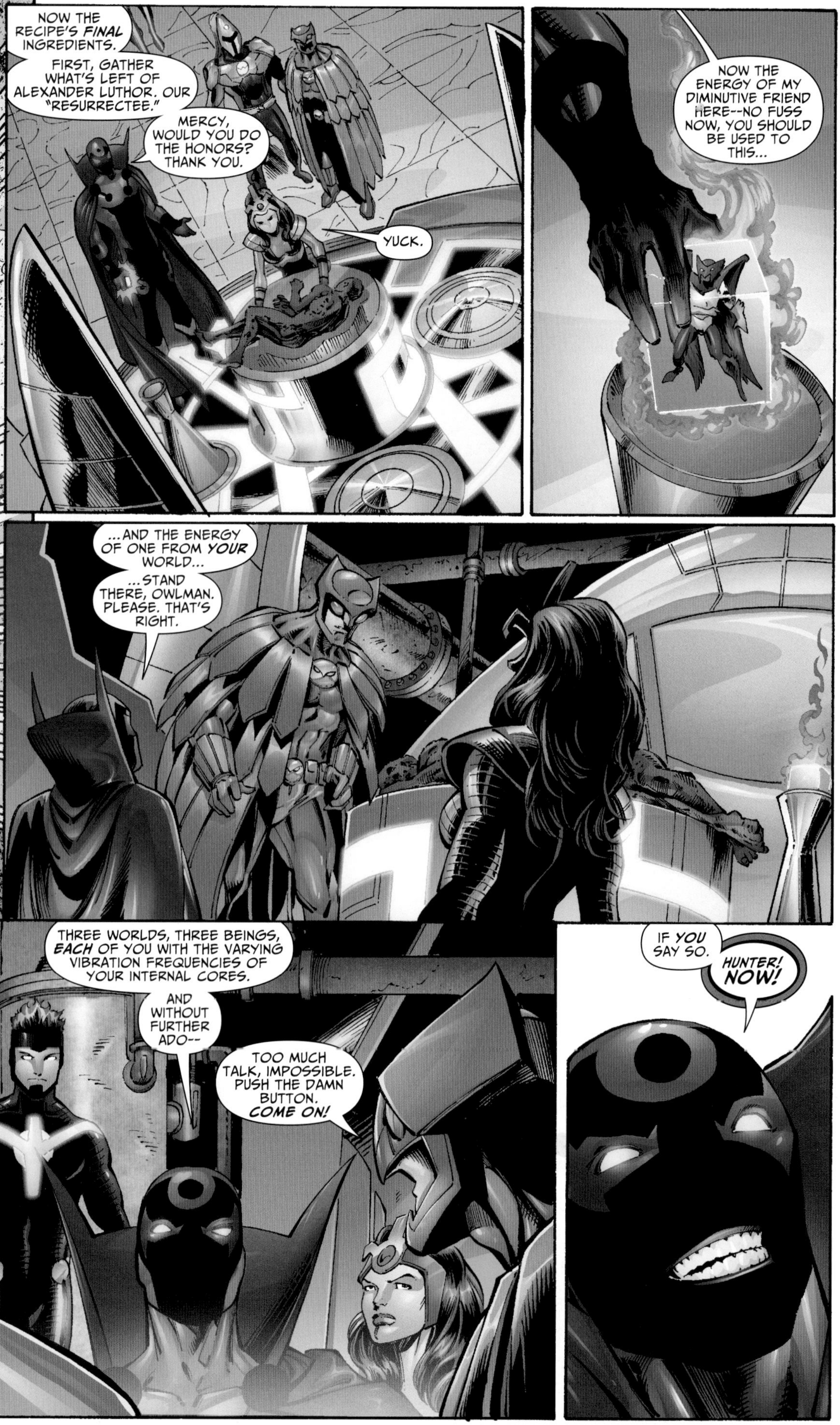
NOW THE RECIPE'S *FINAL* INGREDIENTS.
FIRST, GATHER WHAT'S LEFT OF ALEXANDER LUTHOR. OUR "RESURRECTEE."
MERCY, WOULD YOU DO THE HONORS? THANK YOU.
YUCK.
NOW THE ENERGY OF MY DIMINUTIVE FRIEND HERE--NO FUSS NOW, YOU SHOULD BE USED TO THIS...
...AND THE ENERGY OF ONE FROM *YOUR* WORLD...
...STAND THERE, OWLMAN. PLEASE. THAT'S RIGHT.
THREE WORLDS, THREE BEINGS, *EACH* OF YOU WITH THE VARYING VIBRATION FREQUENCIES OF YOUR INTERNAL CORES.
AND WITHOUT FURTHER ADO--
TOO MUCH TALK, IMPOSSIBLE. PUSH THE DAMN BUTTON. *COME ON!*
IF *YOU* SAY SO.
HUNTER! NOW!

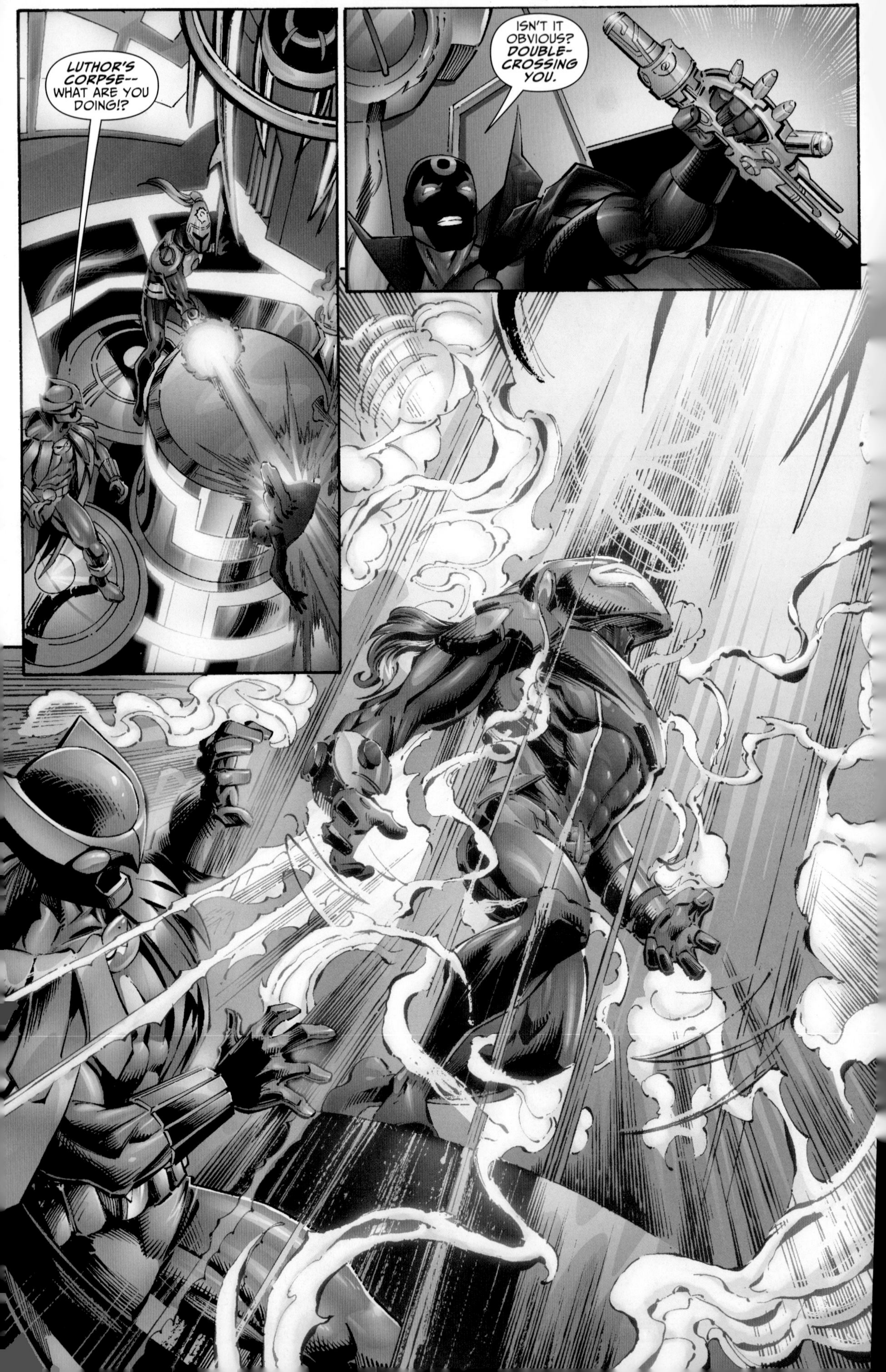
LUTHOR'S CORPSE-- WHAT ARE YOU DOING!?
ISN'T IT OBVIOUS? DOUBLE-CROSSING YOU.

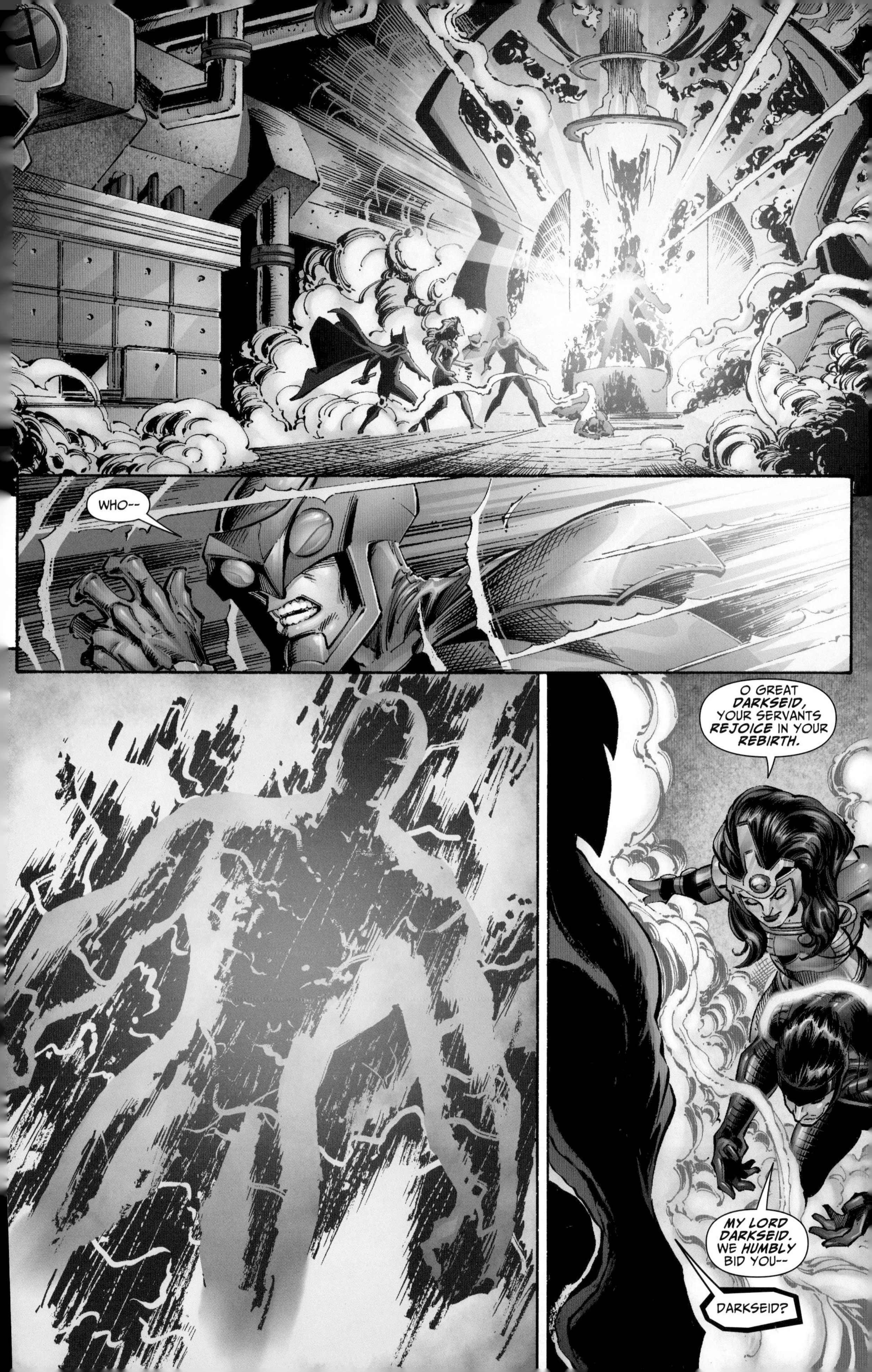
WHO--
O GREAT DARKSEID, YOUR SERVANTS REJOICE IN YOUR REBIRTH.
MY LORD DARKSEID. WE HUMBLY BID YOU--
DARKSEID?

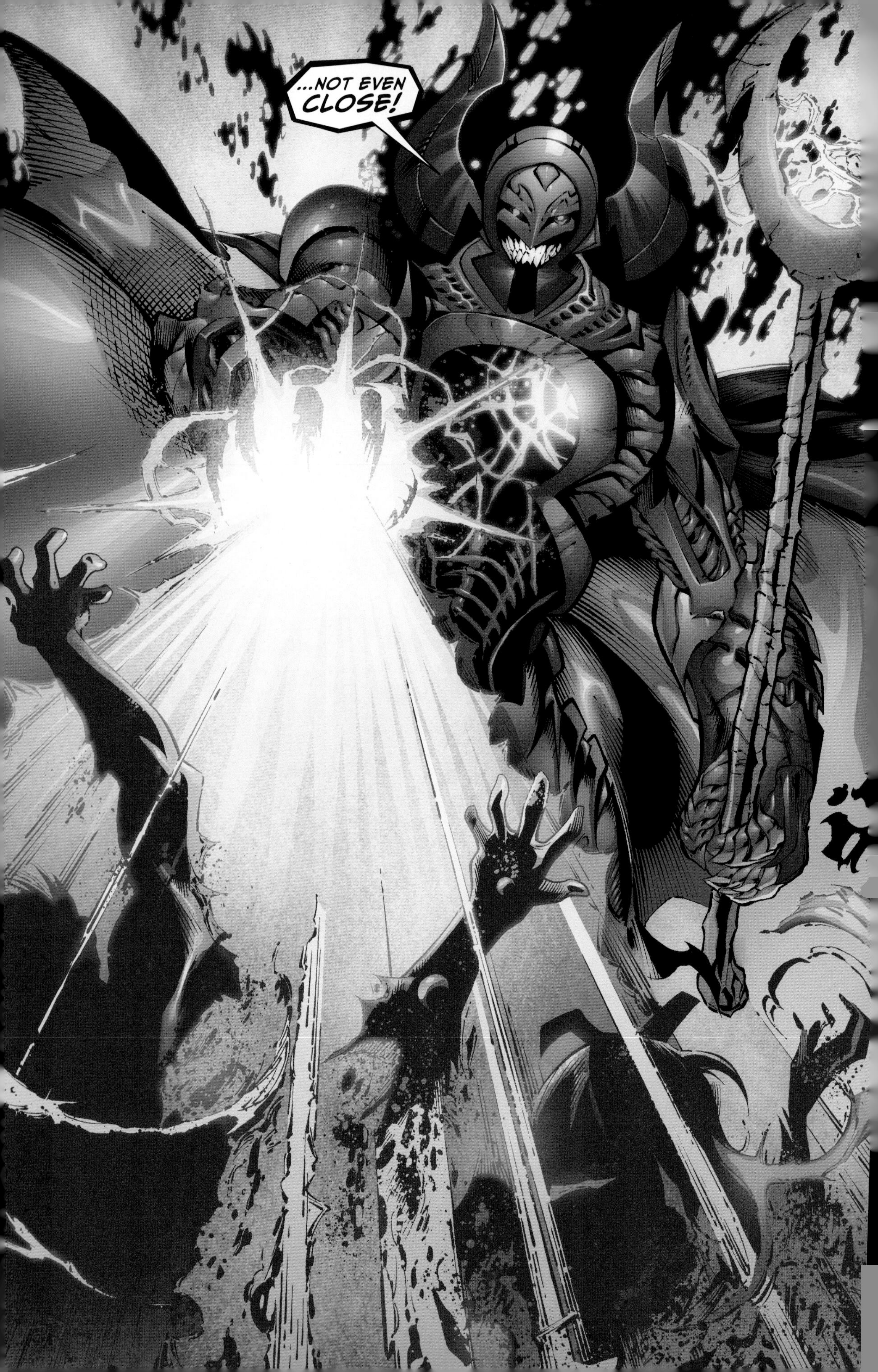
...NOT EVEN CLOSE!

JUSTICE LEAGUE OF AMERICA 51
cover by Mark Bagley, Rob Hunter & Hi-Fi

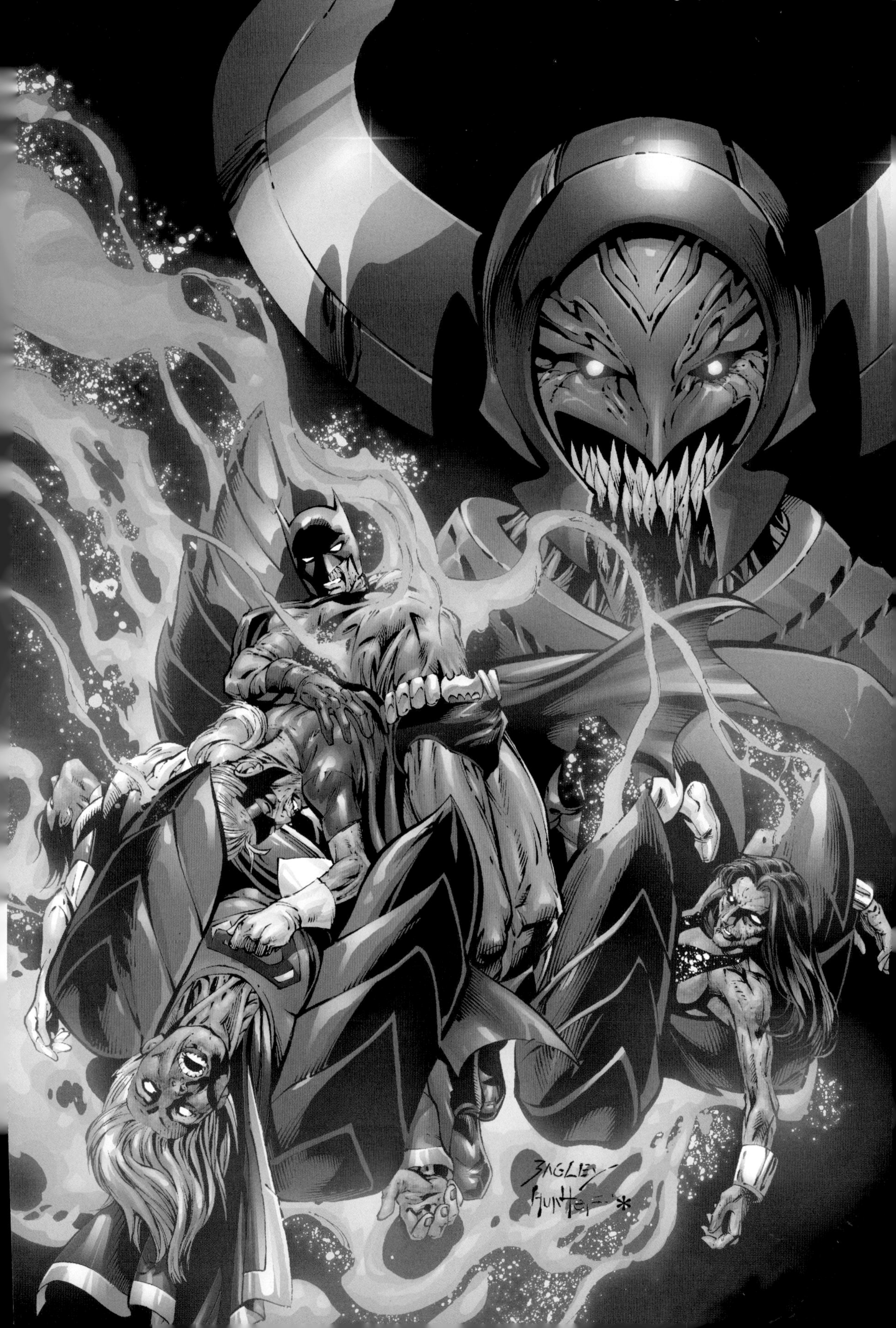

JUSTICE LEAGUE OF AMERICA 51
variant by David Mack

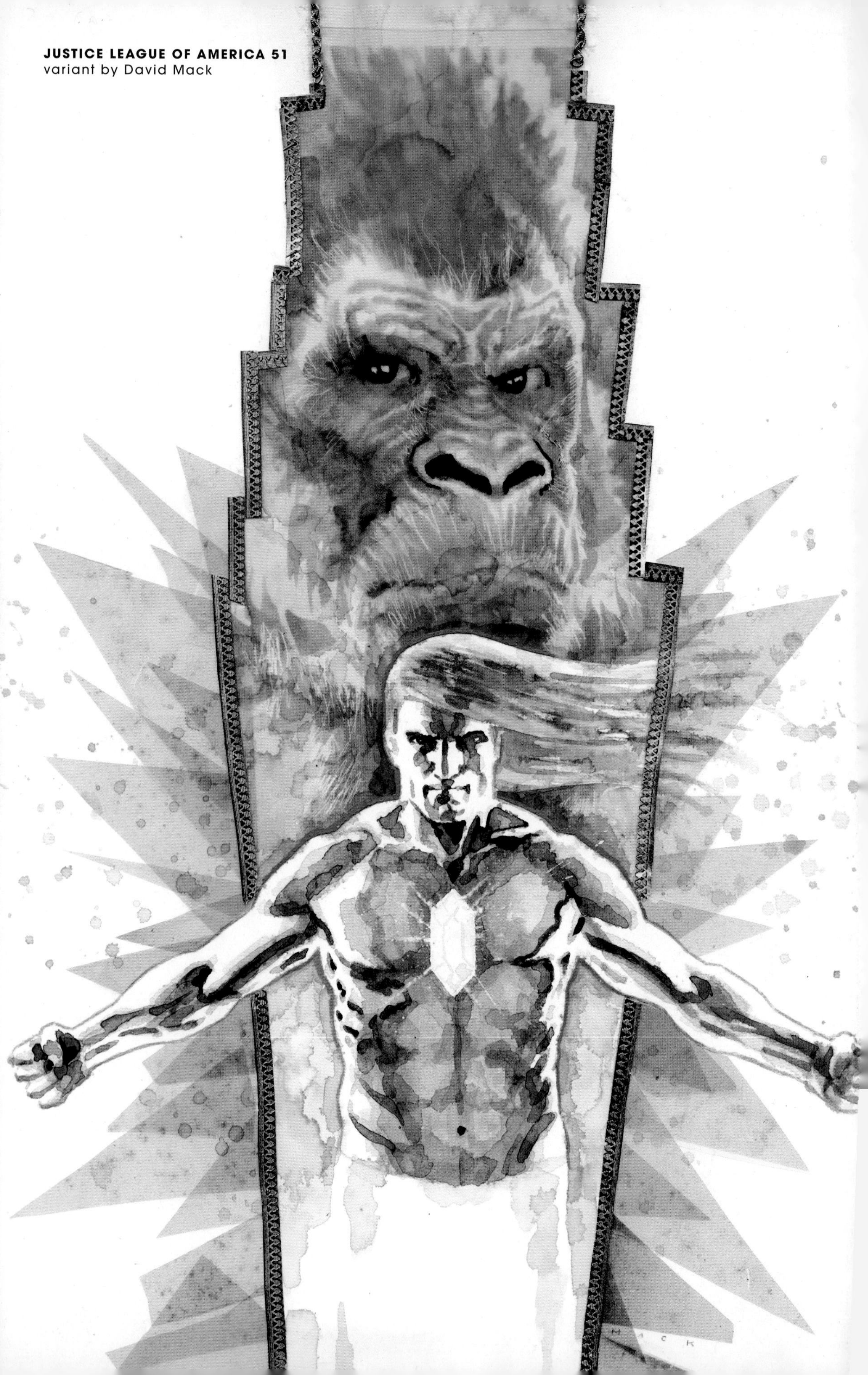
MACK

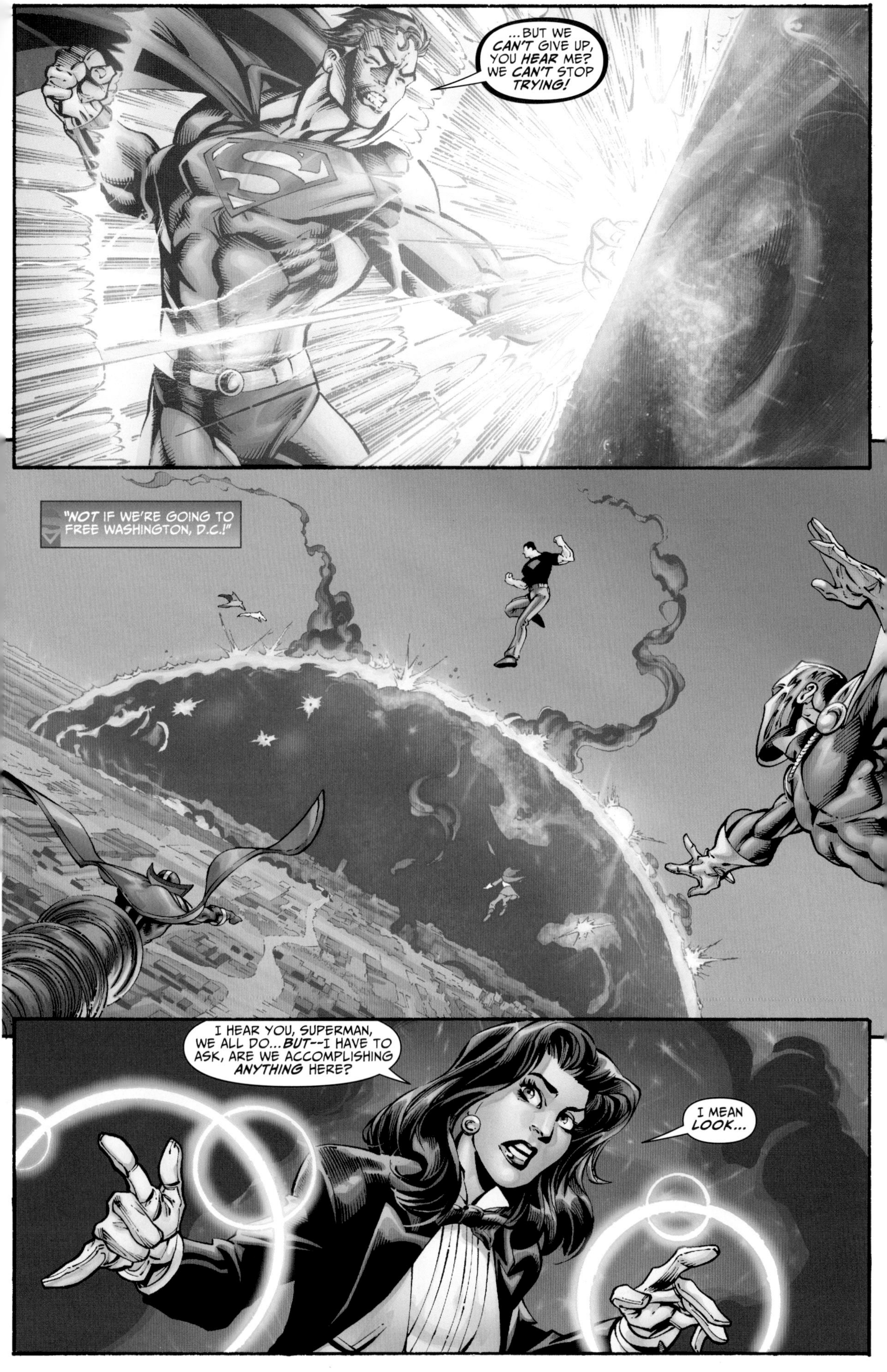
...BUT WE CAN'T GIVE UP, YOU HEAR ME? WE CAN'T STOP TRYING!
"NOT IF WE'RE GOING TO FREE WASHINGTON, D.C.!"
I HEAR YOU, SUPERMAN, WE ALL DO...BUT--I HAVE TO ASK, ARE WE ACCOMPLISHING ANYTHING HERE?
I MEAN LOOK...

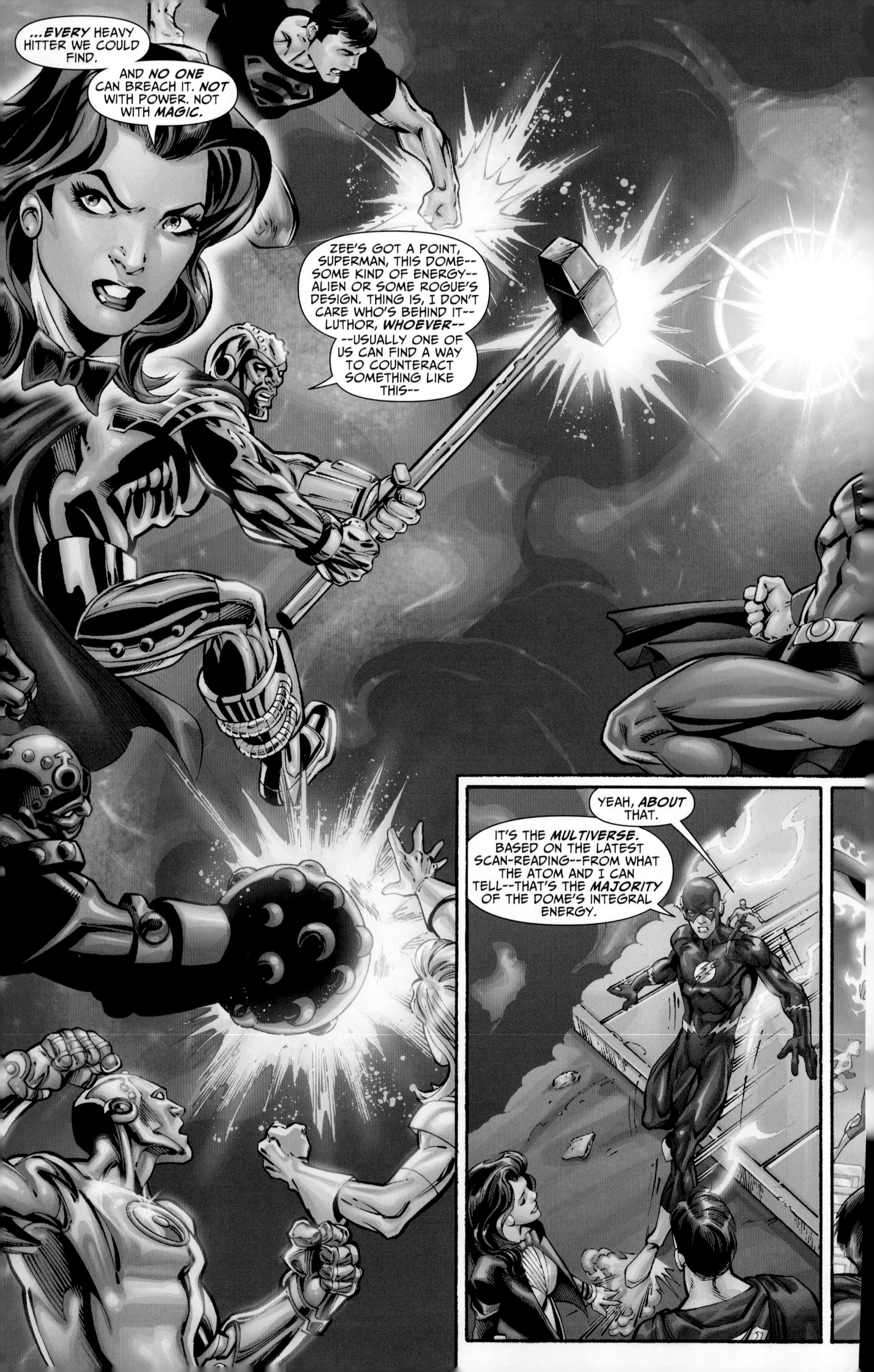
...EVERY HEAVY HITTER WE COULD FIND.
AND NO ONE CAN BREACH IT. NOT WITH POWER. NOT WITH MAGIC.
ZEE'S GOT A POINT, SUPERMAN, THIS DOME-- SOME KIND OF ENERGY-- ALIEN OR SOME ROGUE'S DESIGN. THING IS, I DON'T CARE WHO'S BEHIND IT-- LUTHOR, WHOEVER--
--USUALLY ONE OF US CAN FIND A WAY TO COUNTERACT SOMETHING LIKE THIS--
YEAH, ABOUT THAT.
IT'S THE MULTIVERSE. BASED ON THE LATEST SCAN-READING--FROM WHAT THE ATOM AND I CAN TELL--THAT'S THE MAJORITY OF THE DOME'S INTEGRAL ENERGY.

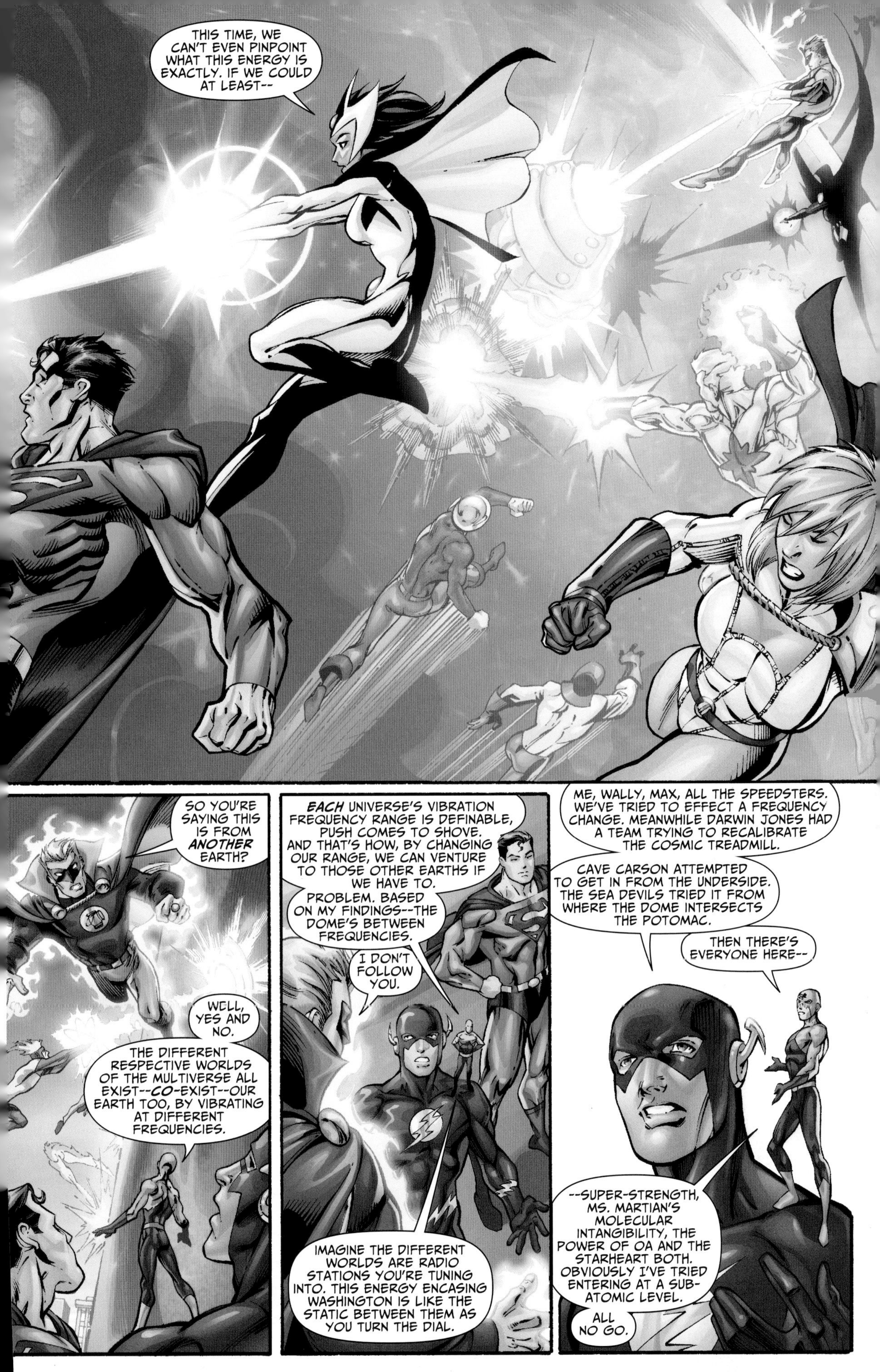
THIS TIME, WE CAN'T EVEN PINPOINT WHAT THIS ENERGY IS EXACTLY. IF WE COULD AT LEAST--
SO YOU'RE SAYING THIS IS FROM ANOTHER EARTH?
WELL, YES AND NO.
THE DIFFERENT RESPECTIVE WORLDS OF THE MULTIVERSE ALL EXIST--CO-EXIST--OUR EARTH TOO, BY VIBRATING AT DIFFERENT FREQUENCIES.
EACH UNIVERSE'S VIBRATION FREQUENCY RANGE IS DEFINABLE, PUSH COMES TO SHOVE. AND THAT'S HOW, BY CHANGING OUR RANGE, WE CAN VENTURE TO THOSE OTHER EARTHS IF WE HAVE TO.
PROBLEM. BASED ON MY FINDINGS--THE DOME'S BETWEEN FREQUENCIES.
I DON'T FOLLOW YOU.
IMAGINE THE DIFFERENT WORLDS ARE RADIO STATIONS YOU'RE TUNING INTO. THIS ENERGY ENCASING WASHINGTON IS LIKE THE STATIC BETWEEN THEM AS YOU TURN THE DIAL.
ME, WALLY, MAX, ALL THE SPEEDSTERS. WE'VE TRIED TO EFFECT A FREQUENCY CHANGE. MEANWHILE DARWIN JONES HAD A TEAM TRYING TO RECALIBRATE THE COSMIC TREADMILL.
CAVE CARSON ATTEMPTED TO GET IN FROM THE UNDERSIDE. THE SEA DEVILS TRIED IT FROM WHERE THE DOME INTERSECTS THE POTOMAC.
THEN THERE'S EVERYONE HERE--
--SUPER-STRENGTH, MS. MARTIAN'S MOLECULAR INTANGIBILITY, THE POWER OF OA AND THE STARHEART BOTH. OBVIOUSLY I'VE TRIED ENTERING AT A SUB-ATOMIC LEVEL.
ALL NO GO.

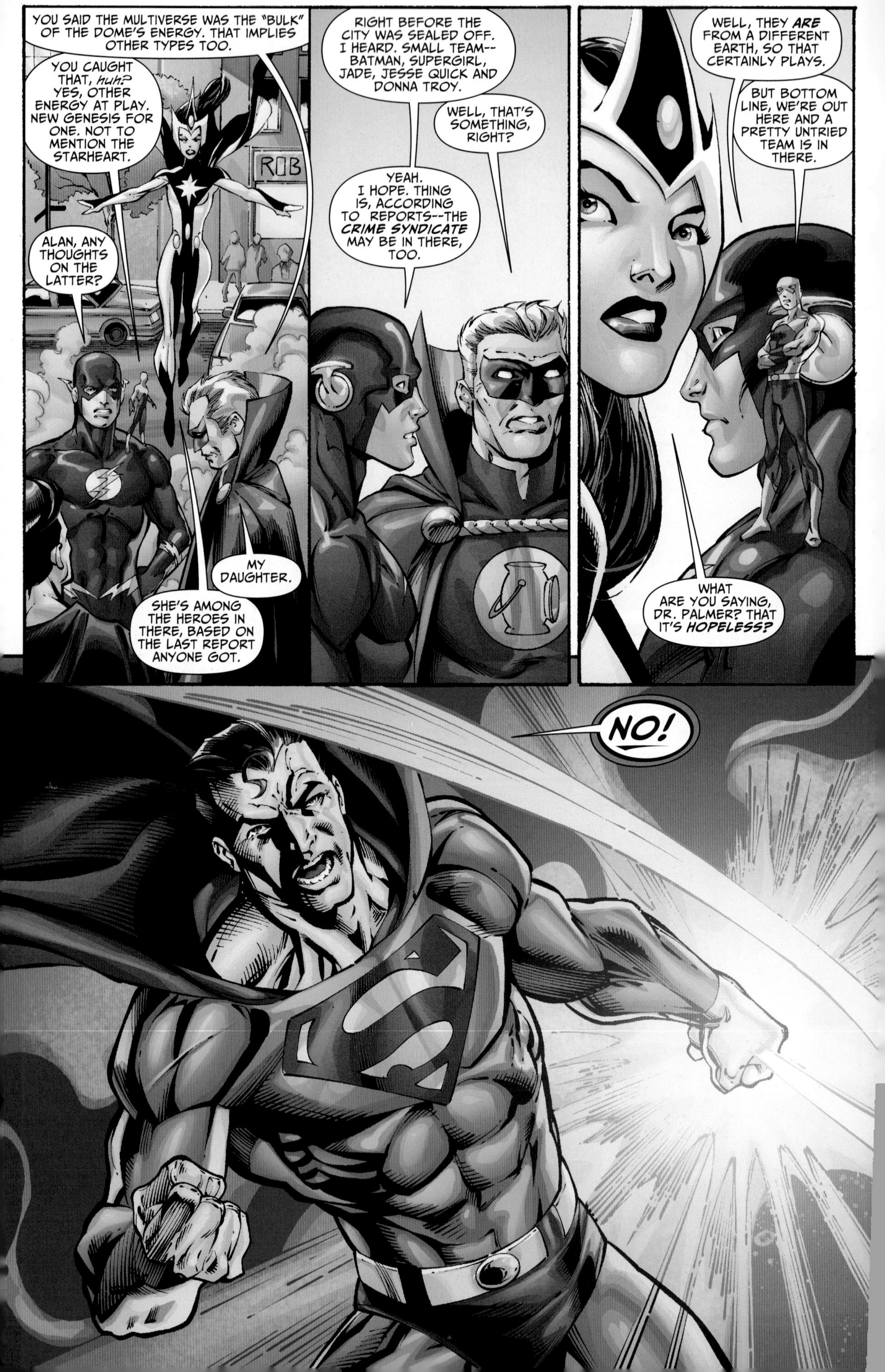

YOU SAID THE MULTIVERSE WAS THE "BULK" OF THE DOME'S ENERGY. THAT IMPLIES OTHER TYPES TOO.
YOU CAUGHT THAT, *huh?* YES, OTHER ENERGY AT PLAY. NEW GENESIS FOR ONE. NOT TO MENTION THE STARHEART.
ROB
ALAN, ANY THOUGHTS ON THE LATTER?
MY DAUGHTER.
SHE'S AMONG THE HEROES IN THERE, BASED ON THE LAST REPORT ANYONE GOT.
RIGHT BEFORE THE CITY WAS SEALED OFF. I HEARD. SMALL TEAM-- BATMAN, SUPERGIRL, JADE, JESSE QUICK AND DONNA TROY.
WELL, THAT'S SOMETHING, RIGHT?
YEAH. I HOPE. THING IS, ACCORDING TO REPORTS--THE ***CRIME SYNDICATE*** MAY BE IN THERE, TOO.
WELL, THEY ***ARE*** FROM A DIFFERENT EARTH, SO THAT CERTAINLY PLAYS.
BUT BOTTOM LINE, WE'RE OUT HERE AND A PRETTY UNTRIED TEAM IS IN THERE.
WHAT ARE YOU SAYING, DR. PALMER? THAT IT'S ***HOPELESS?***
NO!

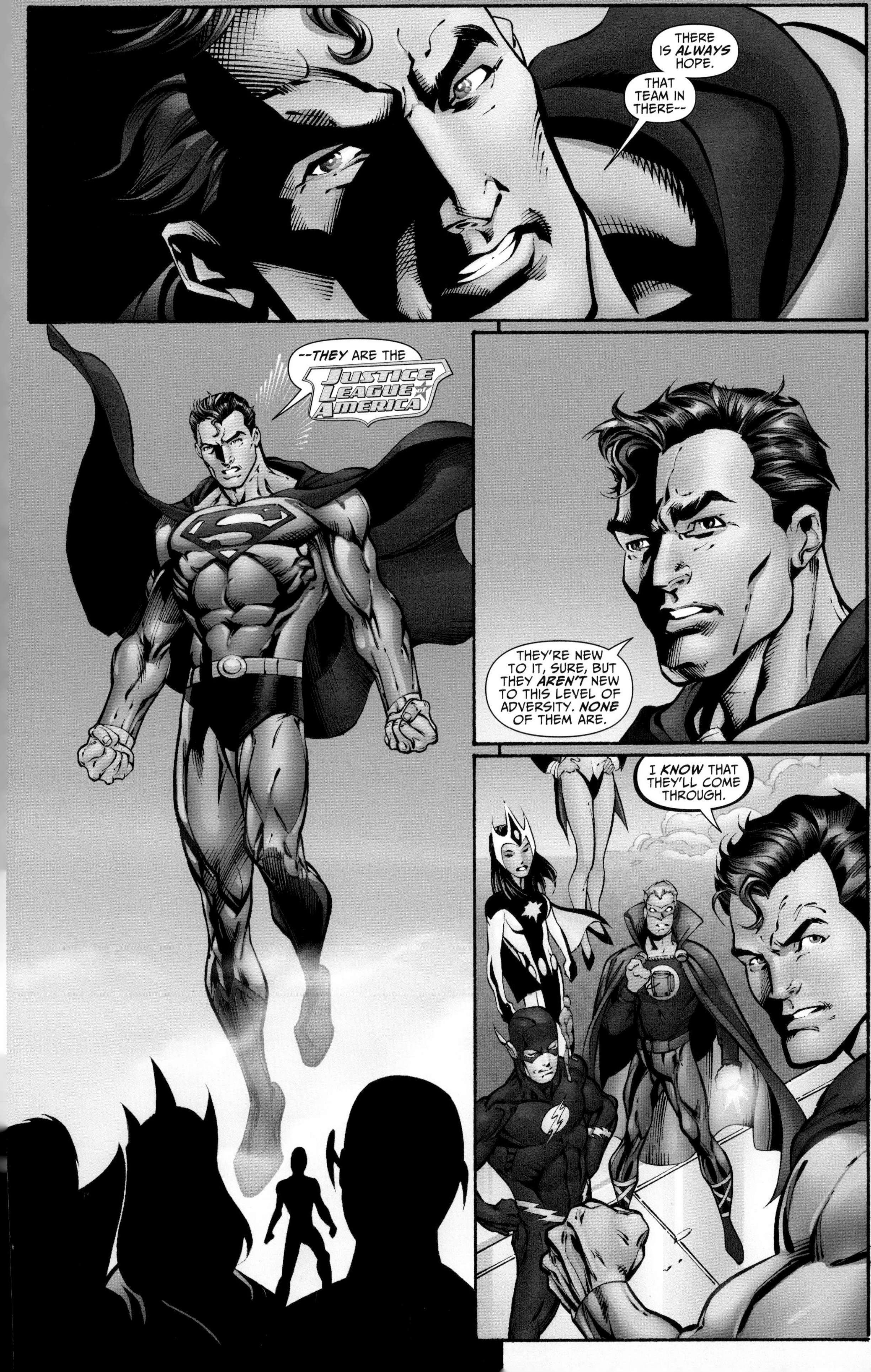
THERE IS ALWAYS HOPE.
THAT TEAM IN THERE--
--THEY ARE THE JUSTICE LEAGUE of AMERICA
THEY'RE NEW TO IT, SURE, BUT THEY AREN'T NEW TO THIS LEVEL OF ADVERSITY. NONE OF THEM ARE.
I KNOW THAT THEY'LL COME THROUGH.

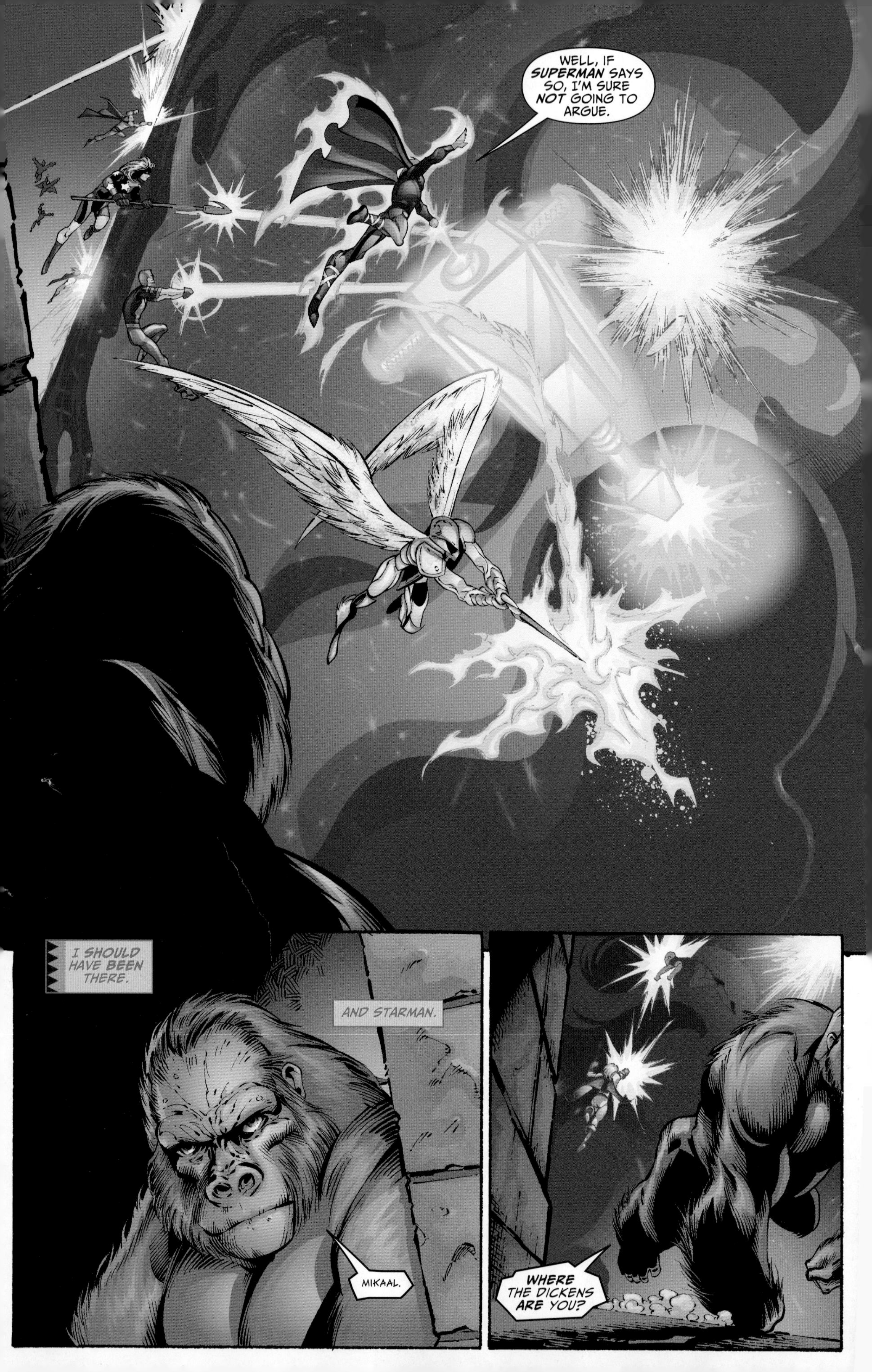
WELL, IF SUPERMAN SAYS SO, I'M SURE NOT GOING TO ARGUE.
I SHOULD HAVE BEEN THERE.
AND STARMAN.
MIKAAL.
WHERE THE DICKENS ARE YOU?

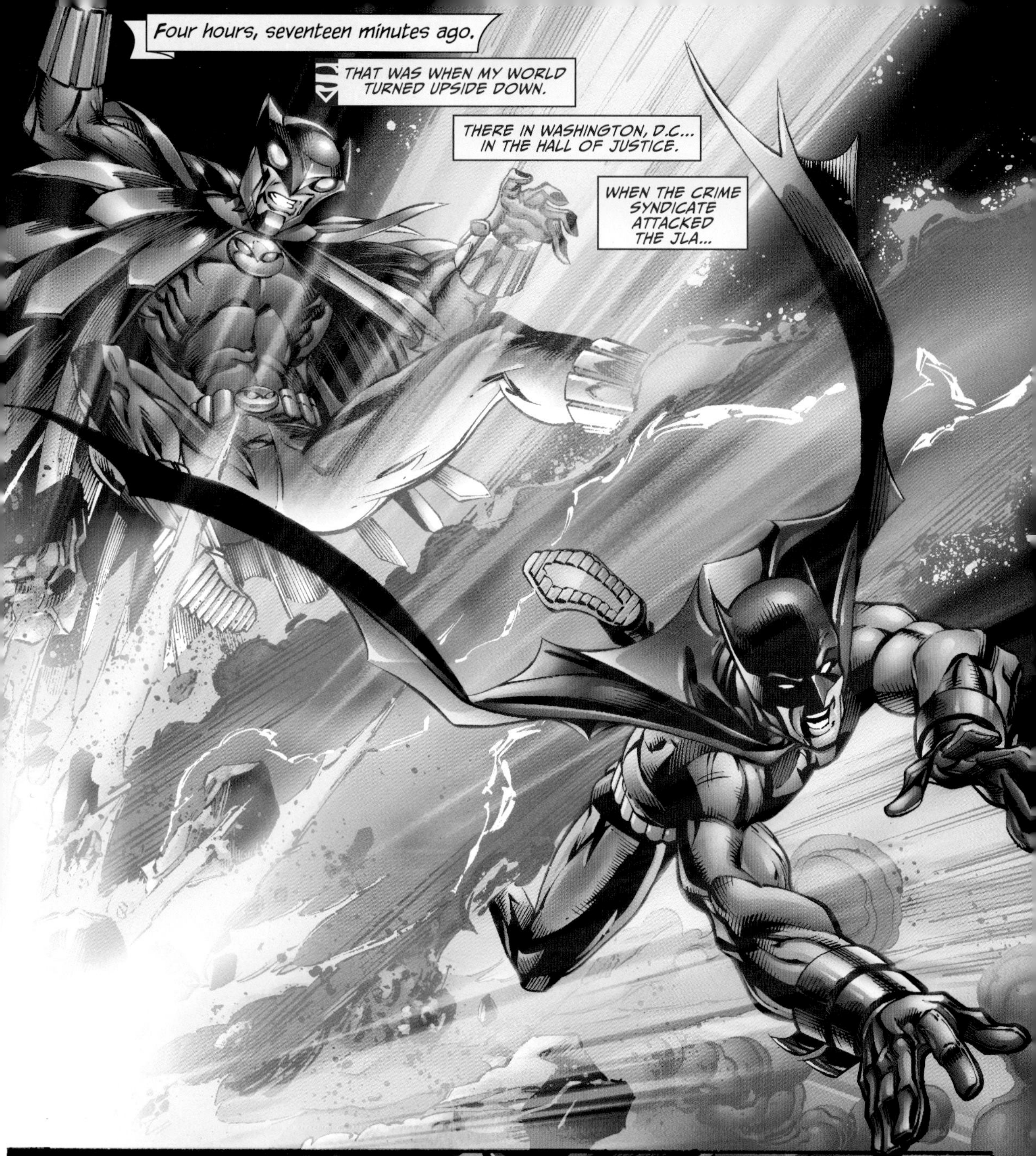
Four hours, seventeen minutes ago.
THAT WAS WHEN MY WORLD TURNED UPSIDE DOWN.
THERE IN WASHINGTON, D.C... IN THE HALL OF JUSTICE.
WHEN THE CRIME SYNDICATE ATTACKED THE JLA...

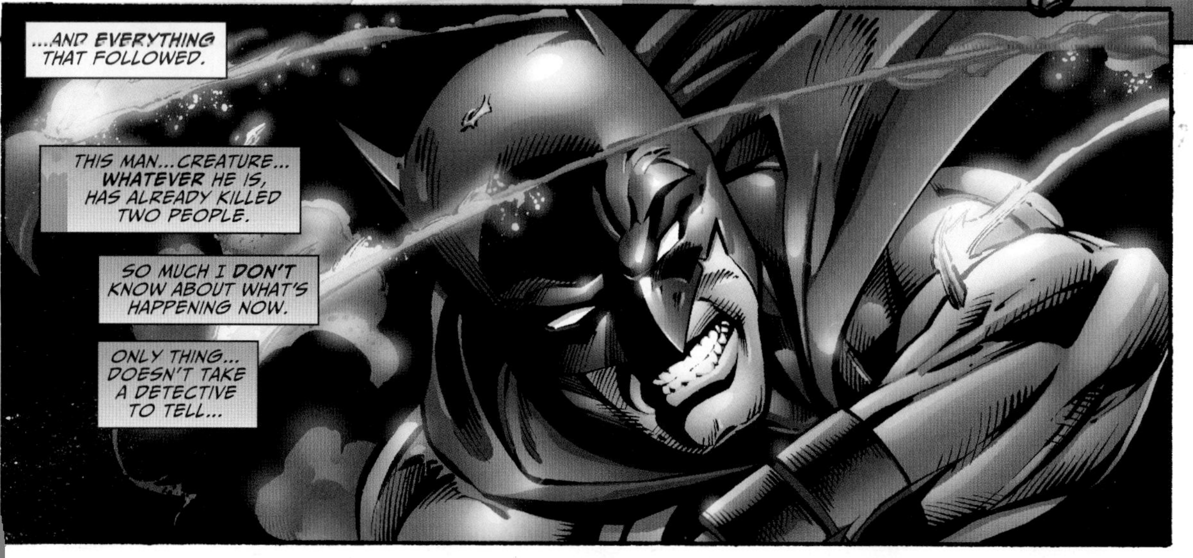
...AND EVERYTHING THAT FOLLOWED.
THIS MAN...CREATURE... WHATEVER HE IS, HAS ALREADY KILLED TWO PEOPLE.
SO MUCH I DON'T KNOW ABOUT WHAT'S HAPPENING NOW.
ONLY THING... DOESN'T TAKE A DETECTIVE TO TELL...

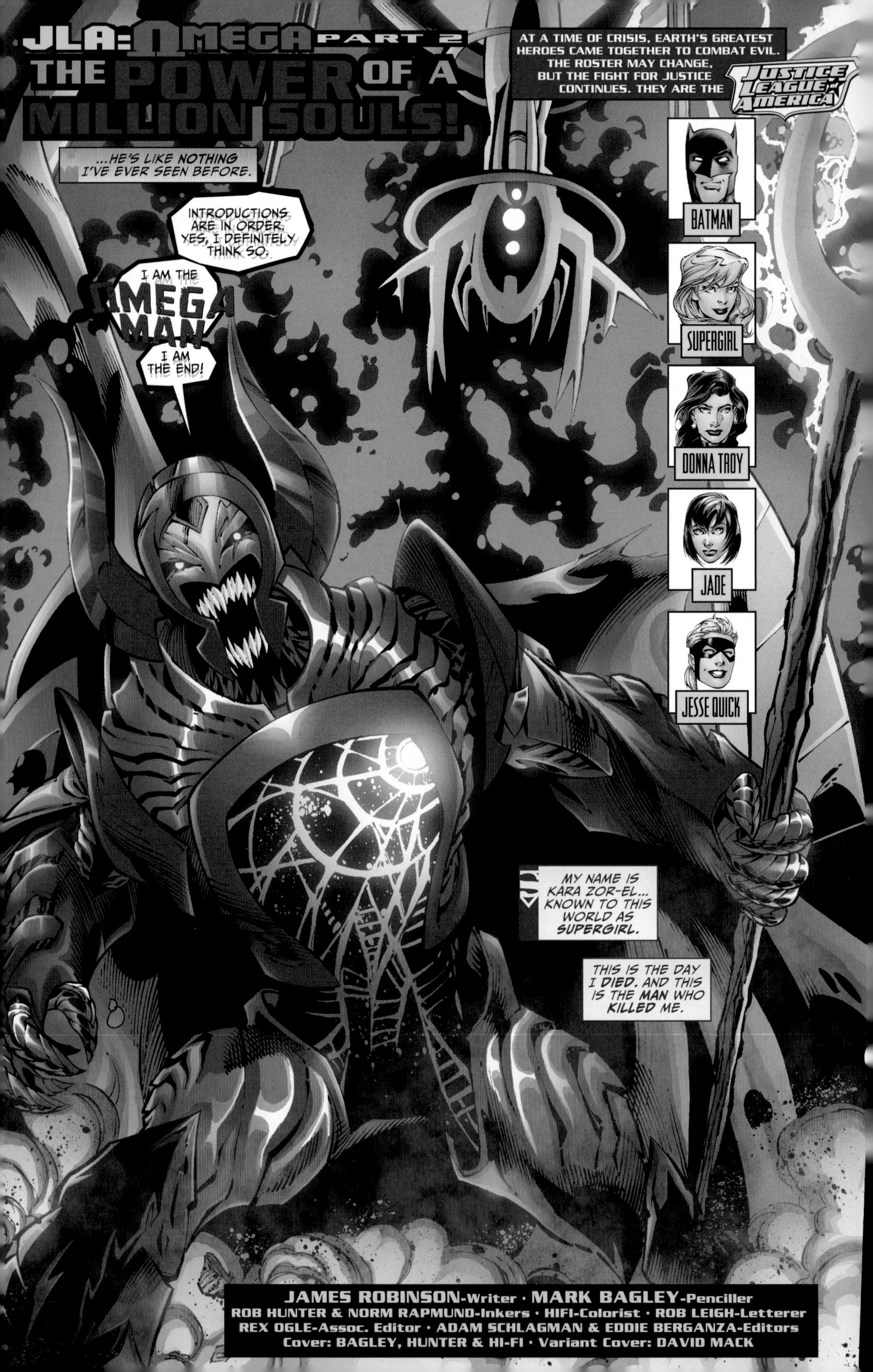

JLA: OMEGA PART 2
THE POWER OF A MILLION SOULS!
AT A TIME OF CRISIS, EARTH'S GREATEST HEROES CAME TOGETHER TO COMBAT EVIL. THE ROSTER MAY CHANGE, BUT THE FIGHT FOR JUSTICE CONTINUES. THEY ARE THE
JUSTICE LEAGUE OF AMERICA
BATMAN
SUPERGIRL
DONNA TROY
JADE
JESSE QUICK
...HE'S LIKE NOTHING I'VE EVER SEEN BEFORE.
INTRODUCTIONS ARE IN ORDER. YES, I DEFINITELY THINK SO.
I AM THE OMEGA MAN
I AM THE END!
MY NAME IS KARA ZOR-EL... KNOWN TO THIS WORLD AS SUPERGIRL.
THIS IS THE DAY I DIED. AND THIS IS THE MAN WHO KILLED ME.
JAMES ROBINSON-Writer · MARK BAGLEY-Penciller
ROB HUNTER & NORM RAPMUND-Inkers · HIFI-Colorist · ROB LEIGH-Letterer
REX OGLE-Assoc. Editor · ADAM SCHLAGMAN & EDDIE BERGANZA-Editors
Cover: BAGLEY, HUNTER & HI-FI · Variant Cover: DAVID MACK

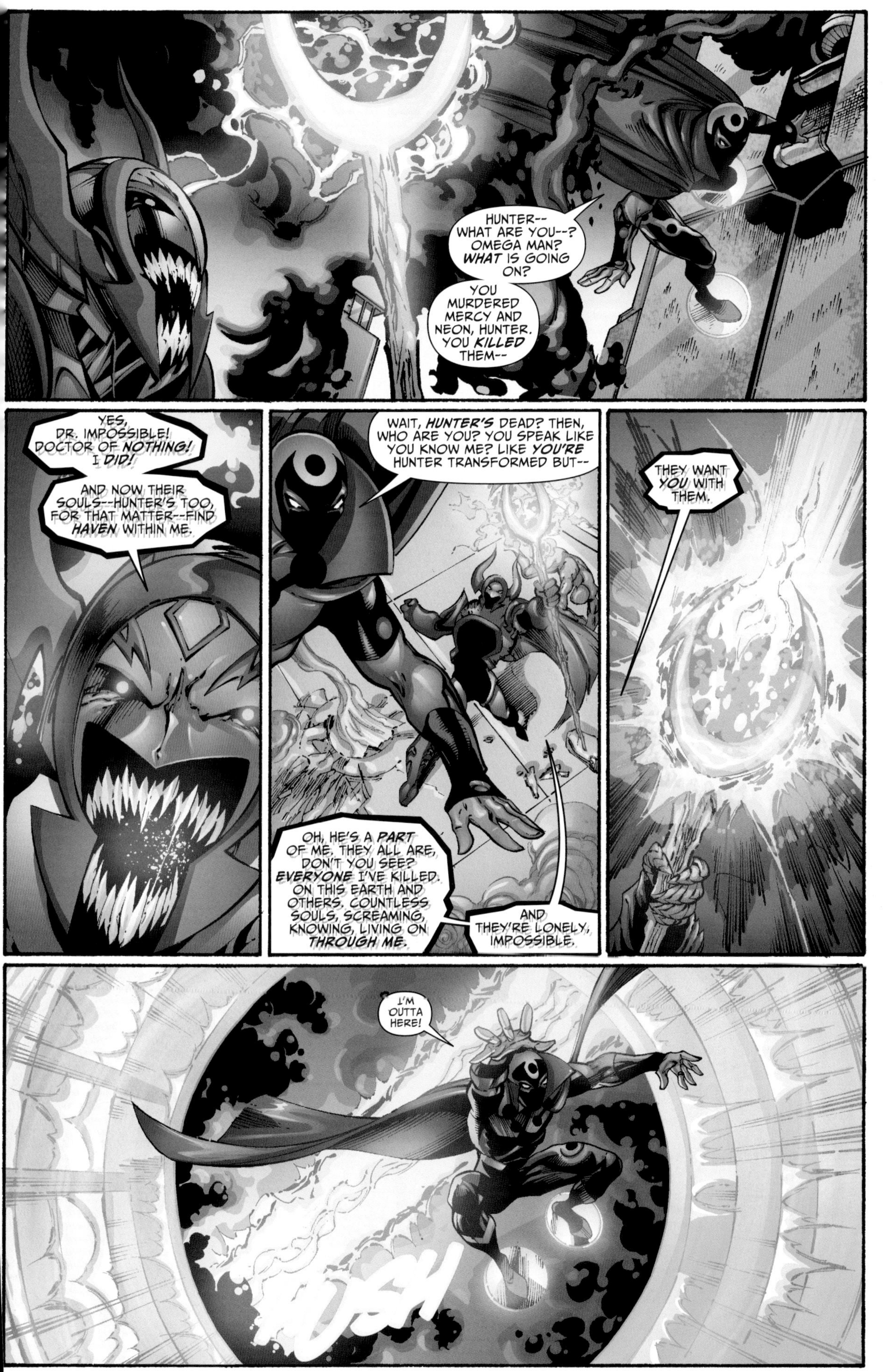
HUNTER-- WHAT ARE YOU--? OMEGA MAN? WHAT IS GOING ON?
YOU MURDERED MERCY AND NEON, HUNTER. YOU KILLED THEM--
YES, DR. IMPOSSIBLE! DOCTOR OF NOTHING! I DID!
AND NOW THEIR SOULS--HUNTER'S TOO, FOR THAT MATTER--FIND HAVEN WITHIN ME.
WAIT, HUNTER'S DEAD? THEN, WHO ARE YOU? YOU SPEAK LIKE YOU KNOW ME? LIKE YOU'RE HUNTER TRANSFORMED BUT--
OH, HE'S A PART OF ME. THEY ALL ARE, DON'T YOU SEE? EVERYONE I'VE KILLED. ON THIS EARTH AND OTHERS. COUNTLESS SOULS, SCREAMING, KNOWING, LIVING ON THROUGH ME.
AND THEY'RE LONELY, IMPOSSIBLE.
THEY WANT YOU WITH THEM.
I'M OUTTA HERE!

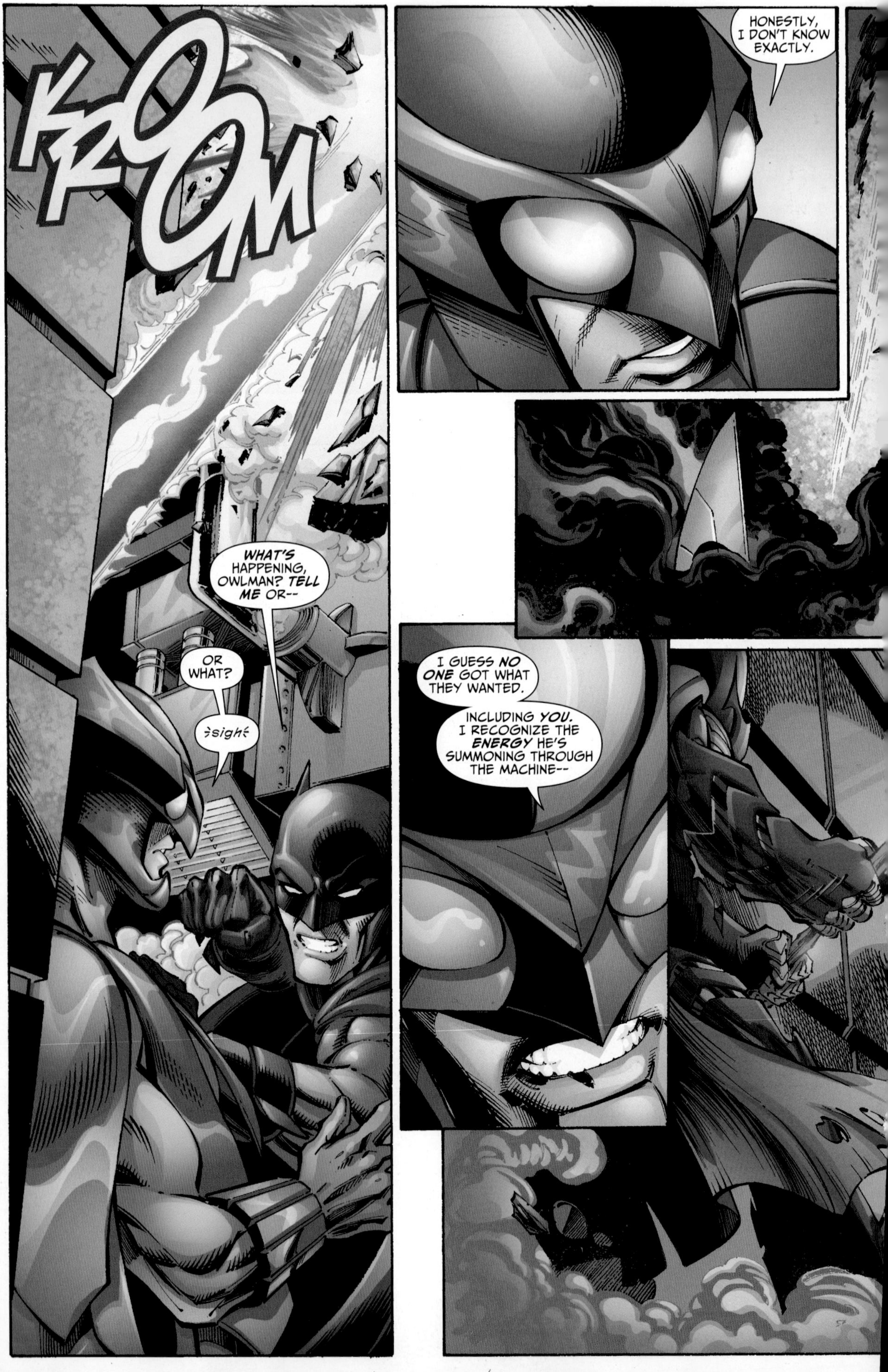
KROOM
HONESTLY, I DON'T KNOW EXACTLY.
WHAT'S HAPPENING, OWLMAN? TELL ME OR--
OR WHAT?
sigh
I GUESS NO ONE GOT WHAT THEY WANTED.
INCLUDING YOU. I RECOGNIZE THE ENERGY HE'S SUMMONING THROUGH THE MACHINE--

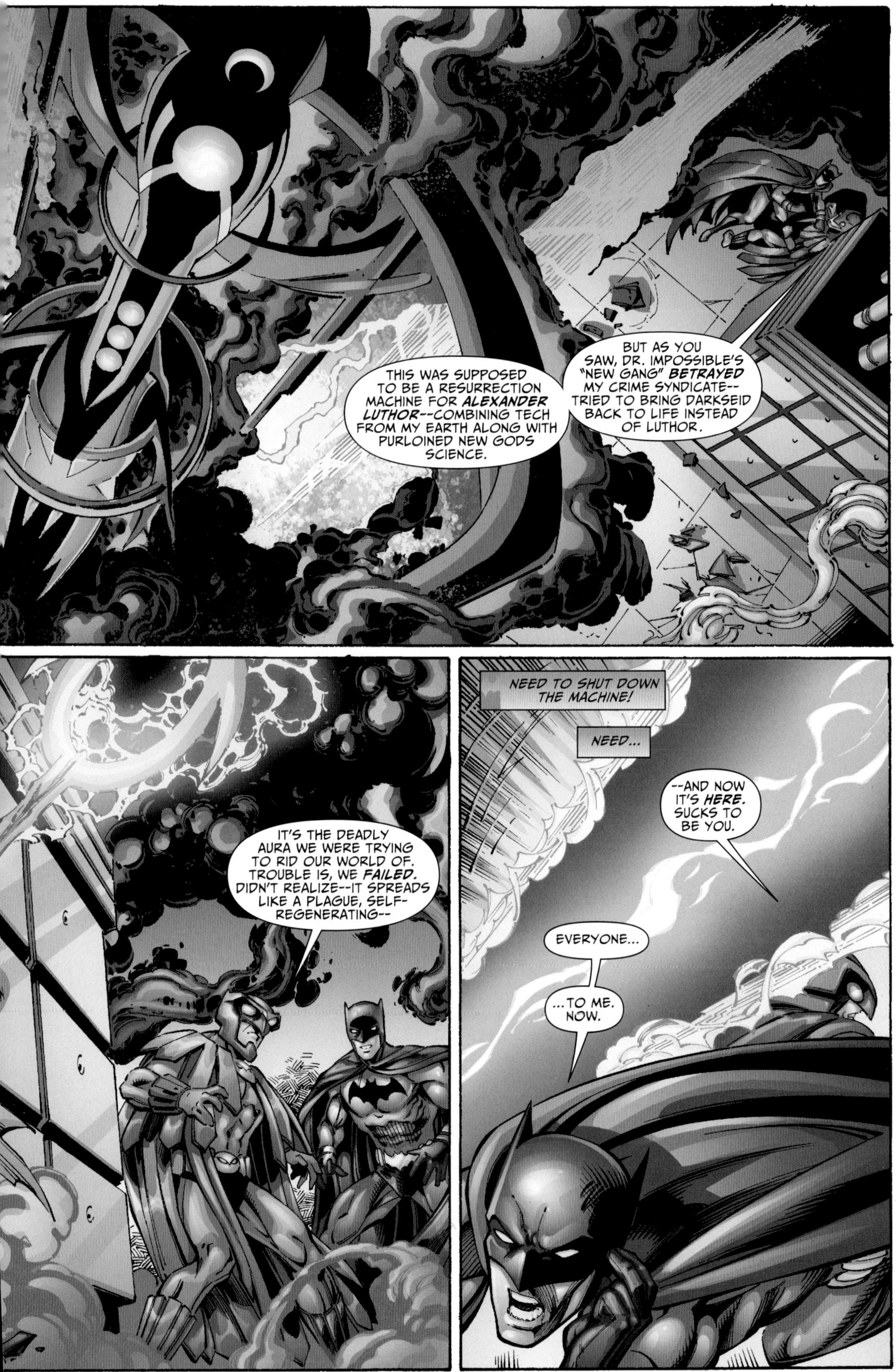
THIS WAS SUPPOSED TO BE A RESURRECTION MACHINE FOR ALEXANDER LUTHOR--COMBINING TECH FROM MY EARTH ALONG WITH PURLOINED NEW GODS SCIENCE.
BUT AS YOU SAW, DR. IMPOSSIBLE'S "NEW GANG" BETRAYED MY CRIME SYNDICATE--TRIED TO BRING DARKSEID BACK TO LIFE INSTEAD OF LUTHOR.
IT'S THE DEADLY AURA WE WERE TRYING TO RID OUR WORLD OF. TROUBLE IS, WE FAILED. DIDN'T REALIZE--IT SPREADS LIKE A PLAGUE, SELF-REGENERATING--
NEED TO SHUT DOWN THE MACHINE!
NEED...
--AND NOW IT'S HERE. SUCKS TO BE YOU.
EVERYONE...
...TO ME. NOW.

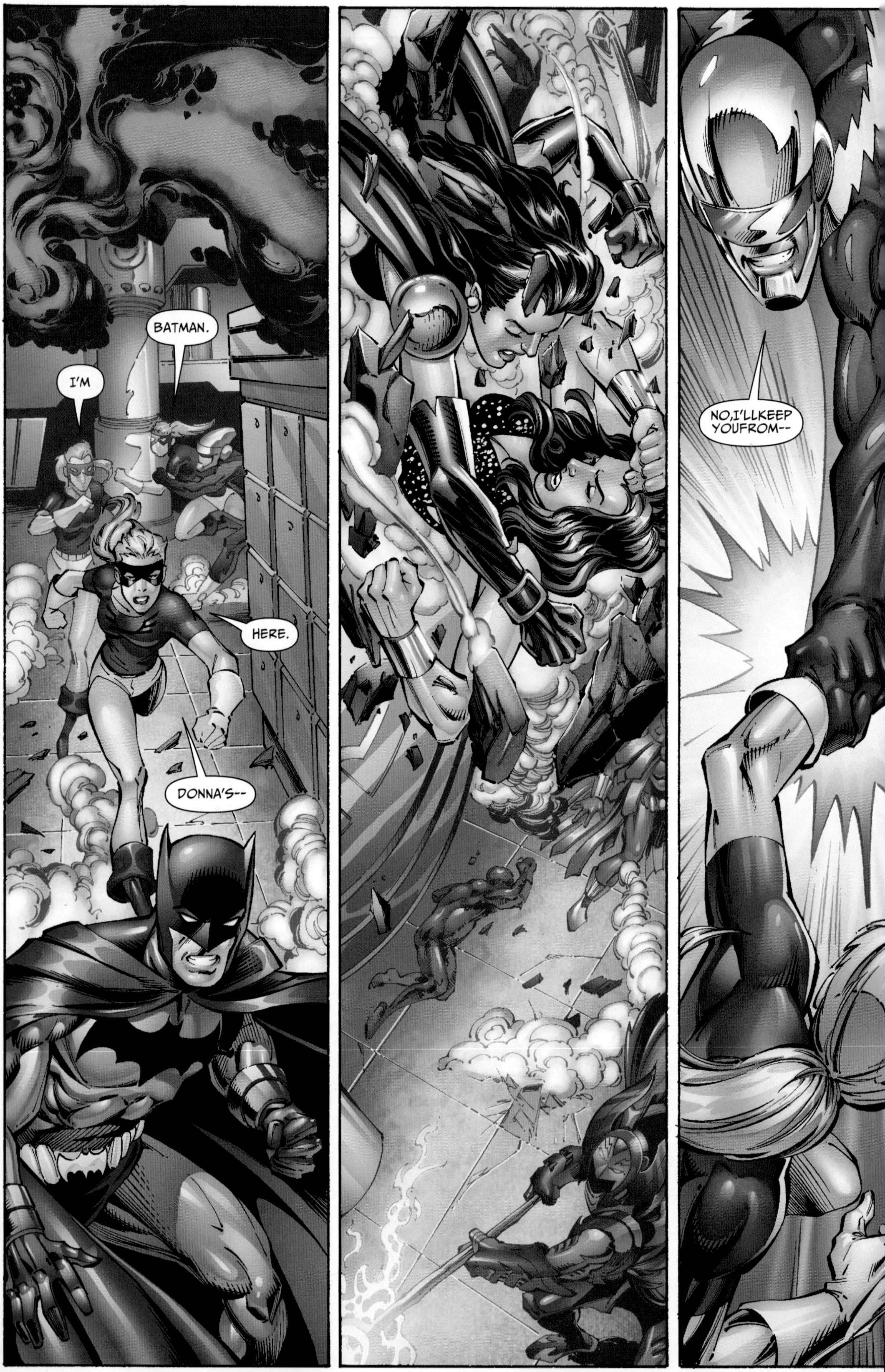
BATMAN.
I'M
HERE.
DONNA'S--
NO, I'LL KEEP YOU FROM--

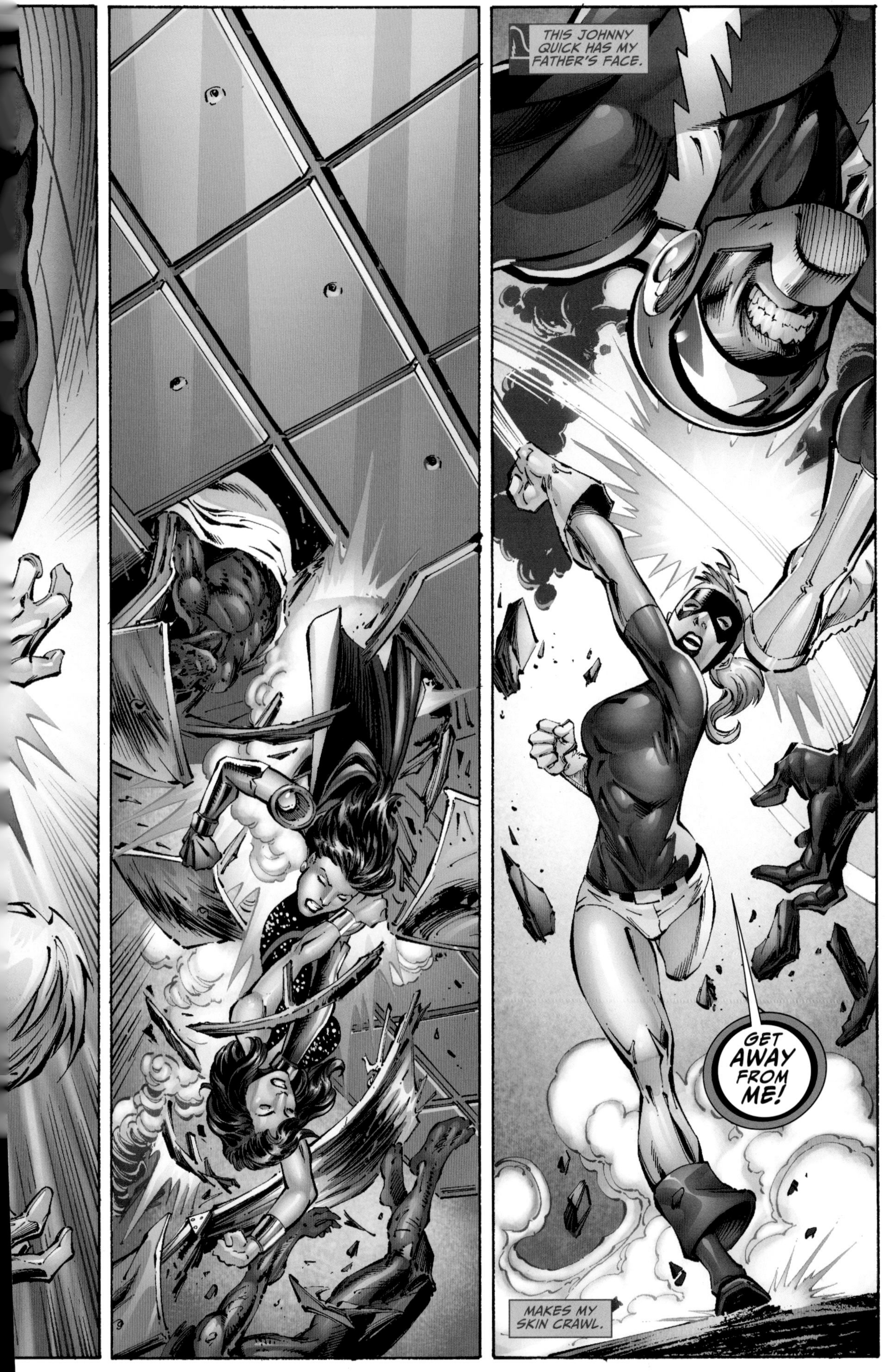
THIS JOHNNY QUICK HAS MY FATHER'S FACE.
GET AWAY FROM ME!
MAKES MY SKIN CRAWL.

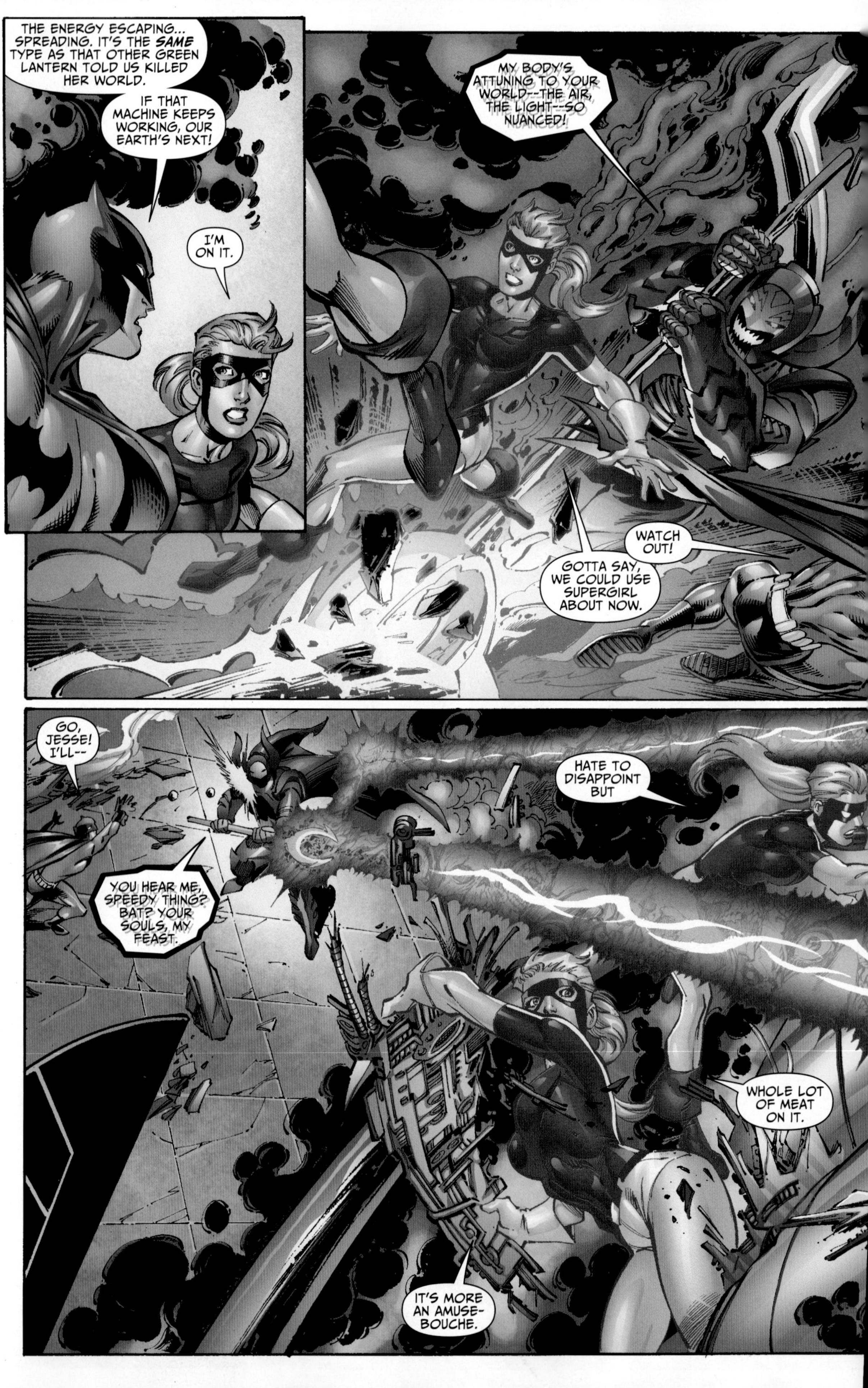
THE ENERGY ESCAPING... SPREADING. IT'S THE SAME TYPE AS THAT OTHER GREEN LANTERN TOLD US KILLED HER WORLD.
IF THAT MACHINE KEEPS WORKING, OUR EARTH'S NEXT!
I'M ON IT.
MY BODY'S ATTUNING TO YOUR WORLD--THE AIR, THE LIGHT--SO NUANCED!
WATCH OUT!
GOTTA SAY, WE COULD USE SUPERGIRL ABOUT NOW.
GO, JESSE! I'LL--
YOU HEAR ME, SPEEDY THING? BAT? YOUR SOULS, MY FEAST.
HATE TO DISAPPOINT BUT
WHOLE LOT OF MEAT ON IT.
IT'S MORE AN AMUSE-BOUCHE.

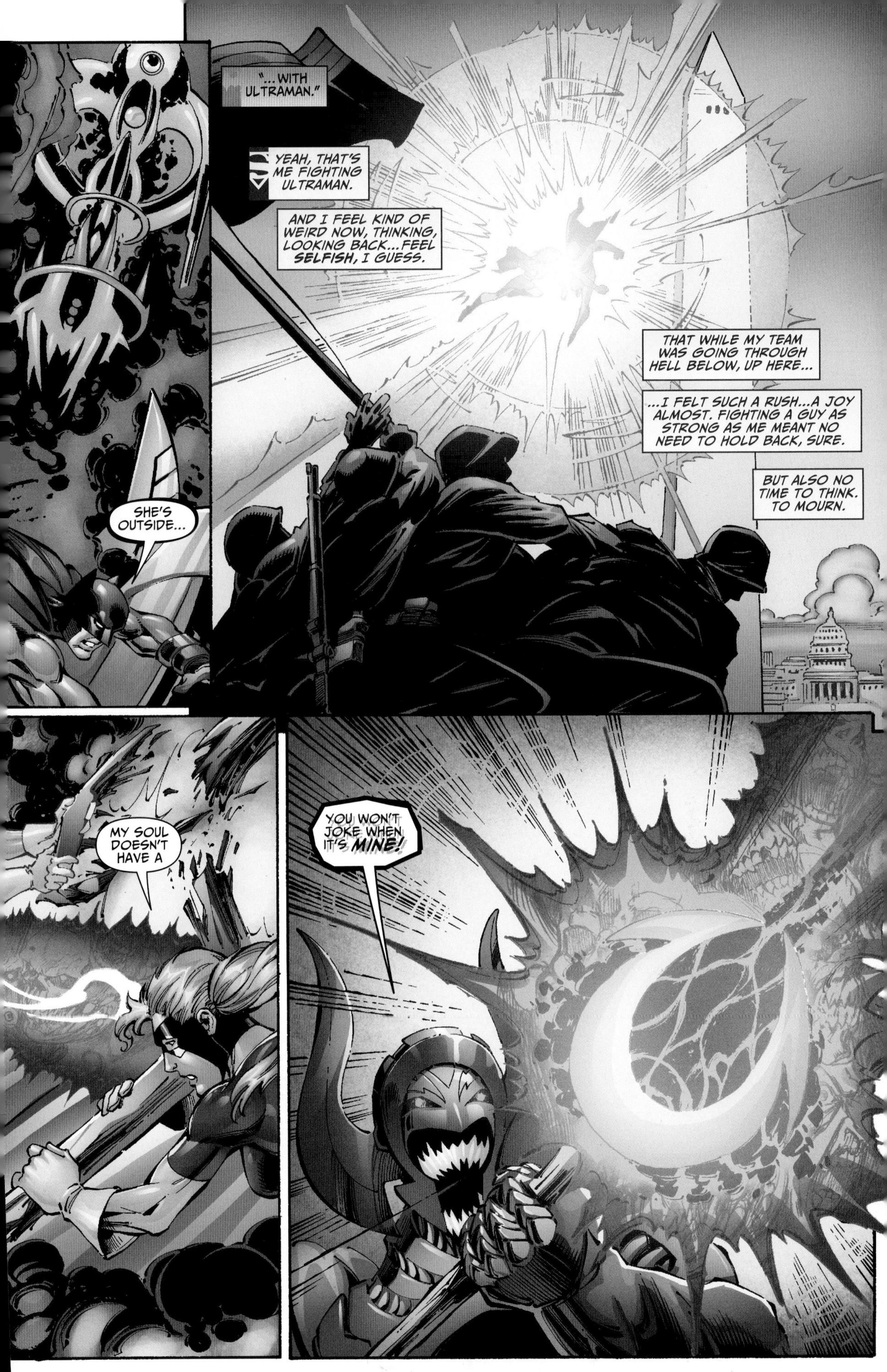
"...WITH ULTRAMAN."
YEAH, THAT'S ME FIGHTING ULTRAMAN.
AND I FEEL KIND OF WEIRD NOW, THINKING, LOOKING BACK...FEEL SELFISH, I GUESS.
THAT WHILE MY TEAM WAS GOING THROUGH HELL BELOW, UP HERE...
...I FELT SUCH A RUSH...A JOY ALMOST. FIGHTING A GUY AS STRONG AS ME MEANT NO NEED TO HOLD BACK, SURE.
BUT ALSO NO TIME TO THINK. TO MOURN.
SHE'S OUTSIDE...
MY SOUL DOESN'T HAVE A
YOU WON'T JOKE WHEN IT'S MINE!

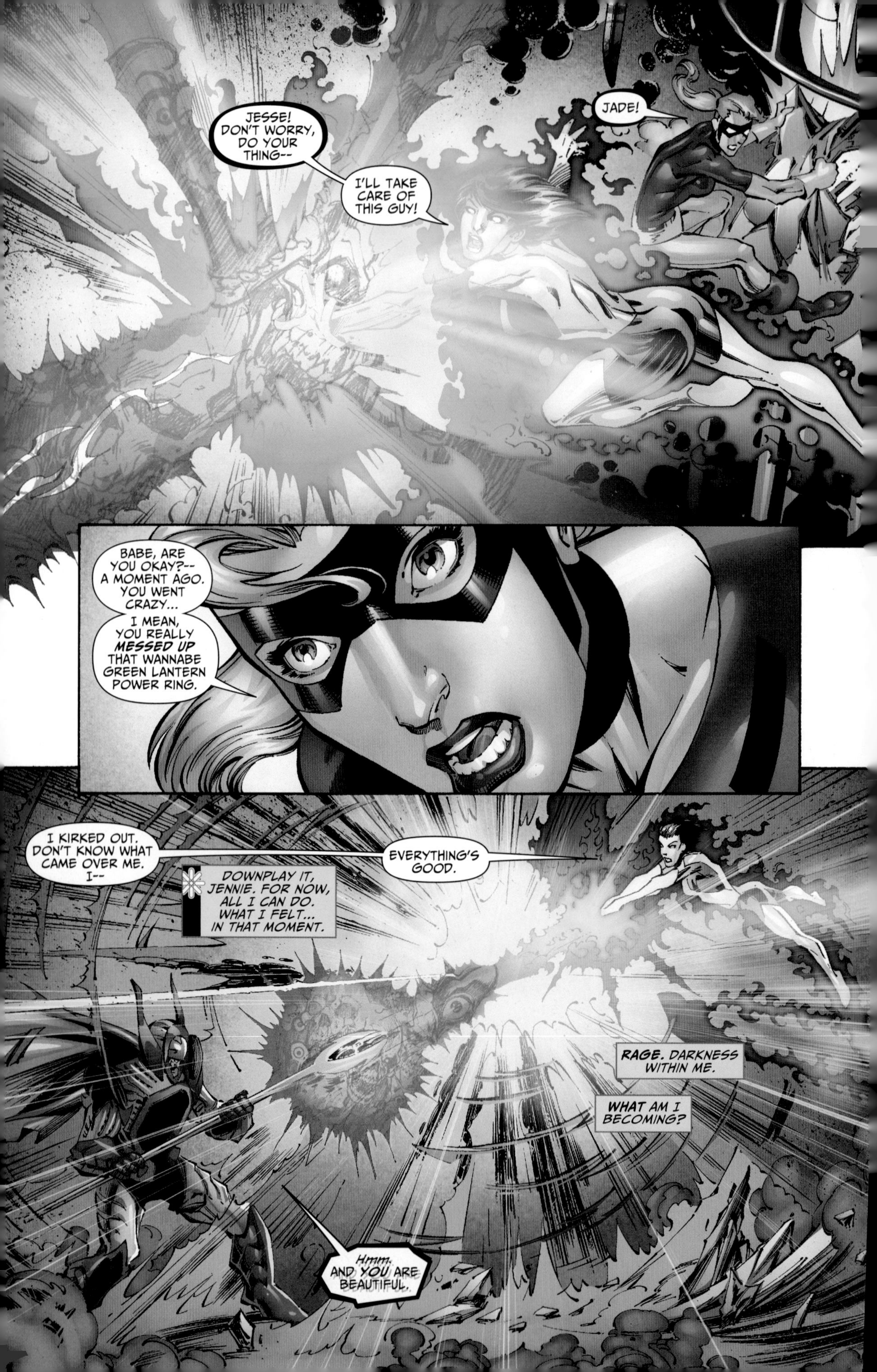
JADE!
JESSE! DON'T WORRY, DO YOUR THING--
I'LL TAKE CARE OF THIS GUY!
BABE, ARE YOU OKAY?-- A MOMENT AGO. YOU WENT CRAZY...
I MEAN, YOU REALLY MESSED UP THAT WANNABE GREEN LANTERN POWER RING.
I KIRKED OUT. DON'T KNOW WHAT CAME OVER ME. I--
EVERYTHING'S GOOD.
DOWNPLAY IT, JENNIE. FOR NOW, ALL I CAN DO. WHAT I FELT... IN THAT MOMENT.
RAGE. DARKNESS WITHIN ME.
WHAT AM I BECOMING?
Hmm. AND YOU ARE BEAUTIFUL.

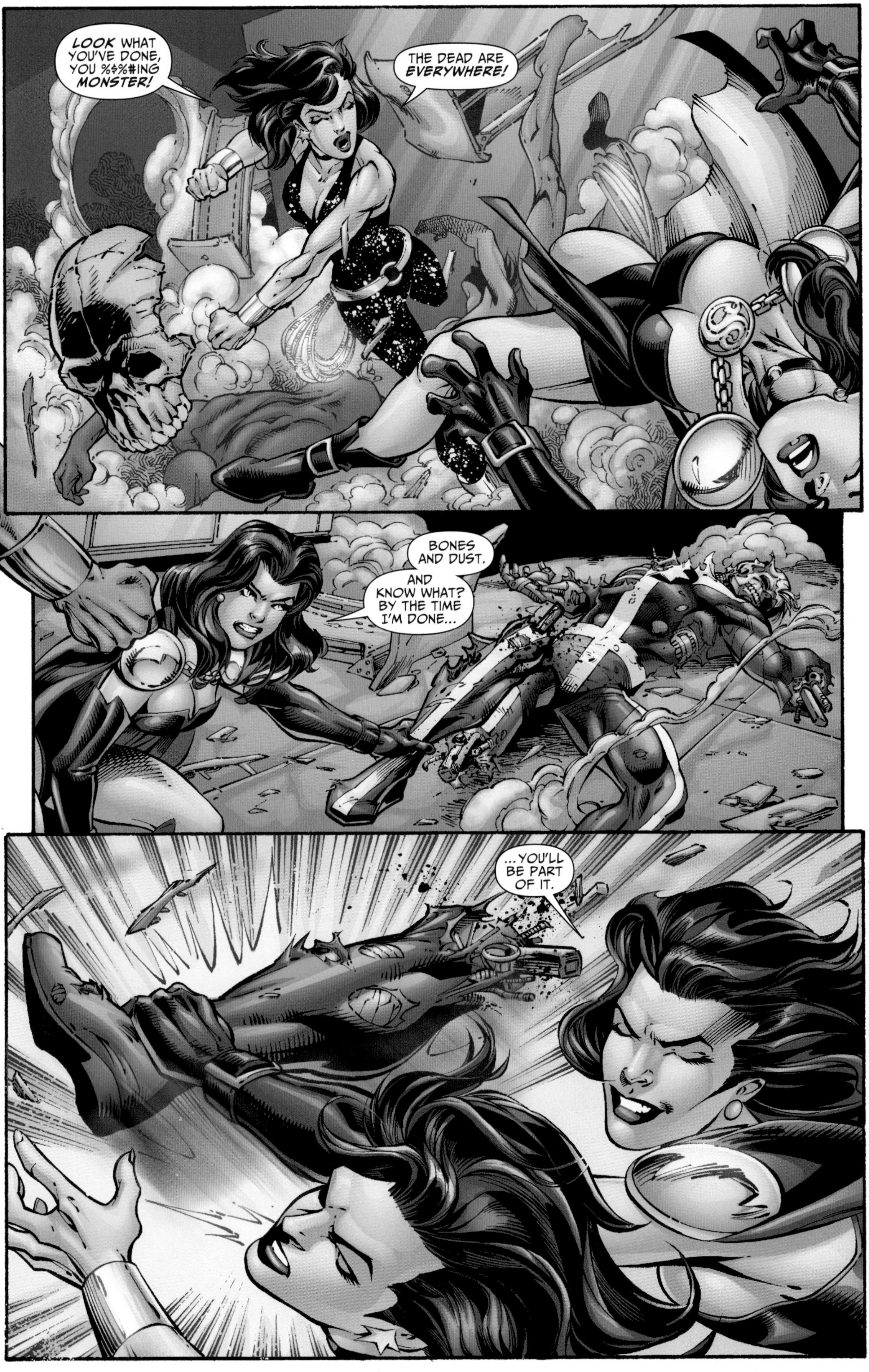
LOOK WHAT YOU'VE DONE, YOU %$%#ING MONSTER!
THE DEAD ARE EVERYWHERE!
BONES AND DUST.
AND KNOW WHAT? BY THE TIME I'M DONE...
...YOU'LL BE PART OF IT.

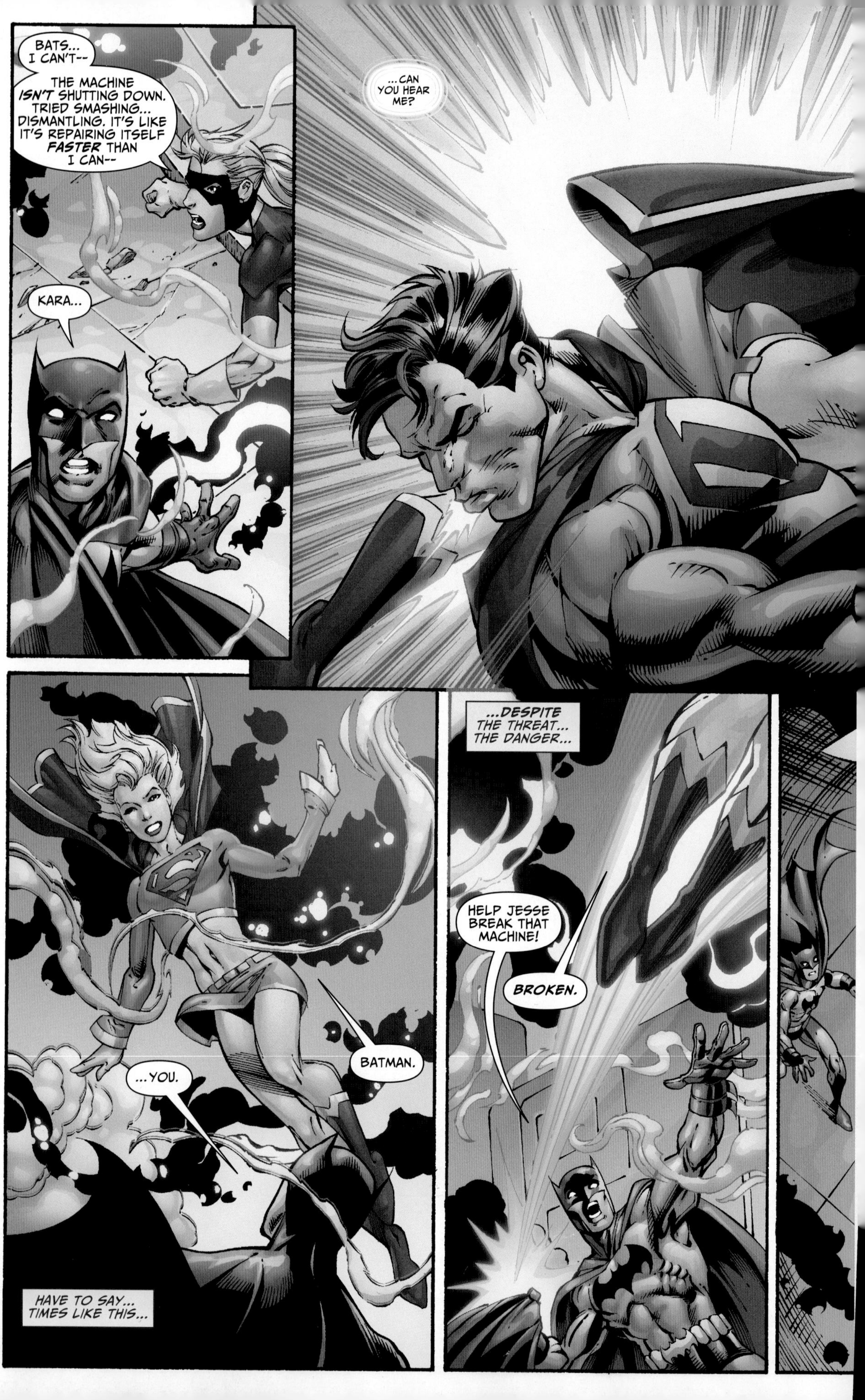
BATS... I CAN'T--
THE MACHINE ISN'T SHUTTING DOWN. TRIED SMASHING... DISMANTLING. IT'S LIKE IT'S REPAIRING ITSELF FASTER THAN I CAN--
KARA...
...CAN YOU HEAR ME?
BATMAN.
...YOU.
HAVE TO SAY... TIMES LIKE THIS...
...DESPITE THE THREAT... THE DANGER...
HELP JESSE BREAK THAT MACHINE!
BROKEN.

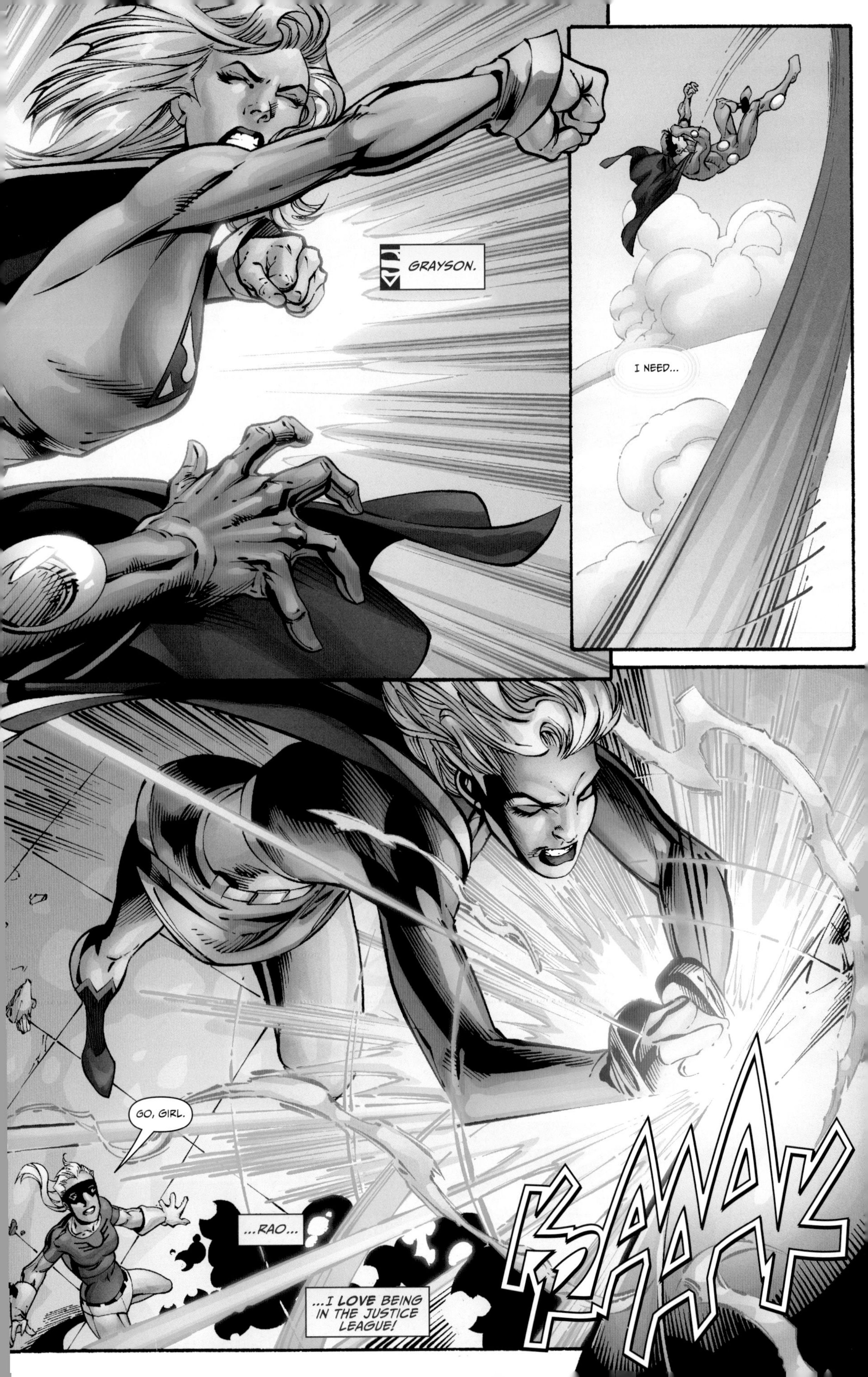
GRAYSON.
I NEED...
GO, GIRL.
...RAO...
...I LOVE BEING IN THE JUSTICE LEAGUE!
KRAAKK

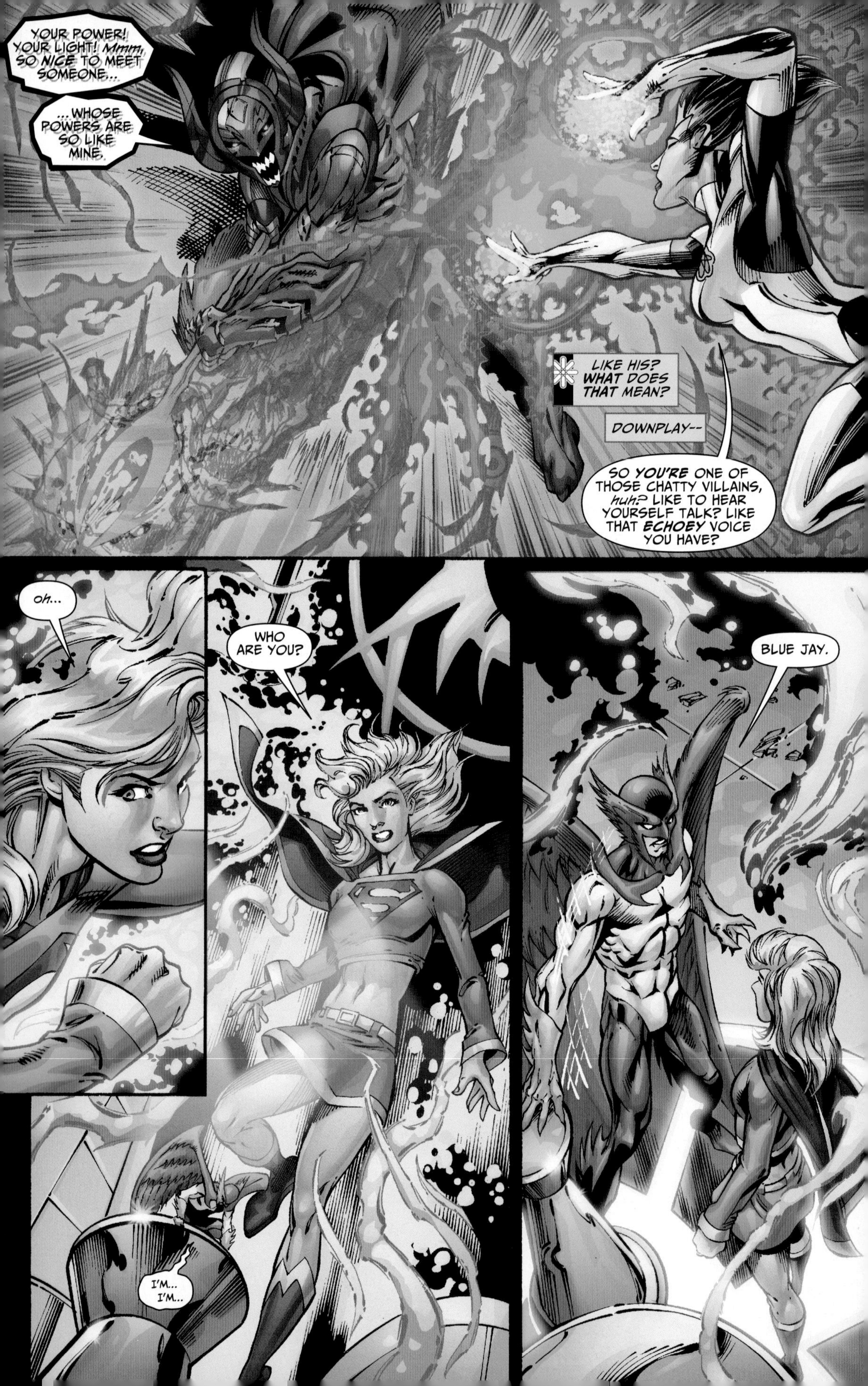
YOUR POWER! YOUR LIGHT! Mmm, SO NICE TO MEET SOMEONE...
...WHOSE POWERS ARE SO LIKE MINE.
LIKE HIS? WHAT DOES THAT MEAN?
DOWNPLAY--
SO YOU'RE ONE OF THOSE CHATTY VILLAINS, huh? LIKE TO HEAR YOURSELF TALK? LIKE THAT ECHOEY VOICE YOU HAVE?
oh...
WHO ARE YOU?
I'M... I'M...
BLUE JAY.

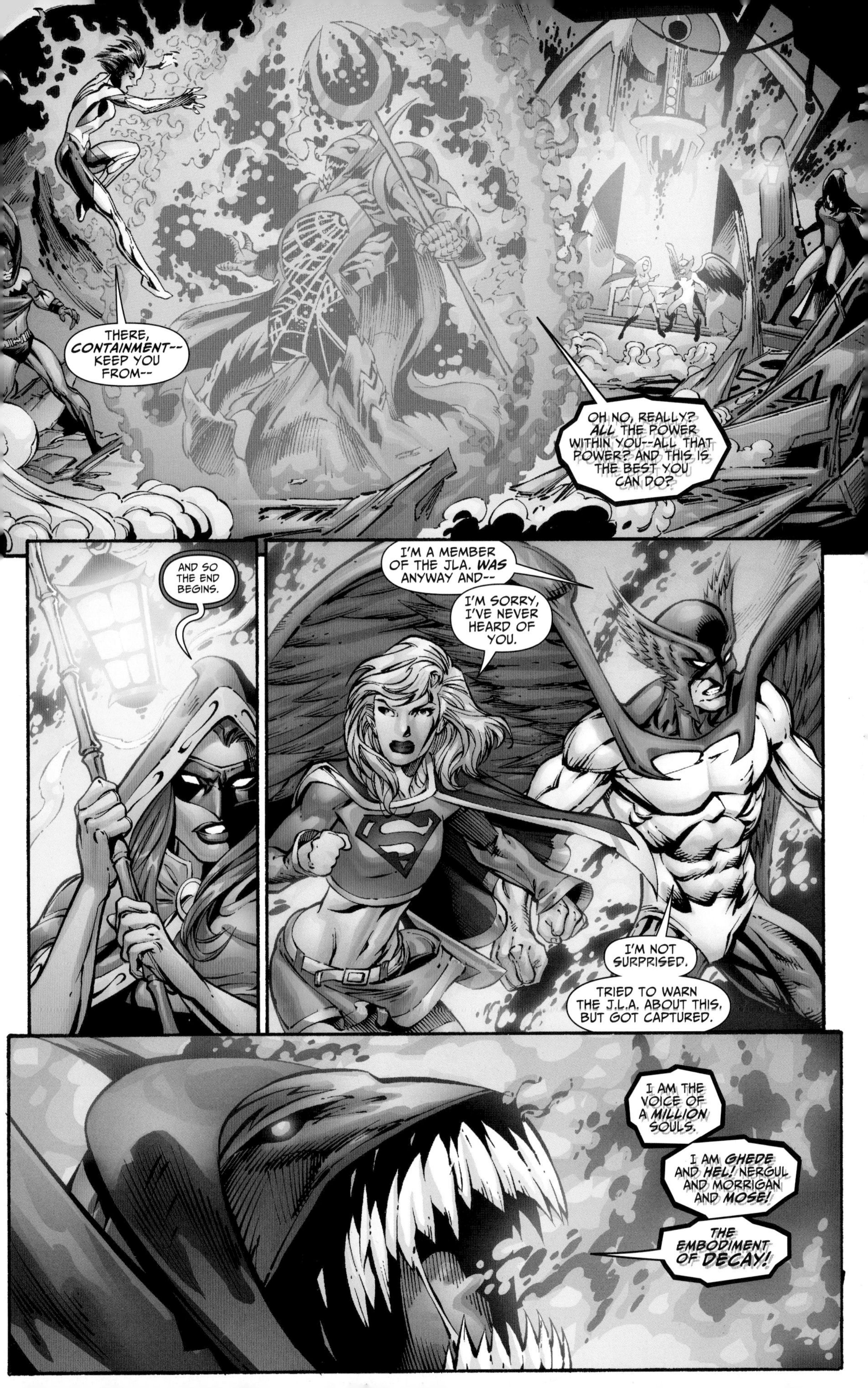
THERE, CONTAINMENT-- KEEP YOU FROM--
OH NO, REALLY? ALL THE POWER WITHIN YOU--ALL THAT POWER? AND THIS IS THE BEST YOU CAN DO?
AND SO THE END BEGINS.
I'M A MEMBER OF THE JLA. WAS ANYWAY AND--
I'M SORRY, I'VE NEVER HEARD OF YOU.
I'M NOT SURPRISED.
TRIED TO WARN THE J.L.A. ABOUT THIS, BUT GOT CAPTURED.
I AM THE VOICE OF A MILLION SOULS.
I AM GHEDE AND HEL! NERGUL AND MORRIGAN AND MOSE!
THE EMBODIMENT OF DECAY!

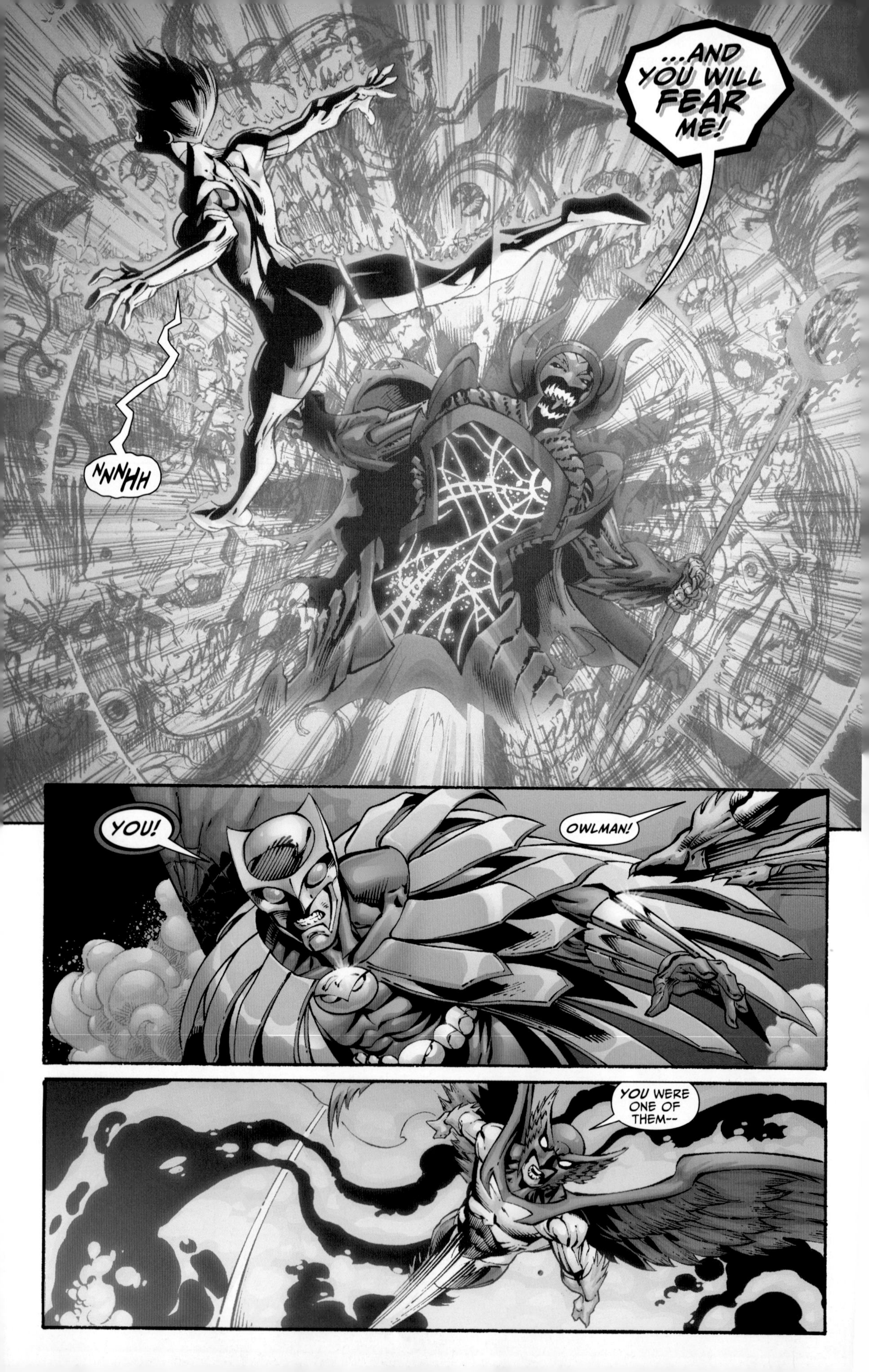
...AND YOU WILL FEAR ME!
NNNHH
YOU!
OWLMAN!
YOU WERE ONE OF THEM--

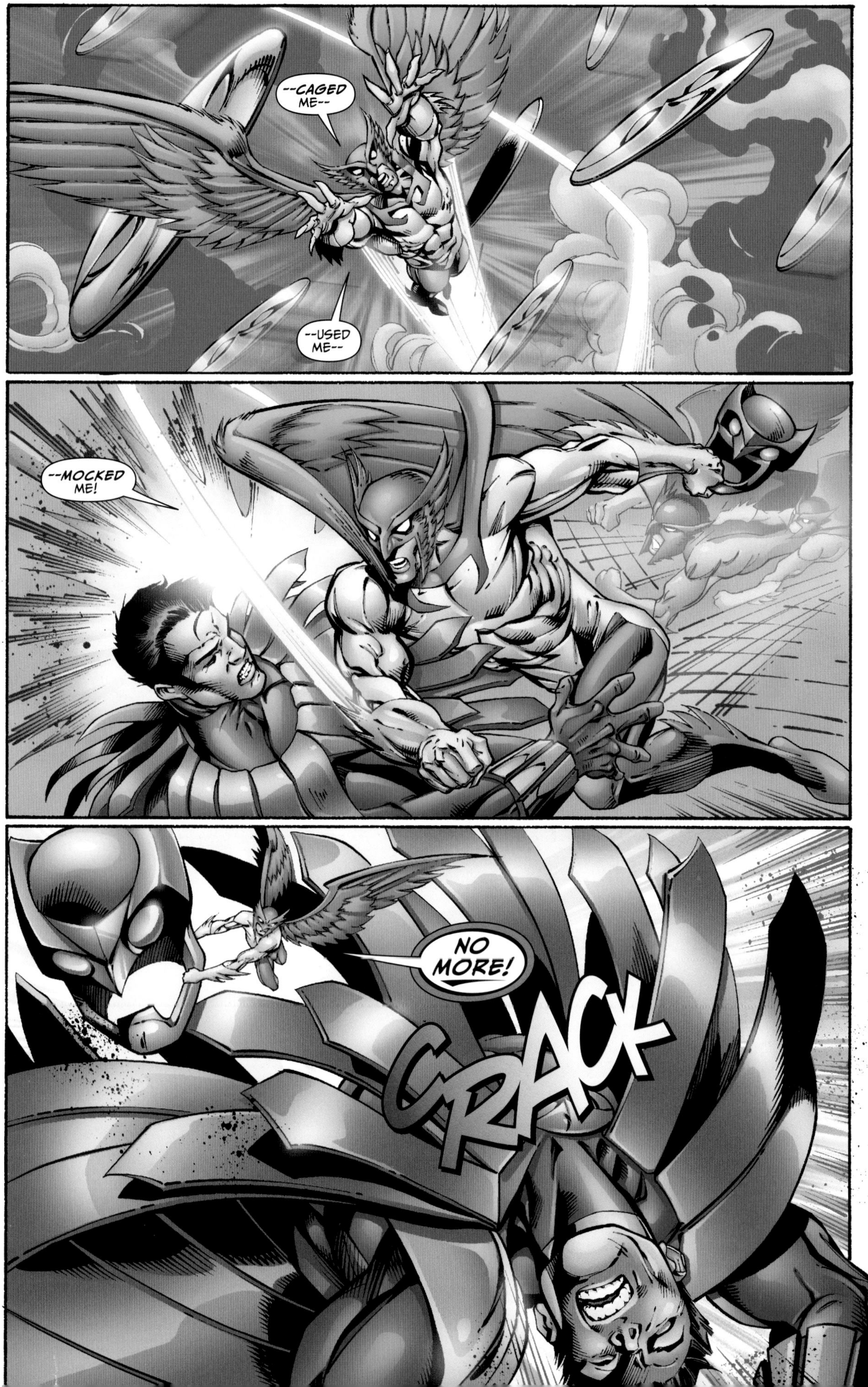
--CAGED ME--
--USED ME--
--MOCKED ME!
NO MORE!
CRACK

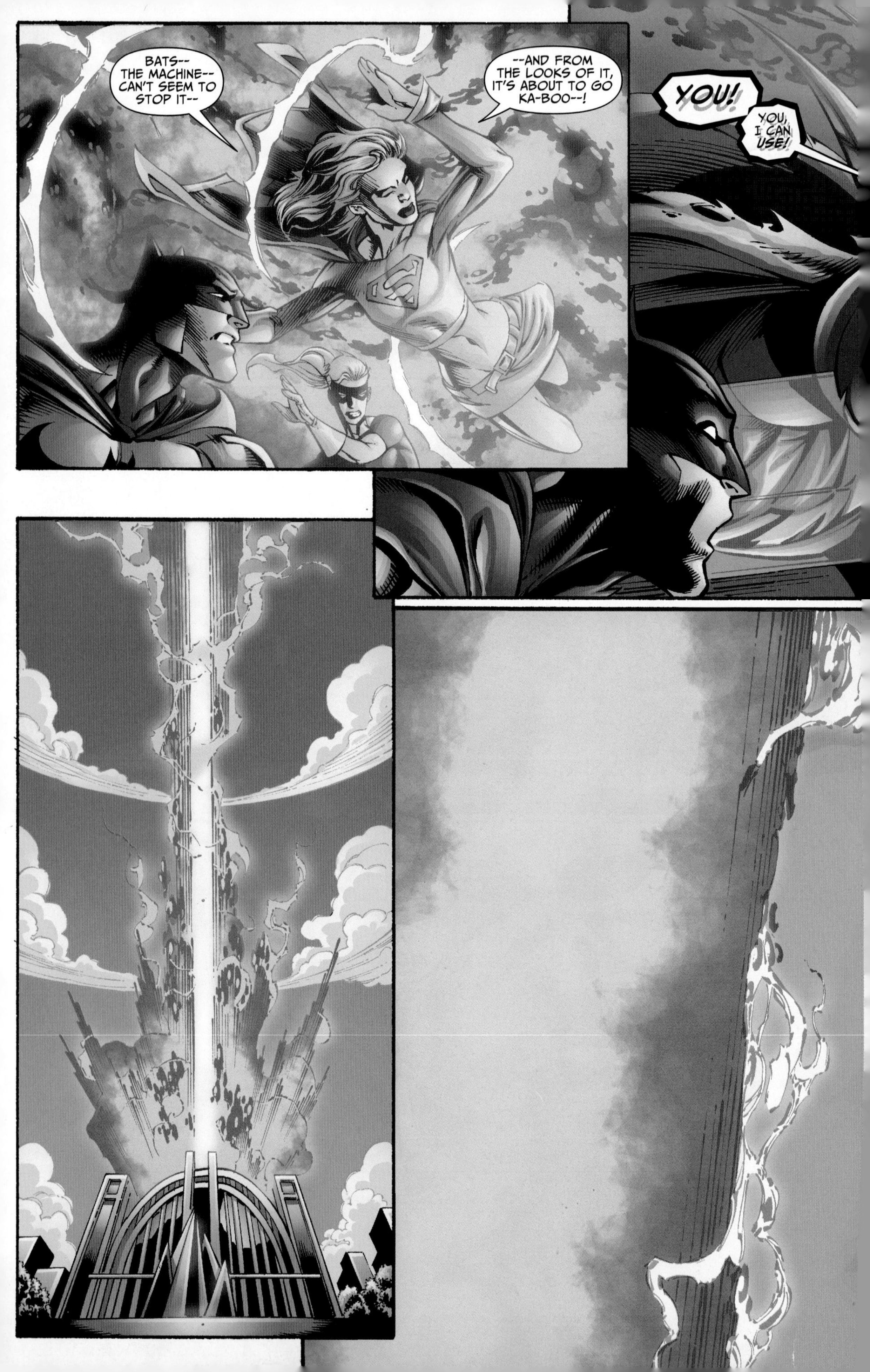
BATS-- THE MACHINE-- CAN'T SEEM TO STOP IT--
--AND FROM THE LOOKS OF IT, IT'S ABOUT TO GO KA-BOO--!
YOU!
YOU, I CAN USE!

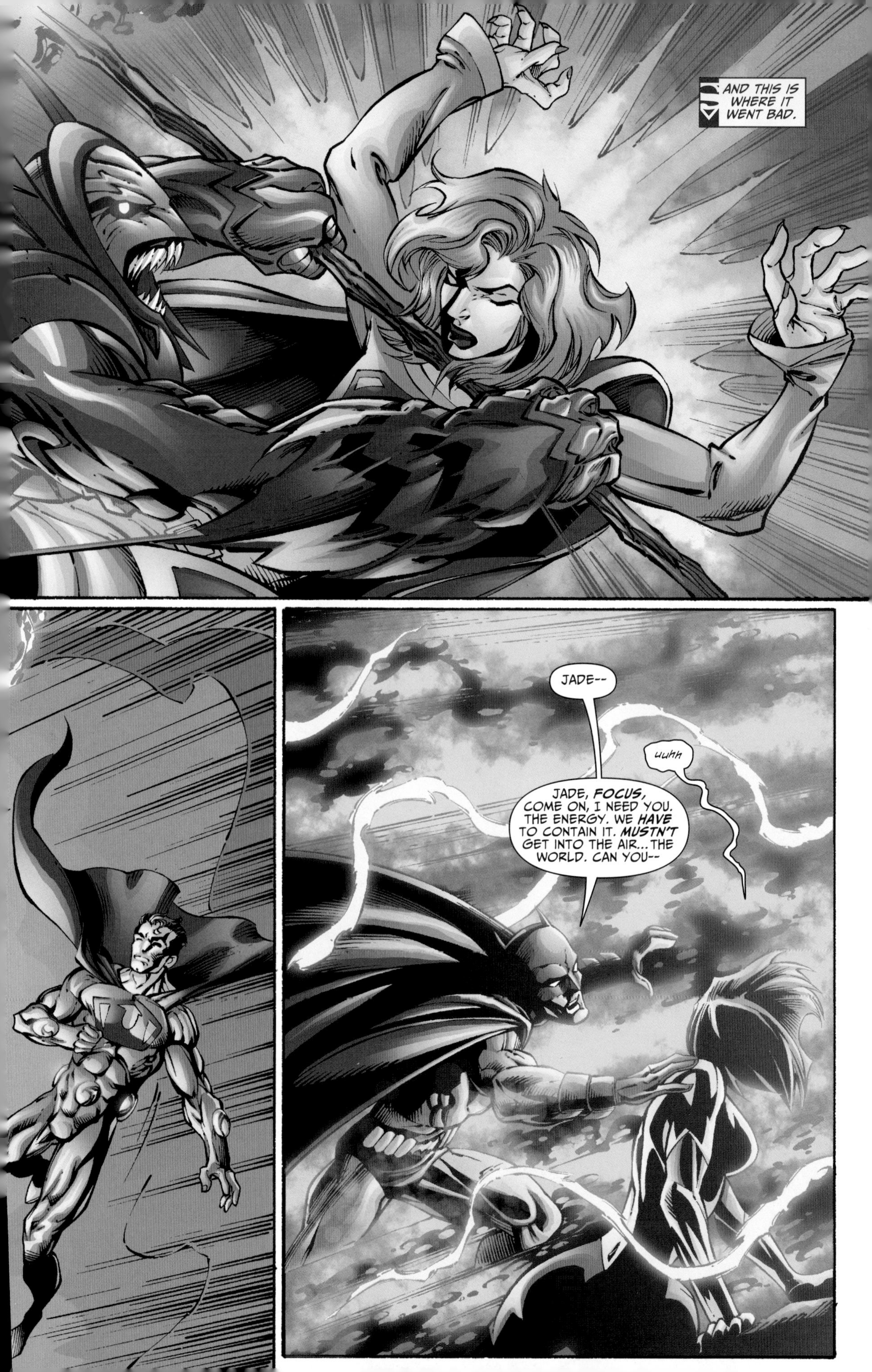
AND THIS IS WHERE IT WENT BAD.
JADE--
uuhh
JADE, FOCUS, COME ON, I NEED YOU. THE ENERGY. WE HAVE TO CONTAIN IT. MUSTN'T GET INTO THE AIR... THE WORLD. CAN YOU--

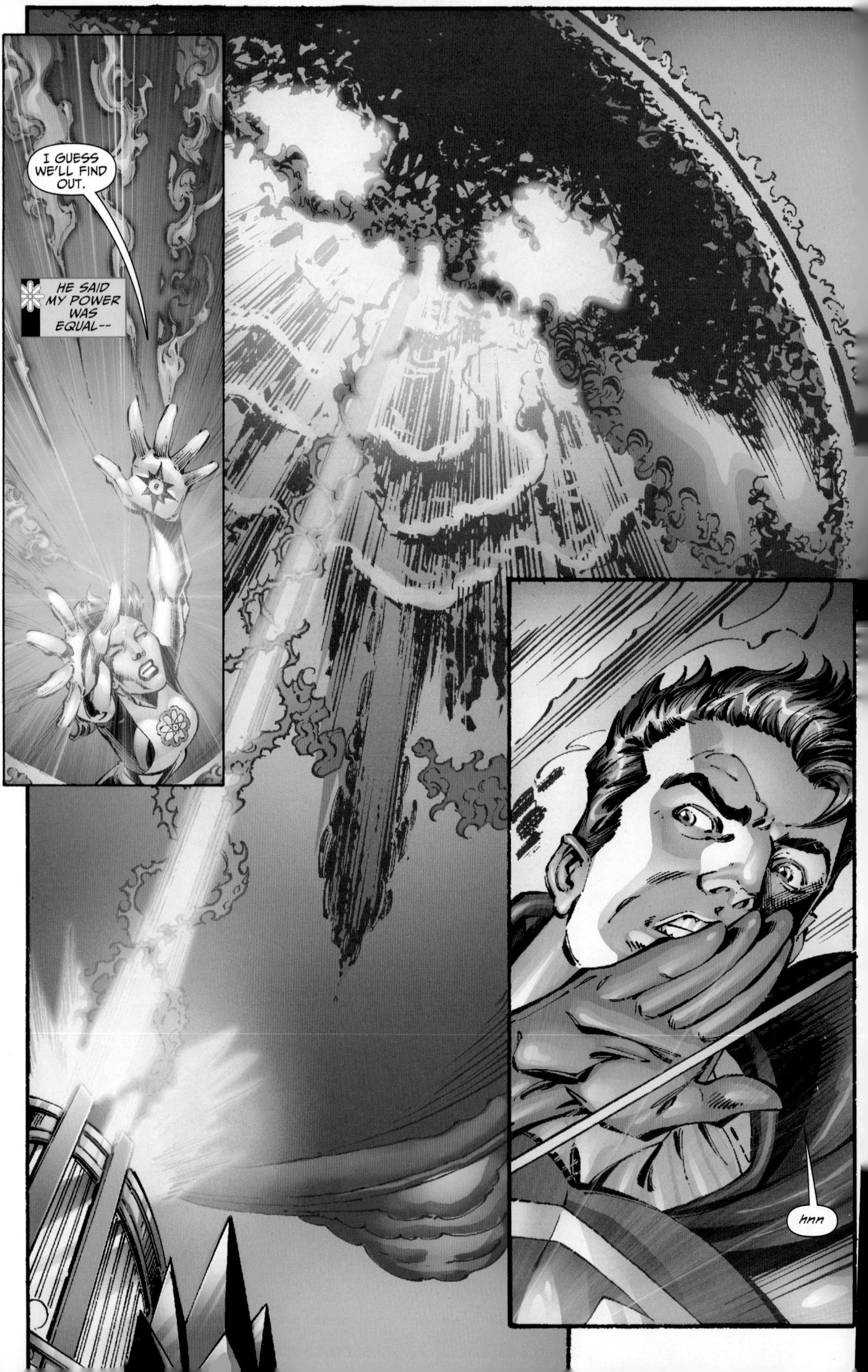
I GUESS WE'LL FIND OUT.
HE SAID MY POWER WAS EQUAL--
hnn

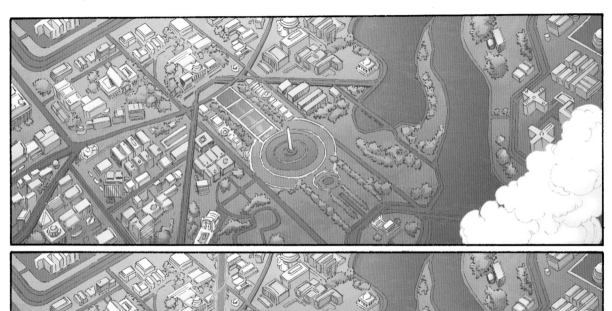

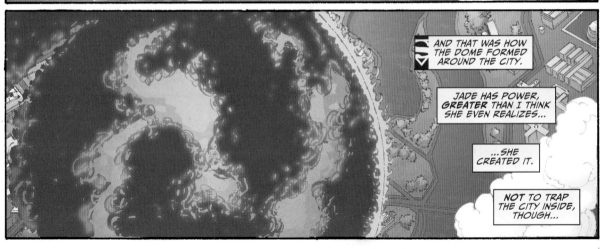

AND THAT WAS HOW THE DOME FORMED AROUND THE CITY.

JADE HAS POWER, *GREATER* THAN I THINK SHE EVEN REALIZES...

...SHE *CREATED* IT.

NOT TO TRAP THE CITY INSIDE, THOUGH...

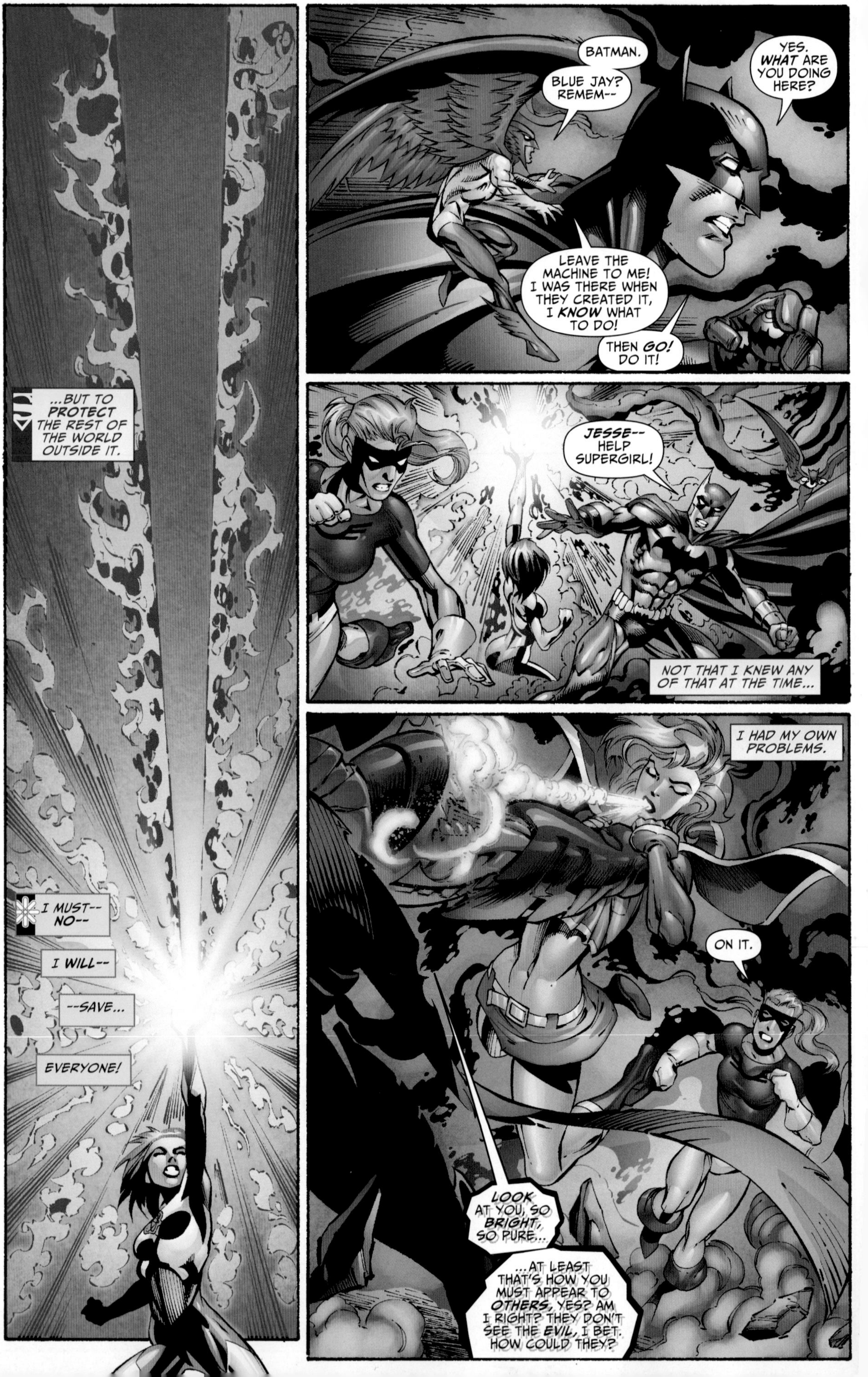
...BUT TO PROTECT THE REST OF THE WORLD OUTSIDE IT.
I MUST-- NO--
I WILL--
--SAVE...
EVERYONE!
BATMAN.
BLUE JAY? REMEM--
YES. WHAT ARE YOU DOING HERE?
LEAVE THE MACHINE TO ME! I WAS THERE WHEN THEY CREATED IT, I KNOW WHAT TO DO!
THEN GO! DO IT!
JESSE-- HELP SUPERGIRL!
NOT THAT I KNEW ANY OF THAT AT THE TIME...
I HAD MY OWN PROBLEMS.
ON IT.
LOOK AT YOU, SO BRIGHT, SO PURE...
...AT LEAST THAT'S HOW YOU MUST APPEAR TO OTHERS, YES? AM I RIGHT? THEY DON'T SEE THE EVIL, I BET. HOW COULD THEY?

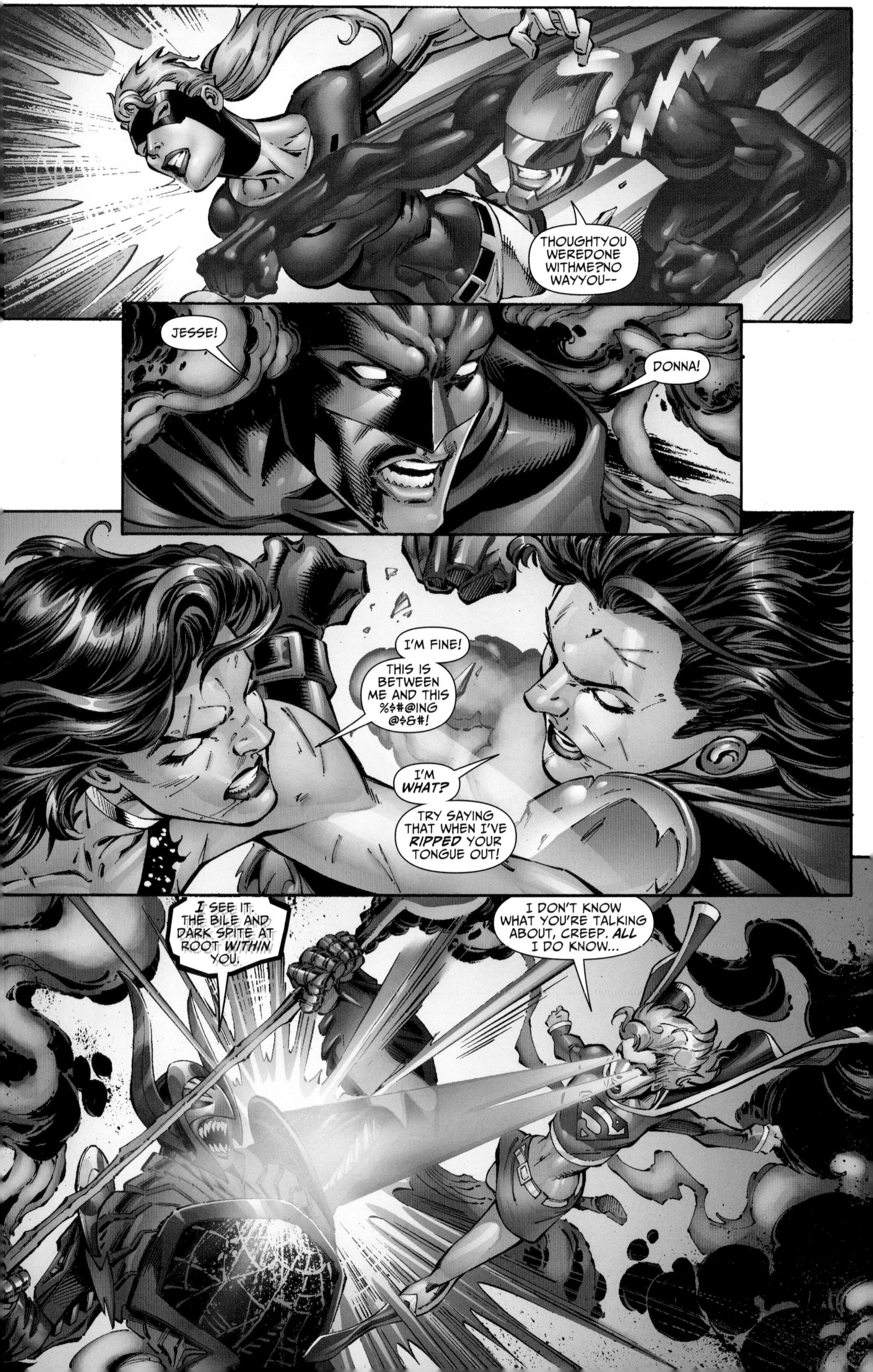
THOUGHTYOU WEREDONE WITHME?NO WAYYOU--
JESSE!
DONNA!
I'M FINE!
THIS IS BETWEEN ME AND THIS %$#@ING @$&#!
I'M WHAT?
TRY SAYING THAT WHEN I'VE RIPPED YOUR TONGUE OUT!
I SEE IT. THE BILE AND DARK SPITE AT ROOT WITHIN YOU.
I DON'T KNOW WHAT YOU'RE TALKING ABOUT, CREEP. ALL I DO KNOW...

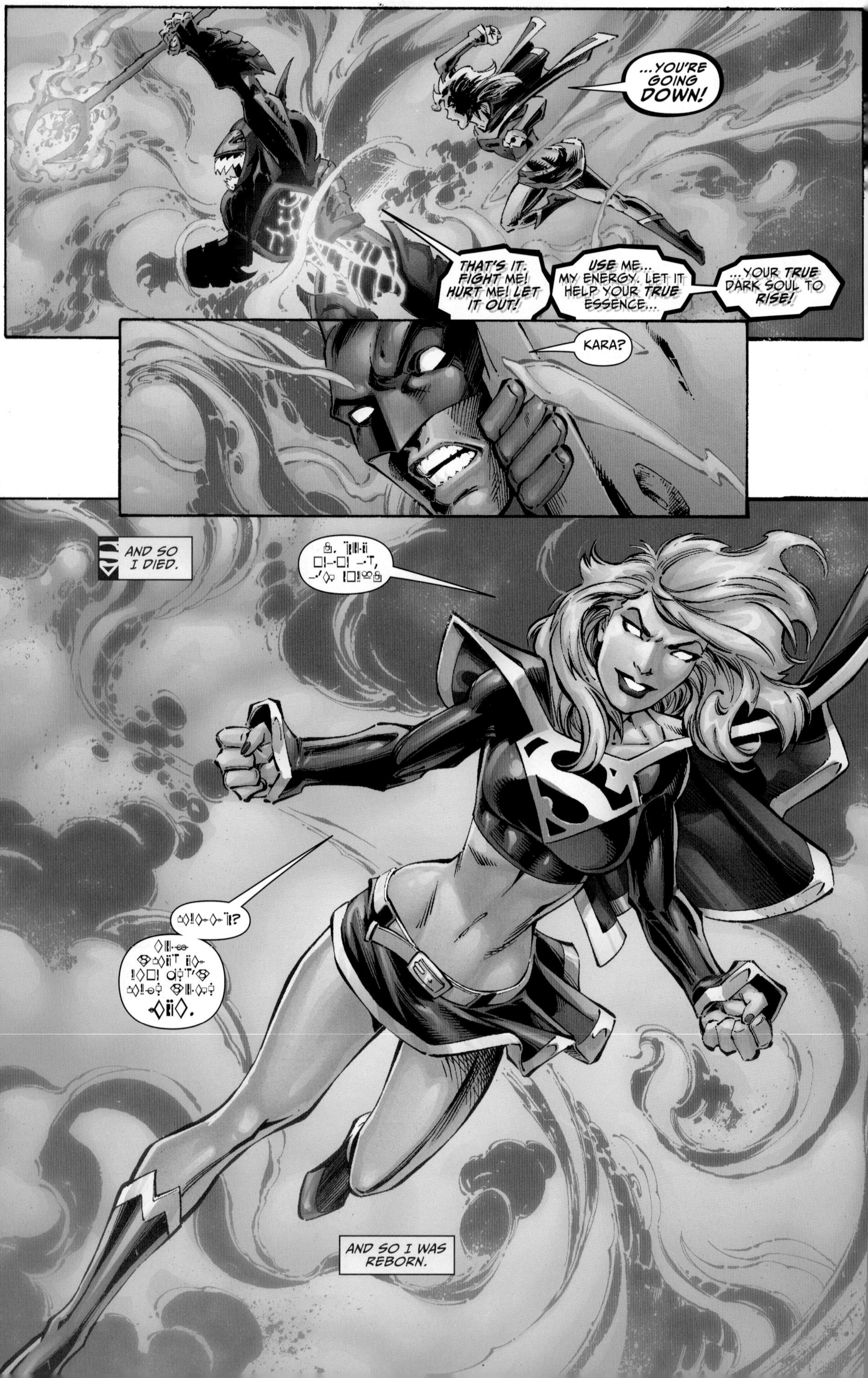
...YOU'RE GOING DOWN!
THAT'S IT. FIGHT ME! HURT ME! LET IT OUT!
USE ME... MY ENERGY. LET IT HELP YOUR TRUE ESSENCE...
...YOUR TRUE DARK SOUL TO RISE!
KARA?
AND SO I DIED.
AND SO I WAS REBORN.

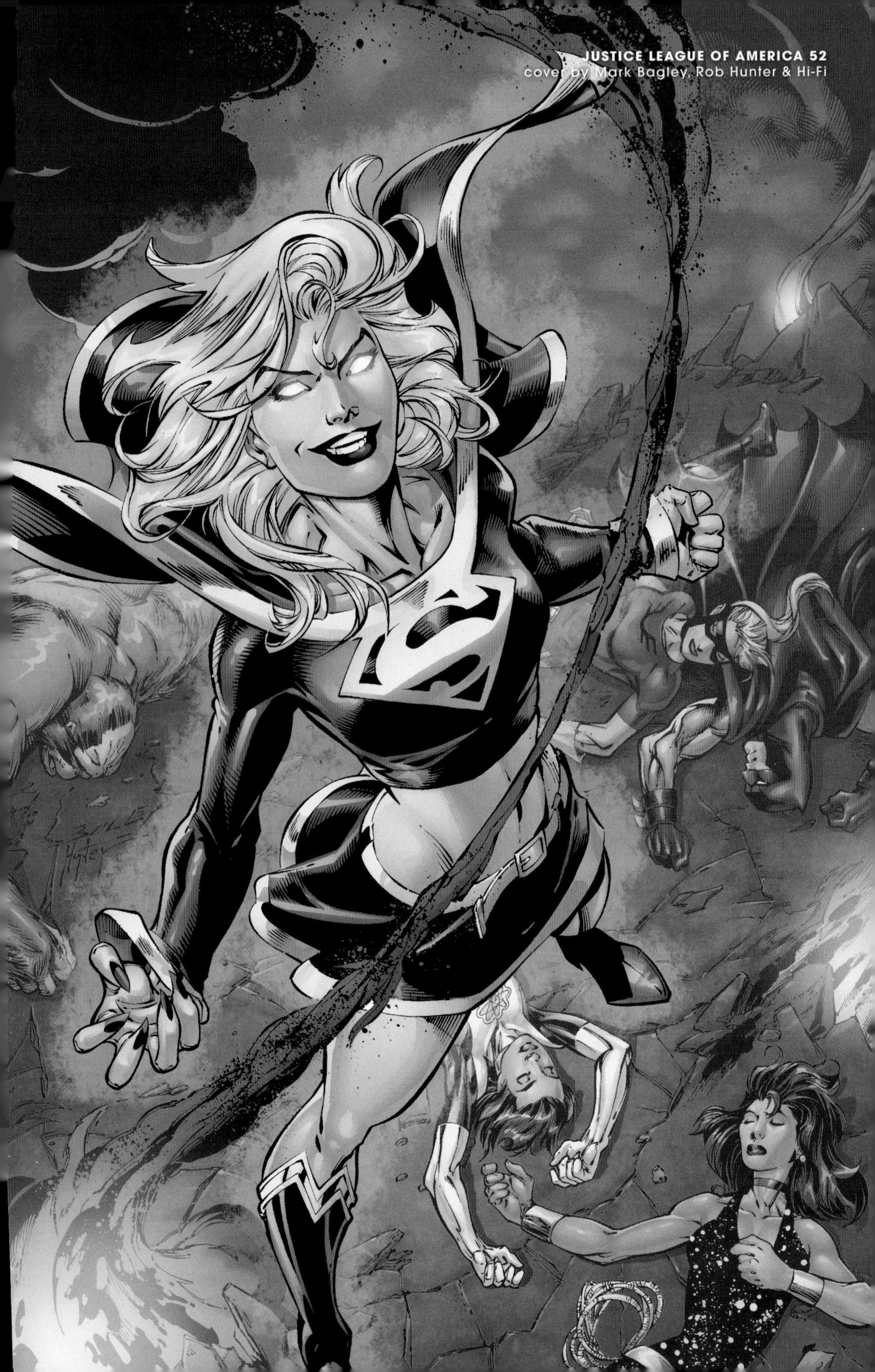

JUSTICE LEAGUE OF AMERICA 52
cover by Mark Bagley, Rob Hunter & Hi-Fi

JUSTICE LEAGUE OF AMERICA 52
variant by David Mack

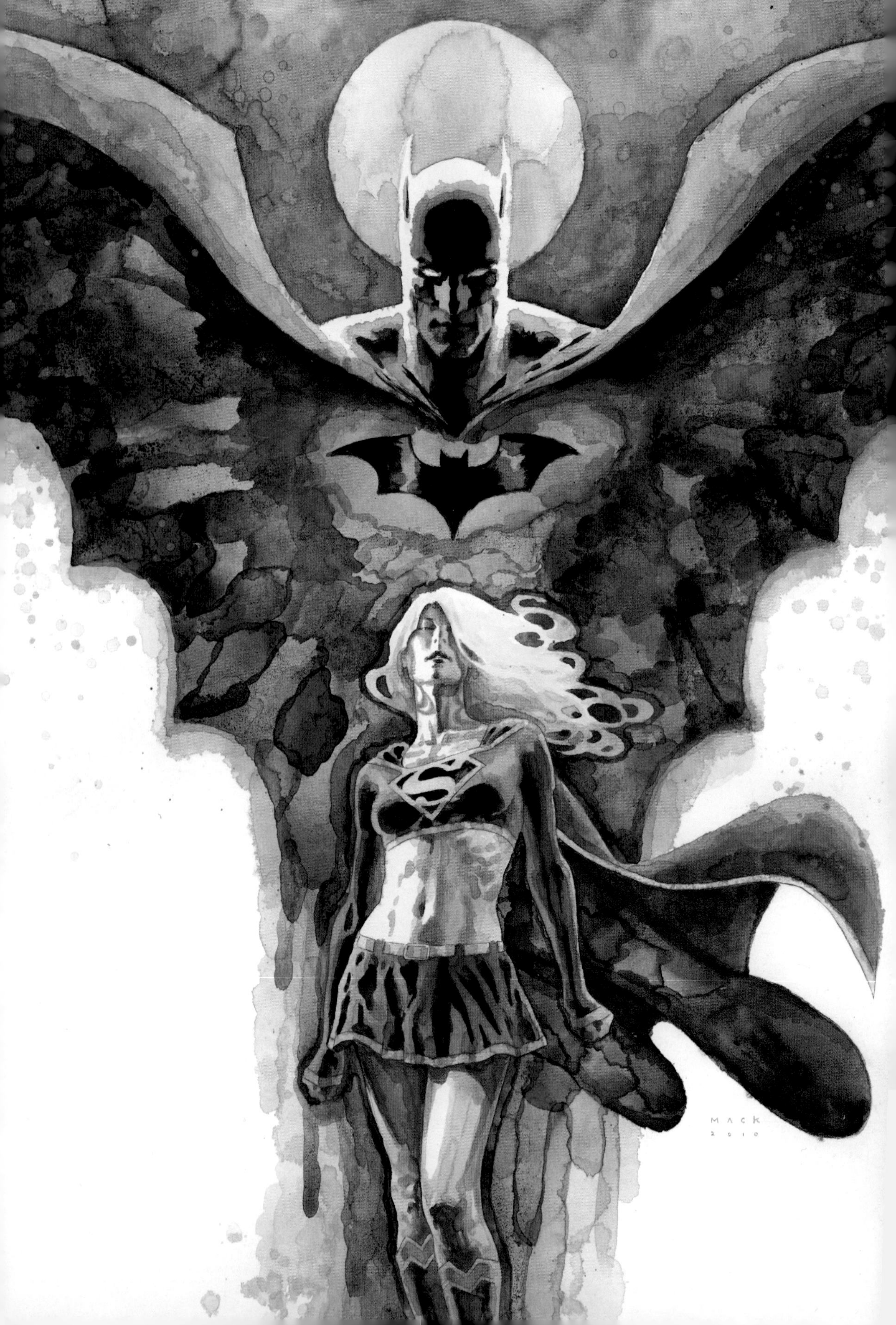
MACK
2010

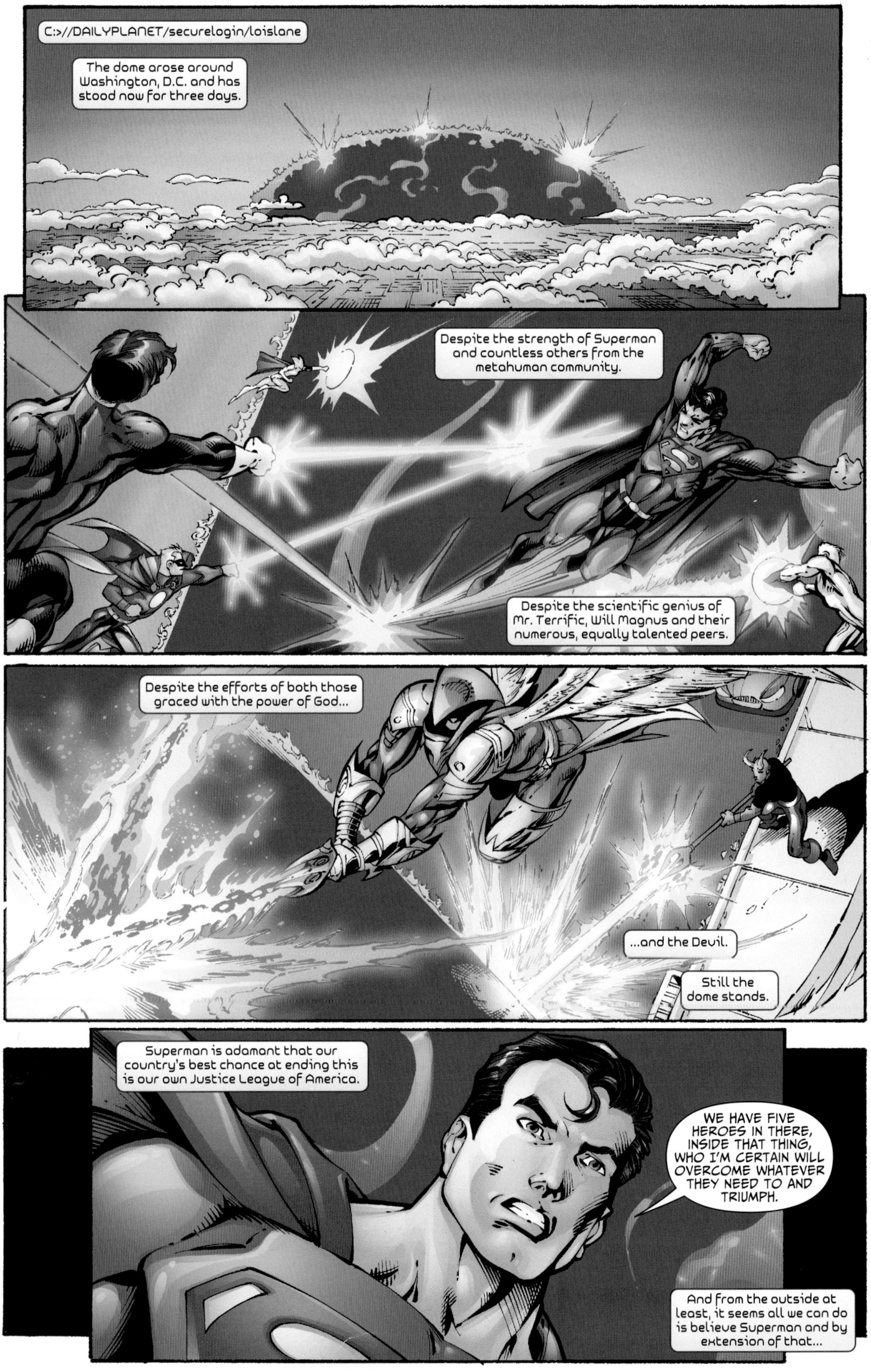
C:>//DAILYPLANET/securelogin/loislane
The dome arose around Washington, D.C. and has stood now for three days.
Despite the strength of Superman and countless others from the metahuman community.
Despite the scientific genius of Mr. Terrific, Will Magnus and their numerous, equally talented peers.
Despite the efforts of both those graced with the power of God...
...and the Devil.
Still the dome stands.
Superman is adamant that our country's best chance at ending this is our own Justice League of America.
WE HAVE FIVE HEROES IN THERE, INSIDE THAT THING, WHO I'M CERTAIN WILL OVERCOME WHATEVER THEY NEED TO AND TRIUMPH.
And from the outside at least, it seems all we can do is believe Superman and by extension of that...

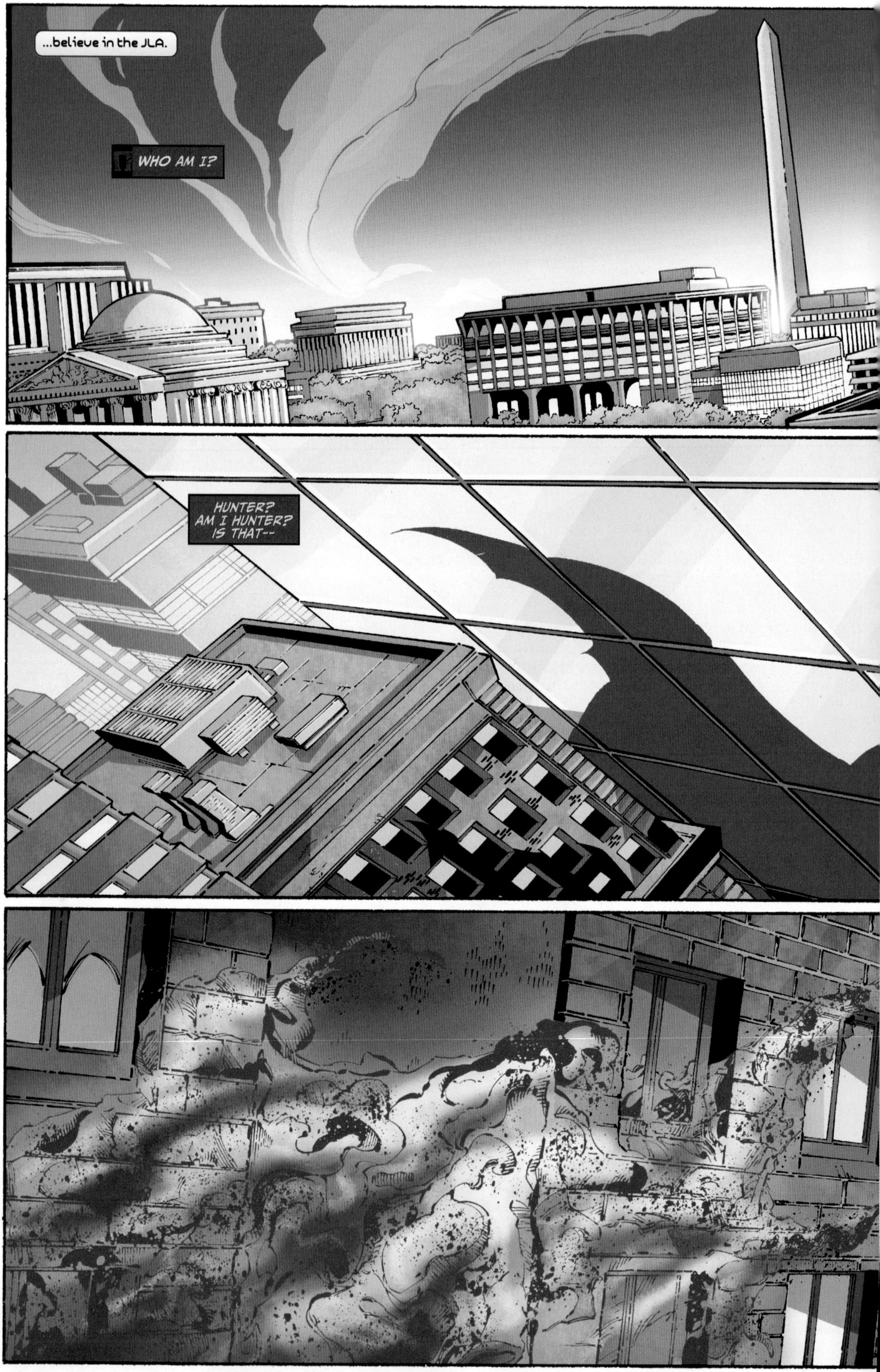
...believe in the JLA.
WHO AM I?
HUNTER?
AM I HUNTER?
IS THAT--

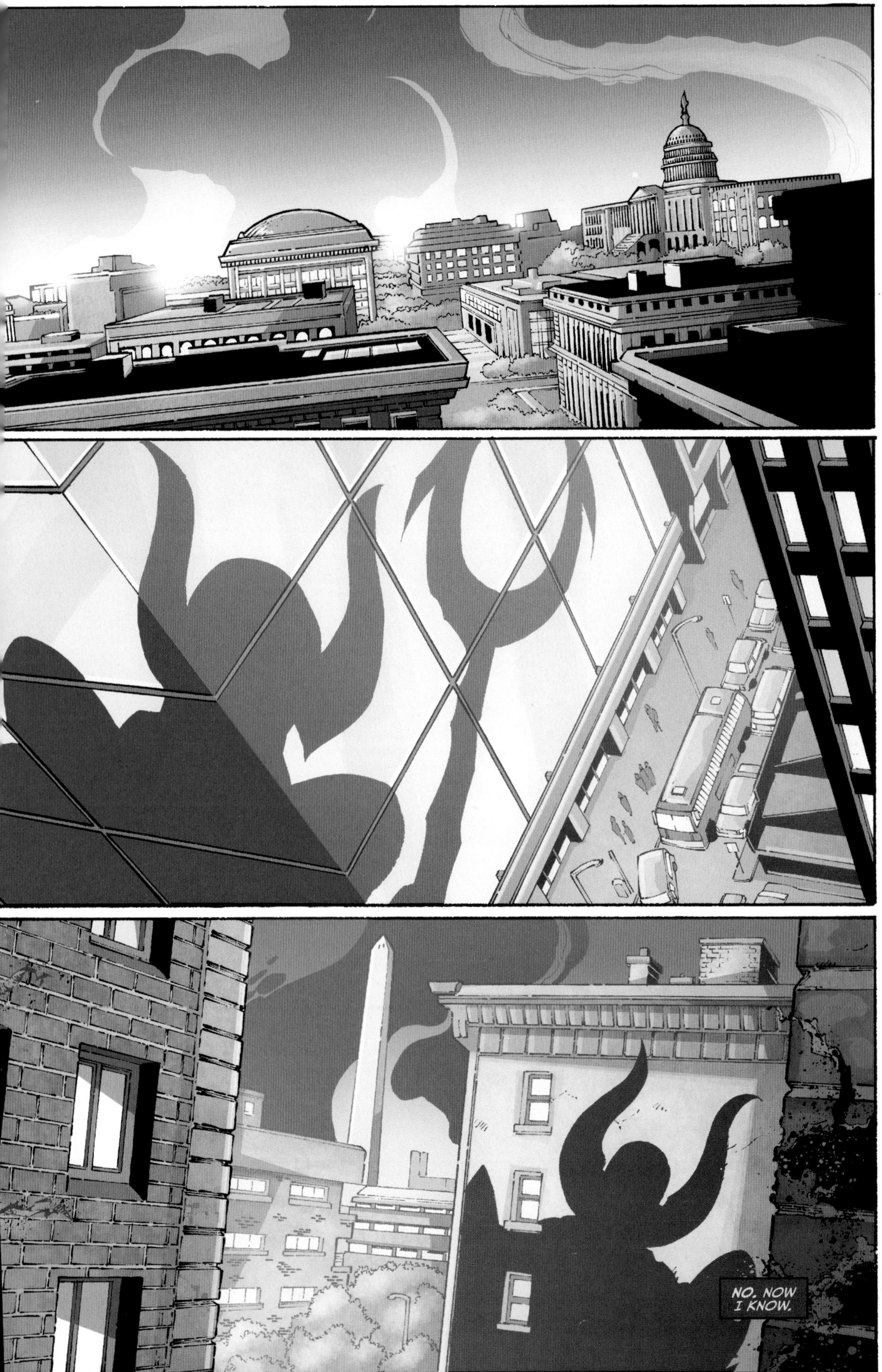
NO. NOW I KNOW.

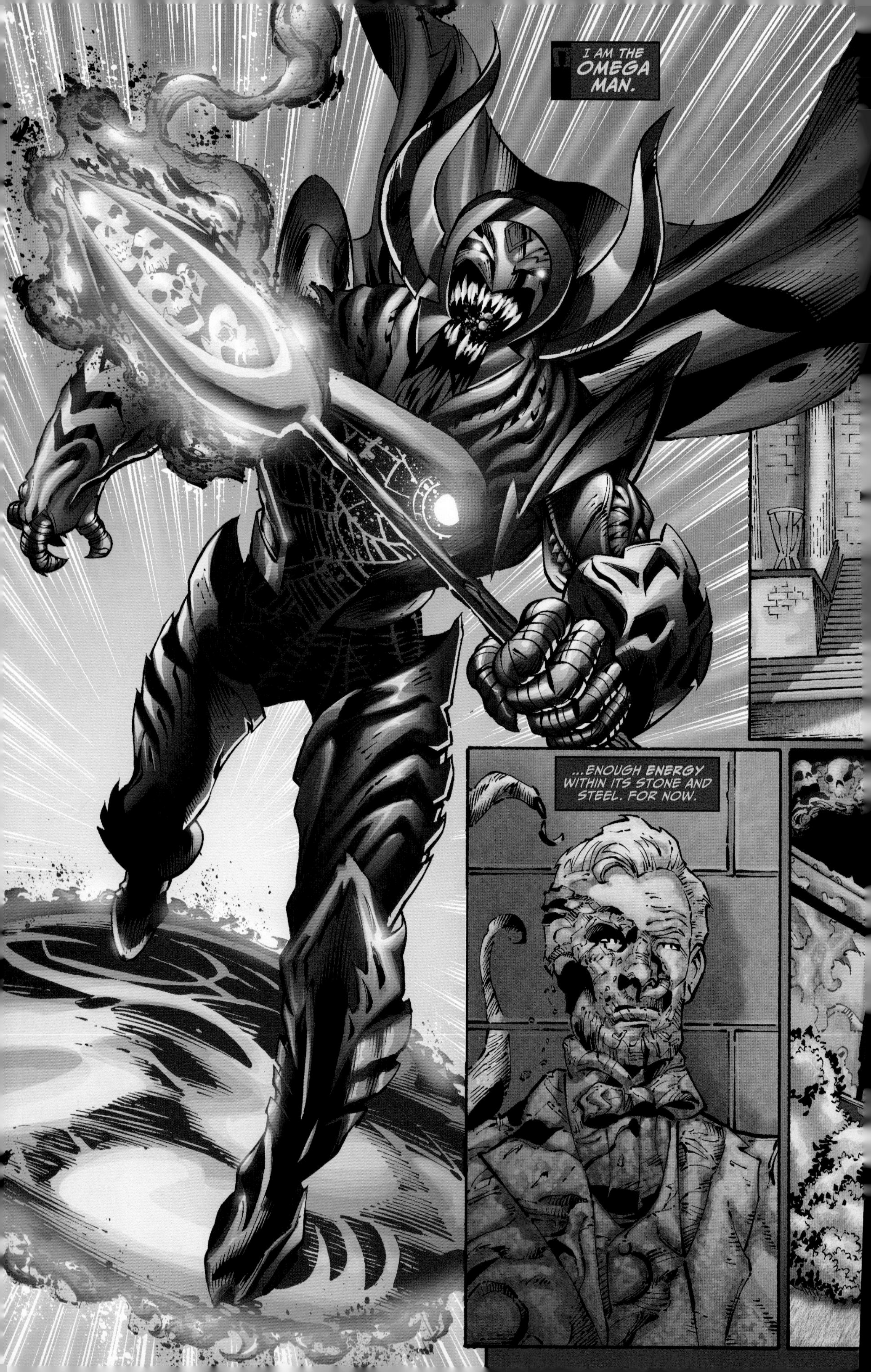

I AM THE OMEGA MAN.
...ENOUGH ENERGY WITHIN ITS STONE AND STEEL. FOR NOW.

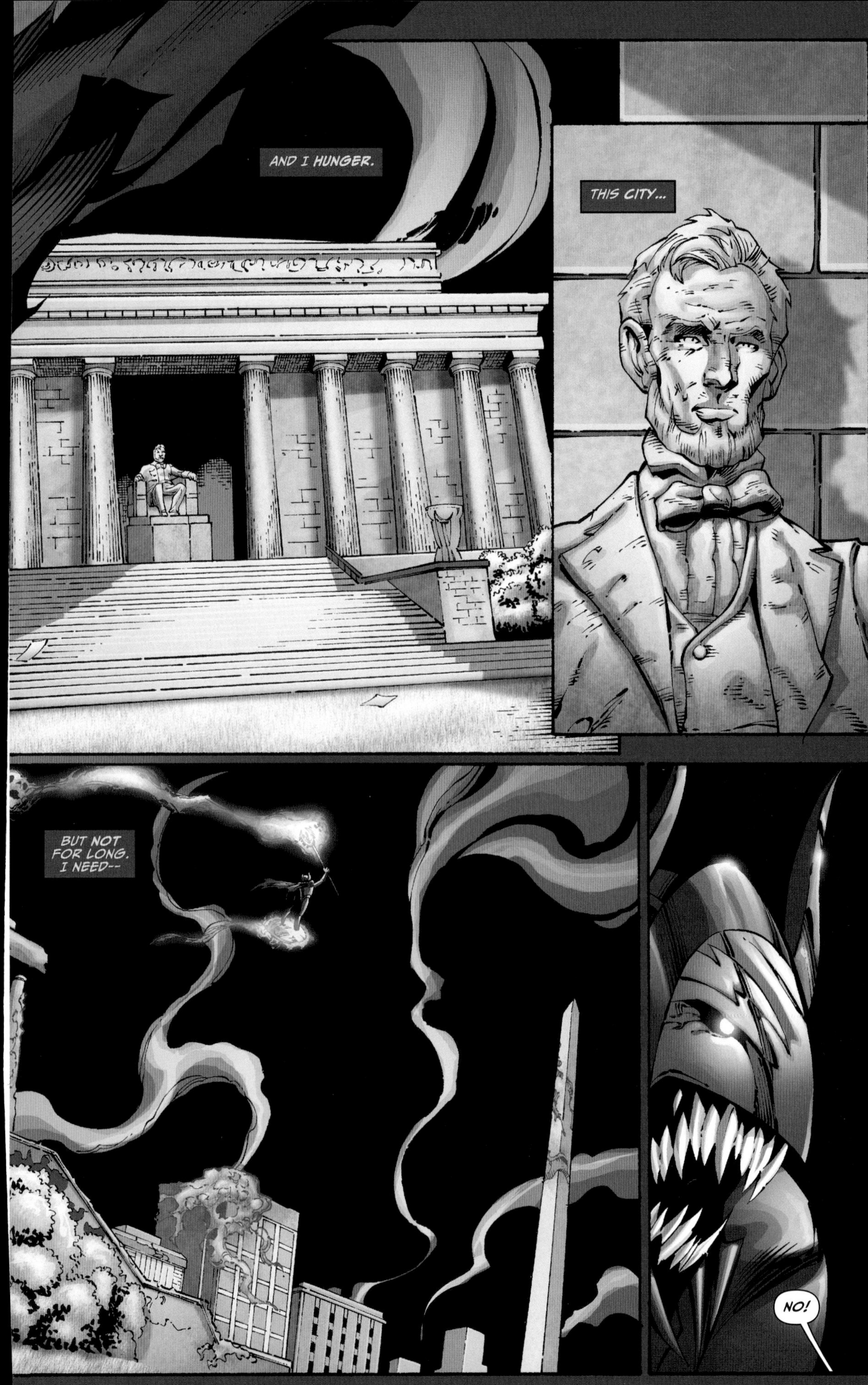
AND I HUNGER.
THIS CITY...
BUT NOT FOR LONG. I NEED--
NO!

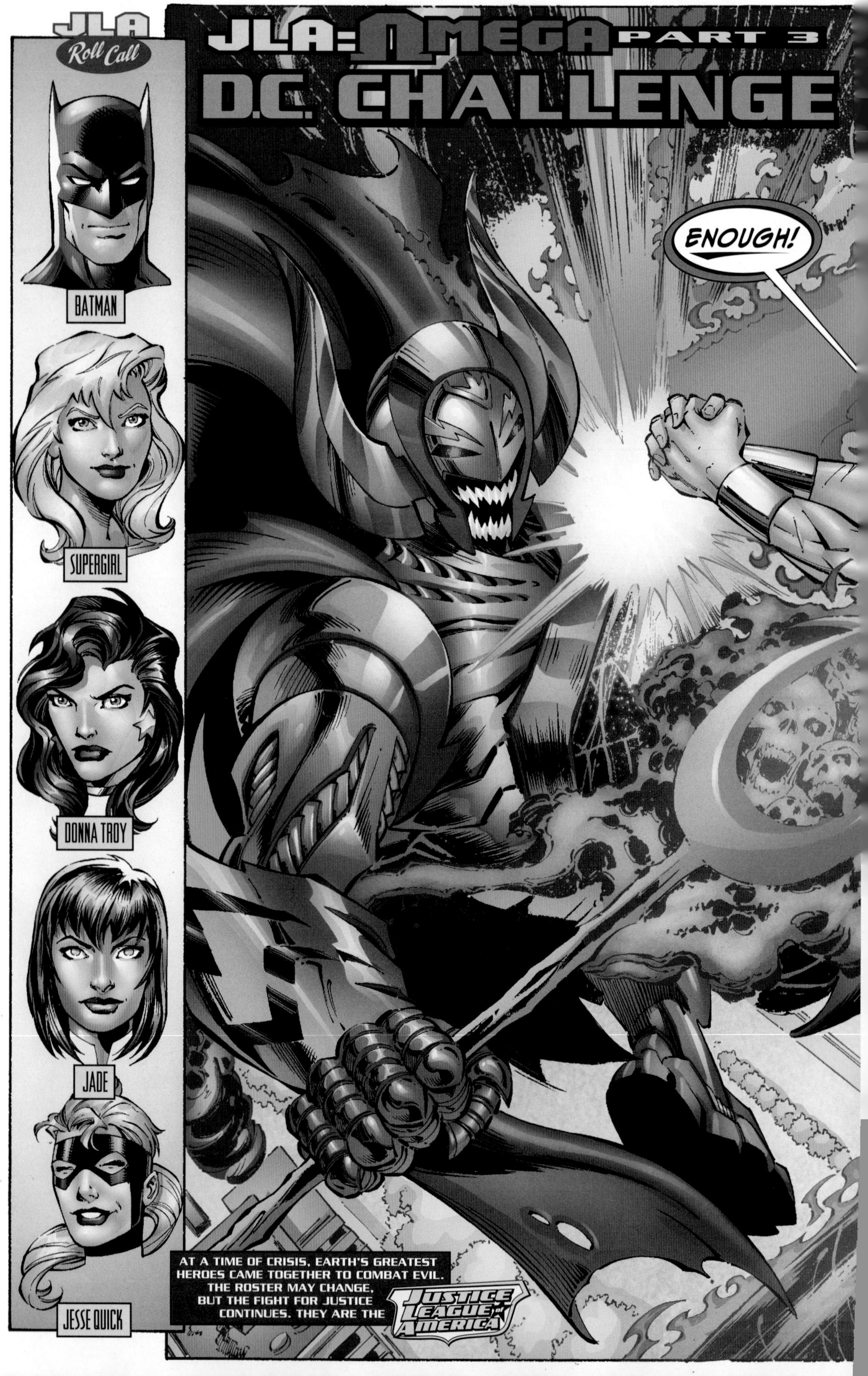
JLA Roll Call
BATMAN
SUPERGIRL
DONNA TROY
JADE
JESSE QUICK
JLA: ΩMEGA PART 3
D.C. CHALLENGE
ENOUGH!
AT A TIME OF CRISIS, EARTH'S GREATEST HEROES CAME TOGETHER TO COMBAT EVIL. THE ROSTER MAY CHANGE, BUT THE FIGHT FOR JUSTICE CONTINUES. THEY ARE THE JUSTICE LEAGUE of AMERICA

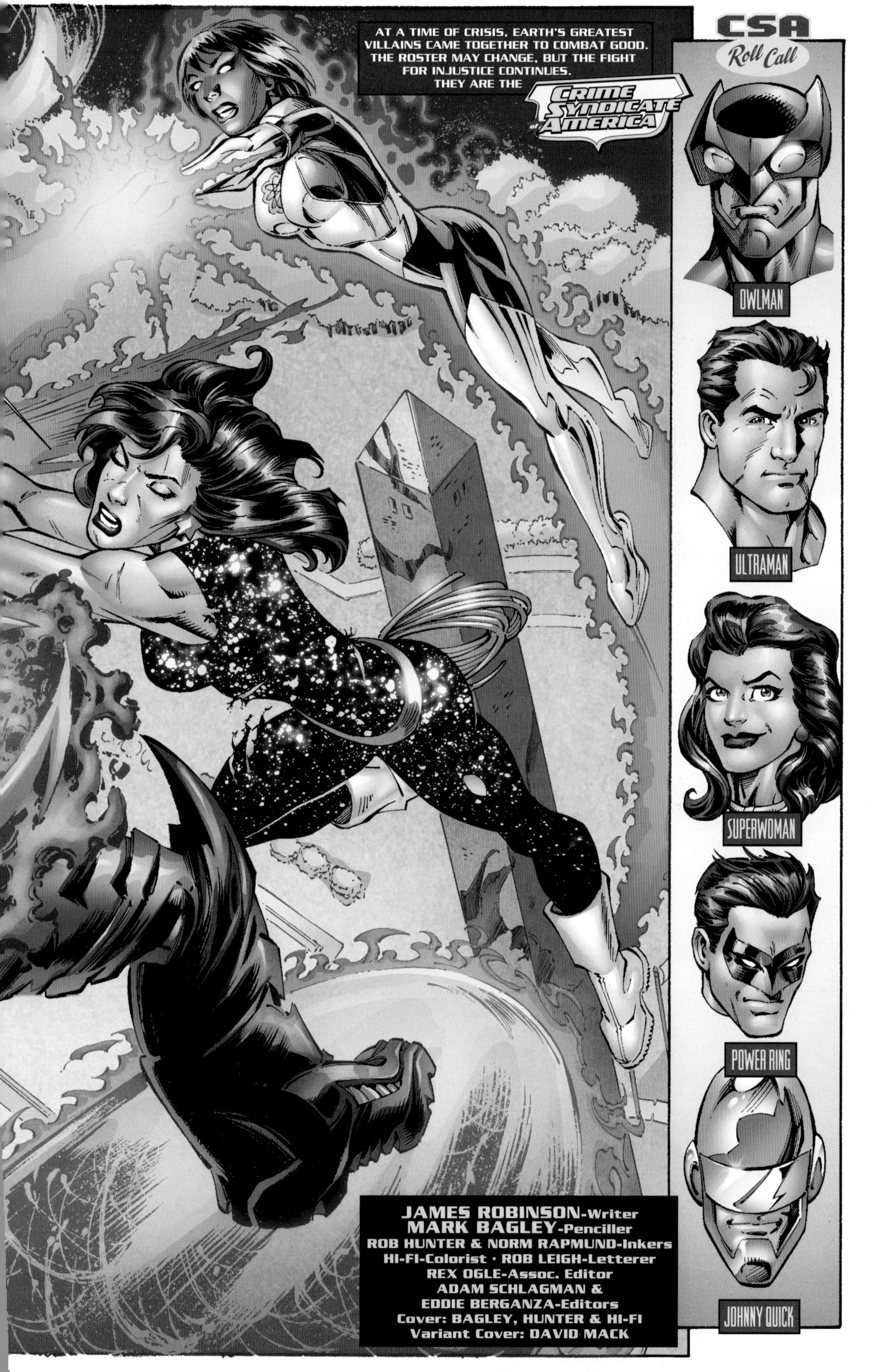
AT A TIME OF CRISIS, EARTH'S GREATEST VILLAINS CAME TOGETHER TO COMBAT GOOD. THE ROSTER MAY CHANGE, BUT THE FIGHT FOR INJUSTICE CONTINUES. THEY ARE THE
CRIME SYNDICATE of AMERICA
CSA
Roll Call
OWLMAN
ULTRAMAN
SUPERWOMAN
POWER RING
JOHNNY QUICK
JAMES ROBINSON-Writer
MARK BAGLEY-Penciller
ROB HUNTER & NORM RAPMUND-Inkers
HI-FI-Colorist · ROB LEIGH-Letterer
REX OGLE-Assoc. Editor
ADAM SCHLAGMAN &
EDDIE BERGANZA-Editors
Cover: BAGLEY, HUNTER & HI-FI
Variant Cover: DAVID MACK

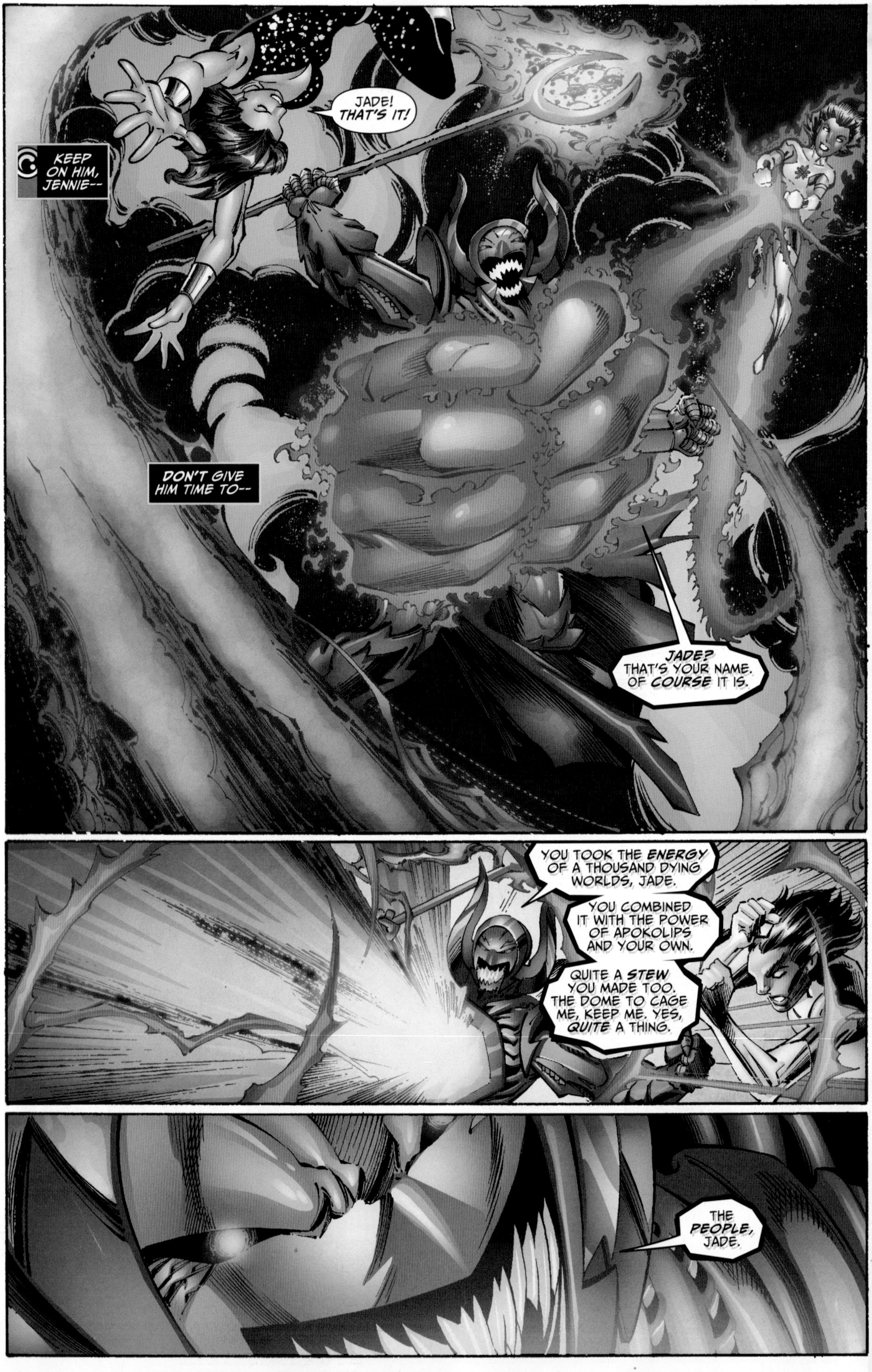
JADE! THAT'S IT!
KEEP ON HIM, JENNIE--
DON'T GIVE HIM TIME TO--
JADE? THAT'S YOUR NAME. OF COURSE IT IS.
YOU TOOK THE ENERGY OF A THOUSAND DYING WORLDS, JADE.
YOU COMBINED IT WITH THE POWER OF APOKOLIPS AND YOUR OWN.
QUITE A STEW YOU MADE TOO. THE DOME TO CAGE ME, KEEP ME. YES, QUITE A THING.
THE PEOPLE, JADE.

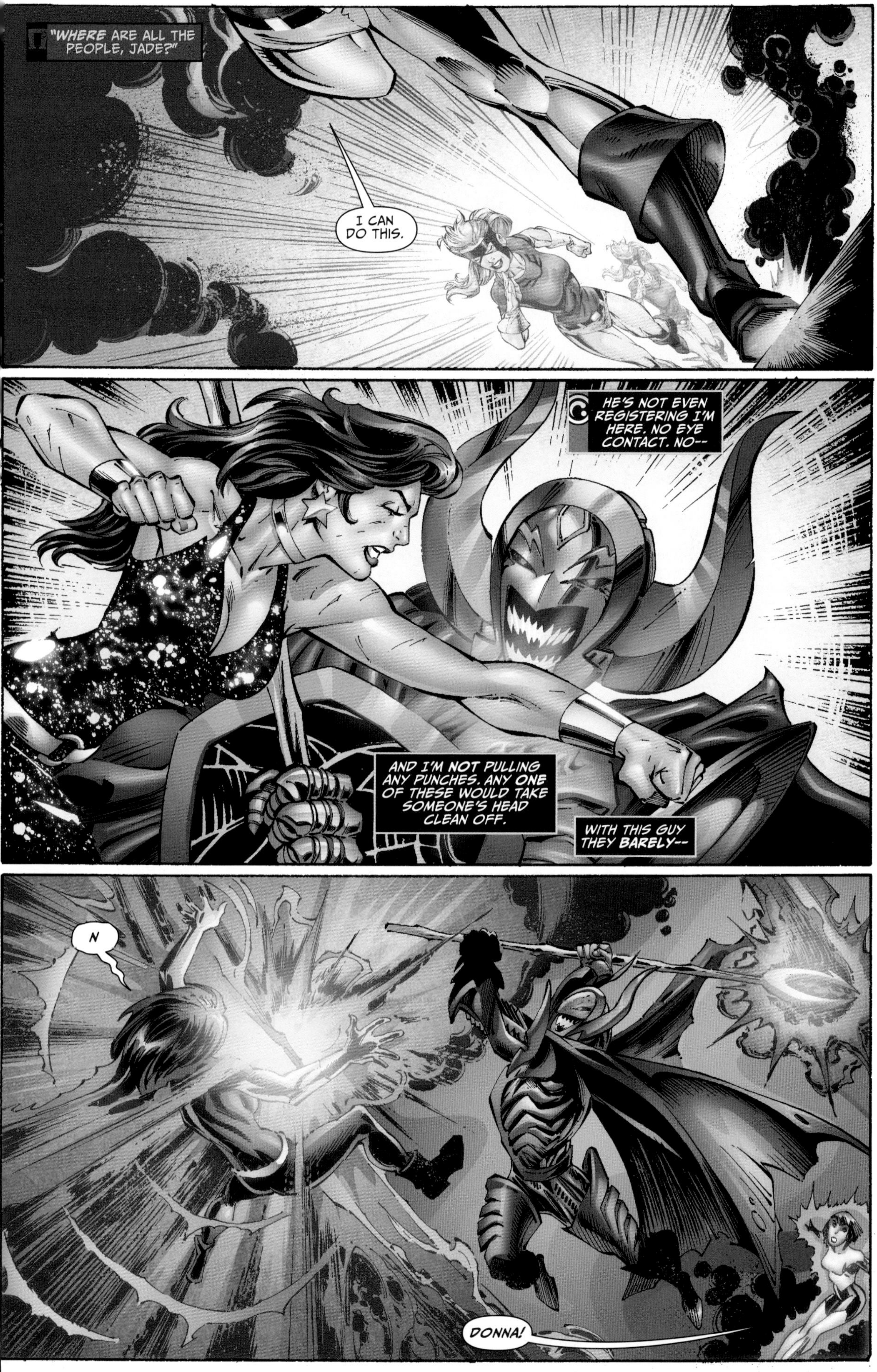
"WHERE ARE ALL THE PEOPLE, JADE?"
I CAN DO THIS.
HE'S NOT EVEN REGISTERING I'M HERE. NO EYE CONTACT. NO--
AND I'M NOT PULLING ANY PUNCHES. ANY ONE OF THESE WOULD TAKE SOMEONE'S HEAD CLEAN OFF.
WITH THIS GUY THEY BARELY--
N
DONNA!

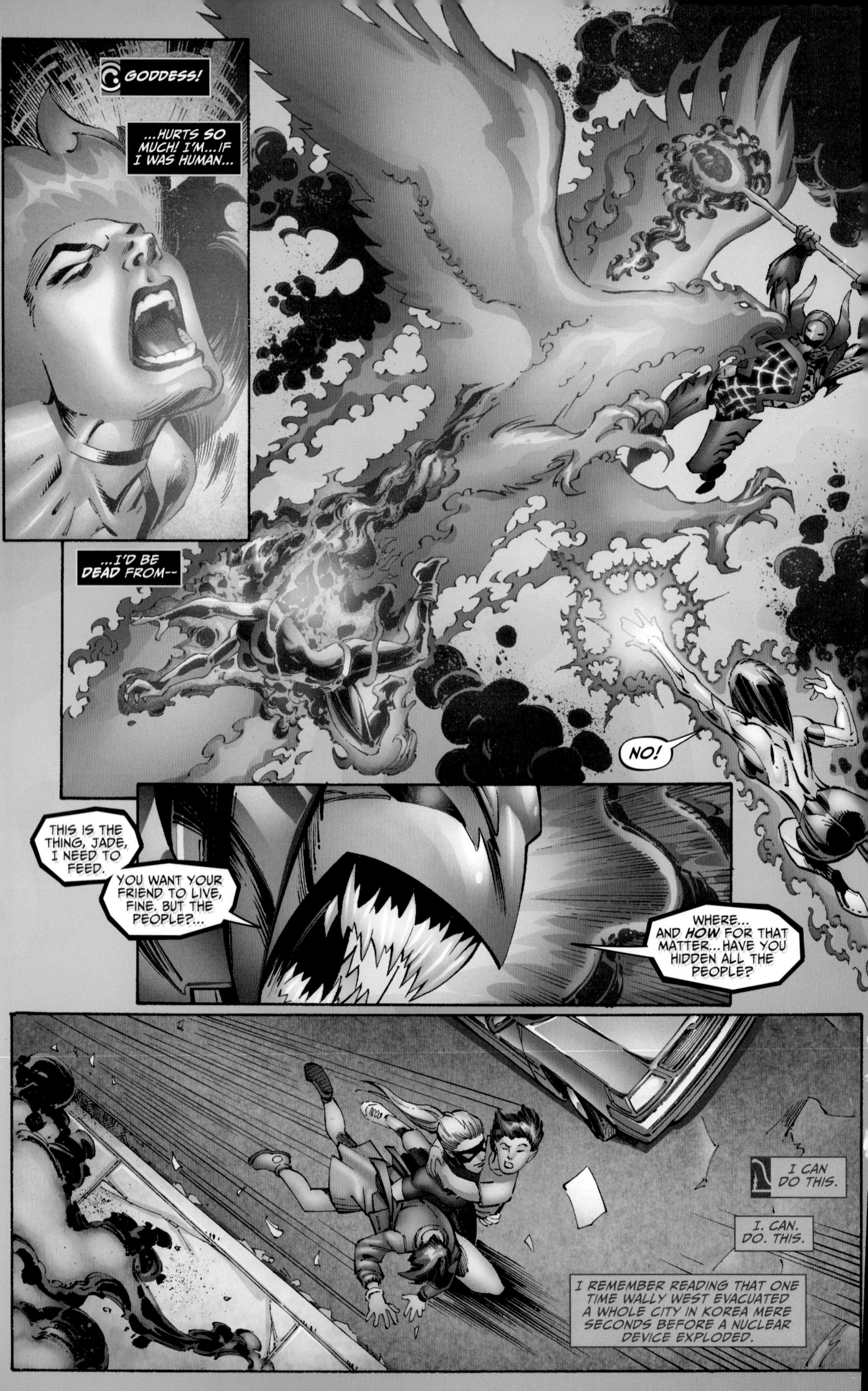
GODDESS!
...HURTS SO MUCH! I'M...IF I WAS HUMAN...
...I'D BE DEAD FROM--
NO!
THIS IS THE THING, JADE, I NEED TO FEED.
YOU WANT YOUR FRIEND TO LIVE, FINE. BUT THE PEOPLE?...
WHERE... AND HOW FOR THAT MATTER... HAVE YOU HIDDEN ALL THE PEOPLE?
I CAN DO THIS.
I. CAN. DO. THIS.
I REMEMBER READING THAT ONE TIME WALLY WEST EVACUATED A WHOLE CITY IN KOREA MERE SECONDS BEFORE A NUCLEAR DEVICE EXPLODED.

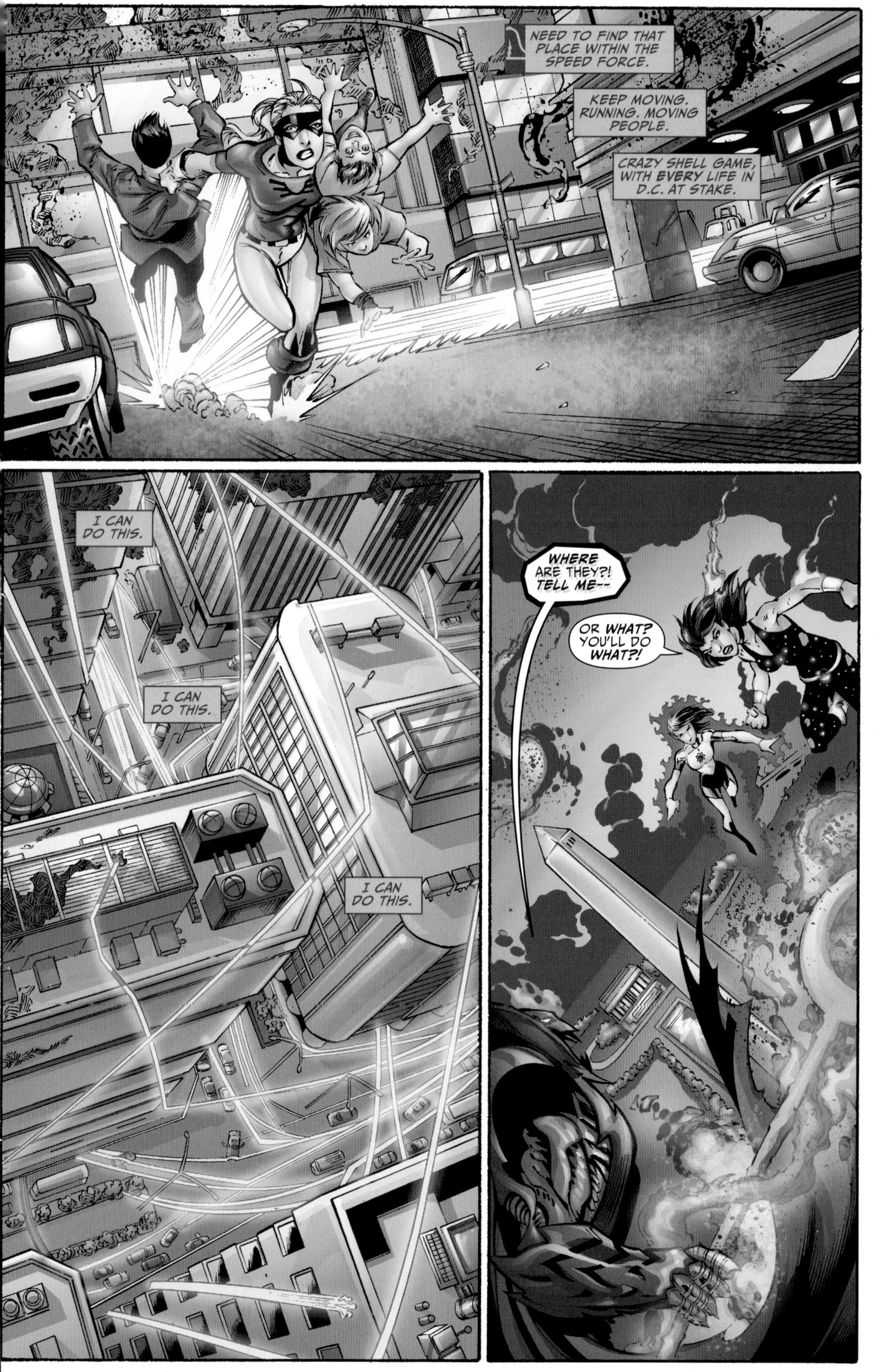
NEED TO FIND THAT PLACE WITHIN THE SPEED FORCE.
KEEP MOVING. RUNNING. MOVING PEOPLE.
CRAZY SHELL GAME, WITH EVERY LIFE IN D.C. AT STAKE.
I CAN DO THIS.
I CAN DO THIS.
I CAN DO THIS.
WHERE ARE THEY?! TELL ME--
OR WHAT? YOU'LL DO WHAT?!

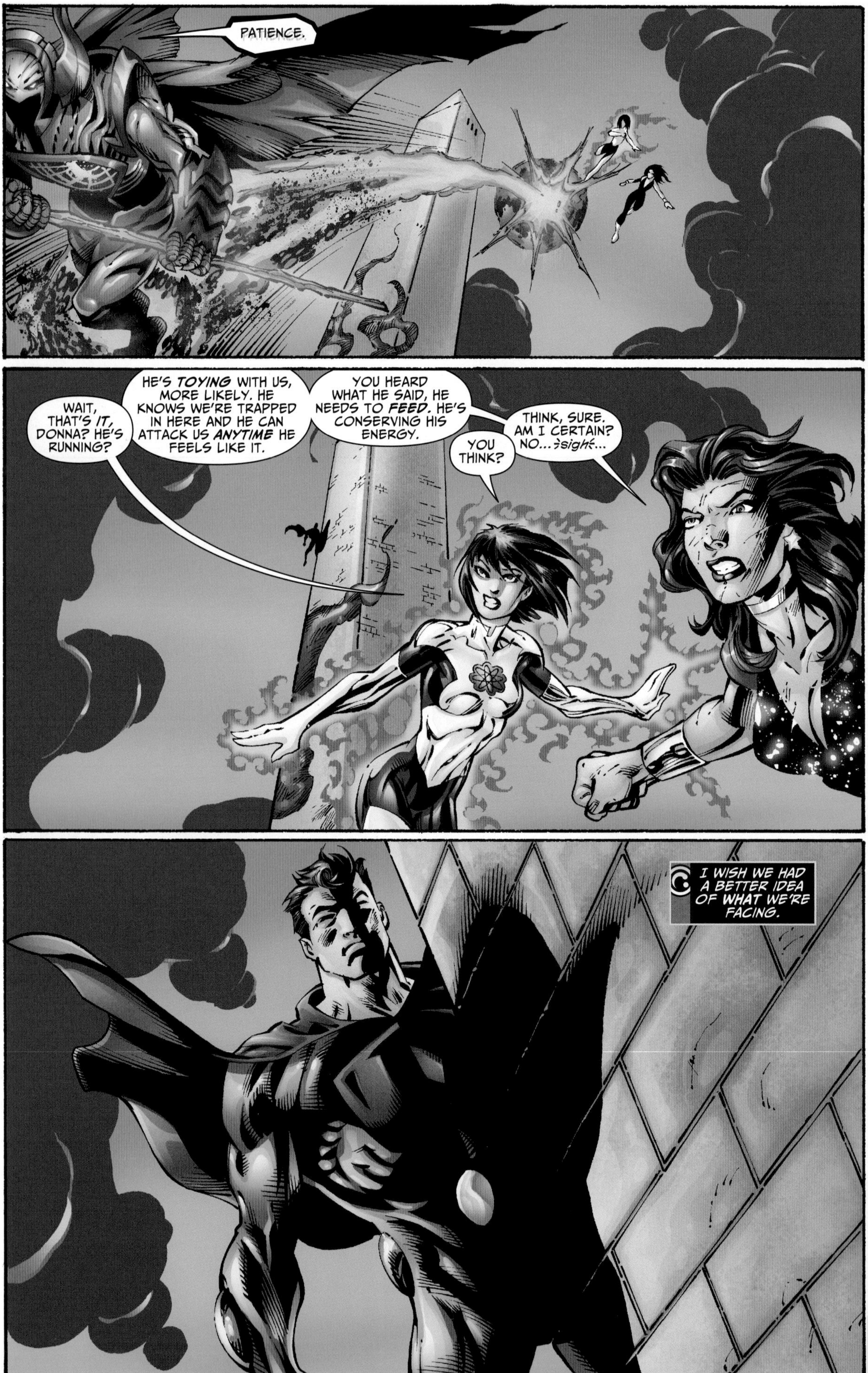
PATIENCE.
WAIT, THAT'S *IT*, DONNA? HE'S RUNNING?
HE'S *TOYING* WITH US, MORE LIKELY. HE KNOWS WE'RE TRAPPED IN HERE AND HE CAN ATTACK US *ANYTIME* HE FEELS LIKE IT.
YOU HEARD WHAT HE SAID, HE NEEDS TO *FEED*. HE'S CONSERVING HIS ENERGY.
YOU THINK?
THINK, SURE. AM I CERTAIN? NO... *sigh*...
I WISH WE HAD A BETTER IDEA OF *WHAT* WE'RE FACING.

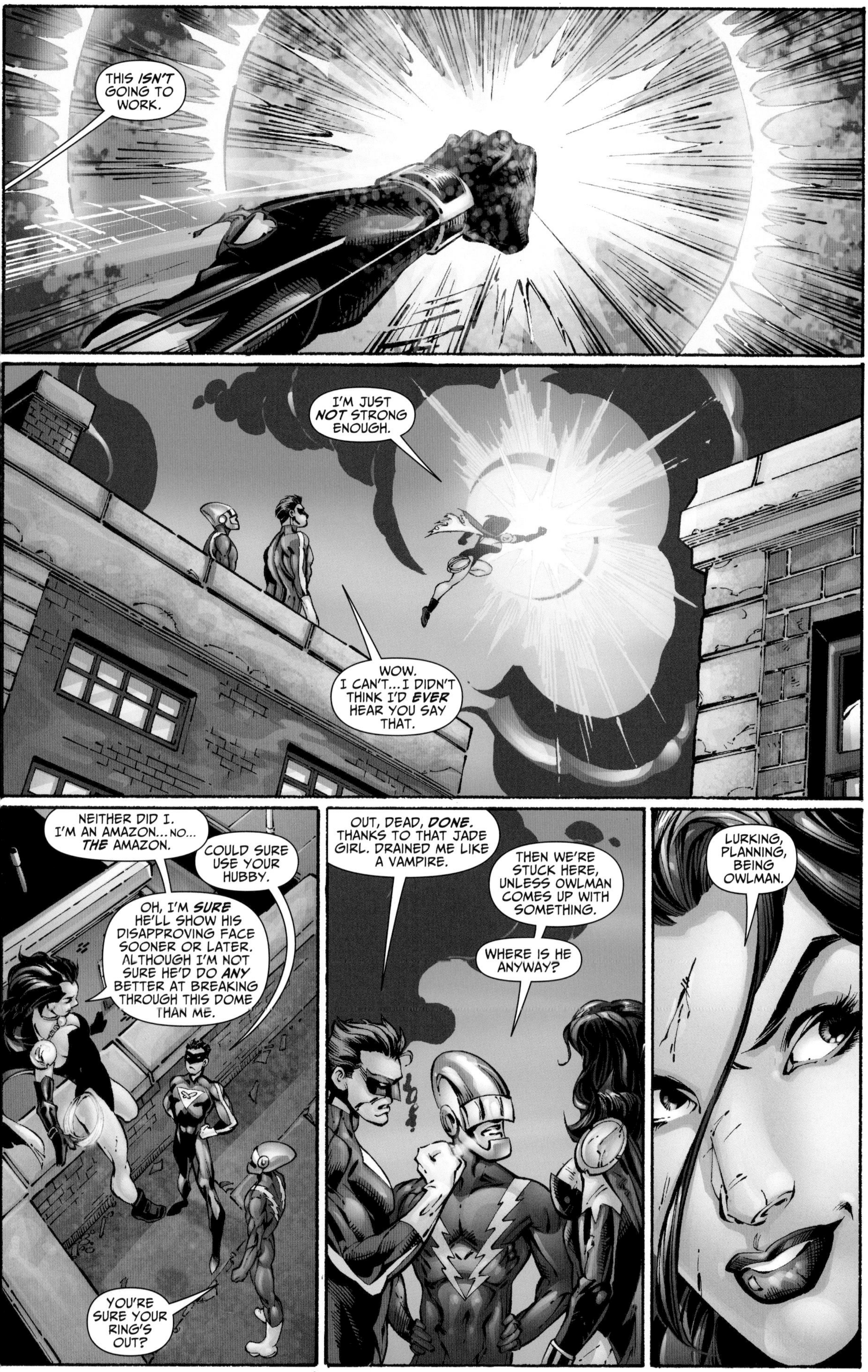
THIS ISN'T GOING TO WORK.
I'M JUST NOT STRONG ENOUGH.
WOW. I CAN'T... I DIDN'T THINK I'D EVER HEAR YOU SAY THAT.
NEITHER DID I. I'M AN AMAZON... NO... THE AMAZON.
COULD SURE USE YOUR HUBBY.
OH, I'M SURE HE'LL SHOW HIS DISAPPROVING FACE SOONER OR LATER. ALTHOUGH I'M NOT SURE HE'D DO ANY BETTER AT BREAKING THROUGH THIS DOME THAN ME.
YOU'RE SURE YOUR RING'S OUT?
OUT, DEAD, DONE. THANKS TO THAT JADE GIRL. DRAINED ME LIKE A VAMPIRE.
THEN WE'RE STUCK HERE, UNLESS OWLMAN COMES UP WITH SOMETHING.
WHERE IS HE ANYWAY?
LURKING, PLANNING, BEING OWLMAN.

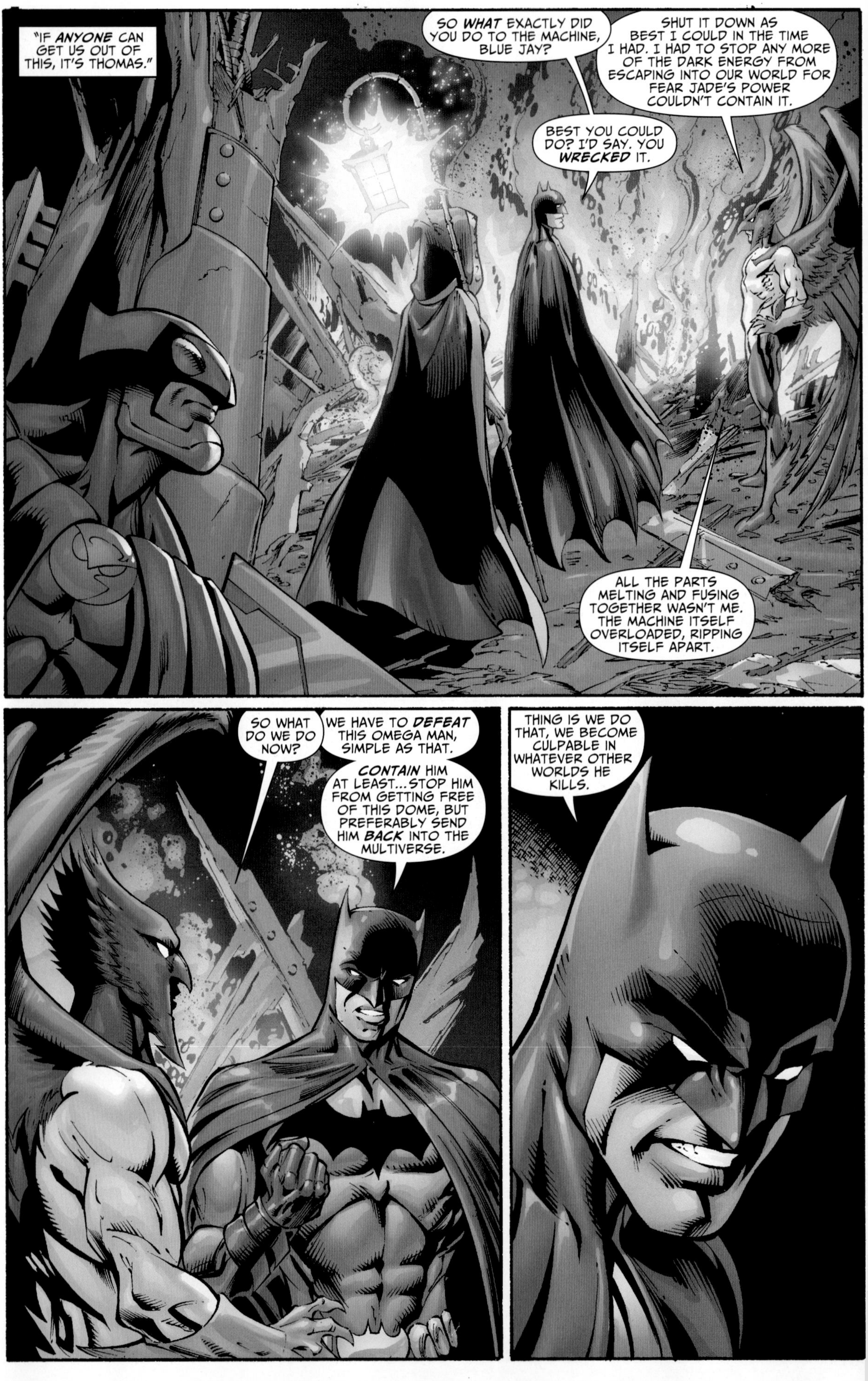
"IF ANYONE CAN GET US OUT OF THIS, IT'S THOMAS."
SO WHAT EXACTLY DID YOU DO TO THE MACHINE, BLUE JAY?
SHUT IT DOWN AS BEST I COULD IN THE TIME I HAD. I HAD TO STOP ANY MORE OF THE DARK ENERGY FROM ESCAPING INTO OUR WORLD FOR FEAR JADE'S POWER COULDN'T CONTAIN IT.
BEST YOU COULD DO? I'D SAY. YOU WRECKED IT.
ALL THE PARTS MELTING AND FUSING TOGETHER WASN'T ME. THE MACHINE ITSELF OVERLOADED, RIPPING ITSELF APART.
SO WHAT DO WE DO NOW?
WE HAVE TO DEFEAT THIS OMEGA MAN, SIMPLE AS THAT.
CONTAIN HIM AT LEAST...STOP HIM FROM GETTING FREE OF THIS DOME, BUT PREFERABLY SEND HIM BACK INTO THE MULTIVERSE.
THING IS WE DO THAT, WE BECOME CULPABLE IN WHATEVER OTHER WORLDS HE KILLS.

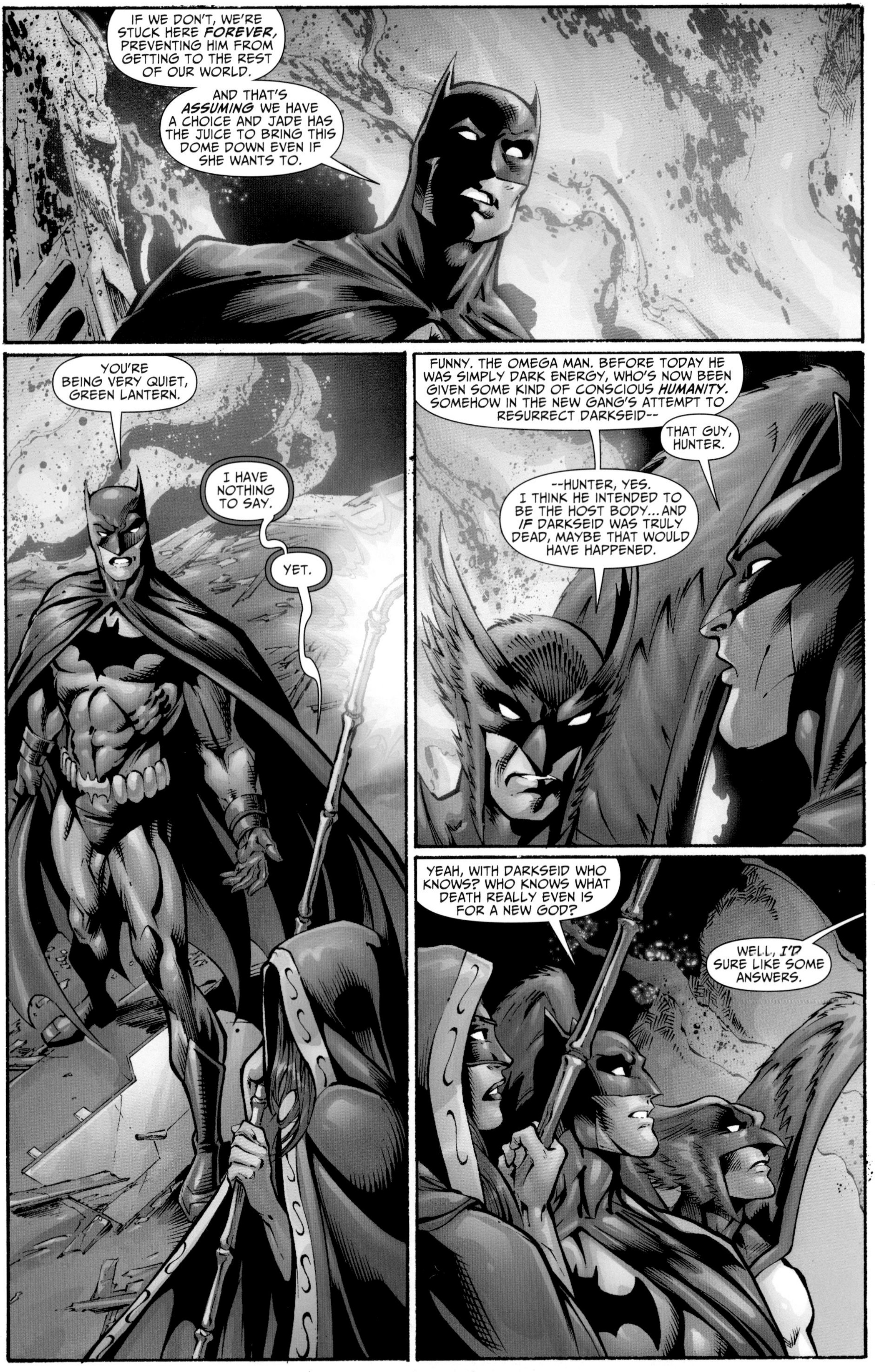
IF WE DON'T, WE'RE STUCK HERE FOREVER, PREVENTING HIM FROM GETTING TO THE REST OF OUR WORLD.
AND THAT'S ASSUMING WE HAVE A CHOICE AND JADE HAS THE JUICE TO BRING THIS DOME DOWN EVEN IF SHE WANTS TO.
YOU'RE BEING VERY QUIET, GREEN LANTERN.
I HAVE NOTHING TO SAY.
YET.
FUNNY. THE OMEGA MAN. BEFORE TODAY HE WAS SIMPLY DARK ENERGY, WHO'S NOW BEEN GIVEN SOME KIND OF CONSCIOUS HUMANITY. SOMEHOW IN THE NEW GANG'S ATTEMPT TO RESURRECT DARKSEID--
THAT GUY, HUNTER.
--HUNTER, YES. I THINK HE INTENDED TO BE THE HOST BODY...AND IF DARKSEID WAS TRULY DEAD, MAYBE THAT WOULD HAVE HAPPENED.
YEAH, WITH DARKSEID WHO KNOWS? WHO KNOWS WHAT DEATH REALLY EVEN IS FOR A NEW GOD?
WELL, I'D SURE LIKE SOME ANSWERS.

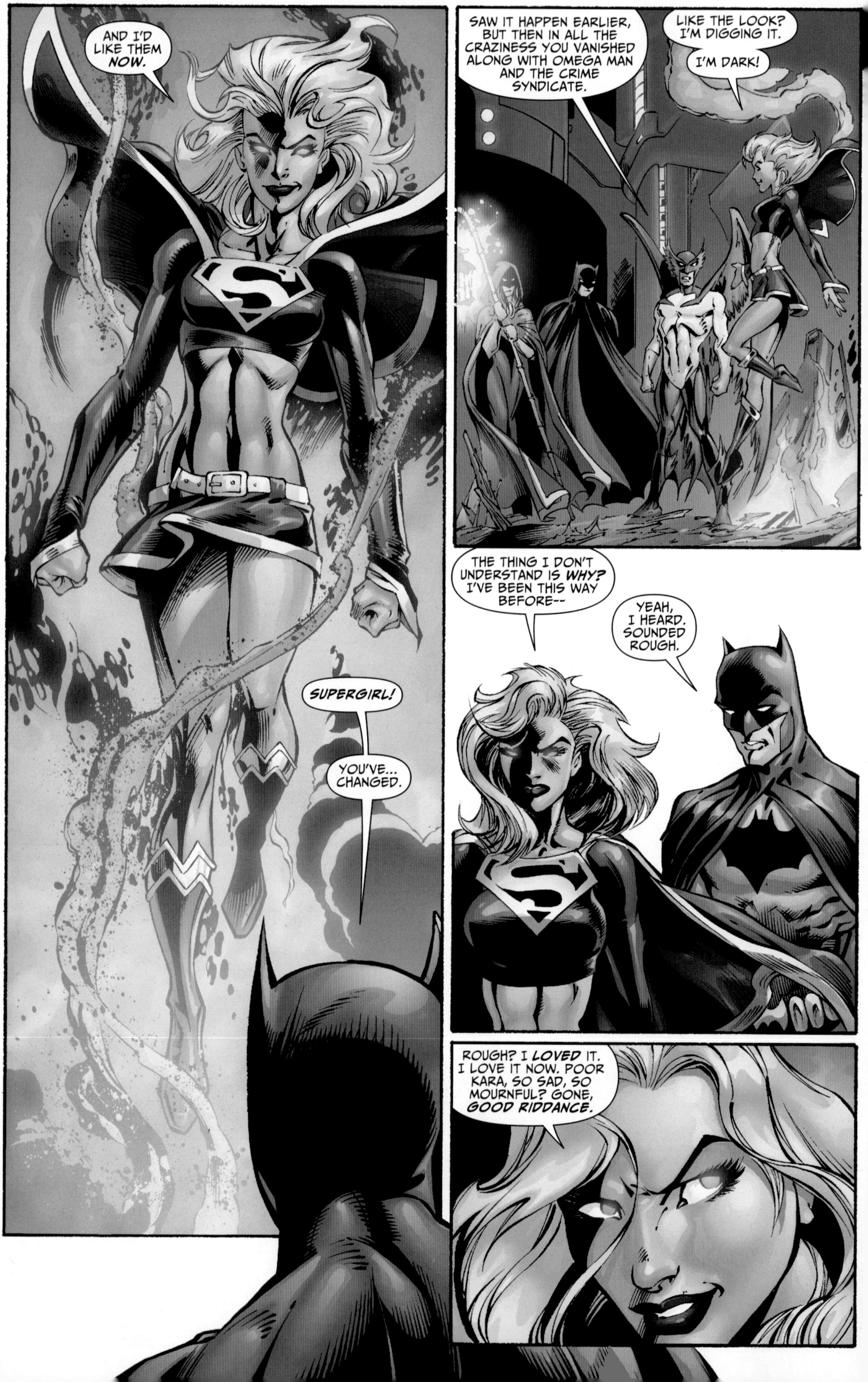
AND I'D LIKE THEM NOW.
SUPERGIRL!
YOU'VE... CHANGED.
SAW IT HAPPEN EARLIER, BUT THEN IN ALL THE CRAZINESS YOU VANISHED ALONG WITH OMEGA MAN AND THE CRIME SYNDICATE.
LIKE THE LOOK? I'M DIGGING IT.
I'M DARK!
THE THING I DON'T UNDERSTAND IS WHY? I'VE BEEN THIS WAY BEFORE--
YEAH, I HEARD. SOUNDED ROUGH.
ROUGH? I LOVED IT. I LOVE IT NOW. POOR KARA, SO SAD, SO MOURNFUL? GONE. GOOD RIDDANCE.

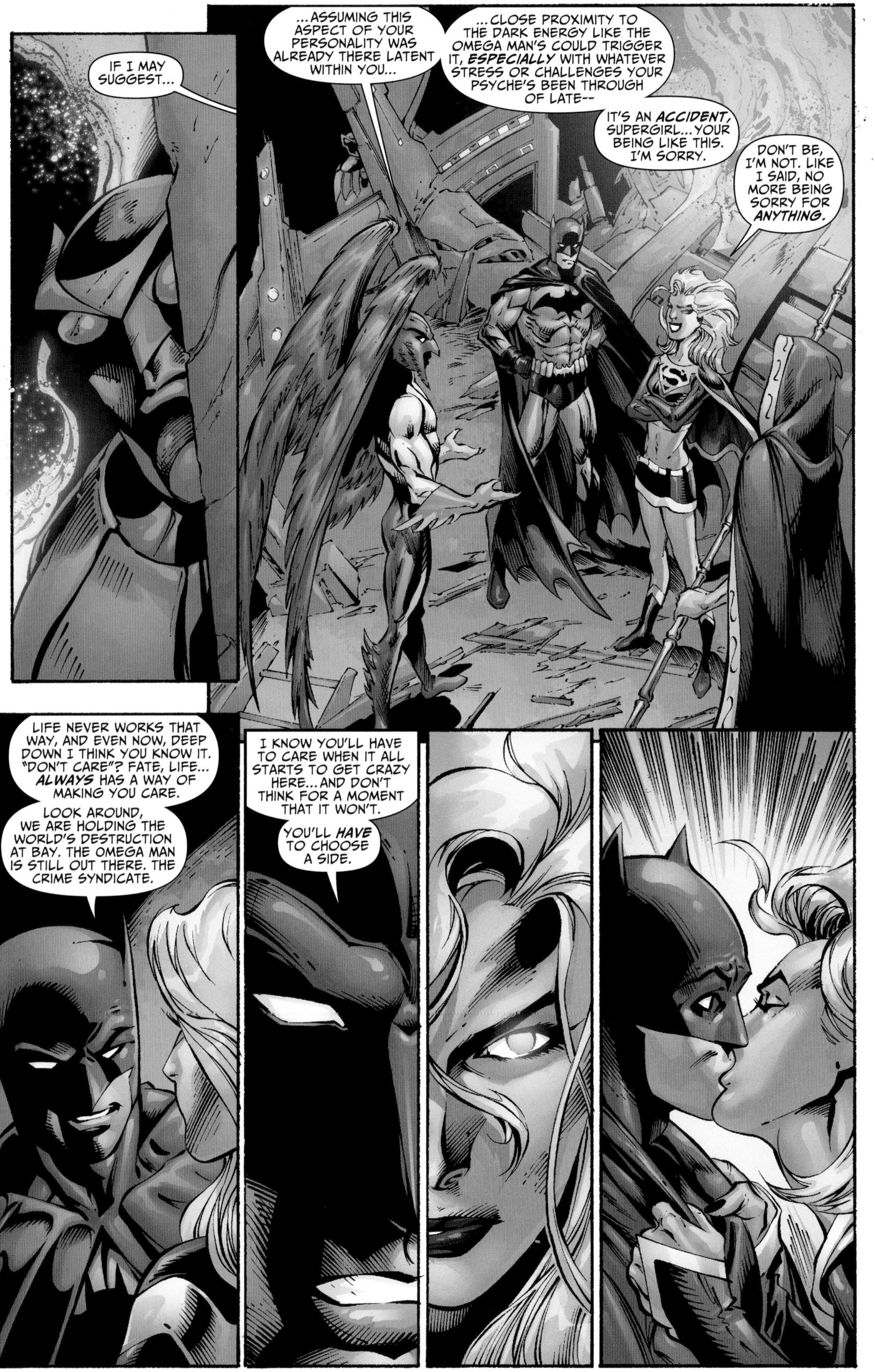
IF I MAY SUGGEST...
...ASSUMING THIS ASPECT OF YOUR PERSONALITY WAS ALREADY THERE LATENT WITHIN YOU...
...CLOSE PROXIMITY TO THE DARK ENERGY LIKE THE OMEGA MAN'S COULD TRIGGER IT, ESPECIALLY WITH WHATEVER STRESS OR CHALLENGES YOUR PSYCHE'S BEEN THROUGH OF LATE--
IT'S AN ACCIDENT, SUPERGIRL...YOUR BEING LIKE THIS. I'M SORRY.
DON'T BE, I'M NOT. LIKE I SAID, NO MORE BEING SORRY FOR ANYTHING.
LIFE NEVER WORKS THAT WAY, AND EVEN NOW, DEEP DOWN I THINK YOU KNOW IT. "DON'T CARE"? FATE, LIFE... ALWAYS HAS A WAY OF MAKING YOU CARE.
LOOK AROUND, WE ARE HOLDING THE WORLD'S DESTRUCTION AT BAY. THE OMEGA MAN IS STILL OUT THERE. THE CRIME SYNDICATE.
I KNOW YOU'LL HAVE TO CARE WHEN IT ALL STARTS TO GET CRAZY HERE...AND DON'T THINK FOR A MOMENT THAT IT WON'T.
YOU'LL HAVE TO CHOOSE A SIDE.

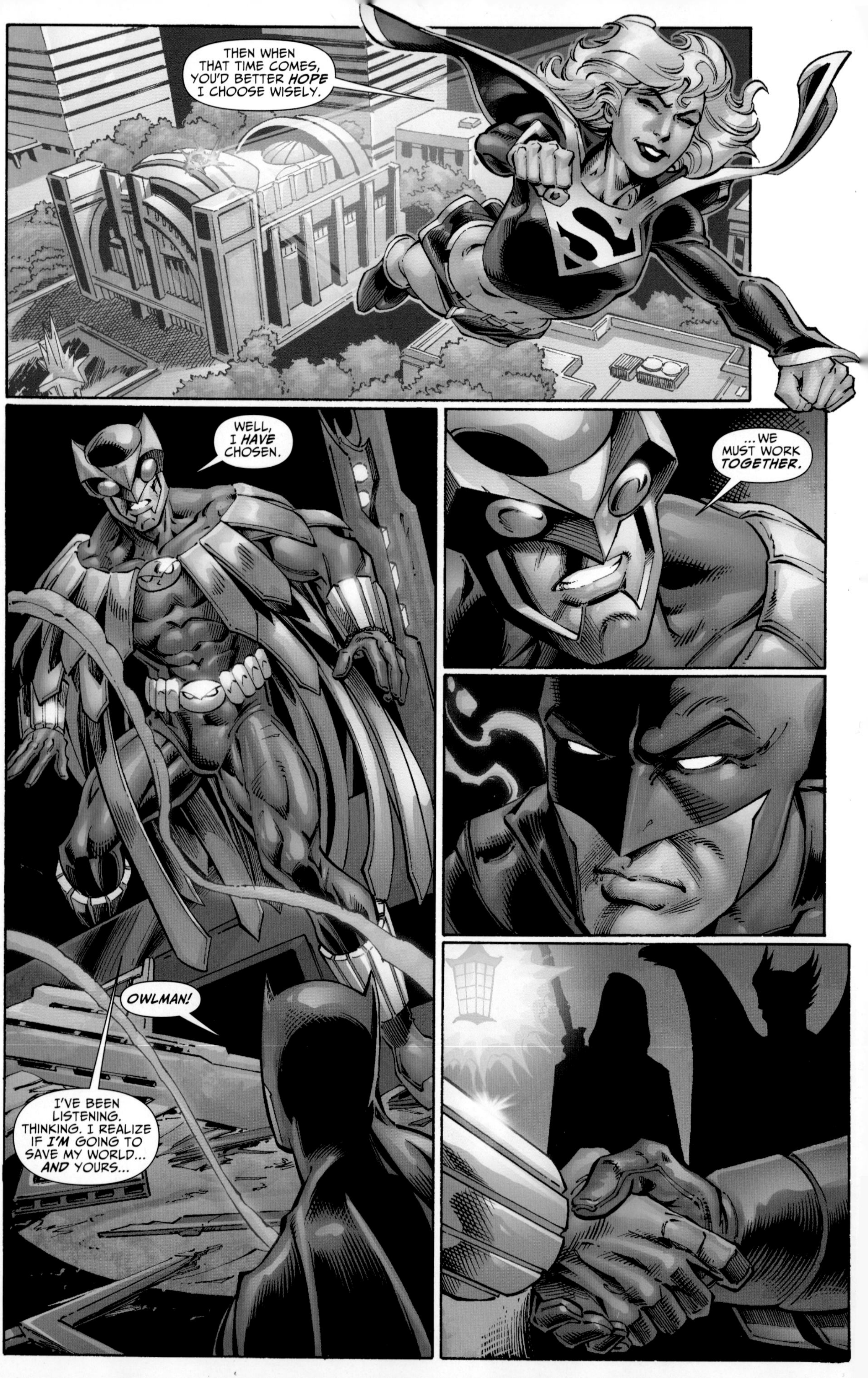
THEN WHEN THAT TIME COMES, YOU'D BETTER *HOPE* I CHOOSE WISELY.
WELL, I *HAVE* CHOSEN.
OWLMAN!
I'VE BEEN LISTENING. THINKING. I REALIZE IF *I'M* GOING TO SAVE MY WORLD... *AND* YOURS...
...WE MUST WORK *TOGETHER.*

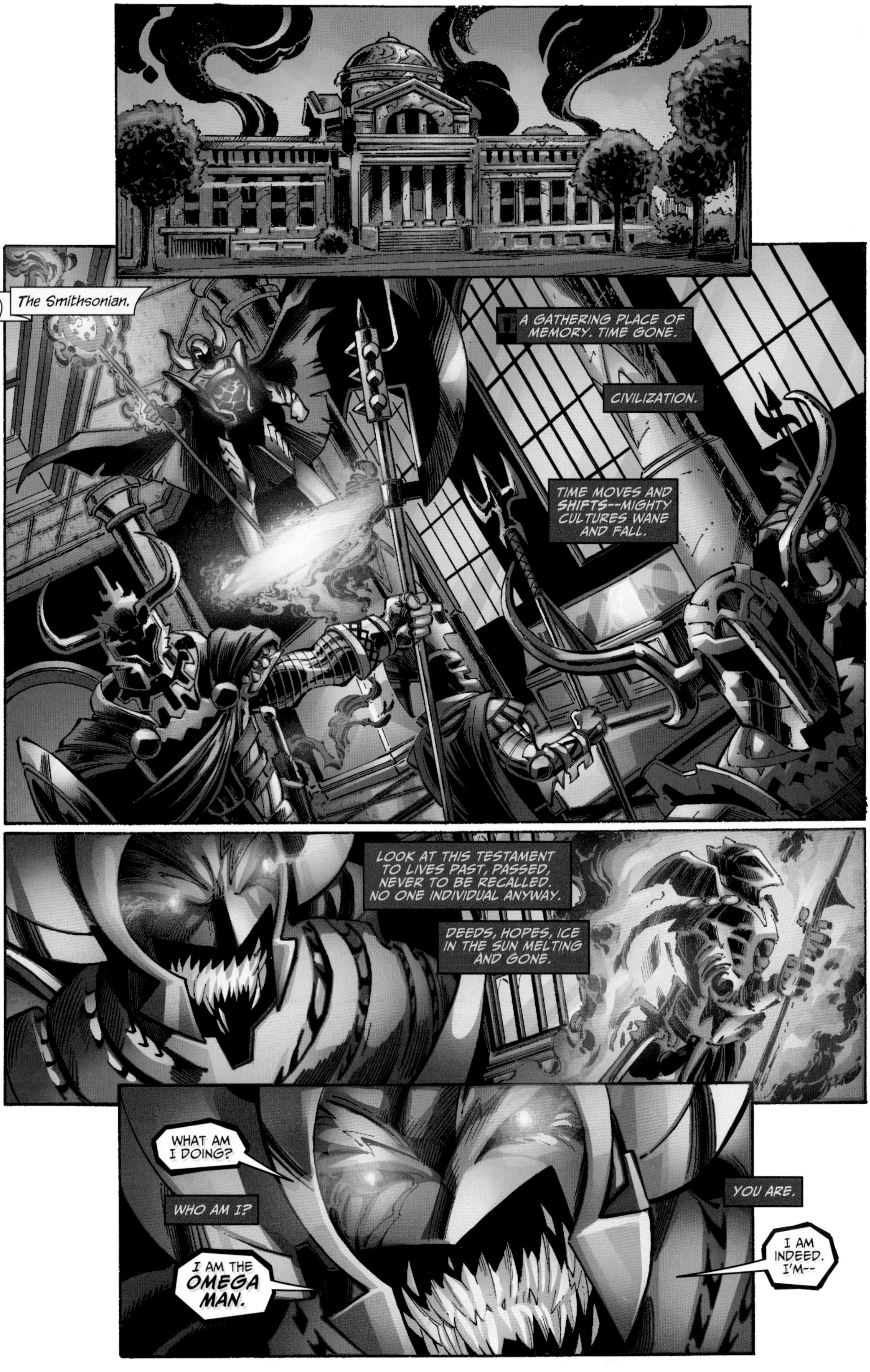

The Smithsonian.
A GATHERING PLACE OF MEMORY. TIME GONE.
CIVILIZATION.
TIME MOVES AND SHIFTS--MIGHTY CULTURES WANE AND FALL.
LOOK AT THIS TESTAMENT TO LIVES PAST, PASSED, NEVER TO BE RECALLED. NO ONE INDIVIDUAL ANYWAY.
DEEDS, HOPES, ICE IN THE SUN MELTING AND GONE.
WHAT AM I DOING?
WHO AM I?
I AM THE OMEGA MAN.
YOU ARE.
I AM INDEED. I'M--

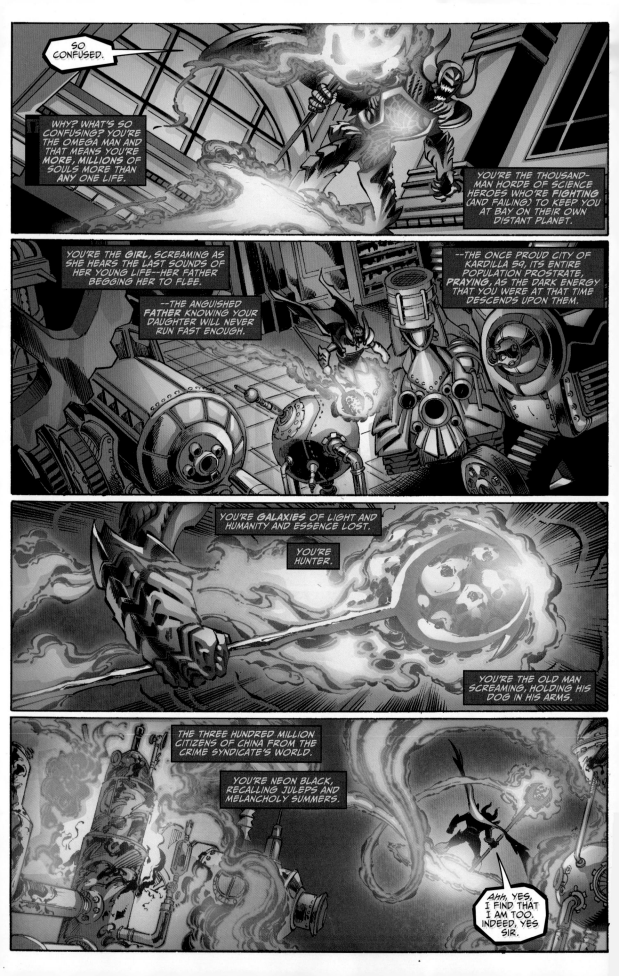

SO CONFUSED.

WHY? WHAT'S SO CONFUSING? YOU'RE THE OMEGA MAN AND THAT MEANS YOU'RE *MORE*, MILLIONS OF SOULS MORE THAN ANY ONE LIFE.

YOU'RE THE THOUSAND-MAN HORDE OF SCIENCE HEROES WHO'RE FIGHTING (AND FAILING) TO KEEP YOU AT BAY ON THEIR OWN DISTANT PLANET.

YOU'RE THE *GIRL*, SCREAMING AS SHE HEARS THE LAST SOUNDS OF HER YOUNG LIFE--HER FATHER BEGGING HER TO FLEE.

--THE ANGUISHED FATHER KNOWING YOUR DAUGHTER WILL NEVER RUN FAST ENOUGH.

--THE ONCE PROUD CITY OF KARDILLA 59, ITS ENTIRE POPULATION PROSTRATE, *PRAYING*, AS THE DARK ENERGY THAT YOU WERE AT THAT TIME DESCENDS UPON THEM.

YOU'RE GALAXIES OF LIGHT AND HUMANITY AND ESSENCE LOST.

YOU'RE HUNTER.

YOU'RE THE OLD MAN SCREAMING, HOLDING HIS DOG IN HIS ARMS.

THE THREE HUNDRED MILLION CITIZENS OF CHINA FROM THE CRIME SYNDICATE'S WORLD.

YOU'RE NEON BLACK, RECALLING JULEPS AND MELANCHOLY SUMMERS.

AHH, YES, I FIND THAT I AM TOO. INDEED, YES SIR.

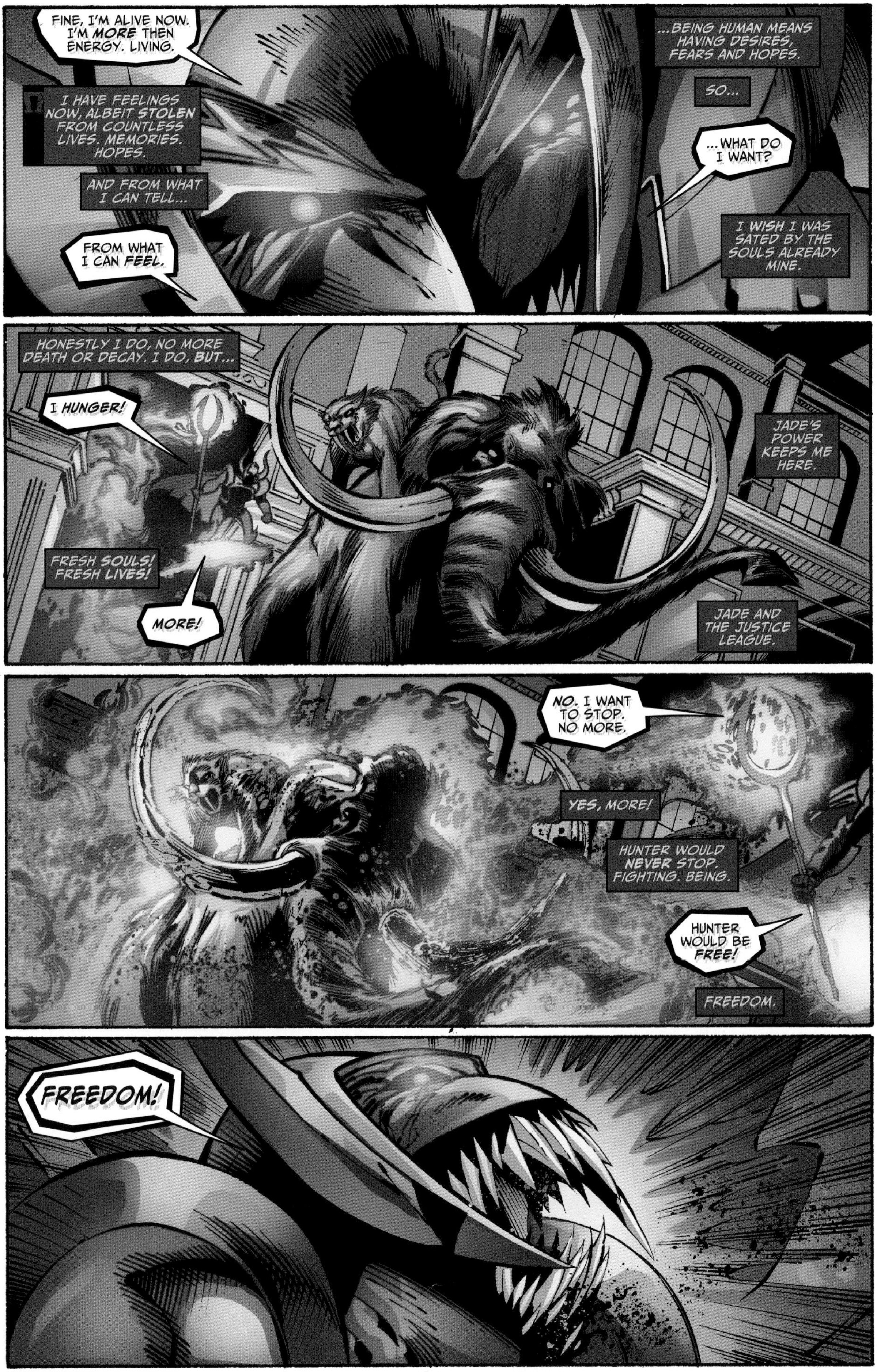
FINE, I'M ALIVE NOW. I'M MORE THEN ENERGY. LIVING.
I HAVE FEELINGS NOW, ALBEIT STOLEN FROM COUNTLESS LIVES. MEMORIES. HOPES.
AND FROM WHAT I CAN TELL...
FROM WHAT I CAN FEEL.
...BEING HUMAN MEANS HAVING DESIRES, FEARS AND HOPES.
SO...
...WHAT DO I WANT?
I WISH I WAS SATED BY THE SOULS ALREADY MINE.
HONESTLY I DO, NO MORE DEATH OR DECAY. I DO, BUT...
I HUNGER!
FRESH SOULS! FRESH LIVES!
MORE!
JADE'S POWER KEEPS ME HERE.
JADE AND THE JUSTICE LEAGUE.
NO. I WANT TO STOP. NO MORE.
YES, MORE!
HUNTER WOULD NEVER STOP. FIGHTING. BEING.
HUNTER WOULD BE FREE!
FREEDOM.
FREEDOM!

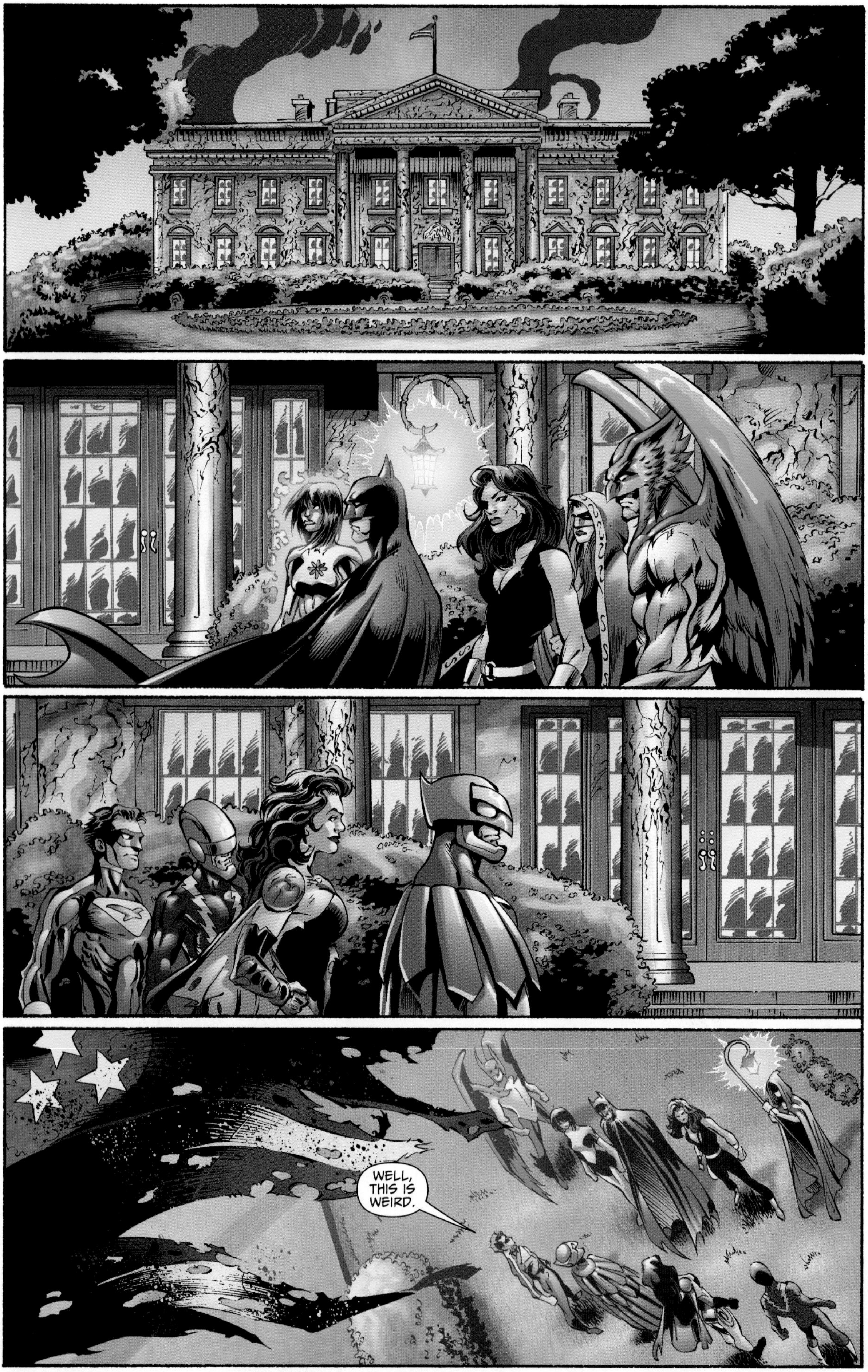
WELL, THIS IS WEIRD.

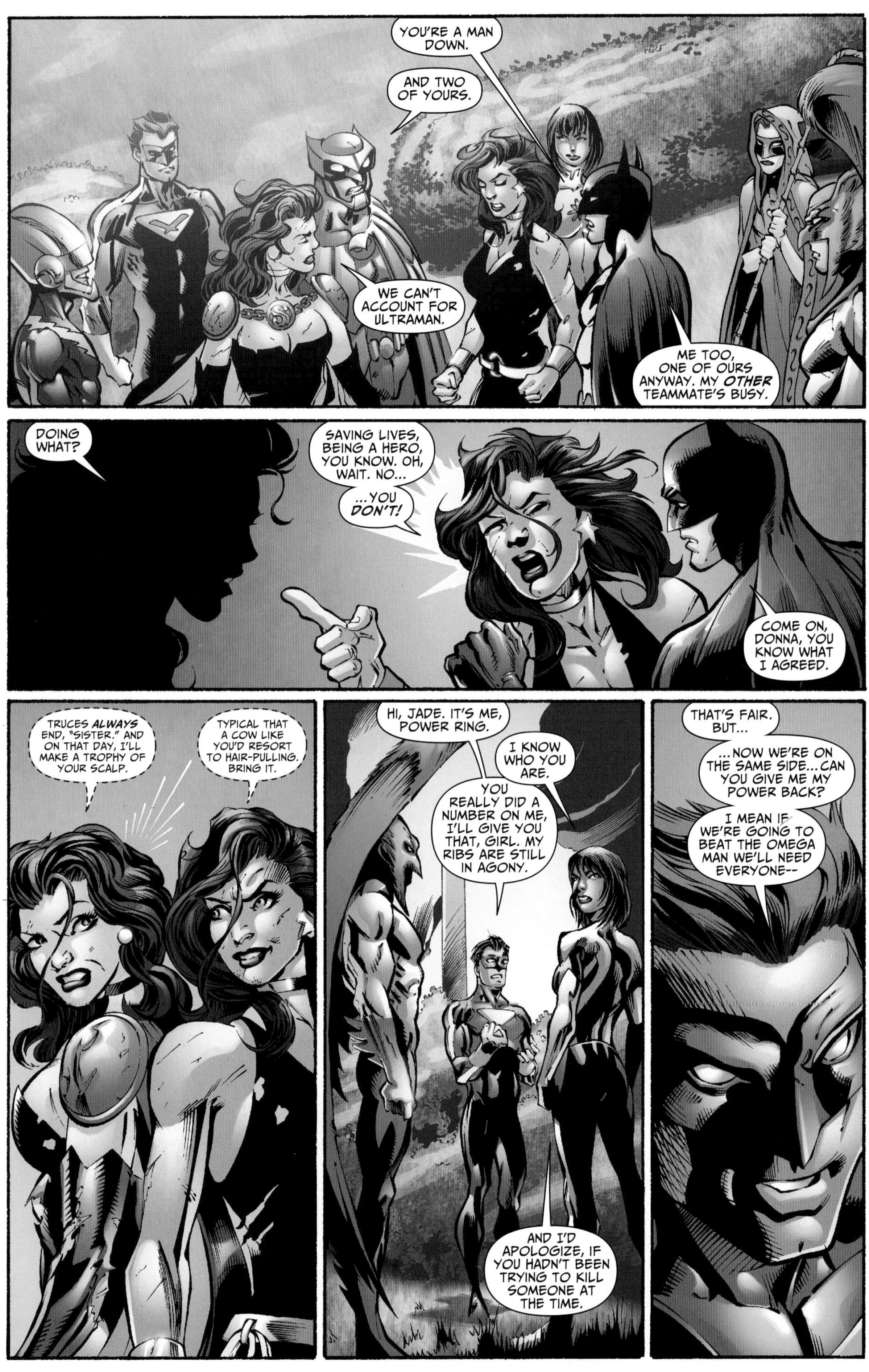
YOU'RE A MAN DOWN.
AND TWO OF YOURS.
WE CAN'T ACCOUNT FOR ULTRAMAN.
ME TOO, ONE OF OURS ANYWAY. MY *OTHER* TEAMMATE'S BUSY.
DOING WHAT?
SAVING LIVES, BEING A HERO, YOU KNOW. OH, WAIT. NO...
...YOU *DON'T!*
COME ON, DONNA, YOU KNOW WHAT I AGREED.
TRUCES *ALWAYS* END, "SISTER." AND ON THAT DAY, I'LL MAKE A TROPHY OF YOUR SCALP.
TYPICAL THAT A COW LIKE YOU'D RESORT TO HAIR-PULLING. BRING IT.
HI, JADE. IT'S ME, POWER RING.
I KNOW WHO YOU ARE.
YOU REALLY DID A NUMBER ON ME, I'LL GIVE YOU THAT, GIRL. MY RIBS ARE STILL IN AGONY.
AND I'D APOLOGIZE, IF YOU HADN'T BEEN TRYING TO KILL SOMEONE AT THE TIME.
THAT'S FAIR. BUT...
...NOW WE'RE ON THE SAME SIDE...CAN YOU GIVE ME MY POWER BACK?
I MEAN IF WE'RE GOING TO BEAT THE OMEGA MAN WE'LL NEED EVERYONE--

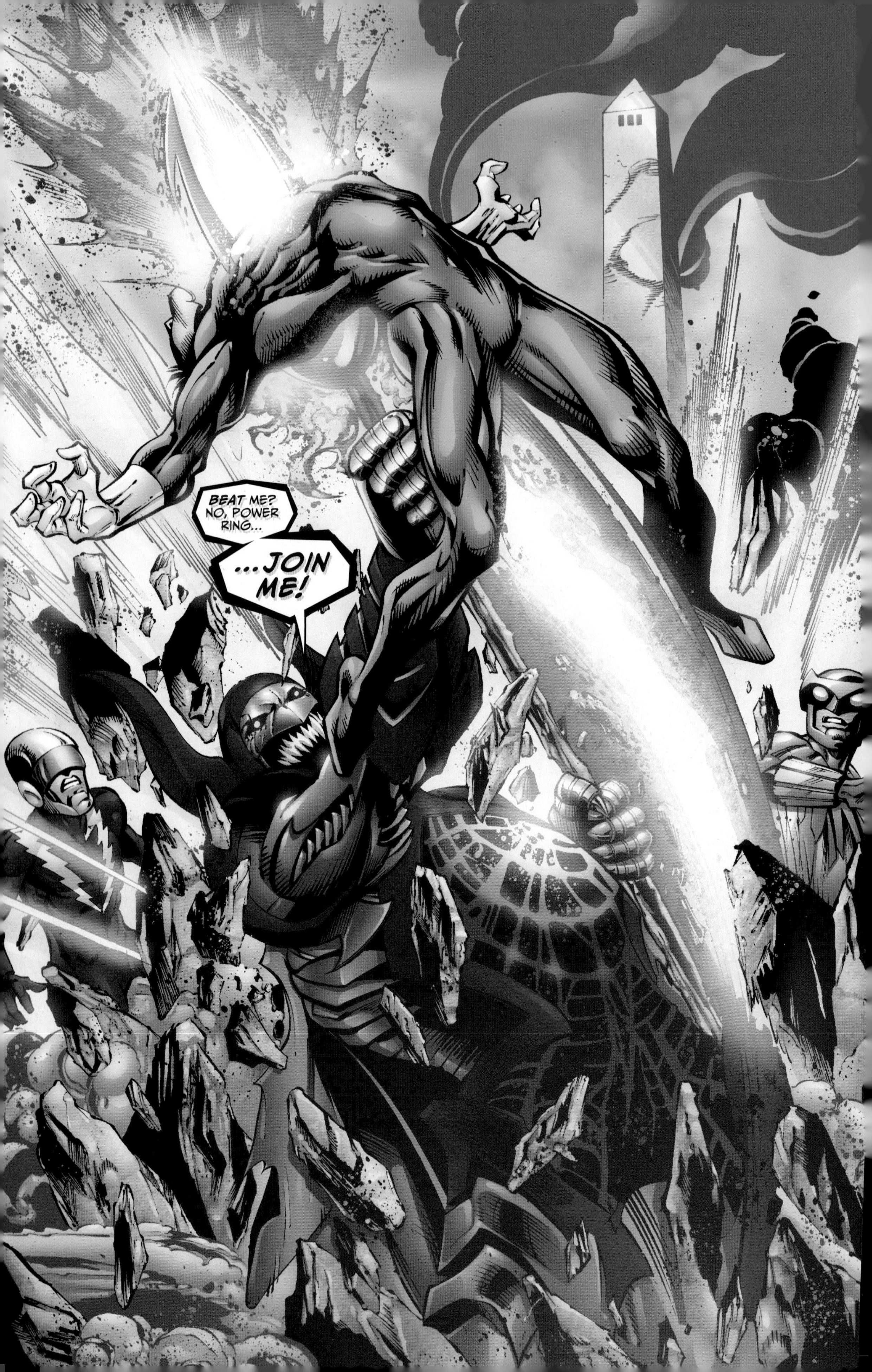
BEAT ME? NO, POWER RING...
...JOIN ME!

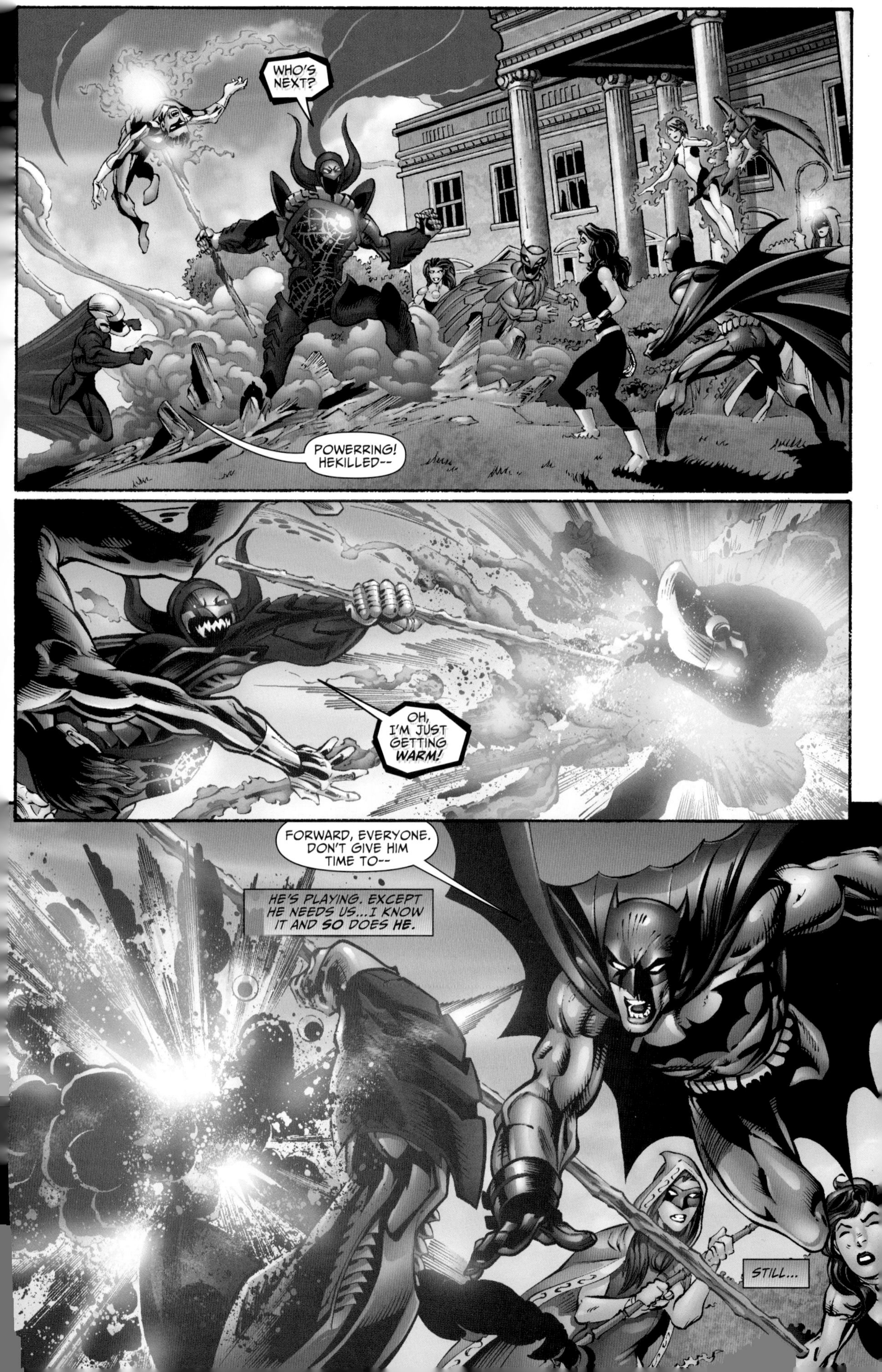
WHO'S NEXT?
POWERRING! HEKILLED--
OH, I'M JUST GETTING WARM!
FORWARD, EVERYONE. DON'T GIVE HIM TIME TO--
HE'S PLAYING. EXCEPT HE NEEDS US...I KNOW IT AND SO DOES HE.
STILL...

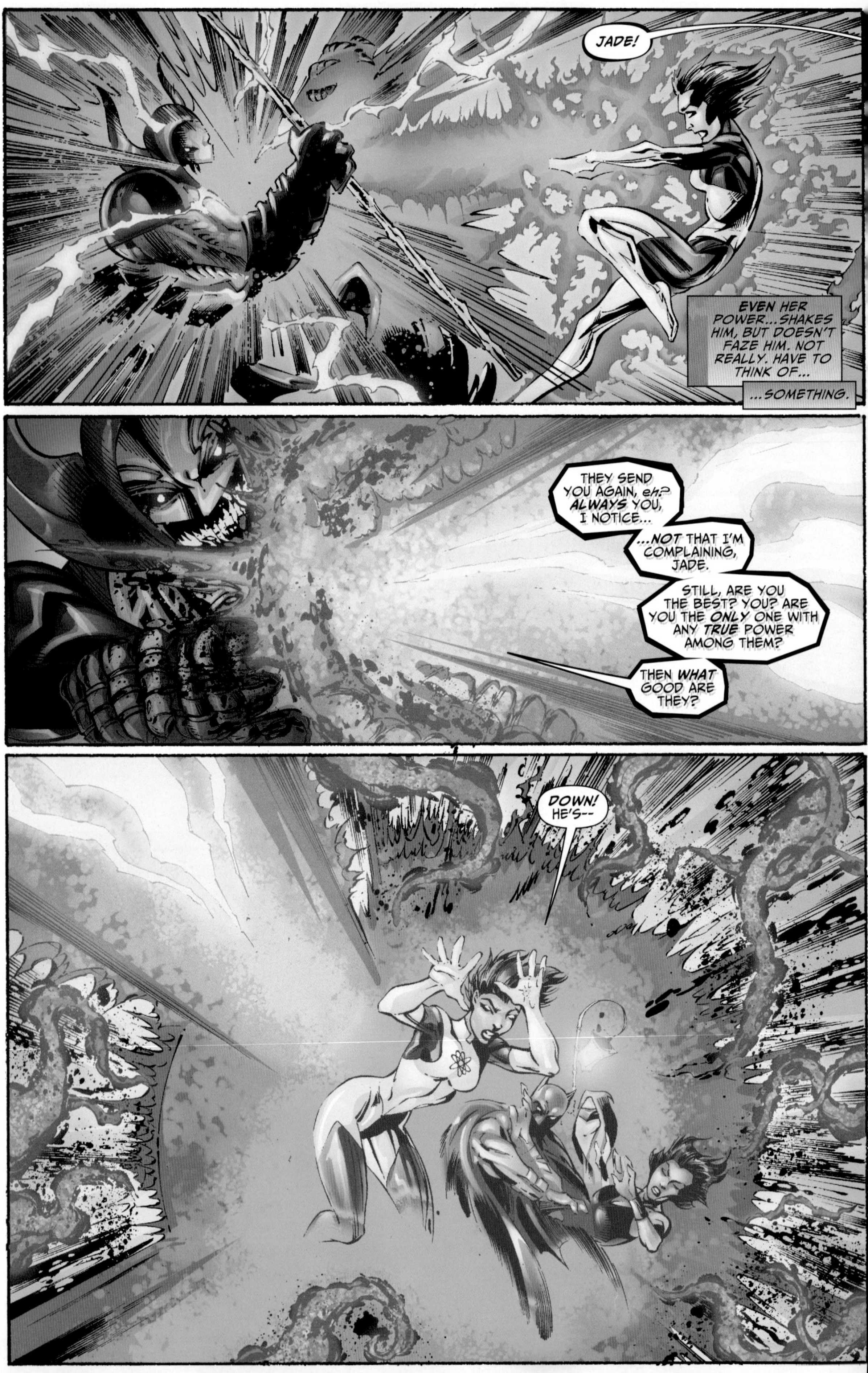
JADE!
EVEN HER POWER...SHAKES HIM, BUT DOESN'T FAZE HIM. NOT REALLY. HAVE TO THINK OF...
...SOMETHING.
THEY SEND YOU AGAIN, eh? ALWAYS YOU, I NOTICE...
...NOT THAT I'M COMPLAINING, JADE.
STILL, ARE YOU THE BEST? YOU? ARE YOU THE ONLY ONE WITH ANY TRUE POWER AMONG THEM?
THEN WHAT GOOD ARE THEY?
DOWN! HE'S--

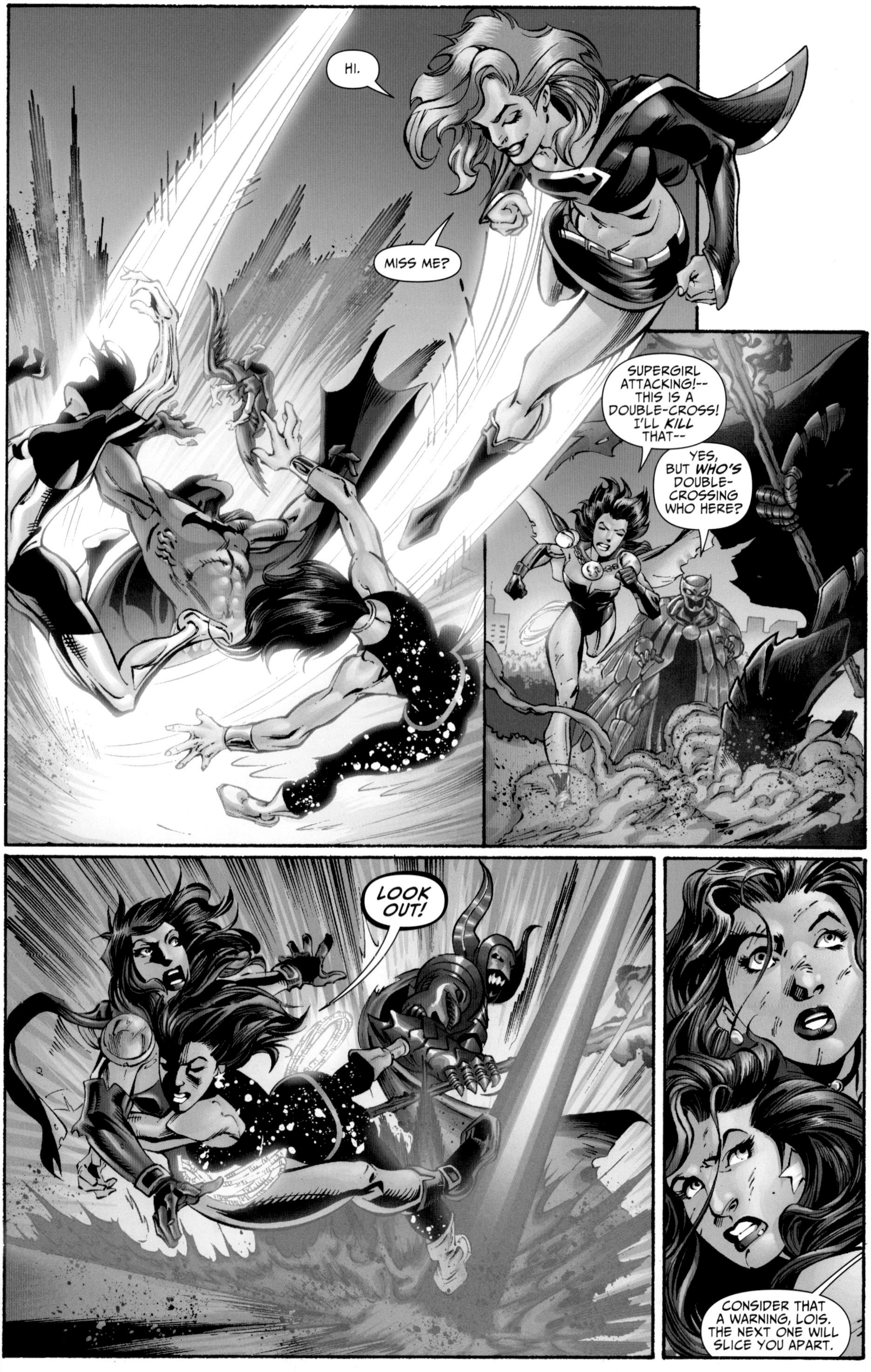
HI.
MISS ME?
SUPERGIRL ATTACKING!-- THIS IS A DOUBLE-CROSS! I'LL KILL THAT--
YES, BUT WHO'S DOUBLE-CROSSING WHO HERE?
LOOK OUT!
CONSIDER THAT A WARNING, LOIS. THE NEXT ONE WILL SLICE YOU APART.

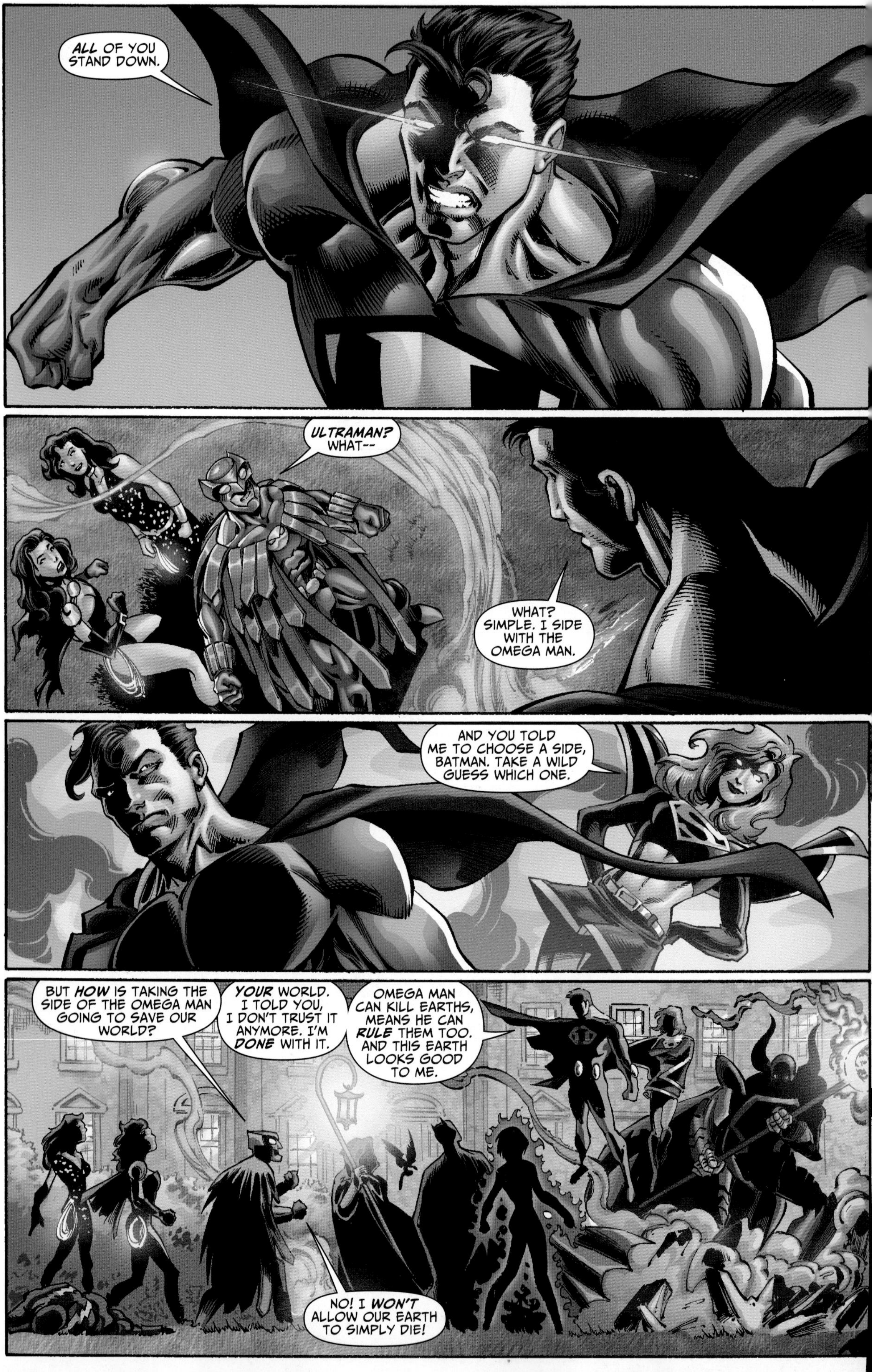
ALL OF YOU STAND DOWN.
ULTRAMAN? WHAT--
WHAT? SIMPLE. I SIDE WITH THE OMEGA MAN.
AND YOU TOLD ME TO CHOOSE A SIDE, BATMAN. TAKE A WILD GUESS WHICH ONE.
BUT HOW IS TAKING THE SIDE OF THE OMEGA MAN GOING TO SAVE OUR WORLD?
YOUR WORLD. I TOLD YOU, I DON'T TRUST IT ANYMORE. I'M DONE WITH IT.
OMEGA MAN CAN KILL EARTHS, MEANS HE CAN RULE THEM TOO. AND THIS EARTH LOOKS GOOD TO ME.
NO! I WON'T ALLOW OUR EARTH TO SIMPLY DIE!

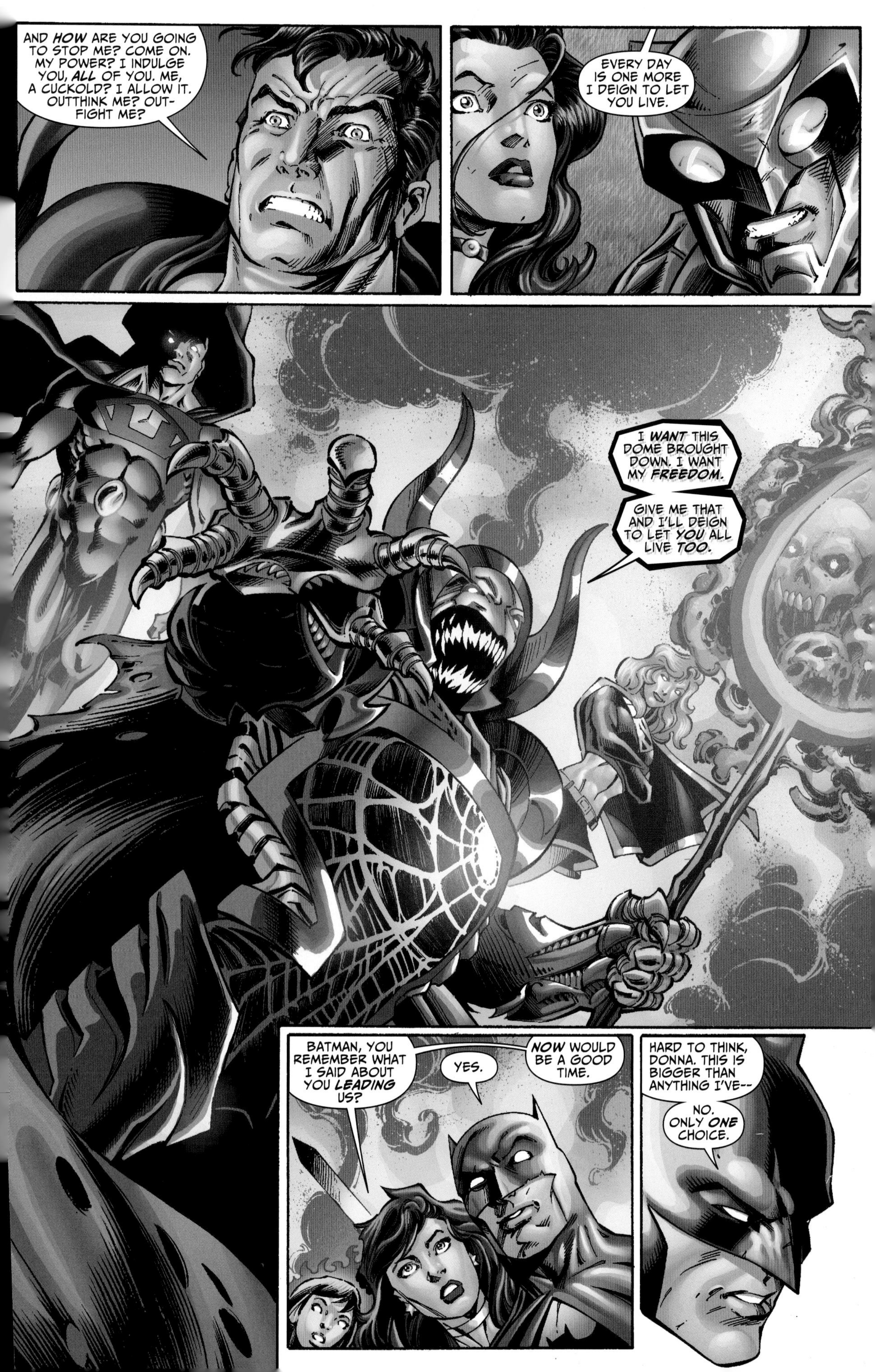
AND HOW ARE YOU GOING TO STOP ME? COME ON. MY POWER? I INDULGE YOU, ALL OF YOU. ME, A CUCKOLD? I ALLOW IT. OUTTHINK ME? OUT-FIGHT ME?
EVERY DAY IS ONE MORE I DEIGN TO LET YOU LIVE.
I WANT THIS DOME BROUGHT DOWN. I WANT MY FREEDOM.
GIVE ME THAT AND I'LL DEIGN TO LET YOU ALL LIVE TOO.
BATMAN, YOU REMEMBER WHAT I SAID ABOUT YOU LEADING US?
YES.
NOW WOULD BE A GOOD TIME.
HARD TO THINK, DONNA. THIS IS BIGGER THAN ANYTHING I'VE--
NO. ONLY ONE CHOICE.

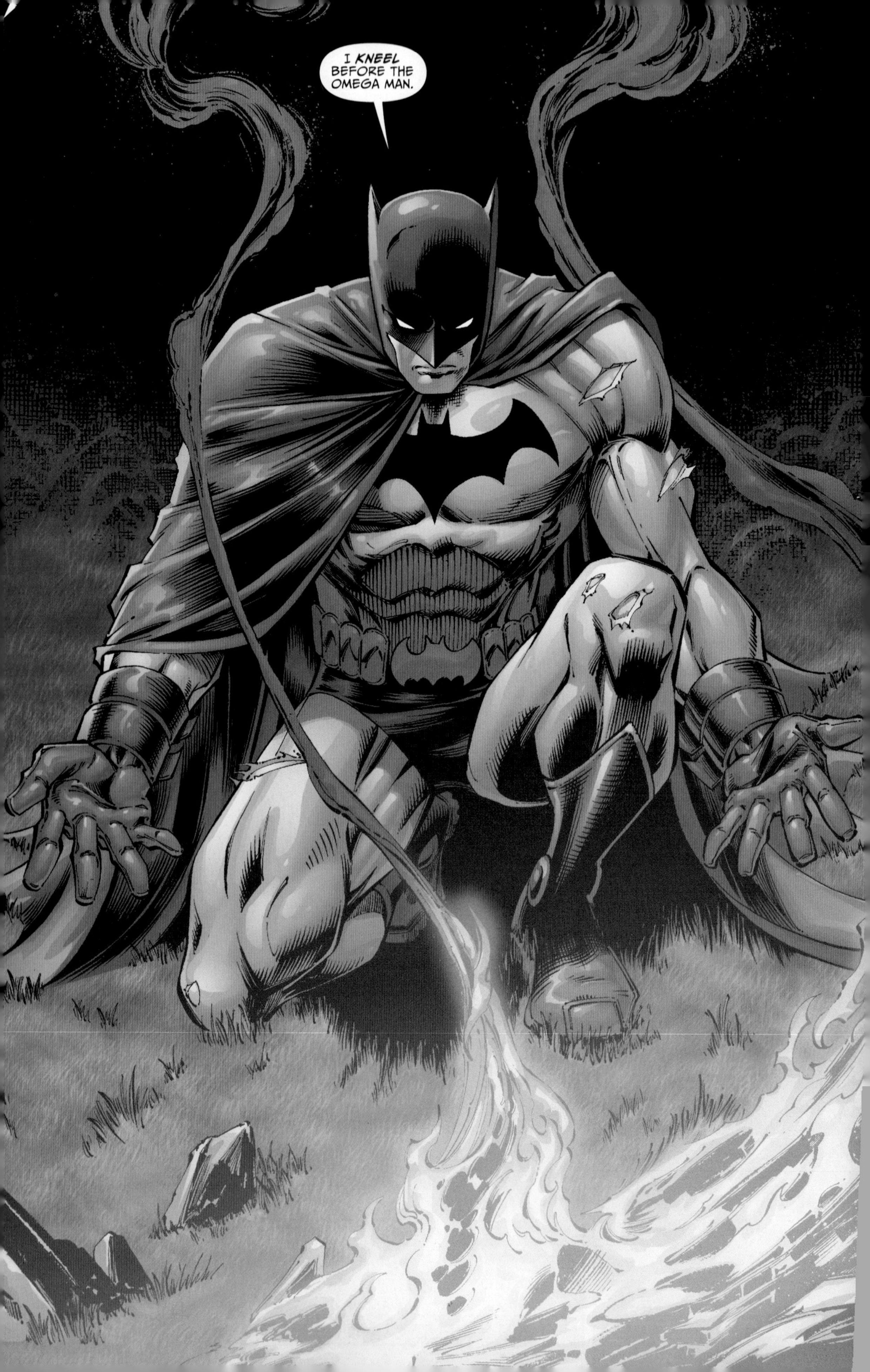
I KNEEL BEFORE THE OMEGA MAN.

STARMAN/CONGORILLA 1
cover by Gene Ha

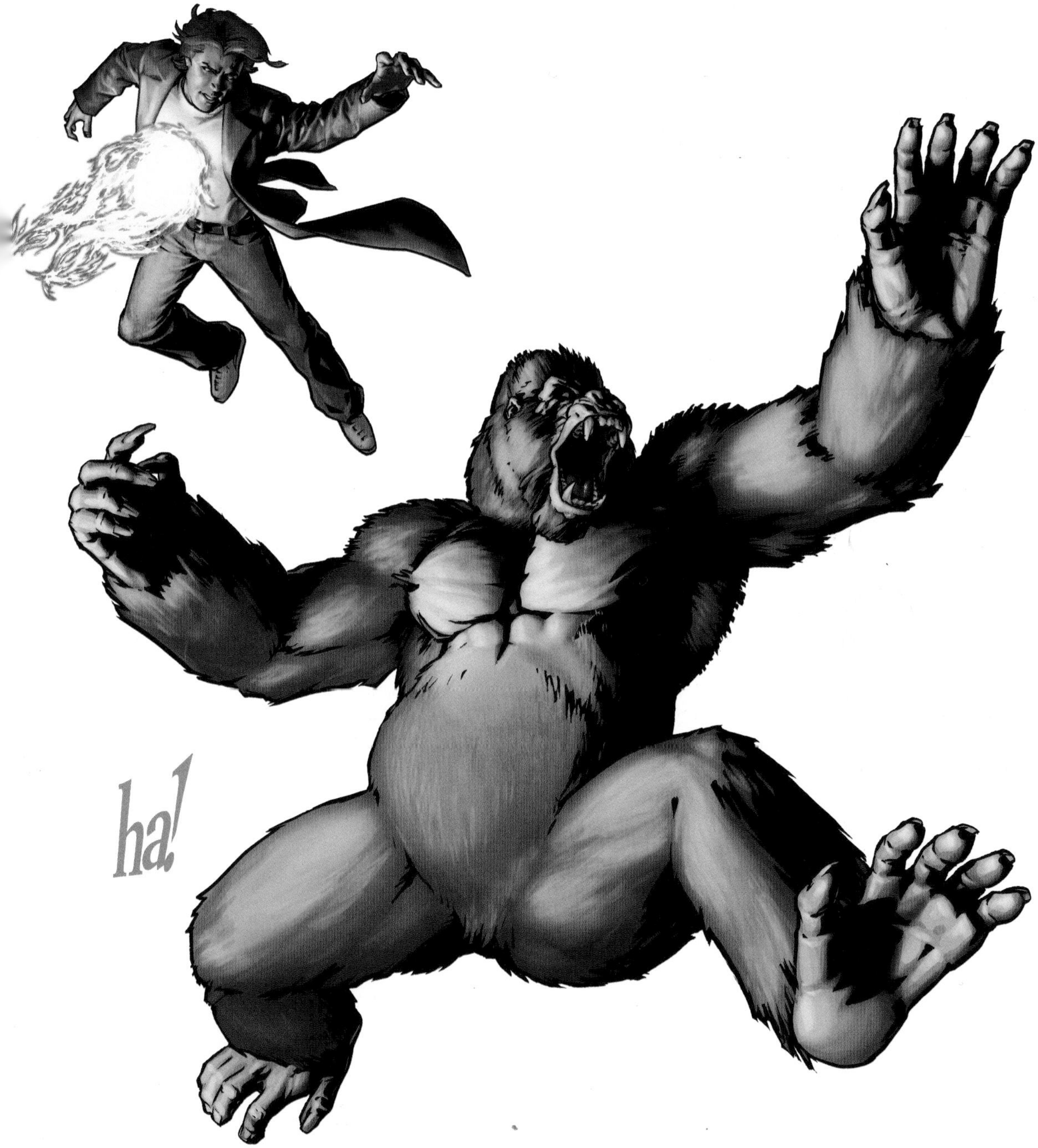
ha!

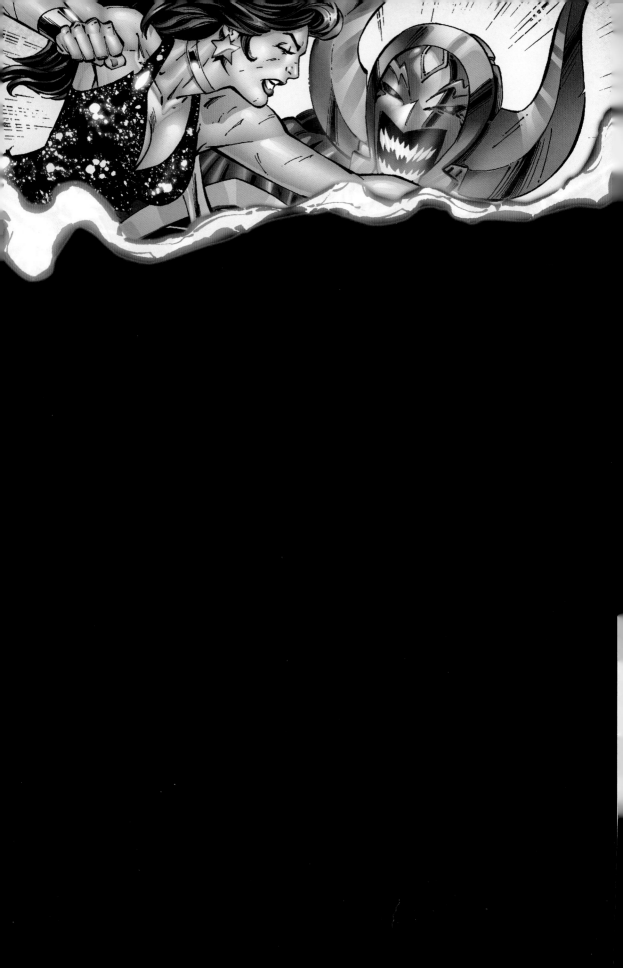

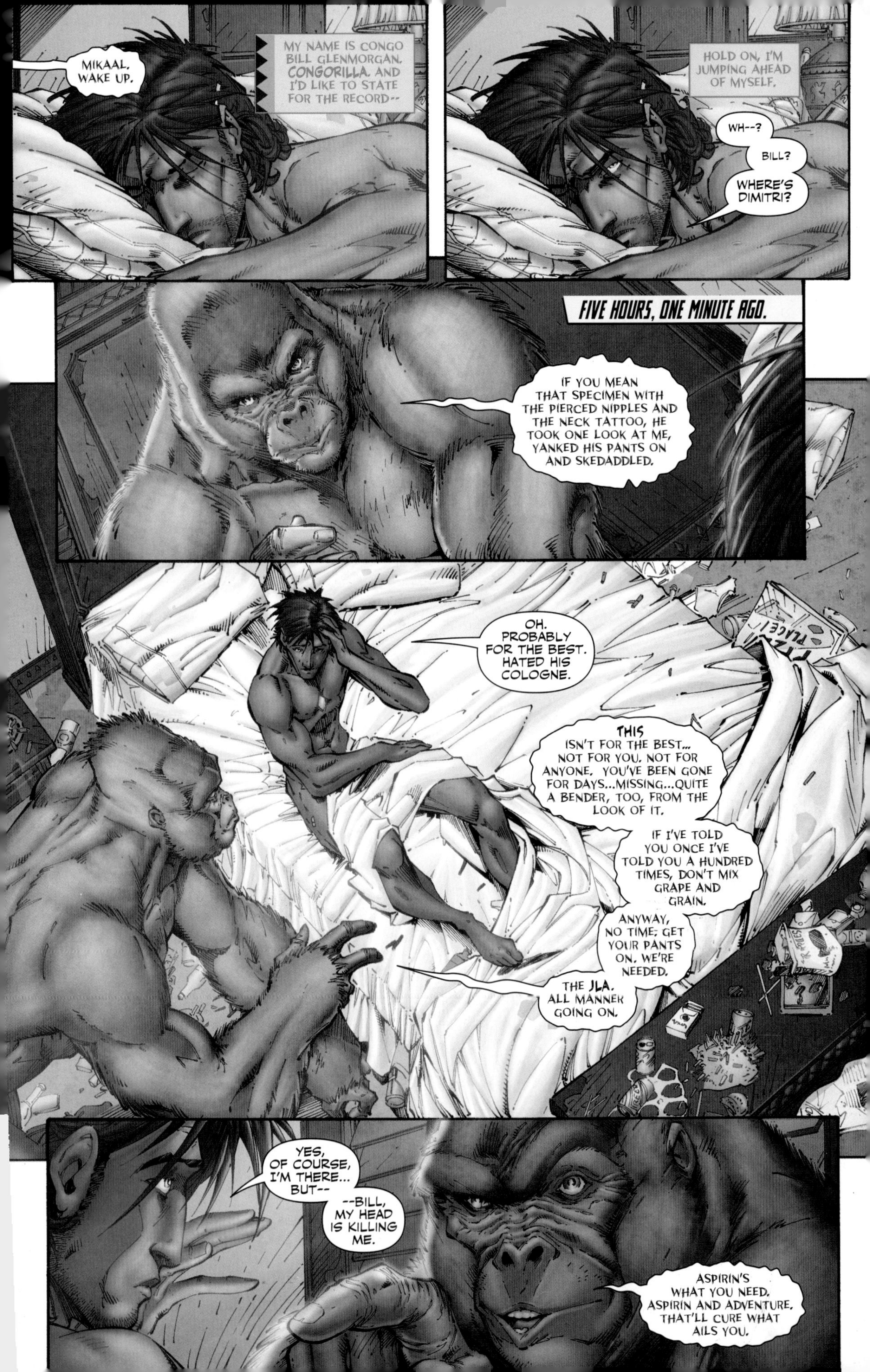
MIKAAL, WAKE UP.
MY NAME IS CONGO BILL GLENMORGAN. CONGORILLA. AND I'D LIKE TO STATE FOR THE RECORD--
HOLD ON, I'M JUMPING AHEAD OF MYSELF.
WH--?
BILL?
WHERE'S DIMITRI?
FIVE HOURS, ONE MINUTE AGO.
IF YOU MEAN THAT SPECIMEN WITH THE PIERCED NIPPLES AND THE NECK TATTOO, HE TOOK ONE LOOK AT ME, YANKED HIS PANTS ON AND SKEDADDLED.
OH. PROBABLY FOR THE BEST. HATED HIS COLOGNE.
THIS ISN'T FOR THE BEST... NOT FOR YOU. NOT FOR ANYONE. YOU'VE BEEN GONE FOR DAYS...MISSING...QUITE A BENDER, TOO, FROM THE LOOK OF IT.
IF I'VE TOLD YOU ONCE I'VE TOLD YOU A HUNDRED TIMES, DON'T MIX GRAPE AND GRAIN.
ANYWAY, NO TIME; GET YOUR PANTS ON. WE'RE NEEDED.
THE JLA. ALL MANNER GOING ON.
YES, OF COURSE, I'M THERE... BUT--
--BILL, MY HEAD IS KILLING ME.
ASPIRIN'S WHAT YOU NEED. ASPIRIN AND ADVENTURE. THAT'LL CURE WHAT AILS YOU.

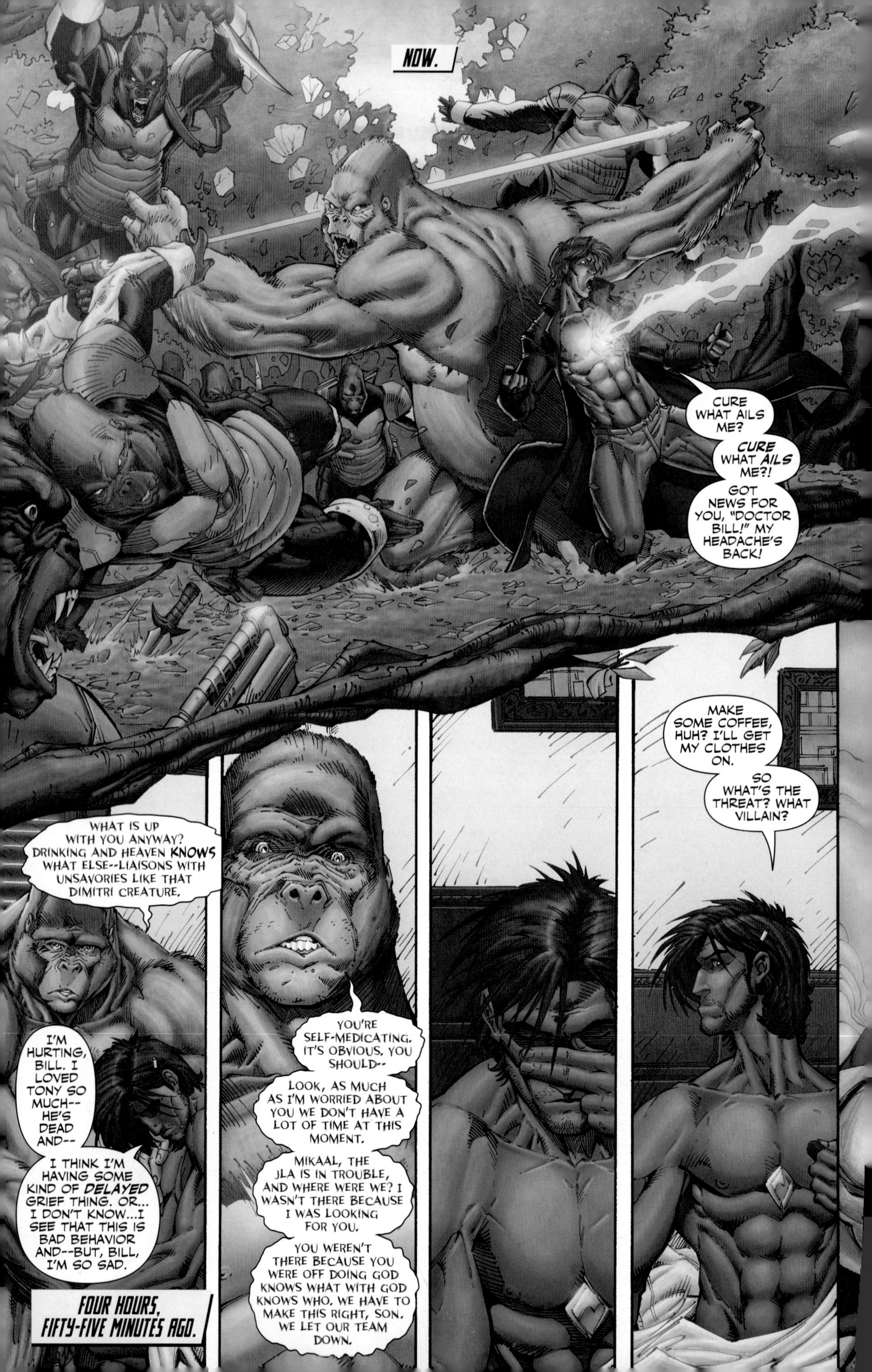
NOW.
CURE WHAT AILS ME?
CURE WHAT AILS ME?!
GOT NEWS FOR YOU, "DOCTOR BILL!" MY HEADACHE'S BACK!
FOUR HOURS, FIFTY-FIVE MINUTES AGO.
WHAT IS UP WITH YOU ANYWAY? DRINKING AND HEAVEN KNOWS WHAT ELSE--LIAISONS WITH UNSAVORIES LIKE THAT DIMITRI CREATURE.
I'M HURTING, BILL. I LOVED TONY SO MUCH-- HE'S DEAD AND--
I THINK I'M HAVING SOME KIND OF DELAYED GRIEF THING. OR... I DON'T KNOW...I SEE THAT THIS IS BAD BEHAVIOR AND--BUT, BILL, I'M SO SAD.
YOU'RE SELF-MEDICATING. IT'S OBVIOUS. YOU SHOULD--
LOOK, AS MUCH AS I'M WORRIED ABOUT YOU WE DON'T HAVE A LOT OF TIME AT THIS MOMENT.
MIKAAL, THE JLA IS IN TROUBLE, AND WHERE WERE WE? I WASN'T THERE BECAUSE I WAS LOOKING FOR YOU.
YOU WEREN'T THERE BECAUSE YOU WERE OFF DOING GOD KNOWS WHAT WITH GOD KNOWS WHO. WE HAVE TO MAKE THIS RIGHT, SON. WE LET OUR TEAM DOWN.
MAKE SOME COFFEE, HUH? I'LL GET MY CLOTHES ON.
SO WHAT'S THE THREAT? WHAT VILLAIN?

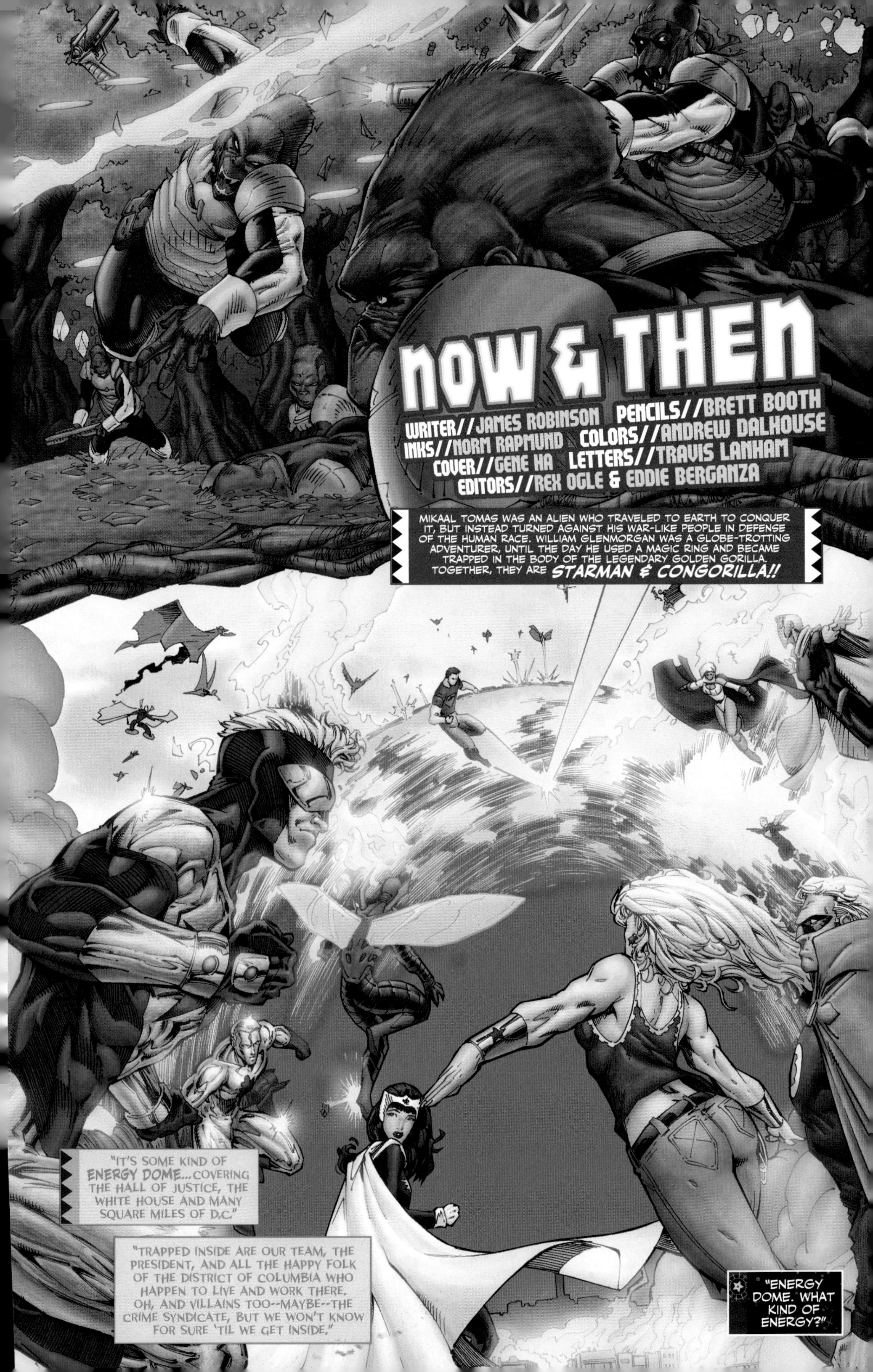
NOW & THEN
WRITER//JAMES ROBINSON PENCILS//BRETT BOOTH
INKS//NORM RAPMUND COLORS//ANDREW DALHOUSE
COVER//GENE HA LETTERS//TRAVIS LANHAM
EDITORS//REX OGLE & EDDIE BERGANZA
MIKAAL TOMAS WAS AN ALIEN WHO TRAVELED TO EARTH TO CONQUER IT, BUT INSTEAD TURNED AGAINST HIS WAR-LIKE PEOPLE IN DEFENSE OF THE HUMAN RACE. WILLIAM GLENMORGAN WAS A GLOBE-TROTTING ADVENTURER, UNTIL THE DAY HE USED A MAGIC RING AND BECAME TRAPPED IN THE BODY OF THE LEGENDARY GOLDEN GORILLA. TOGETHER, THEY ARE STARMAN & CONGORILLA!!
"IT'S SOME KIND OF ENERGY DOME...COVERING THE HALL OF JUSTICE, THE WHITE HOUSE AND MANY SQUARE MILES OF D.C."
"TRAPPED INSIDE ARE OUR TEAM, THE PRESIDENT, AND ALL THE HAPPY FOLK OF THE DISTRICT OF COLUMBIA WHO HAPPEN TO LIVE AND WORK THERE. OH, AND VILLAINS TOO--MAYBE--THE CRIME SYNDICATE, BUT WE WON'T KNOW FOR SURE 'TIL WE GET INSIDE."
"ENERGY DOME. WHAT KIND OF ENERGY?"

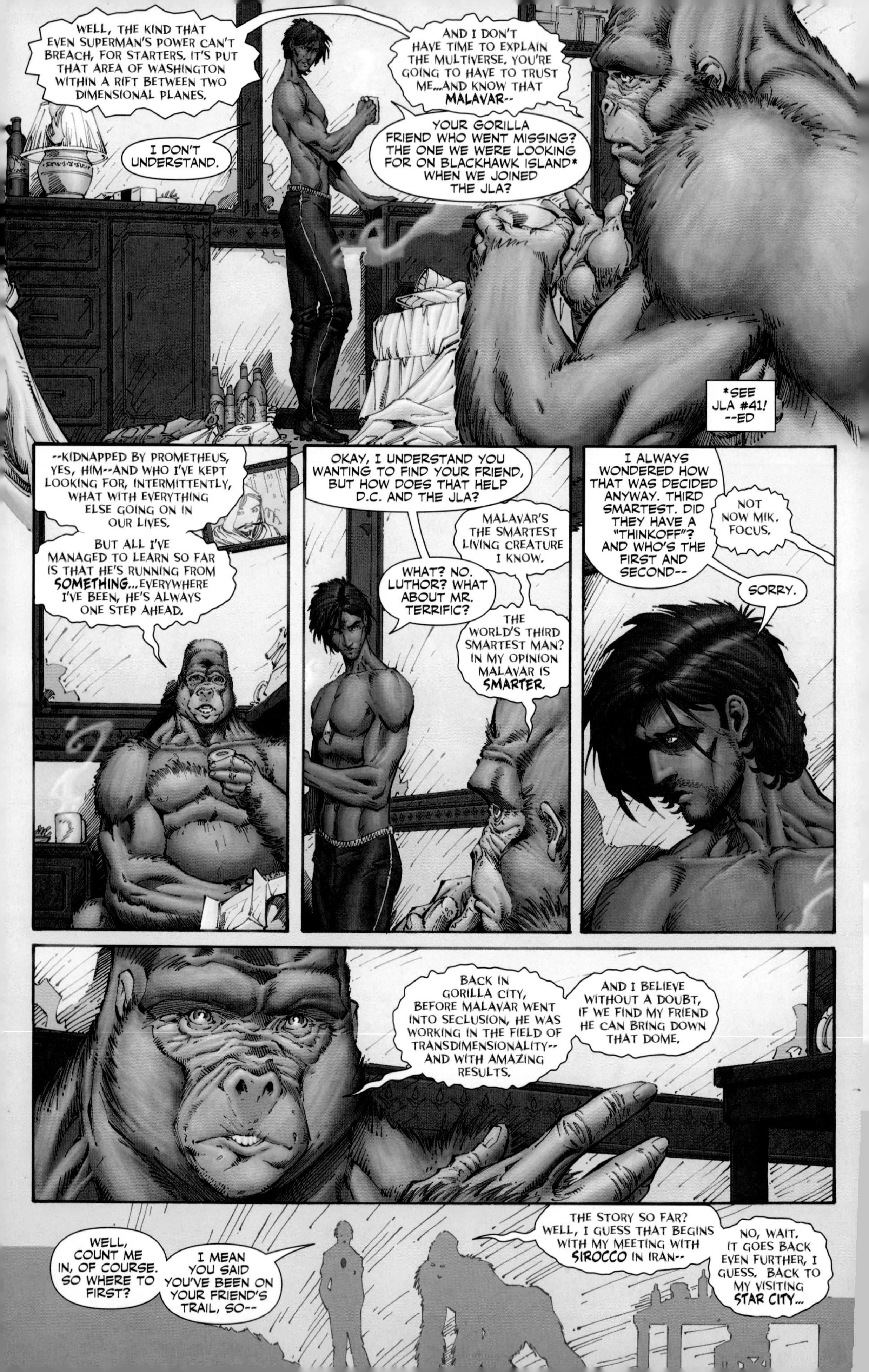
WELL, THE KIND THAT EVEN SUPERMAN'S POWER CAN'T BREACH, FOR STARTERS. IT'S PUT THAT AREA OF WASHINGTON WITHIN A RIFT BETWEEN TWO DIMENSIONAL PLANES.
AND I DON'T HAVE TIME TO EXPLAIN THE MULTIVERSE. YOU'RE GOING TO HAVE TO TRUST ME...AND KNOW THAT MALAVAR--
I DON'T UNDERSTAND.
YOUR GORILLA FRIEND WHO WENT MISSING? THE ONE WE WERE LOOKING FOR ON BLACKHAWK ISLAND* WHEN WE JOINED THE JLA?
*SEE JLA #41! --ED
--KIDNAPPED BY PROMETHEUS, YES, HIM--AND WHO I'VE KEPT LOOKING FOR, INTERMITTENTLY, WHAT WITH EVERYTHING ELSE GOING ON IN OUR LIVES.
BUT ALL I'VE MANAGED TO LEARN SO FAR IS THAT HE'S RUNNING FROM SOMETHING...EVERYWHERE I'VE BEEN, HE'S ALWAYS ONE STEP AHEAD.
OKAY, I UNDERSTAND YOU WANTING TO FIND YOUR FRIEND, BUT HOW DOES THAT HELP D.C. AND THE JLA?
MALAVAR'S THE SMARTEST LIVING CREATURE I KNOW.
WHAT? NO. LUTHOR? WHAT ABOUT MR. TERRIFIC?
THE WORLD'S THIRD SMARTEST MAN? IN MY OPINION MALAVAR IS SMARTER.
I ALWAYS WONDERED HOW THAT WAS DECIDED ANYWAY. THIRD SMARTEST. DID THEY HAVE A "THINKOFF"? AND WHO'S THE FIRST AND SECOND--
NOT NOW MIK. FOCUS.
SORRY.
BACK IN GORILLA CITY, BEFORE MALAVAR WENT INTO SECLUSION, HE WAS WORKING IN THE FIELD OF TRANSDIMENSIONALITY--AND WITH AMAZING RESULTS.
AND I BELIEVE WITHOUT A DOUBT, IF WE FIND MY FRIEND HE CAN BRING DOWN THAT DOME.
WELL, COUNT ME IN, OF COURSE. SO WHERE TO FIRST?
I MEAN YOU SAID YOU'VE BEEN ON YOUR FRIEND'S TRAIL, SO--
THE STORY SO FAR? WELL, I GUESS THAT BEGINS WITH MY MEETING WITH SIROCCO IN IRAN--
NO, WAIT. IT GOES BACK EVEN FURTHER, I GUESS. BACK TO MY VISITING STAR CITY...

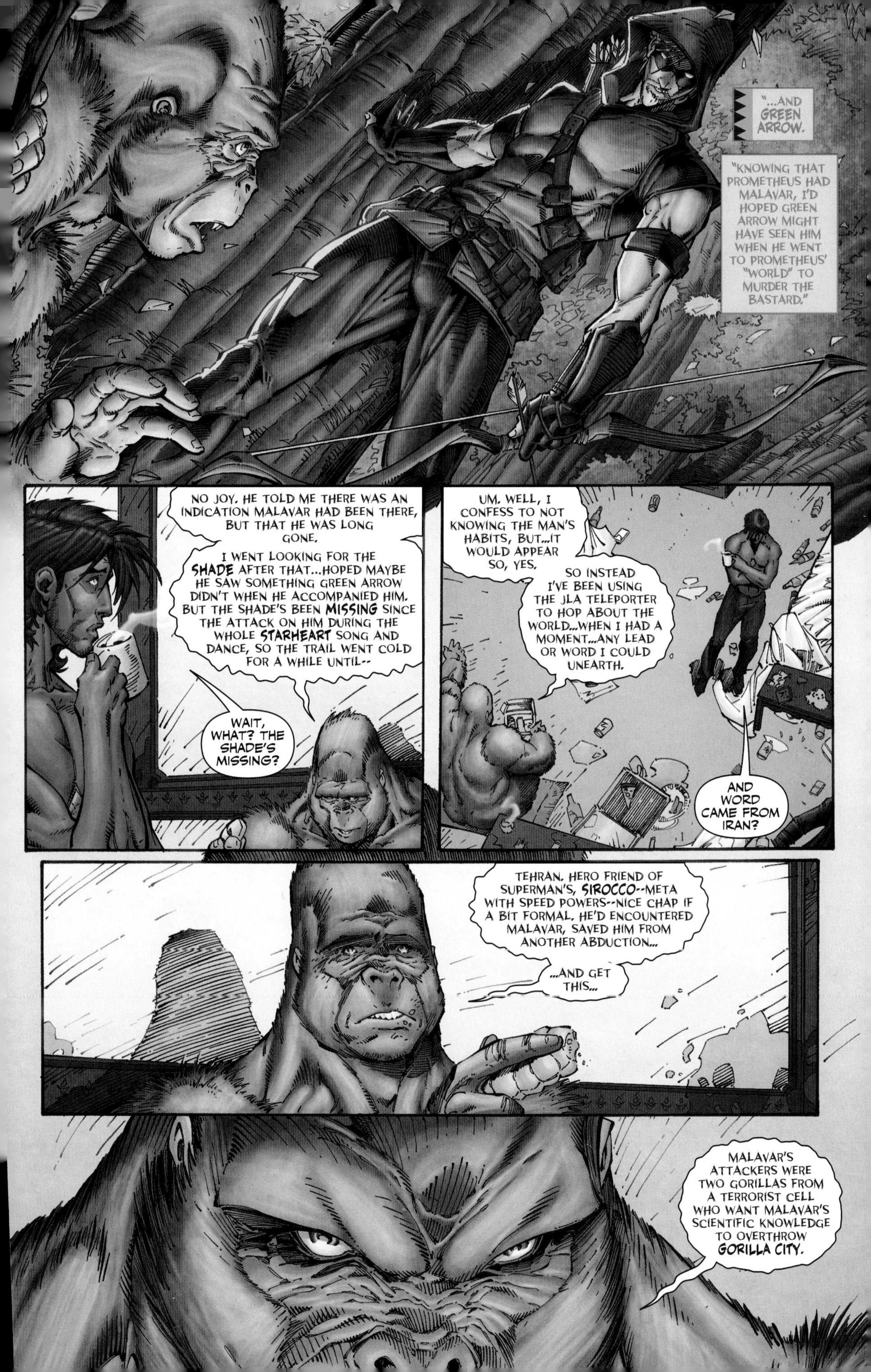
"...AND GREEN ARROW.
"KNOWING THAT PROMETHEUS HAD MALAVAR, I'D HOPED GREEN ARROW MIGHT HAVE SEEN HIM WHEN HE WENT TO PROMETHEUS' "WORLD" TO MURDER THE BASTARD."
NO JOY. HE TOLD ME THERE WAS AN INDICATION MALAVAR HAD BEEN THERE, BUT THAT HE WAS LONG GONE.
I WENT LOOKING FOR THE SHADE AFTER THAT...HOPED MAYBE HE SAW SOMETHING GREEN ARROW DIDN'T WHEN HE ACCOMPANIED HIM. BUT THE SHADE'S BEEN MISSING SINCE THE ATTACK ON HIM DURING THE WHOLE STARHEART SONG AND DANCE, SO THE TRAIL WENT COLD FOR A WHILE UNTIL--
WAIT, WHAT? THE SHADE'S MISSING?
UM, WELL, I CONFESS TO NOT KNOWING THE MAN'S HABITS, BUT...IT WOULD APPEAR SO, YES.
SO INSTEAD I'VE BEEN USING THE JLA TELEPORTER TO HOP ABOUT THE WORLD...WHEN I HAD A MOMENT...ANY LEAD OR WORD I COULD UNEARTH.
AND WORD CAME FROM IRAN?
TEHRAN. HERO FRIEND OF SUPERMAN'S, SIROCCO--META WITH SPEED POWERS--NICE CHAP IF A BIT FORMAL. HE'D ENCOUNTERED MALAVAR, SAVED HIM FROM ANOTHER ABDUCTION...
...AND GET THIS...
MALAVAR'S ATTACKERS WERE TWO GORILLAS FROM A TERRORIST CELL WHO WANT MALAVAR'S SCIENTIFIC KNOWLEDGE TO OVERTHROW GORILLA CITY.

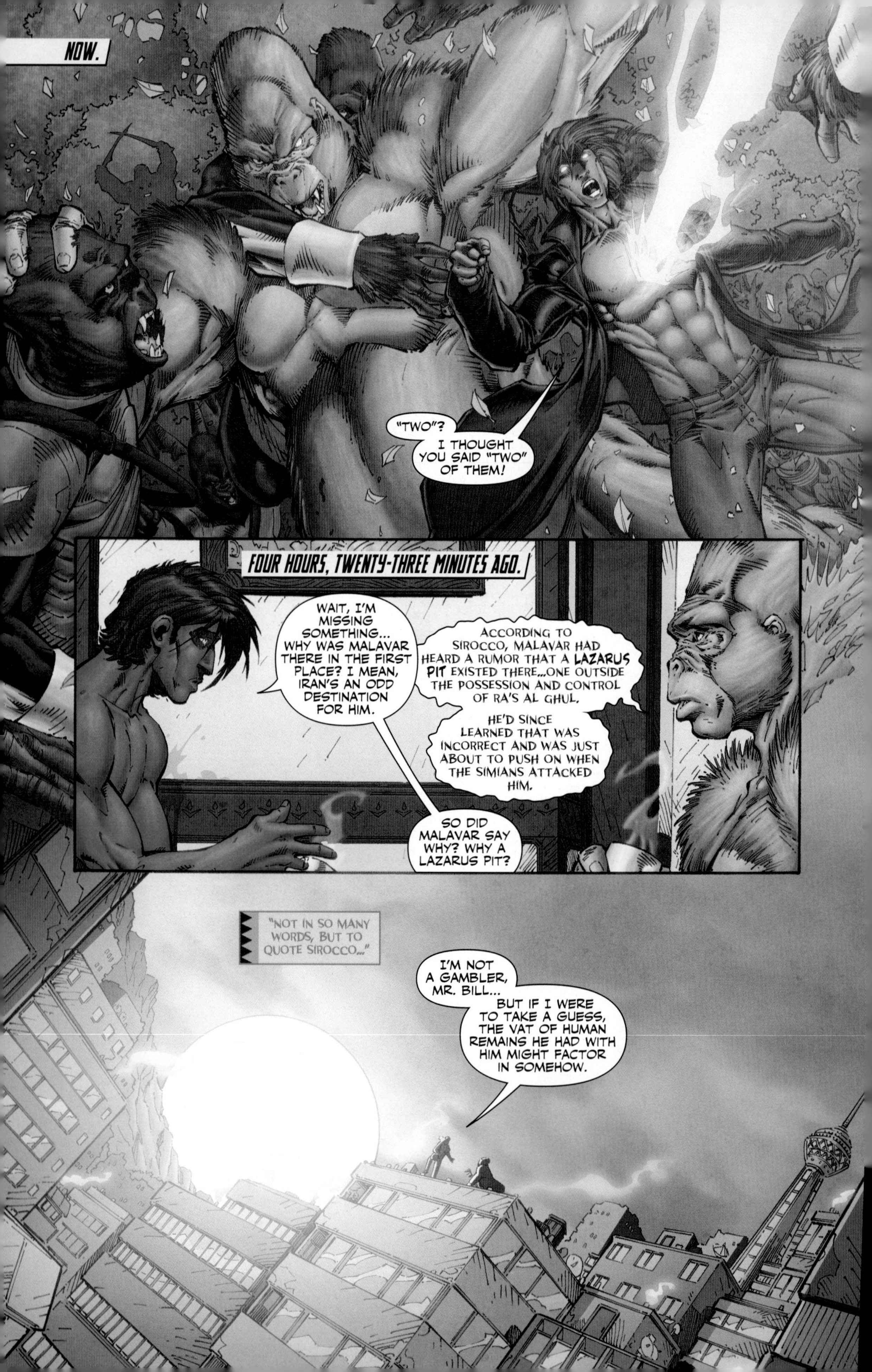
NOW.
"TWO"? I THOUGHT YOU SAID "TWO" OF THEM!
FOUR HOURS, TWENTY-THREE MINUTES AGO.
WAIT, I'M MISSING SOMETHING... WHY WAS MALAVAR THERE IN THE FIRST PLACE? I MEAN, IRAN'S AN ODD DESTINATION FOR HIM.
ACCORDING TO SIROCCO, MALAVAR HAD HEARD A RUMOR THAT A LAZARUS PIT EXISTED THERE...ONE OUTSIDE THE POSSESSION AND CONTROL OF RA'S AL GHUL.
HE'D SINCE LEARNED THAT WAS INCORRECT AND WAS JUST ABOUT TO PUSH ON WHEN THE SIMIANS ATTACKED HIM.
SO DID MALAVAR SAY WHY? WHY A LAZARUS PIT?
"NOT IN SO MANY WORDS, BUT TO QUOTE SIROCCO..."
I'M NOT A GAMBLER, MR. BILL...
BUT IF I WERE TO TAKE A GUESS, THE VAT OF HUMAN REMAINS HE HAD WITH HIM MIGHT FACTOR IN SOMEHOW.

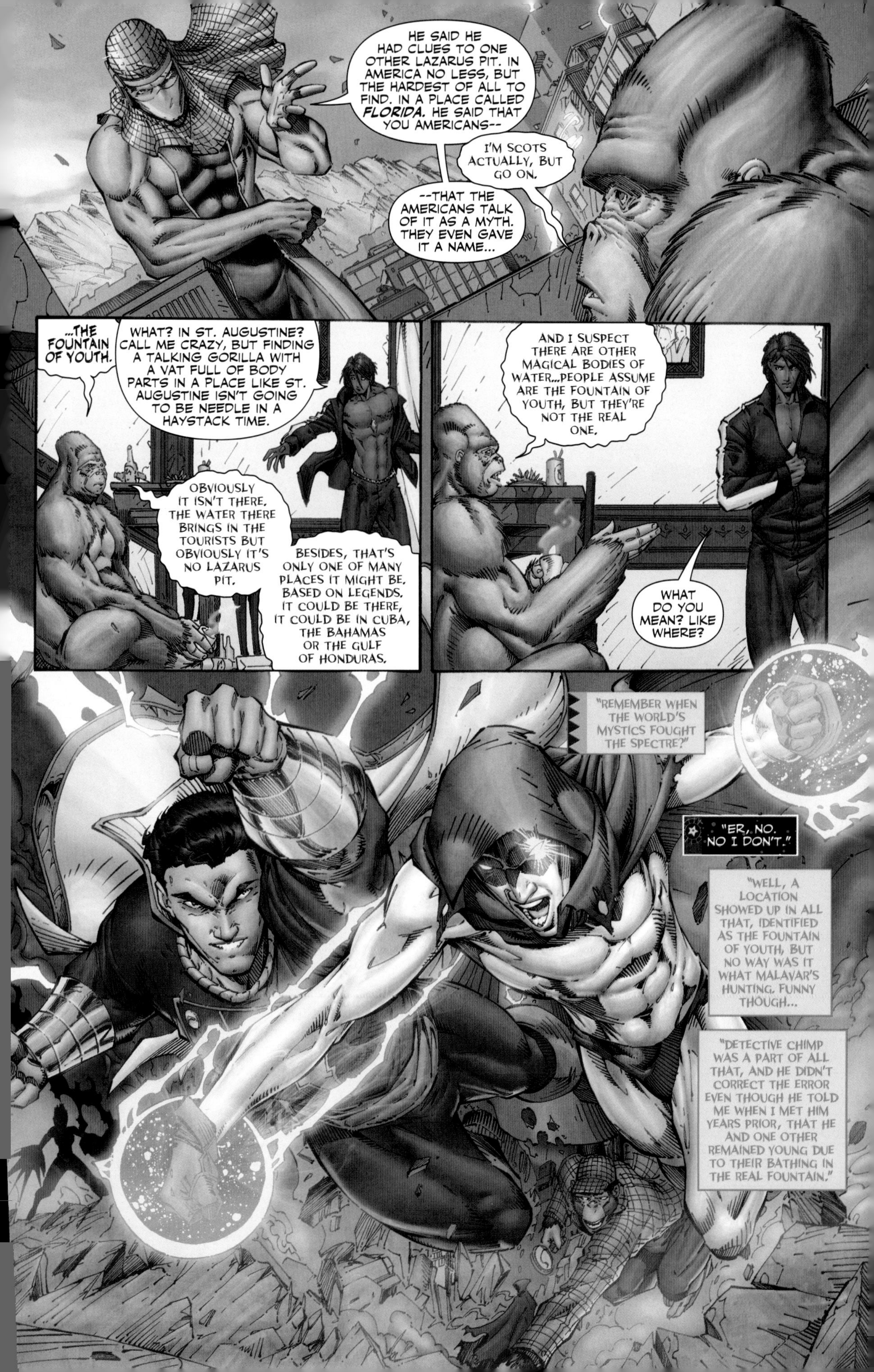
HE SAID HE HAD CLUES TO ONE OTHER LAZARUS PIT. IN AMERICA NO LESS, BUT THE HARDEST OF ALL TO FIND. IN A PLACE CALLED FLORIDA. HE SAID THAT YOU AMERICANS--
I'M SCOTS ACTUALLY, BUT GO ON.
--THAT THE AMERICANS TALK OF IT AS A MYTH. THEY EVEN GAVE IT A NAME...
...THE FOUNTAIN OF YOUTH.
WHAT? IN ST. AUGUSTINE? CALL ME CRAZY, BUT FINDING A TALKING GORILLA WITH A VAT FULL OF BODY PARTS IN A PLACE LIKE ST. AUGUSTINE ISN'T GOING TO BE NEEDLE IN A HAYSTACK TIME.
OBVIOUSLY IT ISN'T THERE. THE WATER THERE BRINGS IN THE TOURISTS BUT OBVIOUSLY IT'S NO LAZARUS PIT.
BESIDES, THAT'S ONLY ONE OF MANY PLACES IT MIGHT BE, BASED ON LEGENDS. IT COULD BE THERE, IT COULD BE IN CUBA, THE BAHAMAS OR THE GULF OF HONDURAS.
AND I SUSPECT THERE ARE OTHER MAGICAL BODIES OF WATER...PEOPLE ASSUME ARE THE FOUNTAIN OF YOUTH, BUT THEY'RE NOT THE REAL ONE.
WHAT DO YOU MEAN? LIKE WHERE?
"REMEMBER WHEN THE WORLD'S MYSTICS FOUGHT THE SPECTRE?"
"ER, NO. NO I DON'T."
"WELL, A LOCATION SHOWED UP IN ALL THAT, IDENTIFIED AS THE FOUNTAIN OF YOUTH, BUT NO WAY WAS IT WHAT MALAVAR'S HUNTING. FUNNY THOUGH...
"DETECTIVE CHIMP WAS A PART OF ALL THAT, AND HE DIDN'T CORRECT THE ERROR EVEN THOUGH HE TOLD ME WHEN I MET HIM YEARS PRIOR, THAT HE AND ONE OTHER REMAINED YOUNG DUE TO THEIR BATHING IN THE REAL FOUNTAIN."

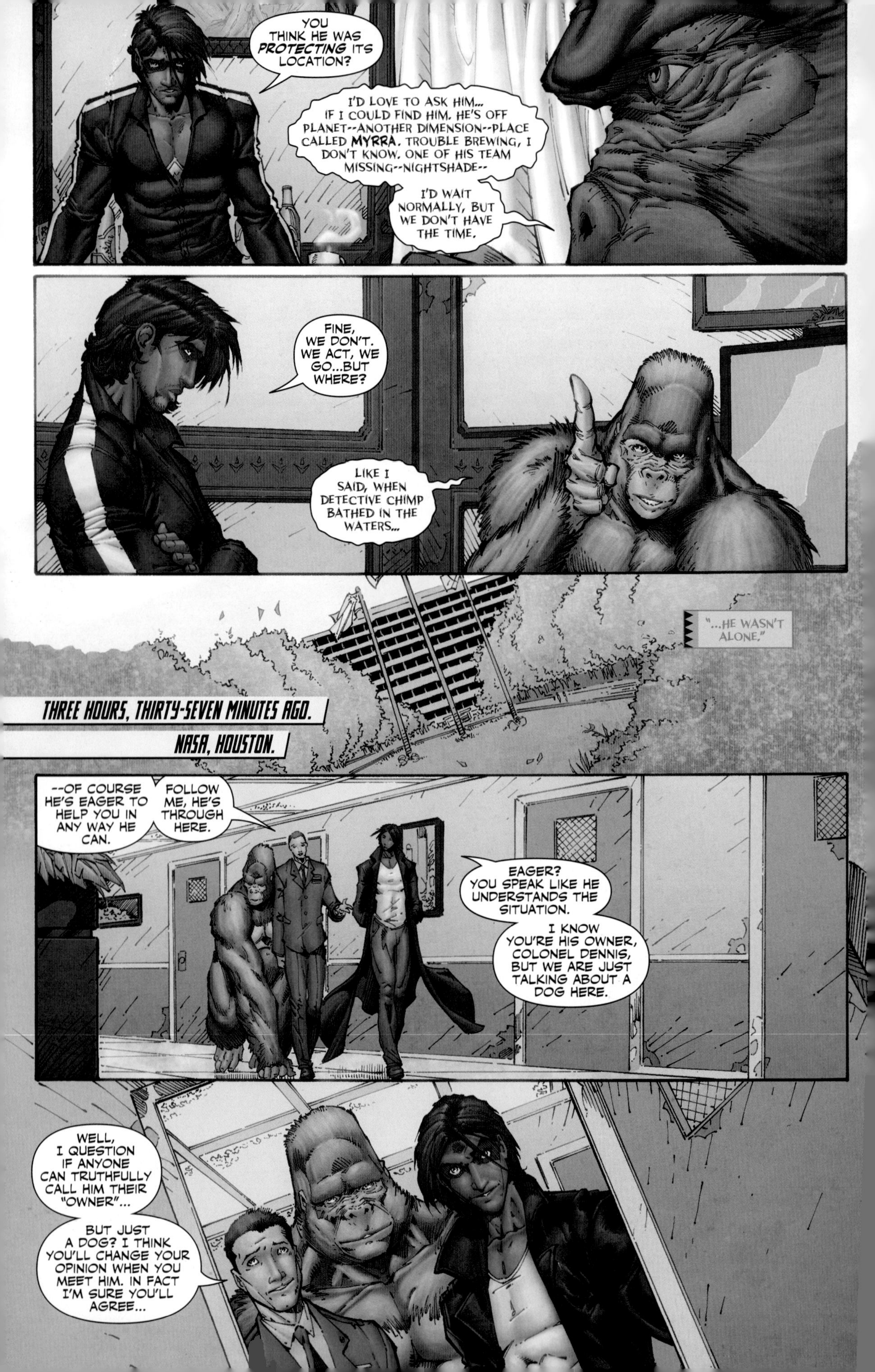
YOU THINK HE WAS PROTECTING ITS LOCATION?
I'D LOVE TO ASK HIM... IF I COULD FIND HIM. HE'S OFF PLANET--ANOTHER DIMENSION--PLACE CALLED MYRRA. TROUBLE BREWING, I DON'T KNOW. ONE OF HIS TEAM MISSING--NIGHTSHADE--
I'D WAIT NORMALLY, BUT WE DON'T HAVE THE TIME.
FINE, WE DON'T. WE ACT, WE GO...BUT WHERE?
LIKE I SAID, WHEN DETECTIVE CHIMP BATHED IN THE WATERS...
"...HE WASN'T ALONE."
THREE HOURS, THIRTY-SEVEN MINUTES AGO.
NASA, HOUSTON.
--OF COURSE HE'S EAGER TO HELP YOU IN ANY WAY HE CAN.
FOLLOW ME, HE'S THROUGH HERE.
EAGER? YOU SPEAK LIKE HE UNDERSTANDS THE SITUATION.
I KNOW YOU'RE HIS OWNER, COLONEL DENNIS, BUT WE ARE JUST TALKING ABOUT A DOG HERE.
WELL, I QUESTION IF ANYONE CAN TRUTHFULLY CALL HIM THEIR "OWNER"...
BUT JUST A DOG? I THINK YOU'LL CHANGE YOUR OPINION WHEN YOU MEET HIM. IN FACT I'M SURE YOU'LL AGREE...

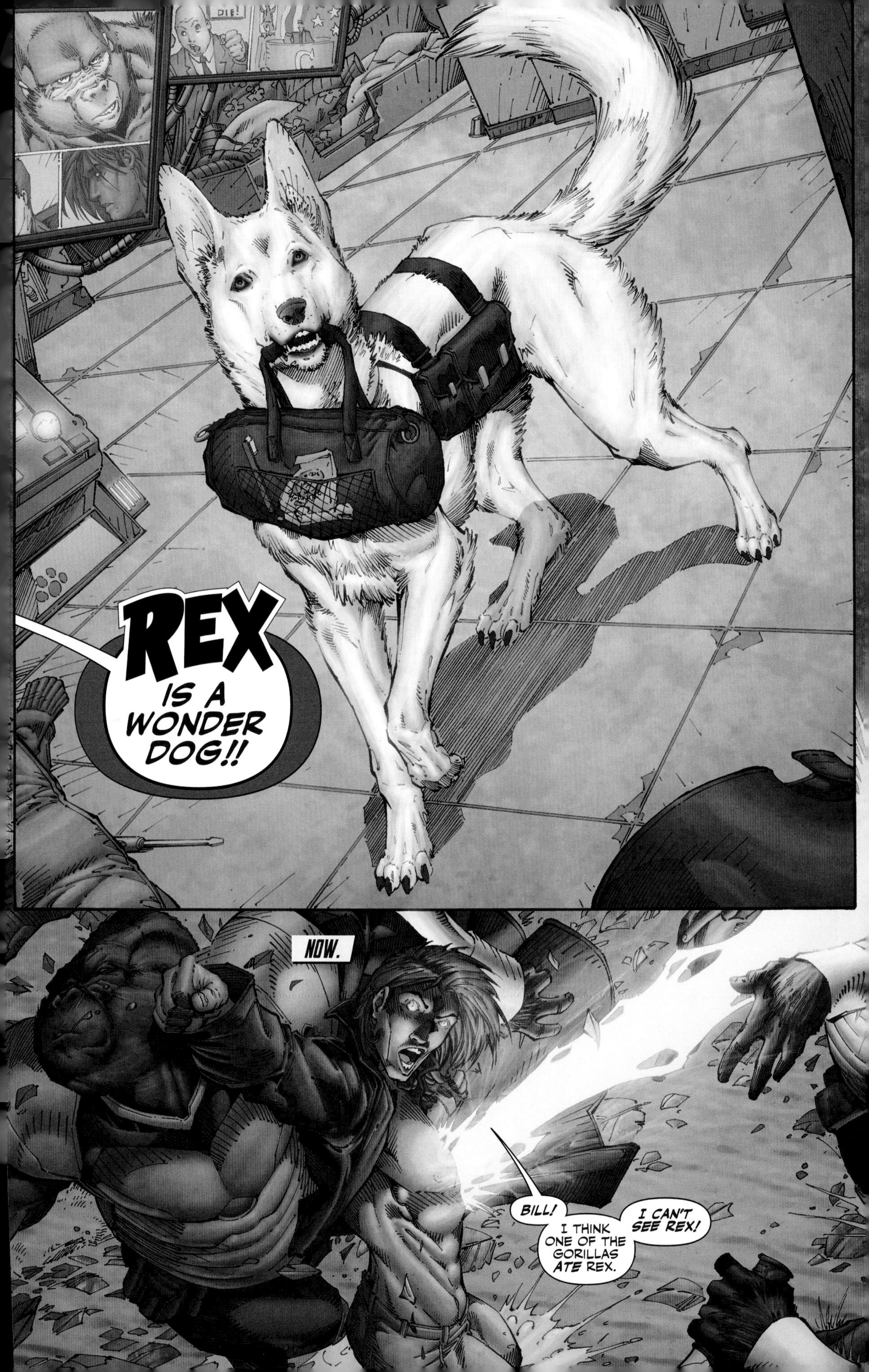
REX IS A WONDER DOG!!
NOW.
BILL!
I THINK ONE OF THE GORILLAS ATE REX.
I CAN'T SEE REX!

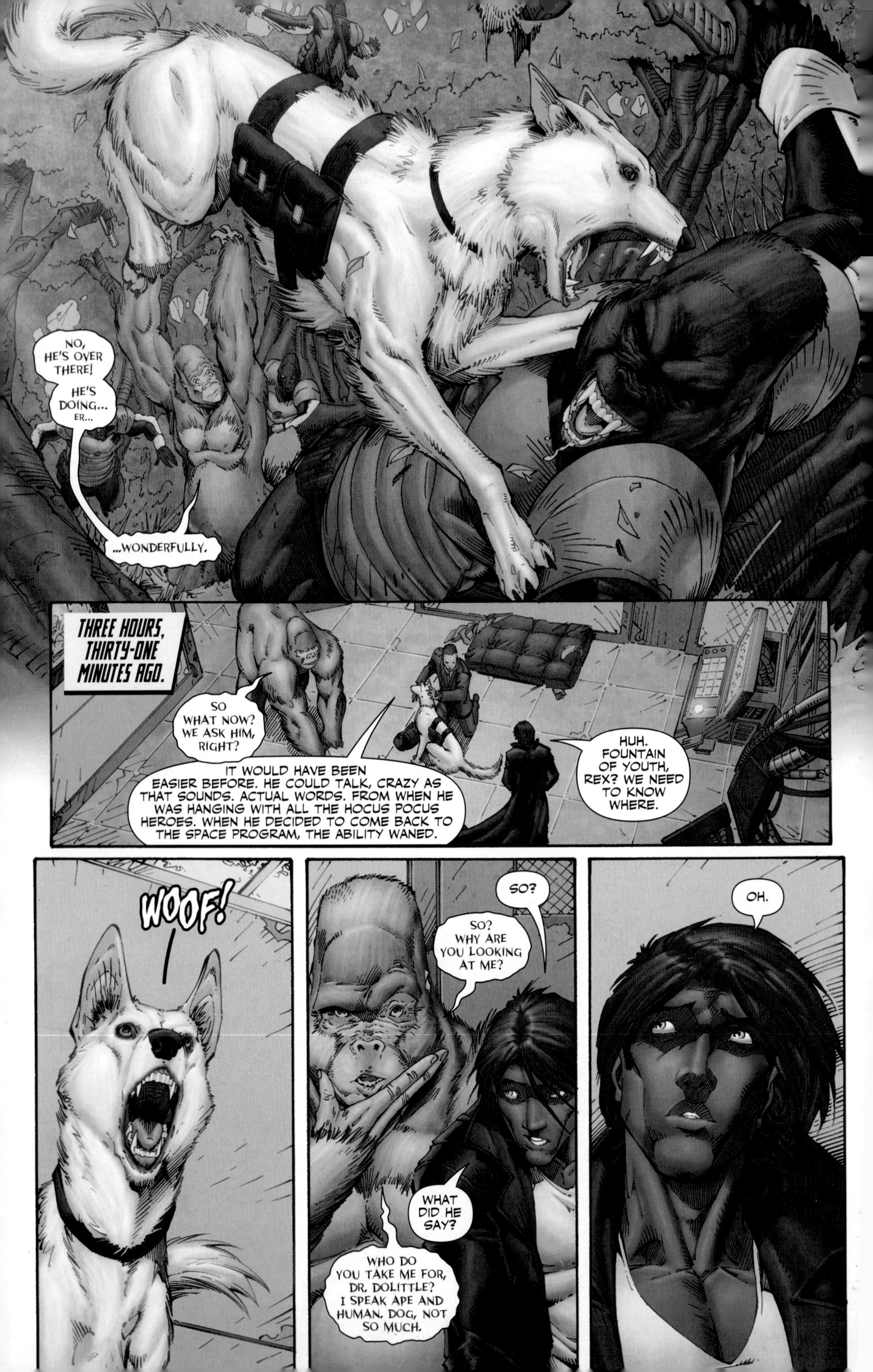
NO, HE'S OVER THERE!
HE'S DOING... ER...
...WONDERFULLY.
THREE HOURS, THIRTY-ONE MINUTES AGO.
SO WHAT NOW? WE ASK HIM, RIGHT?
IT WOULD HAVE BEEN EASIER BEFORE. HE COULD TALK, CRAZY AS THAT SOUNDS. ACTUAL WORDS. FROM WHEN HE WAS HANGING WITH ALL THE HOCUS POCUS HEROES. WHEN HE DECIDED TO COME BACK TO THE SPACE PROGRAM, THE ABILITY WANED.
HUH. FOUNTAIN OF YOUTH, REX? WE NEED TO KNOW WHERE.
WOOF!
SO?
SO? WHY ARE YOU LOOKING AT ME?
WHAT DID HE SAY?
WHO DO YOU TAKE ME FOR, DR. DOLITTLE? I SPEAK APE AND HUMAN. DOG, NOT SO MUCH.
OH.

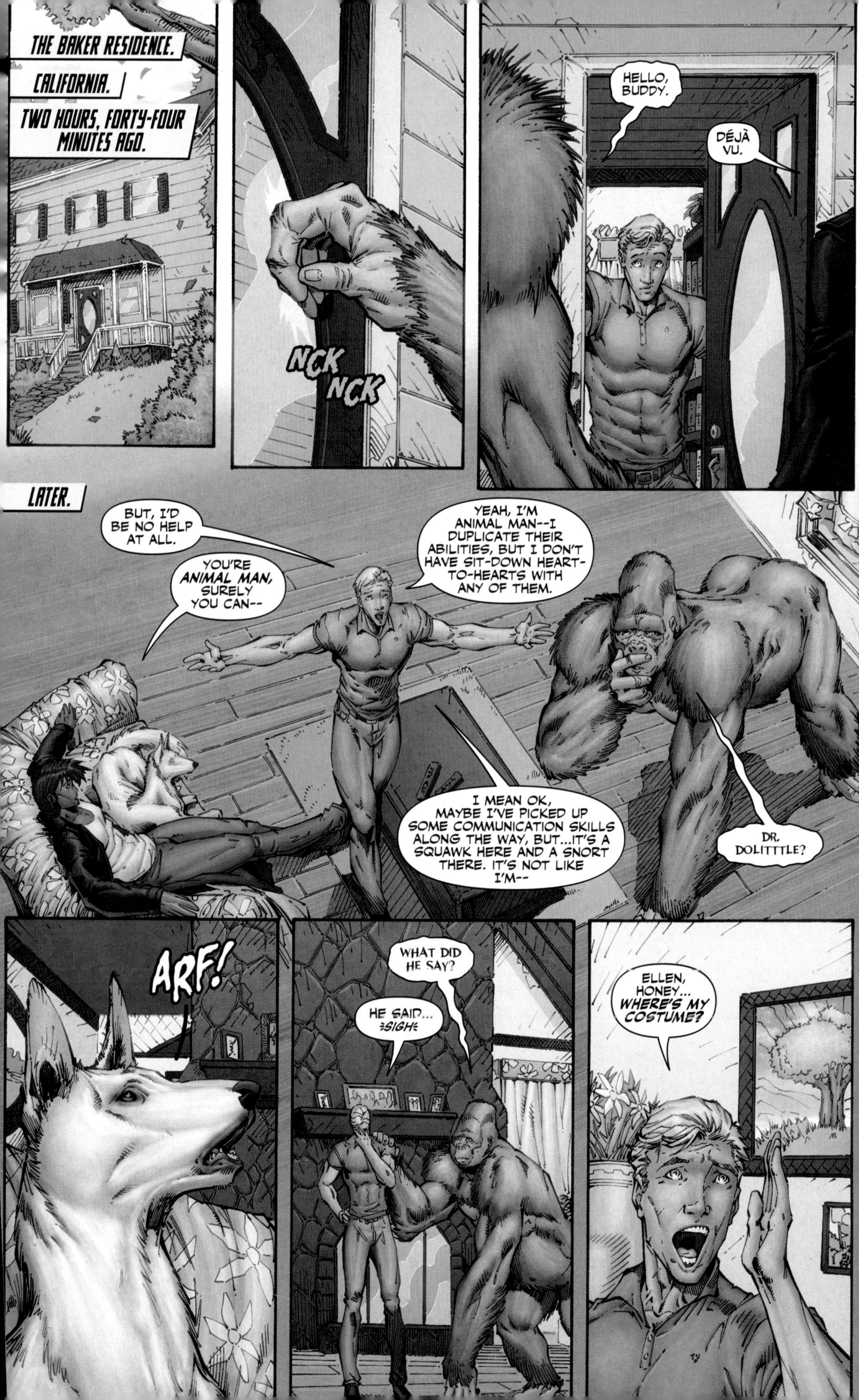
THE BAKER RESIDENCE.
CALIFORNIA.
TWO HOURS, FORTY-FOUR MINUTES AGO.
NCK NCK
HELLO, BUDDY.
DÉJÀ VU.
LATER.
BUT, I'D BE NO HELP AT ALL.
YOU'RE ANIMAL MAN, SURELY YOU CAN--
YEAH, I'M ANIMAL MAN--I DUPLICATE THEIR ABILITIES, BUT I DON'T HAVE SIT-DOWN HEART-TO-HEARTS WITH ANY OF THEM.
I MEAN OK, MAYBE I'VE PICKED UP SOME COMMUNICATION SKILLS ALONG THE WAY, BUT...IT'S A SQUAWK HERE AND A SNORT THERE. IT'S NOT LIKE I'M--
DR. DOLITTTLE?
ARF!
WHAT DID HE SAY?
HE SAID... SIGH
ELLEN, HONEY... WHERE'S MY COSTUME?

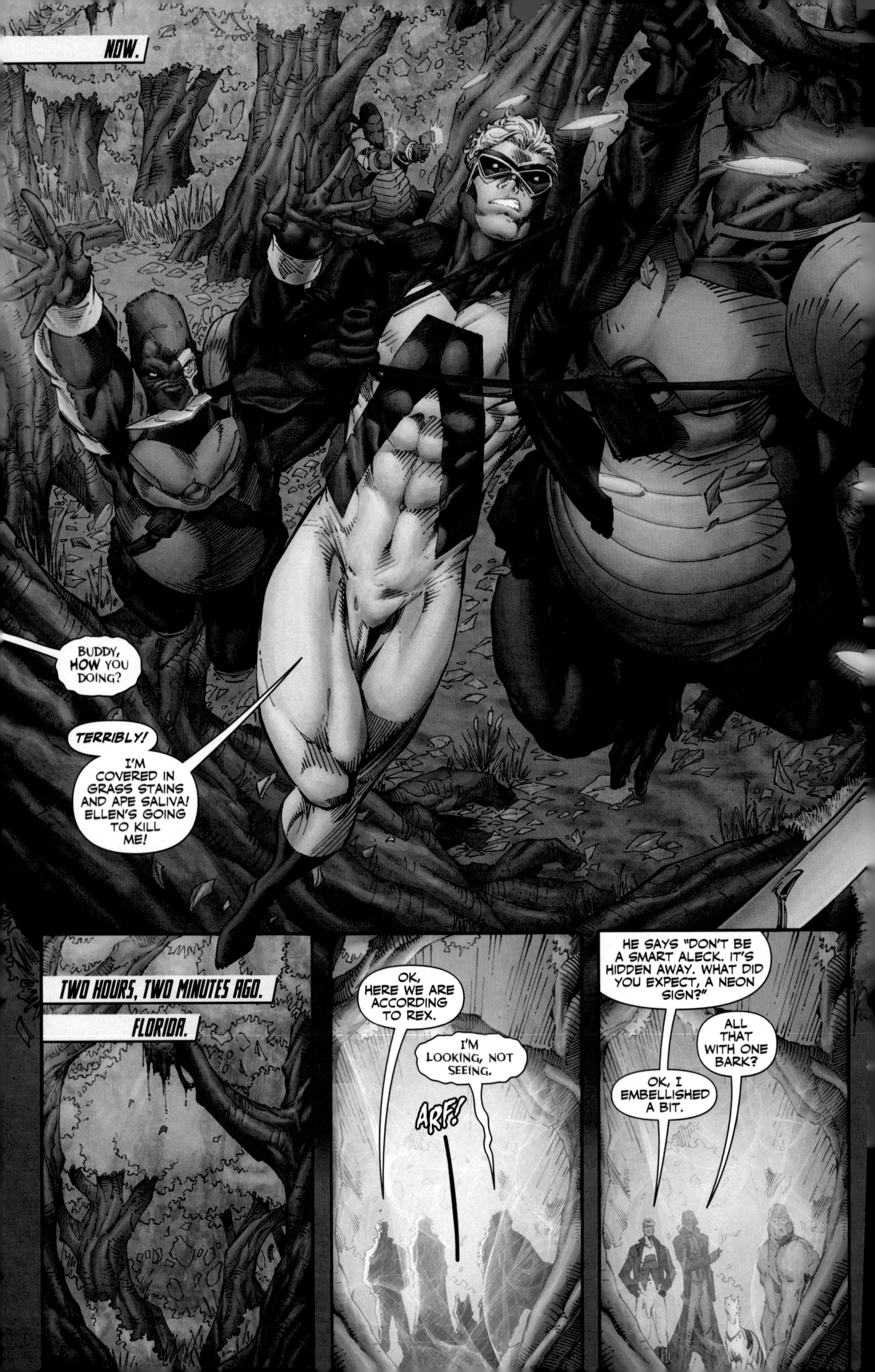
NOW.
BUDDY, HOW YOU DOING?
TERRIBLY! I'M COVERED IN GRASS STAINS AND APE SALIVA! ELLEN'S GOING TO KILL ME!
TWO HOURS, TWO MINUTES AGO.
FLORIDA.
OK, HERE WE ARE ACCORDING TO REX.
I'M LOOKING, NOT SEEING.
ARF!
HE SAYS "DON'T BE A SMART ALECK. IT'S HIDDEN AWAY. WHAT DID YOU EXPECT, A NEON SIGN?"
ALL THAT WITH ONE BARK?
OK, I EMBELLISHED A BIT.

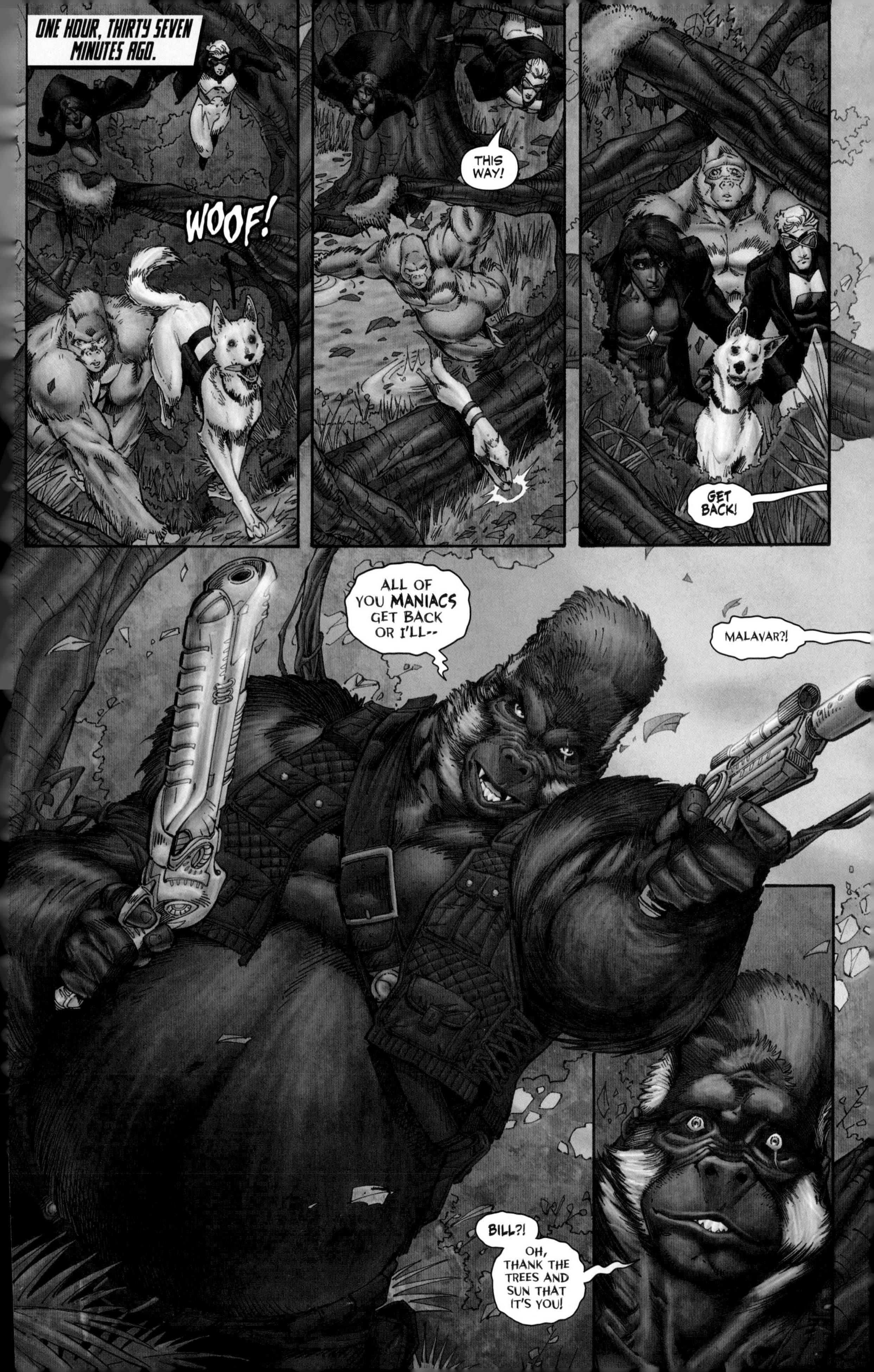
ONE HOUR, THIRTY SEVEN MINUTES AGO.
WOOF!
THIS WAY!
GET BACK!
ALL OF YOU MANIACS GET BACK OR I'LL--
MALAVAR?!
BILL?!
OH, THANK THE TREES AND SUN THAT IT'S YOU!

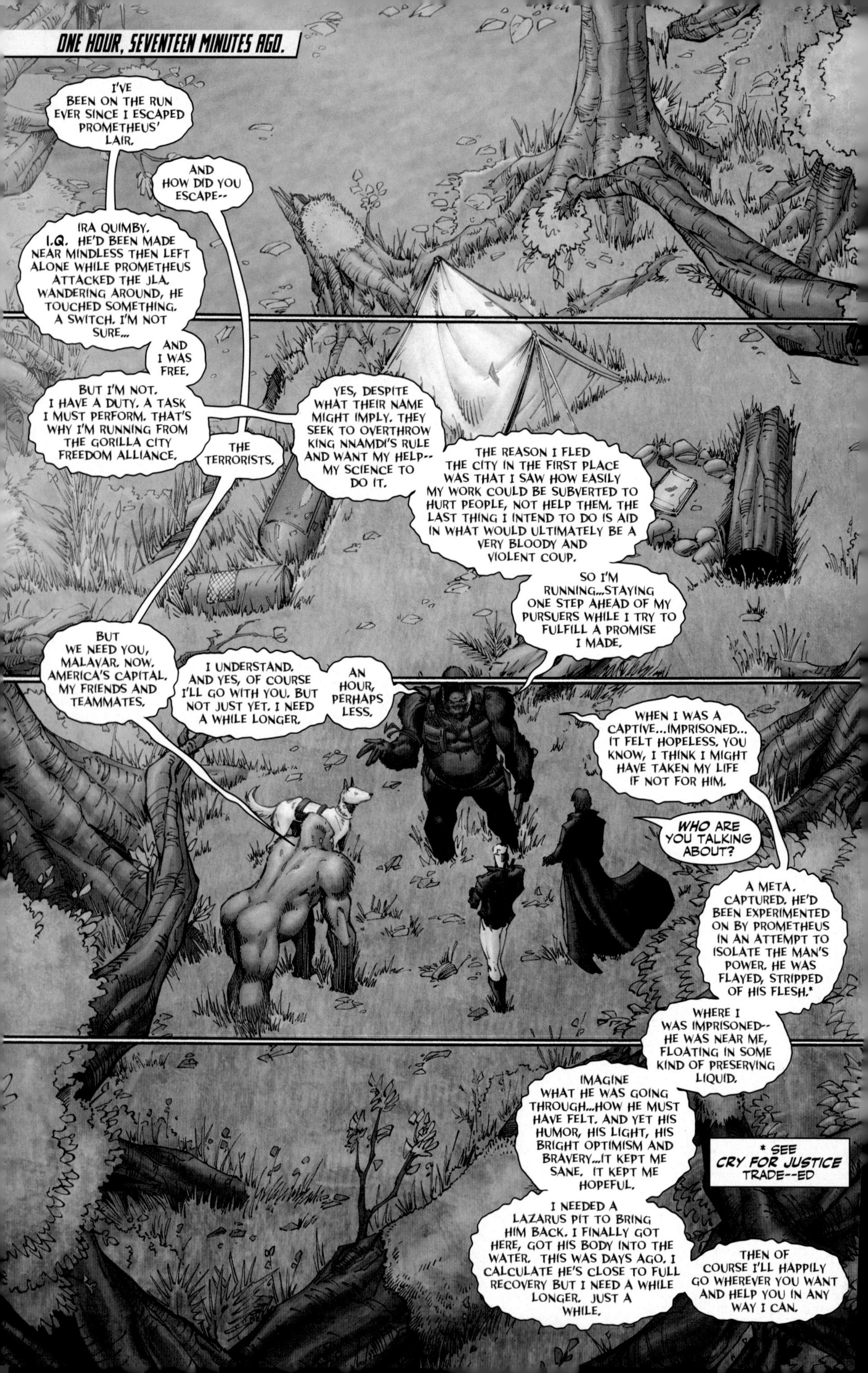
ONE HOUR, SEVENTEEN MINUTES AGO.
I'VE BEEN ON THE RUN EVER SINCE I ESCAPED PROMETHEUS' LAIR.
AND HOW DID YOU ESCAPE--
IRA QUIMBY. I.Q. HE'D BEEN MADE NEAR MINDLESS THEN LEFT ALONE WHILE PROMETHEUS ATTACKED THE JLA. WANDERING AROUND, HE TOUCHED SOMETHING. A SWITCH. I'M NOT SURE...
AND I WAS FREE.
BUT I'M NOT. I HAVE A DUTY. A TASK I MUST PERFORM. THAT'S WHY I'M RUNNING FROM THE GORILLA CITY FREEDOM ALLIANCE.
THE TERRORISTS.
YES, DESPITE WHAT THEIR NAME MIGHT IMPLY. THEY SEEK TO OVERTHROW KING NNAMDI'S RULE AND WANT MY HELP-- MY SCIENCE TO DO IT.
THE REASON I FLED THE CITY IN THE FIRST PLACE WAS THAT I SAW HOW EASILY MY WORK COULD BE SUBVERTED TO HURT PEOPLE, NOT HELP THEM. THE LAST THING I INTEND TO DO IS AID IN WHAT WOULD ULTIMATELY BE A VERY BLOODY AND VIOLENT COUP.
SO I'M RUNNING...STAYING ONE STEP AHEAD OF MY PURSUERS WHILE I TRY TO FULFILL A PROMISE I MADE.
BUT WE NEED YOU, MALAVAR. NOW. AMERICA'S CAPITAL. MY FRIENDS AND TEAMMATES.
I UNDERSTAND. AND YES, OF COURSE I'LL GO WITH YOU. BUT NOT JUST YET. I NEED A WHILE LONGER.
AN HOUR, PERHAPS LESS.
WHEN I WAS A CAPTIVE...IMPRISONED... IT FELT HOPELESS. YOU KNOW, I THINK I MIGHT HAVE TAKEN MY LIFE IF NOT FOR HIM.
WHO ARE YOU TALKING ABOUT?
A META. CAPTURED. HE'D BEEN EXPERIMENTED ON BY PROMETHEUS IN AN ATTEMPT TO ISOLATE THE MAN'S POWER. HE WAS FLAYED, STRIPPED OF HIS FLESH.*
WHERE I WAS IMPRISONED-- HE WAS NEAR ME, FLOATING IN SOME KIND OF PRESERVING LIQUID.
IMAGINE WHAT HE WAS GOING THROUGH...HOW HE MUST HAVE FELT. AND YET HIS HUMOR, HIS LIGHT, HIS BRIGHT OPTIMISM AND BRAVERY...IT KEPT ME SANE. IT KEPT ME HOPEFUL.
* SEE CRY FOR JUSTICE TRADE--ED
I NEEDED A LAZARUS PIT TO BRING HIM BACK. I FINALLY GOT HERE, GOT HIS BODY INTO THE WATER. THIS WAS DAYS AGO. I CALCULATE HE'S CLOSE TO FULL RECOVERY BUT I NEED A WHILE LONGER. JUST A WHILE.
THEN OF COURSE I'LL HAPPILY GO WHEREVER YOU WANT AND HELP YOU IN ANY WAY I CAN.

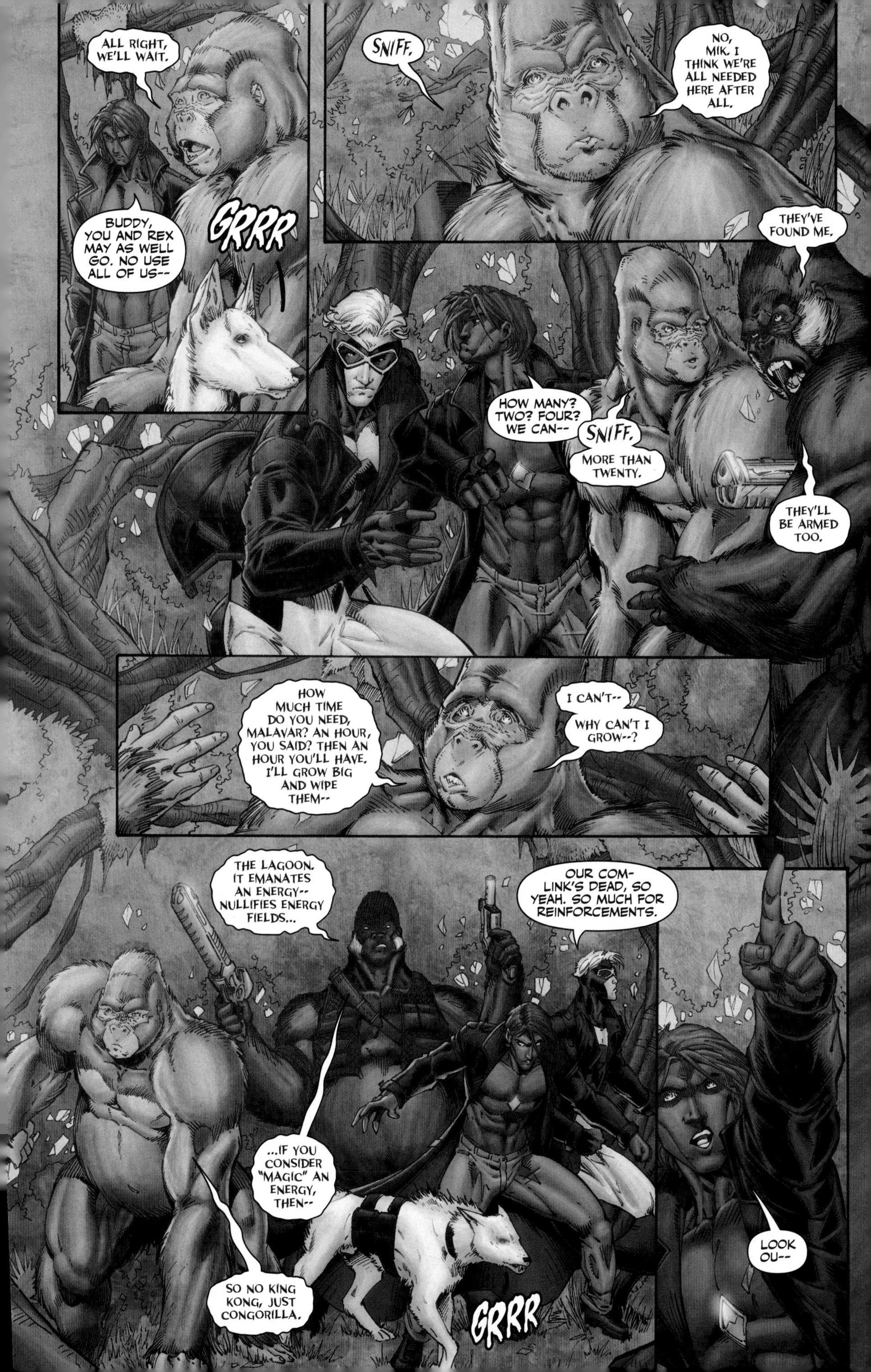
ALL RIGHT, WE'LL WAIT.
BUDDY, YOU AND REX MAY AS WELL GO. NO USE ALL OF US--
GRRR
SNIFF.
NO, MIK. I THINK WE'RE ALL NEEDED HERE AFTER ALL.
THEY'VE FOUND ME.
HOW MANY? TWO? FOUR? WE CAN--
SNIFF.
MORE THAN TWENTY.
THEY'LL BE ARMED TOO.
HOW MUCH TIME DO YOU NEED, MALAVAR? AN HOUR, YOU SAID? THEN AN HOUR YOU'LL HAVE. I'LL GROW BIG AND WIPE THEM--
I CAN'T--
WHY CAN'T I GROW--?
THE LAGOON. IT EMANATES AN ENERGY-- NULLIFIES ENERGY FIELDS...
OUR COM-LINK'S DEAD, SO YEAH. SO MUCH FOR REINFORCEMENTS.
...IF YOU CONSIDER "MAGIC" AN ENERGY, THEN--
SO NO KING KONG, JUST CONGORILLA.
GRRR
LOOK OU--

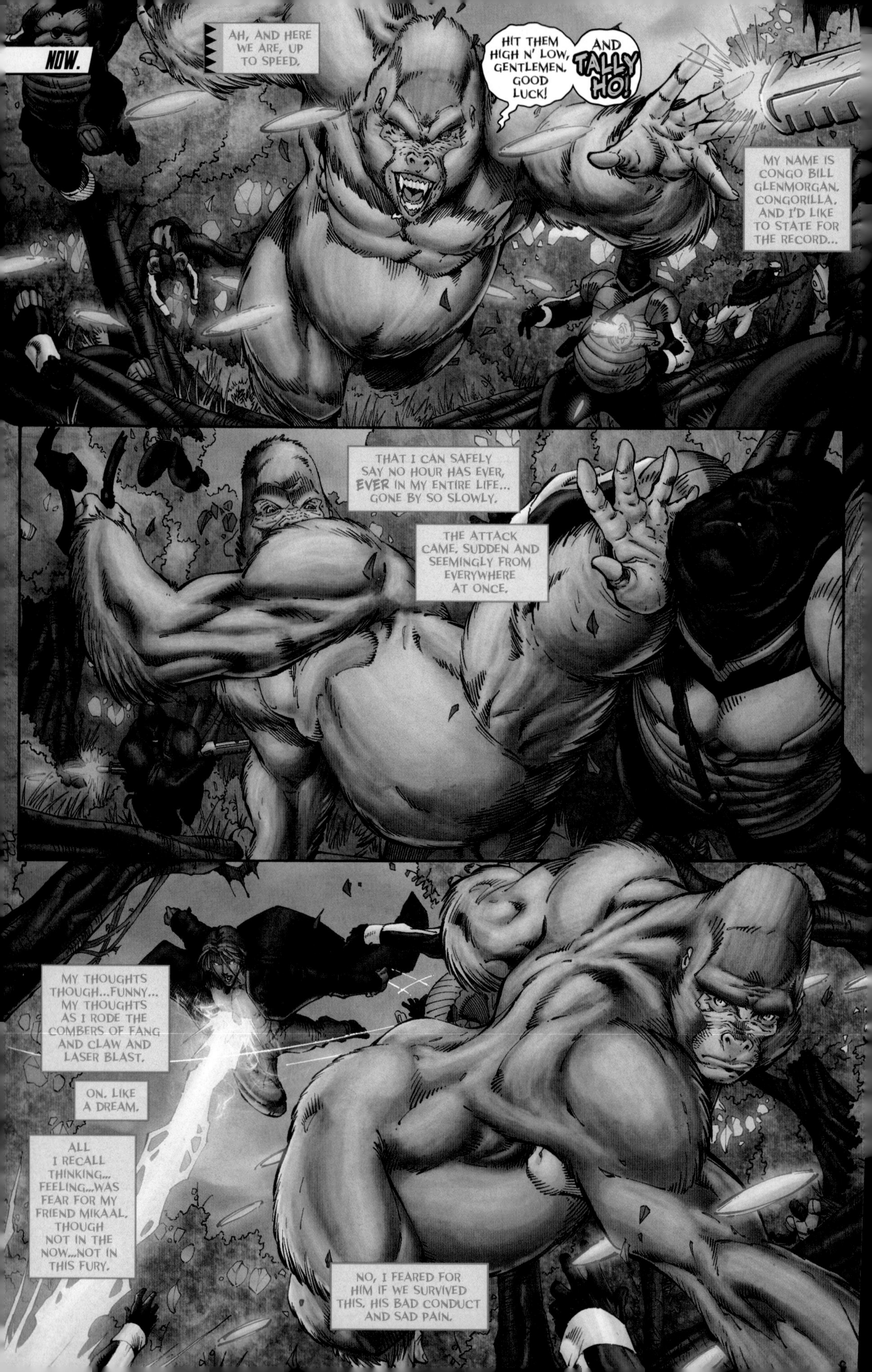
NOW.
AH, AND HERE WE ARE, UP TO SPEED.
HIT THEM HIGH N' LOW, GENTLEMEN. GOOD LUCK!
AND TALLY HO!
MY NAME IS CONGO BILL GLENMORGAN. CONGORILLA. AND I'D LIKE TO STATE FOR THE RECORD...
THAT I CAN SAFELY SAY NO HOUR HAS EVER, EVER IN MY ENTIRE LIFE... GONE BY SO SLOWLY.
THE ATTACK CAME, SUDDEN AND SEEMINGLY FROM EVERYWHERE AT ONCE.
MY THOUGHTS THOUGH...FUNNY... MY THOUGHTS AS I RODE THE COMBERS OF FANG AND CLAW AND LASER BLAST.
ON. LIKE A DREAM.
ALL I RECALL THINKING... FEELING...WAS FEAR FOR MY FRIEND MIKAAL. THOUGH NOT IN THE NOW...NOT IN THIS FURY.
NO, I FEARED FOR HIM IF WE SURVIVED THIS. HIS BAD CONDUCT AND SAD PAIN.

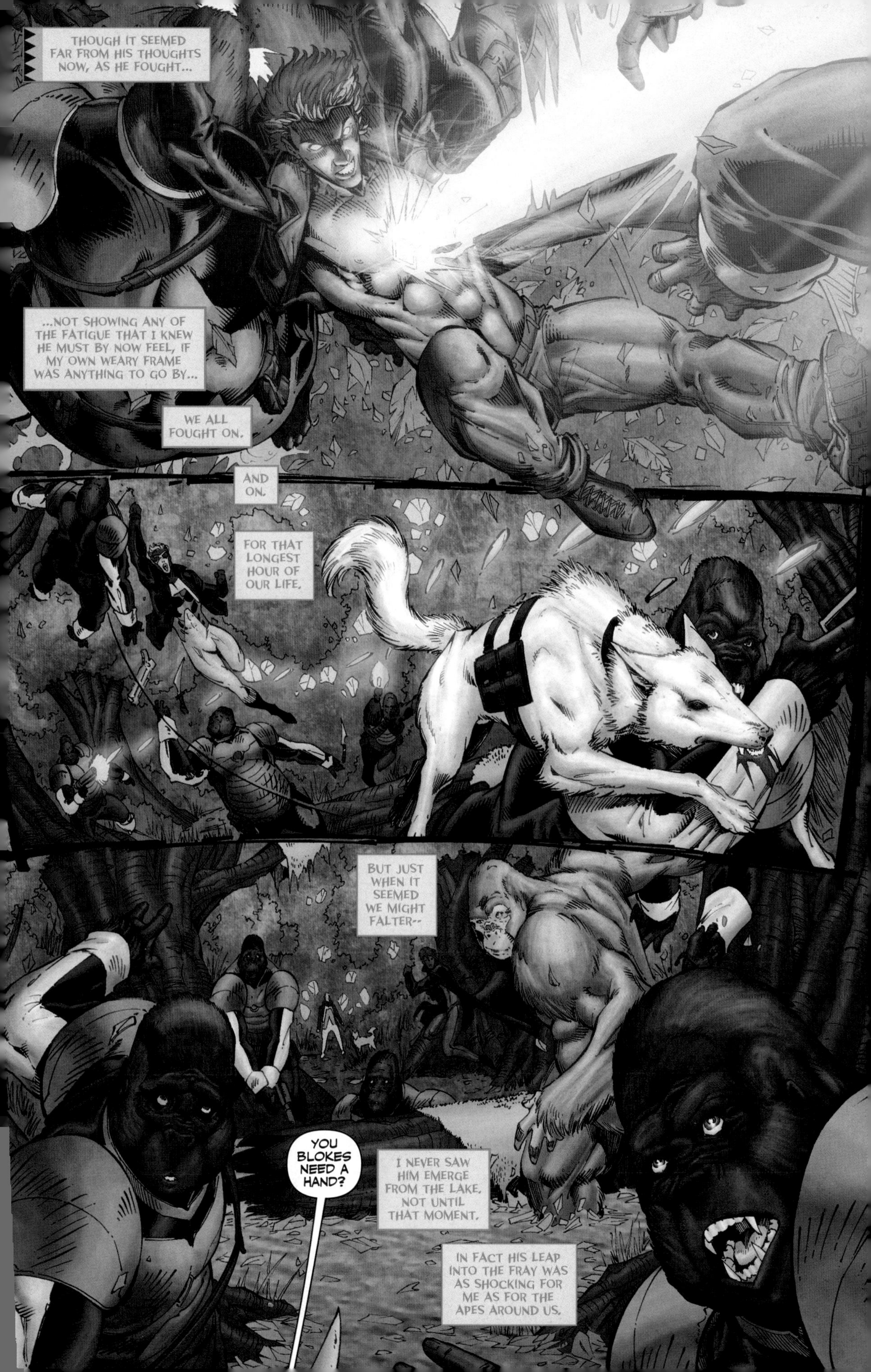
THOUGH IT SEEMED FAR FROM HIS THOUGHTS NOW, AS HE FOUGHT...
...NOT SHOWING ANY OF THE FATIGUE THAT I KNEW HE MUST BY NOW FEEL, IF MY OWN WEARY FRAME WAS ANYTHING TO GO BY...
WE ALL FOUGHT ON.
AND ON.
FOR THAT LONGEST HOUR OF OUR LIFE.
BUT JUST WHEN IT SEEMED WE MIGHT FALTER--
YOU BLOKES NEED A HAND?
I NEVER SAW HIM EMERGE FROM THE LAKE, NOT UNTIL THAT MOMENT.
IN FACT HIS LEAP INTO THE FRAY WAS AS SHOCKING FOR ME AS FOR THE APES AROUND US.

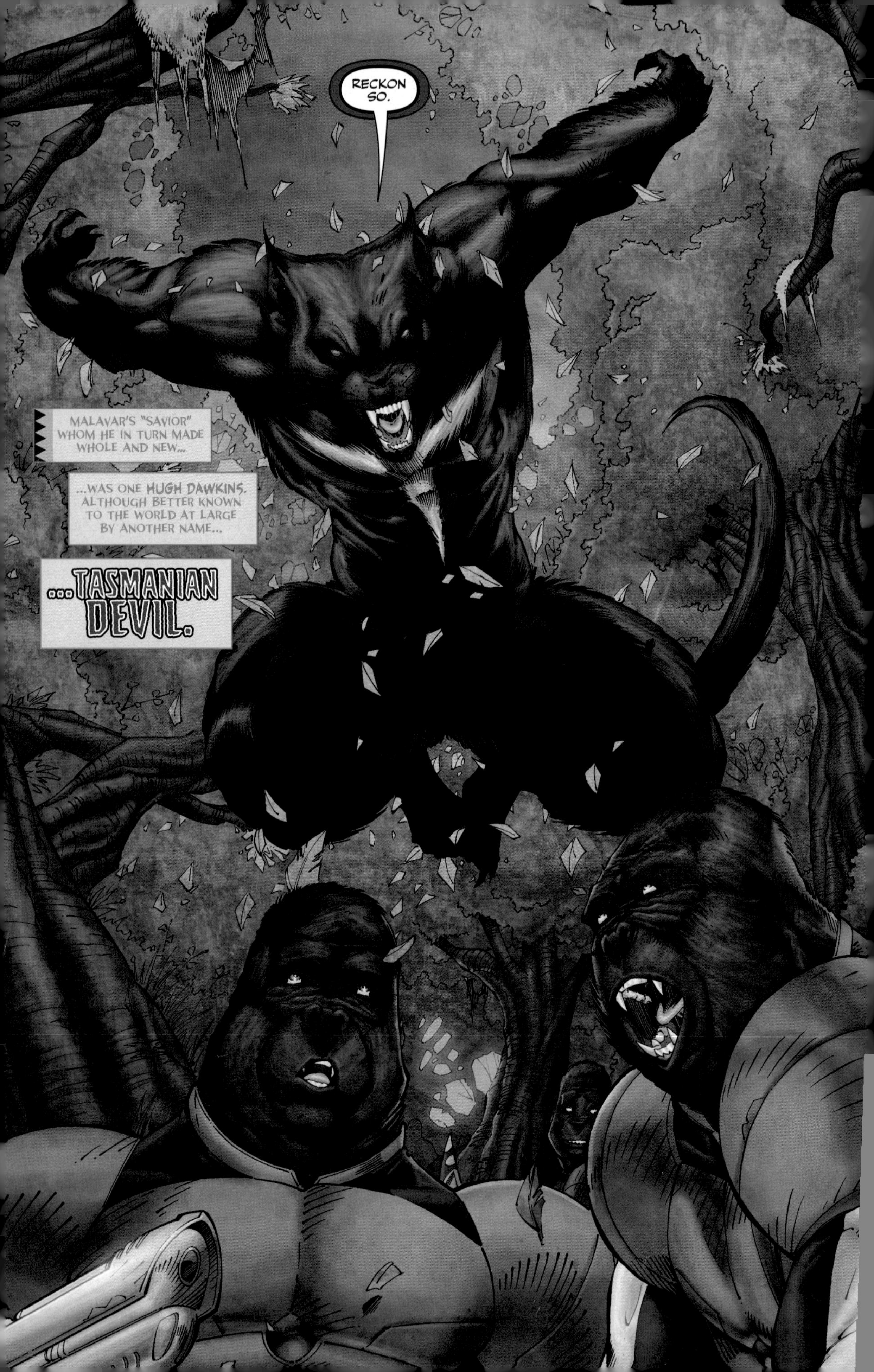
RECKON SO.
MALAVAR'S "SAVIOR" WHOM HE IN TURN MADE WHOLE AND NEW...
...WAS ONE HUGH DAWKINS. ALTHOUGH BETTER KNOWN TO THE WORLD AT LARGE BY ANOTHER NAME...
...TASMANIAN DEVIL.

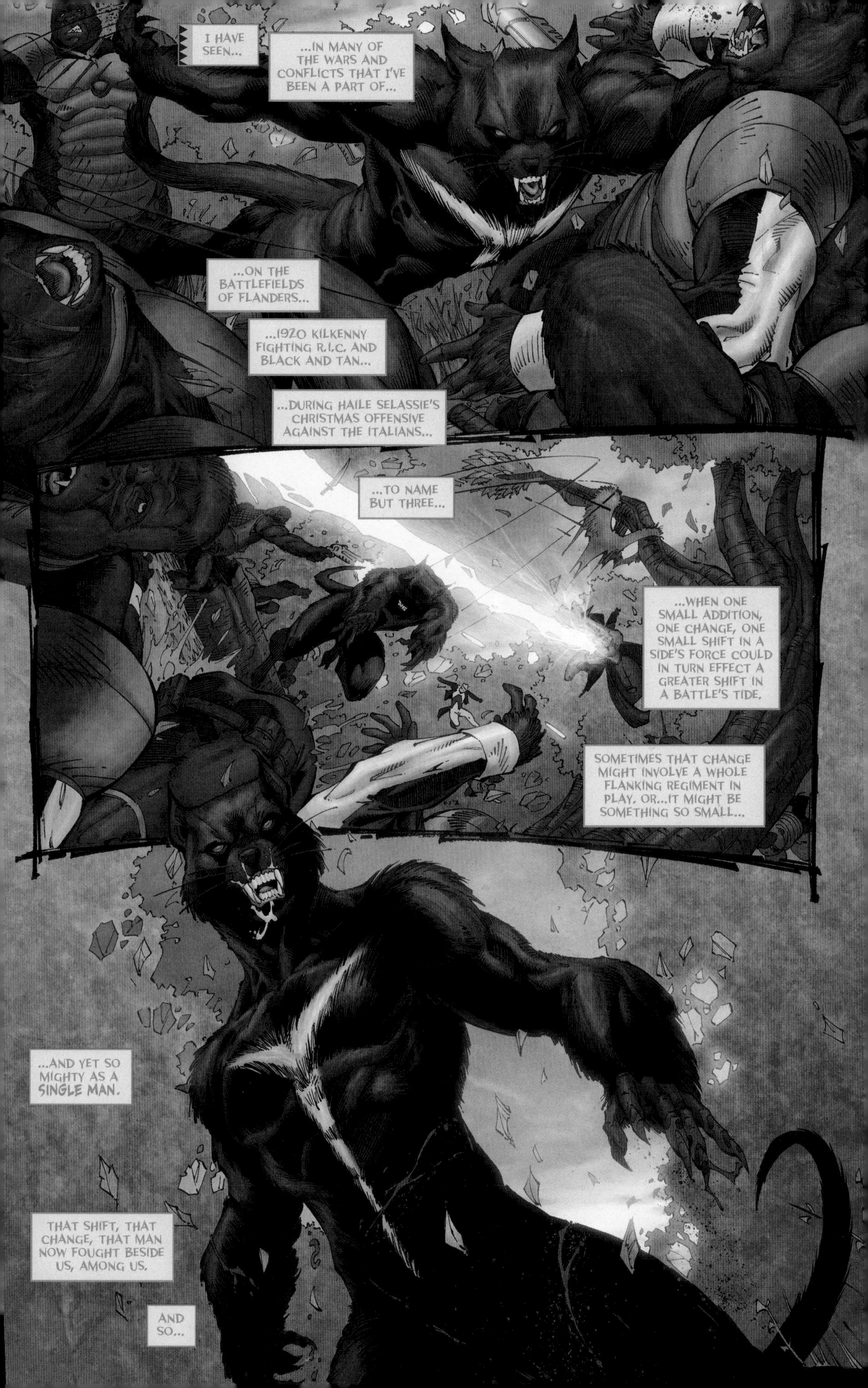
I HAVE SEEN...
...IN MANY OF THE WARS AND CONFLICTS THAT I'VE BEEN A PART OF...
...ON THE BATTLEFIELDS OF FLANDERS...
...1920 KILKENNY FIGHTING R.I.C. AND BLACK AND TAN...
...DURING HAILE SELASSIE'S CHRISTMAS OFFENSIVE AGAINST THE ITALIANS...
...TO NAME BUT THREE...
...WHEN ONE SMALL ADDITION, ONE CHANGE, ONE SMALL SHIFT IN A SIDE'S FORCE COULD IN TURN EFFECT A GREATER SHIFT IN A BATTLE'S TIDE.
SOMETIMES THAT CHANGE MIGHT INVOLVE A WHOLE FLANKING REGIMENT IN PLAY. OR...IT MIGHT BE SOMETHING SO SMALL...
...AND YET SO MIGHTY AS A SINGLE MAN.
THAT SHIFT, THAT CHANGE, THAT MAN NOW FOUGHT BESIDE US, AMONG US.
AND SO...

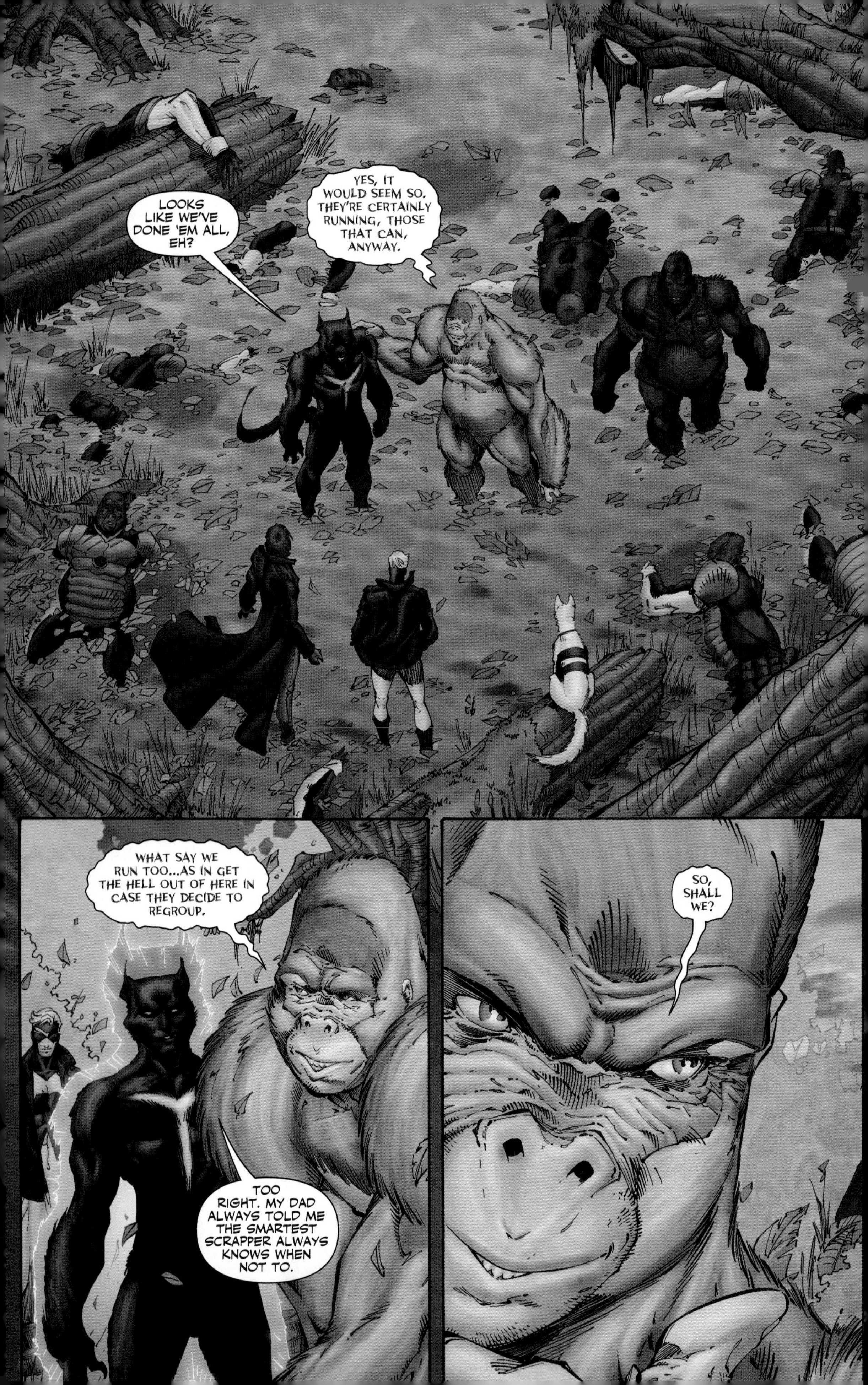
LOOKS LIKE WE'VE DONE 'EM ALL, EH?
YES, IT WOULD SEEM SO. THEY'RE CERTAINLY RUNNING, THOSE THAT CAN, ANYWAY.
WHAT SAY WE RUN TOO...AS IN GET THE HELL OUT OF HERE IN CASE THEY DECIDE TO REGROUP.
TOO RIGHT. MY DAD ALWAYS TOLD ME THE SMARTEST SCRAPPER ALWAYS KNOWS WHEN NOT TO.
SO, SHALL WE?

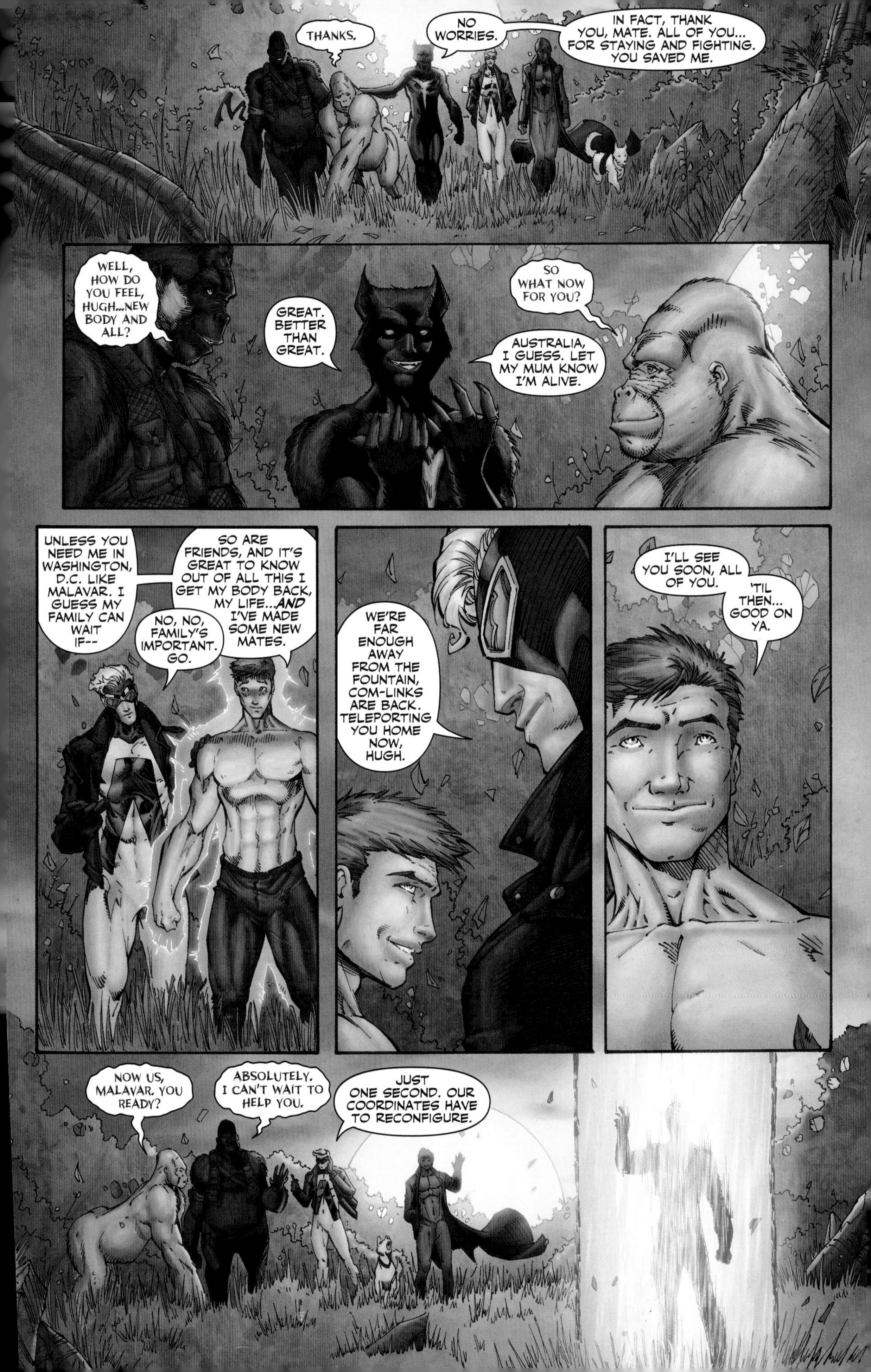
THANKS.
NO WORRIES.
IN FACT, THANK YOU, MATE. ALL OF YOU... FOR STAYING AND FIGHTING. YOU SAVED ME.
WELL, HOW DO YOU FEEL, HUGH...NEW BODY AND ALL?
GREAT. BETTER THAN GREAT.
SO WHAT NOW FOR YOU?
AUSTRALIA, I GUESS. LET MY MUM KNOW I'M ALIVE.
UNLESS YOU NEED ME IN WASHINGTON, D.C. LIKE MALAVAR. I GUESS MY FAMILY CAN WAIT IF--
NO, NO, FAMILY'S IMPORTANT. GO.
SO ARE FRIENDS, AND IT'S GREAT TO KNOW OUT OF ALL THIS I GET MY BODY BACK, MY LIFE...AND I'VE MADE SOME NEW MATES.
WE'RE FAR ENOUGH AWAY FROM THE FOUNTAIN, COM-LINKS ARE BACK. TELEPORTING YOU HOME NOW, HUGH.
I'LL SEE YOU SOON, ALL OF YOU.
'TIL THEN... GOOD ON YA.
NOW US, MALAVAR. YOU READY?
ABSOLUTELY. I CAN'T WAIT TO HELP YOU.
JUST ONE SECOND. OUR COORDINATES HAVE TO RECONFIGURE.

HE'S GAY, YOU KNOW.

WHO?

TASMANIAN DEVIL.

SO?

SO? HE'S GAY, YOU'RE GAY.

WE'RE BOTH GAY AND WE'RE BOTH METAS, WE TAKE ONE LOOK AT EACH OTHER, PUT A SYLVESTER LP ON THE TURNTABLE, SPLASH ON SOME PACO RABANNE, AND IT'S OFF TO THE RACES? YOU THINK THAT'S HOW IT WORKS?

MIK, I HAVE NO IDEA HOW IT WORKS.

SHALL I TELL YOU?

PLEASE DON'T.

LOOK, MIK, YOU'RE MY FRIEND, I CARE ABOUT YOU, THAT'S ALL. YOU'RE SAD AND IT'S MAKING YOU SELF-DESTRUCTIVE, I JUST WANT YOU HAPPY AND HEALTHY.

AND I APPRECIATE THAT, BILL. I DO. YOU'RE THE BEST FRIEND ANYONE COULD ASK FOR.

=SIGH=

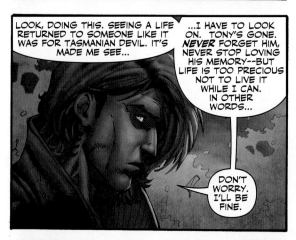

LOOK, DOING THIS. SEEING A LIFE RETURNED TO SOMEONE LIKE IT WAS FOR TASMANIAN DEVIL. IT'S MADE ME SEE...

...I HAVE TO LOOK ON. TONY'S GONE. *NEVER* FORGET HIM, NEVER STOP LOVING HIS MEMORY--BUT LIFE IS TOO PRECIOUS NOT TO LIVE IT WHILE I CAN. IN OTHER WORDS...

DON'T WORRY. I'LL BE FINE.

GOOD, NOW LET'S GO SAVE OUR TEAMMATES.

ABSOLUTELY.

GOTTA SAY THOUGH... WHEN HE ISN'T ALL BIG AND HAIRY, HUGH IS KIND OF HOT.

JUSTICE LEAGUE OF AMERICA 53
cover by Mark Bagley, Rob Hunter & Hi-Fi

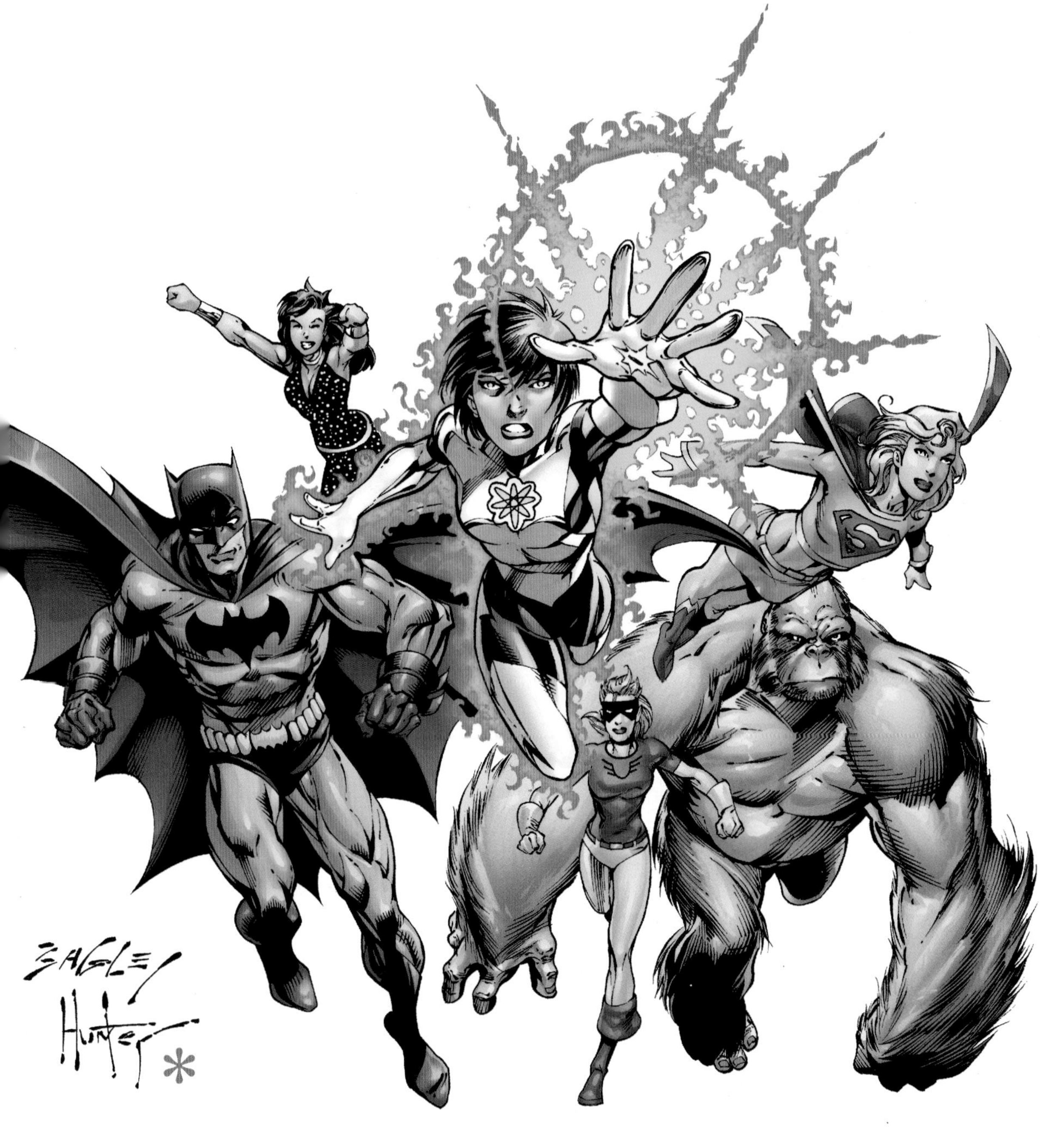
BAGLEY
Hunter

JUSTICE LEAGUE OF AMERICA 53
variant by David Mack

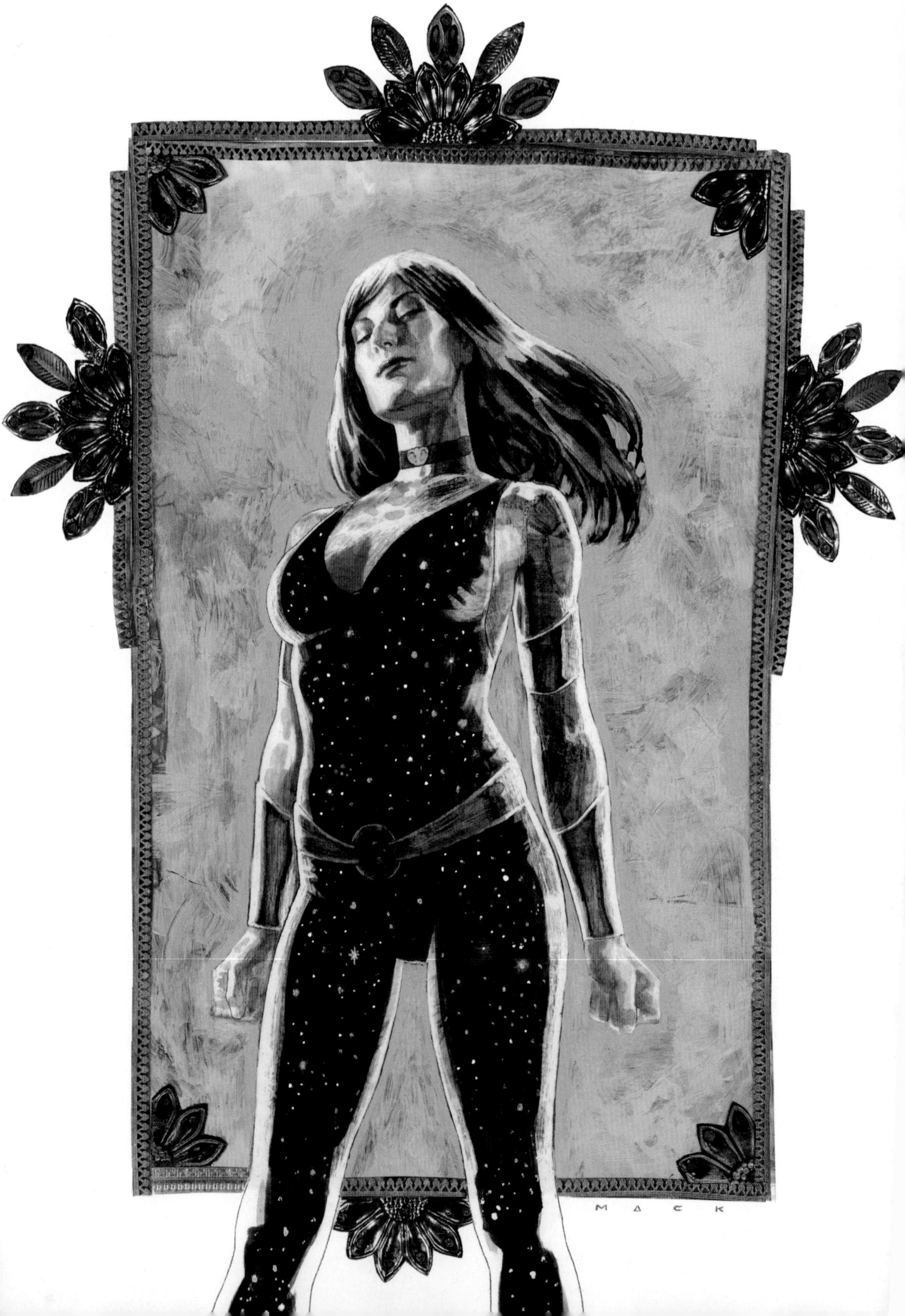
MACK

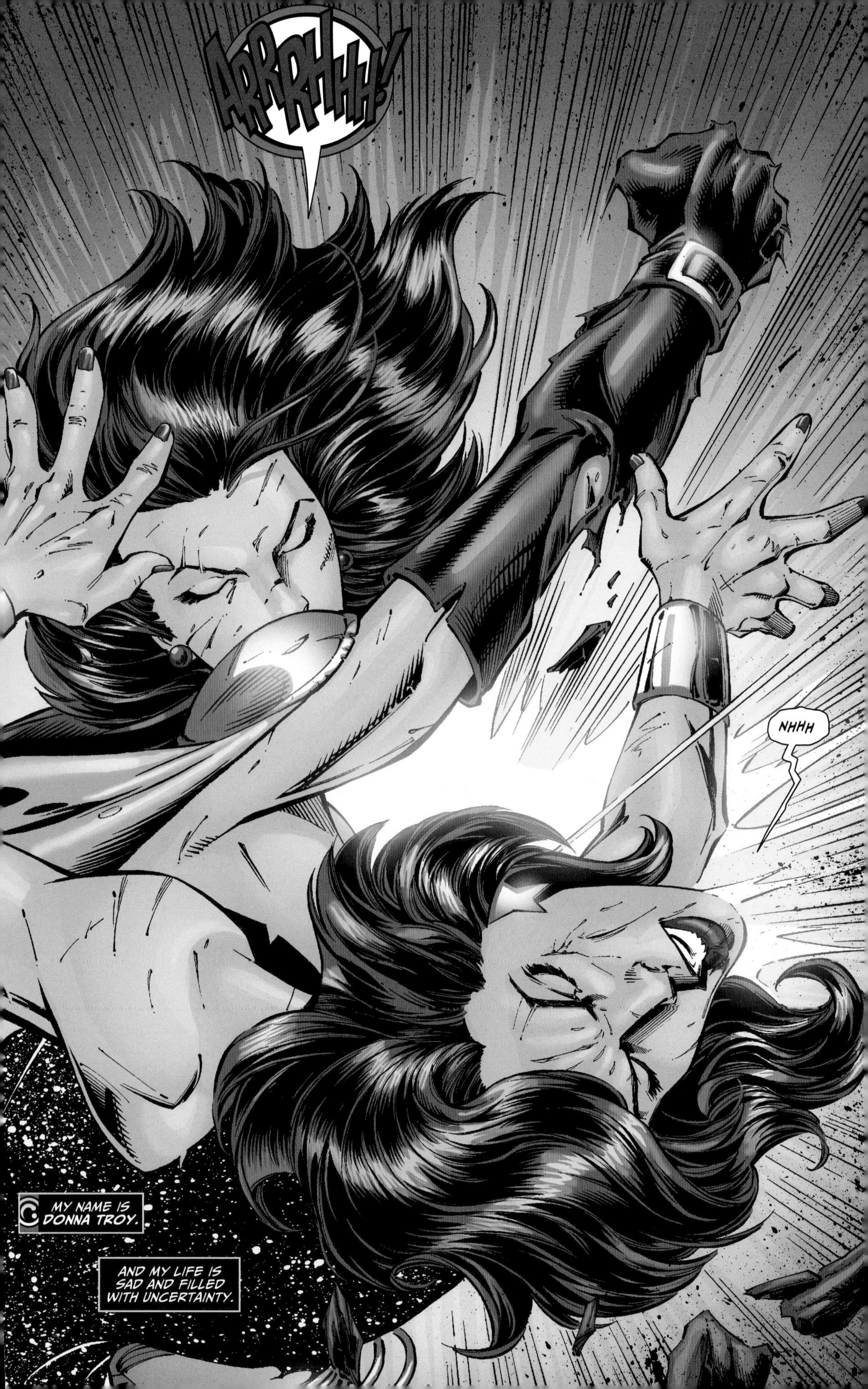
ARRRHHH!
NHHH
MY NAME IS DONNA TROY.
AND MY LIFE IS SAD AND FILLED WITH UNCERTAINTY.

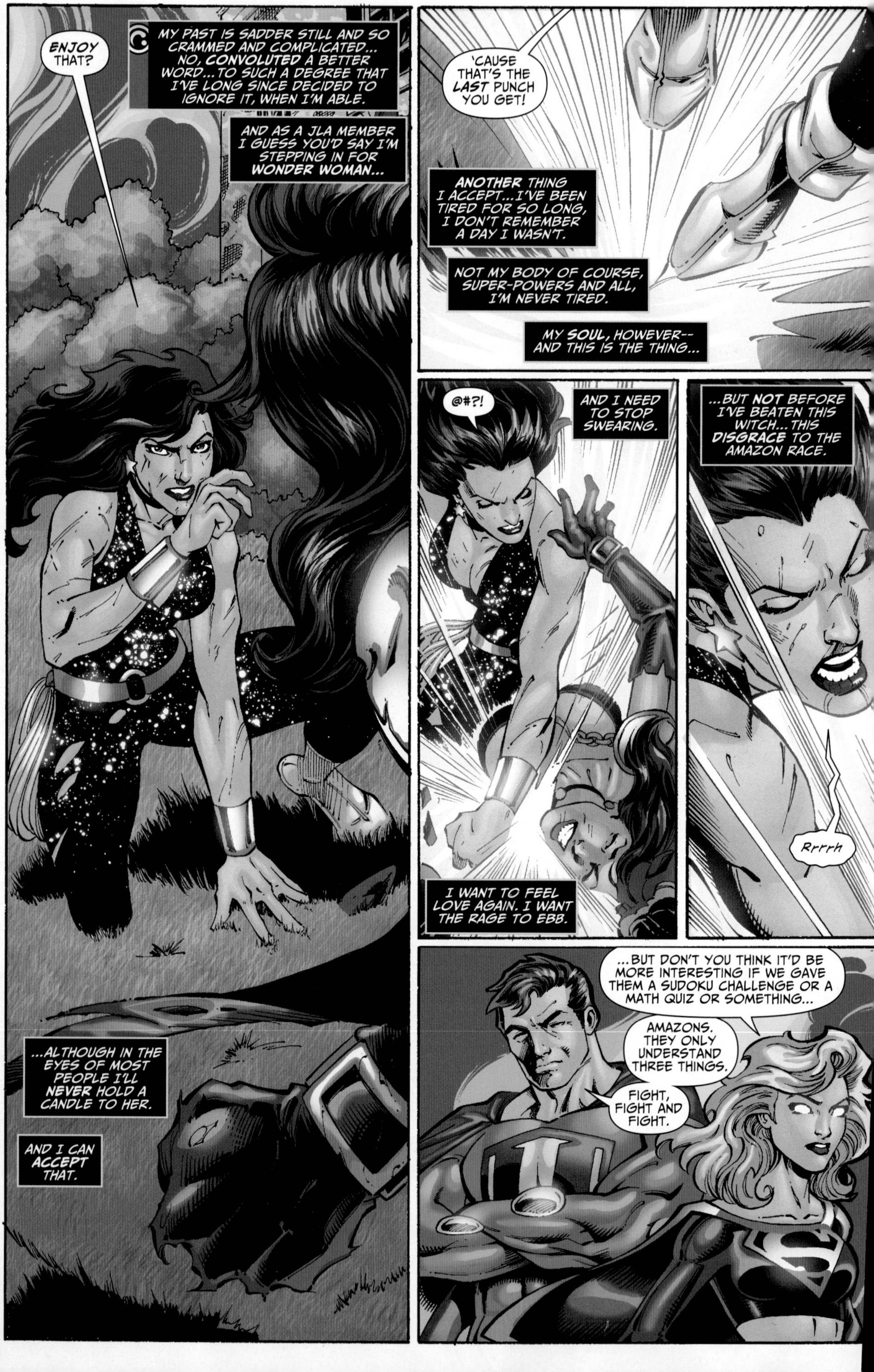

ENJOY THAT?
MY PAST IS SADDER STILL AND SO CRAMMED AND COMPLICATED... NO, CONVOLUTED A BETTER WORD...TO SUCH A DEGREE THAT I'VE LONG SINCE DECIDED TO IGNORE IT, WHEN I'M ABLE.
AND AS A JLA MEMBER I GUESS YOU'D SAY I'M STEPPING IN FOR WONDER WOMAN...
...ALTHOUGH IN THE EYES OF MOST PEOPLE I'LL NEVER HOLD A CANDLE TO HER.
AND I CAN ACCEPT THAT.
'CAUSE THAT'S THE LAST PUNCH YOU GET!
ANOTHER THING I ACCEPT...I'VE BEEN TIRED FOR SO LONG, I DON'T REMEMBER A DAY I WASN'T.
NOT MY BODY OF COURSE, SUPER-POWERS AND ALL, I'M NEVER TIRED.
MY SOUL, HOWEVER-- AND THIS IS THE THING...
@#?!
AND I NEED TO STOP SWEARING.
I WANT TO FEEL LOVE AGAIN. I WANT THE RAGE TO EBB.
...BUT NOT BEFORE I'VE BEATEN THIS WITCH...THIS DISGRACE TO THE AMAZON RACE.
Rrrrh
...BUT DON'T YOU THINK IT'D BE MORE INTERESTING IF WE GAVE THEM A SUDOKU CHALLENGE OR A MATH QUIZ OR SOMETHING...
AMAZONS. THEY ONLY UNDERSTAND THREE THINGS.
FIGHT, FIGHT AND FIGHT.

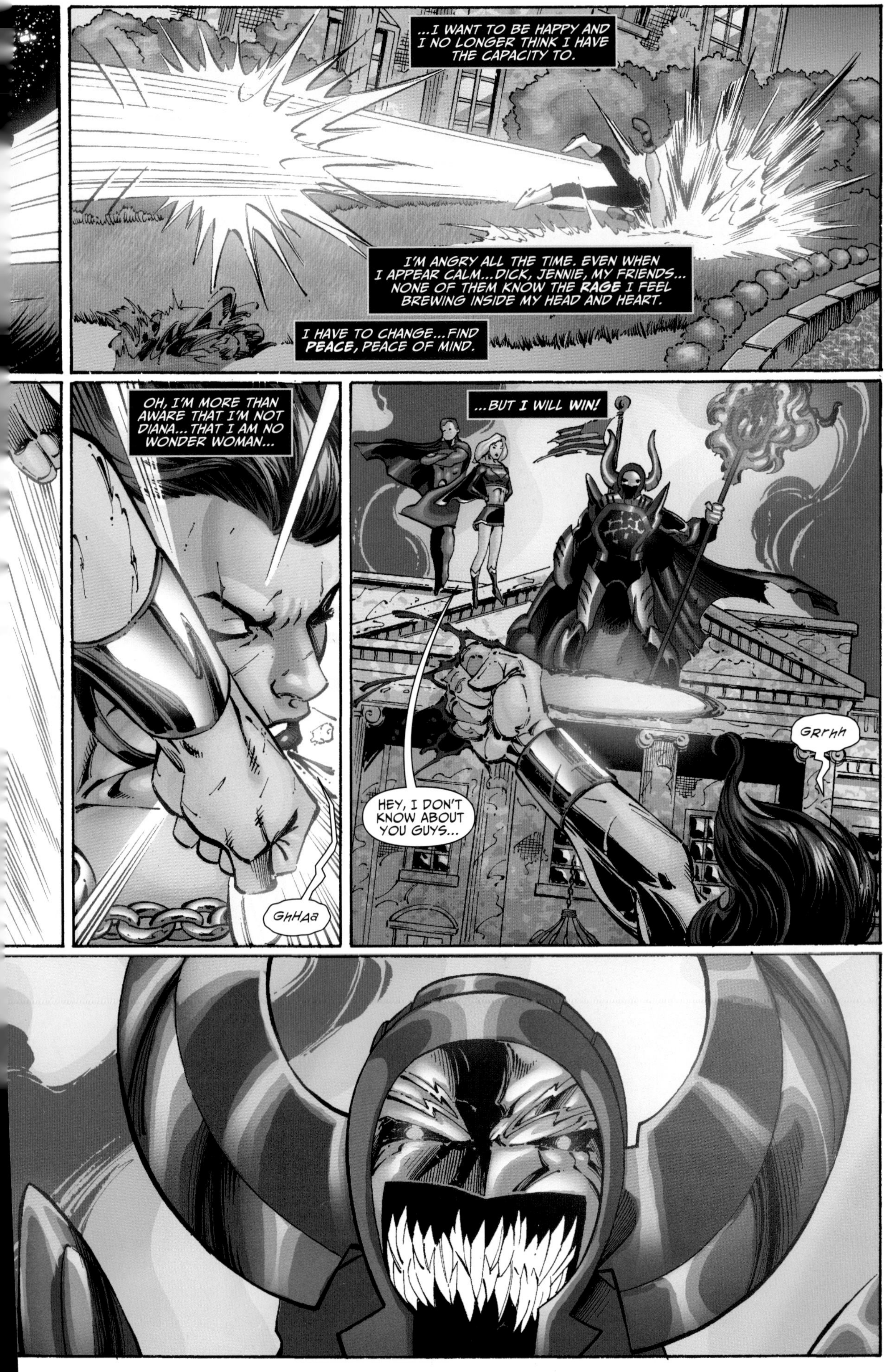
...I WANT TO BE HAPPY AND I NO LONGER THINK I HAVE THE CAPACITY TO.
I'M ANGRY ALL THE TIME. EVEN WHEN I APPEAR CALM...DICK, JENNIE, MY FRIENDS... NONE OF THEM KNOW THE RAGE I FEEL BREWING INSIDE MY HEAD AND HEART.
I HAVE TO CHANGE...FIND PEACE, PEACE OF MIND.
OH, I'M MORE THAN AWARE THAT I'M NOT DIANA...THAT I AM NO WONDER WOMAN...
GhHAa
...BUT I WILL WIN!
HEY, I DON'T KNOW ABOUT YOU GUYS...
Grrhh

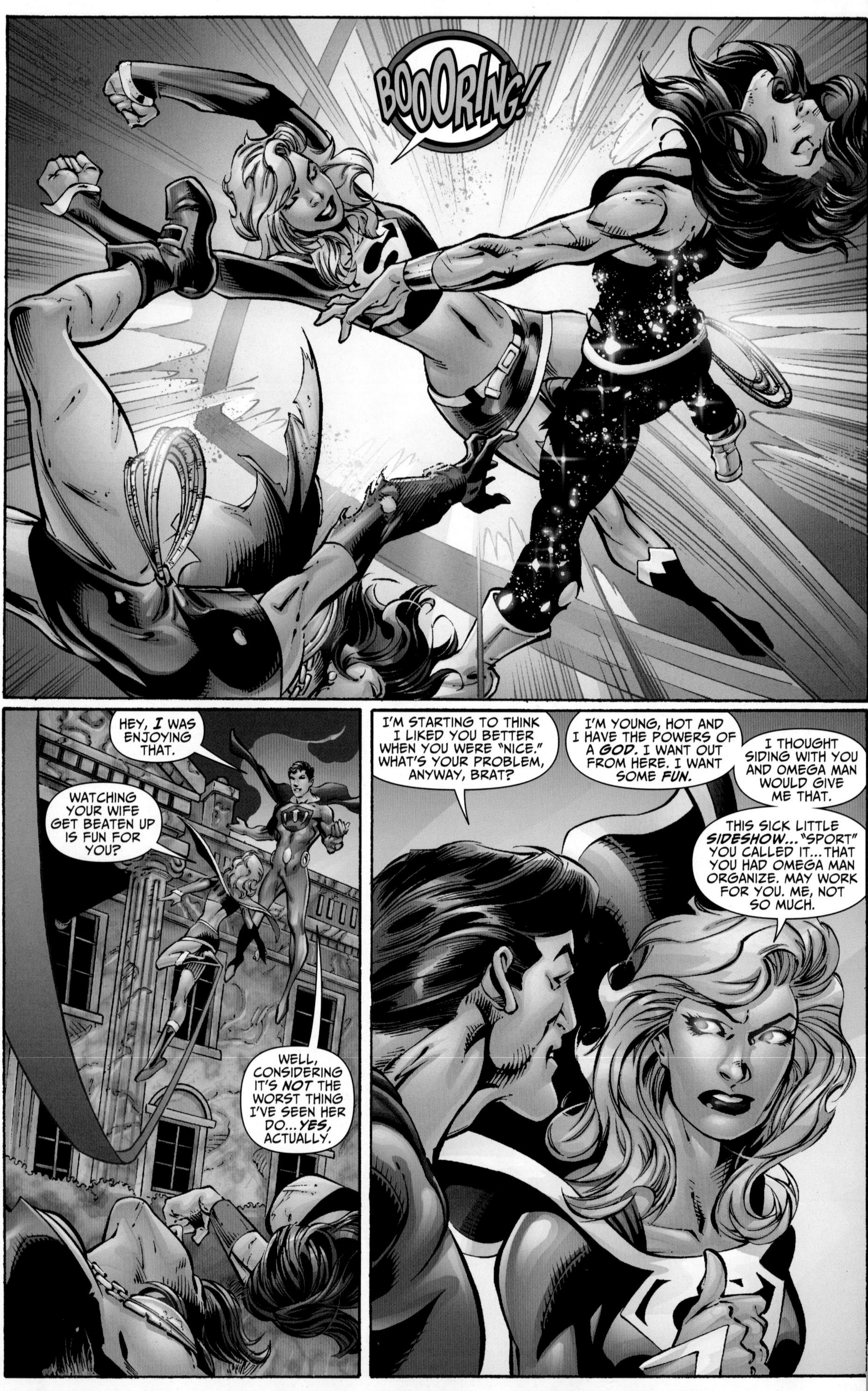
BOOORING!
HEY, I WAS ENJOYING THAT.
WATCHING YOUR WIFE GET BEATEN UP IS FUN FOR YOU?
WELL, CONSIDERING IT'S NOT THE WORST THING I'VE SEEN HER DO...YES, ACTUALLY.
I'M STARTING TO THINK I LIKED YOU BETTER WHEN YOU WERE "NICE." WHAT'S YOUR PROBLEM, ANYWAY, BRAT?
I'M YOUNG, HOT AND I HAVE THE POWERS OF A GOD. I WANT OUT FROM HERE. I WANT SOME FUN.
I THOUGHT SIDING WITH YOU AND OMEGA MAN WOULD GIVE ME THAT.
THIS SICK LITTLE SIDESHOW... "SPORT" YOU CALLED IT... THAT YOU HAD OMEGA MAN ORGANIZE. MAY WORK FOR YOU. ME, NOT SO MUCH.

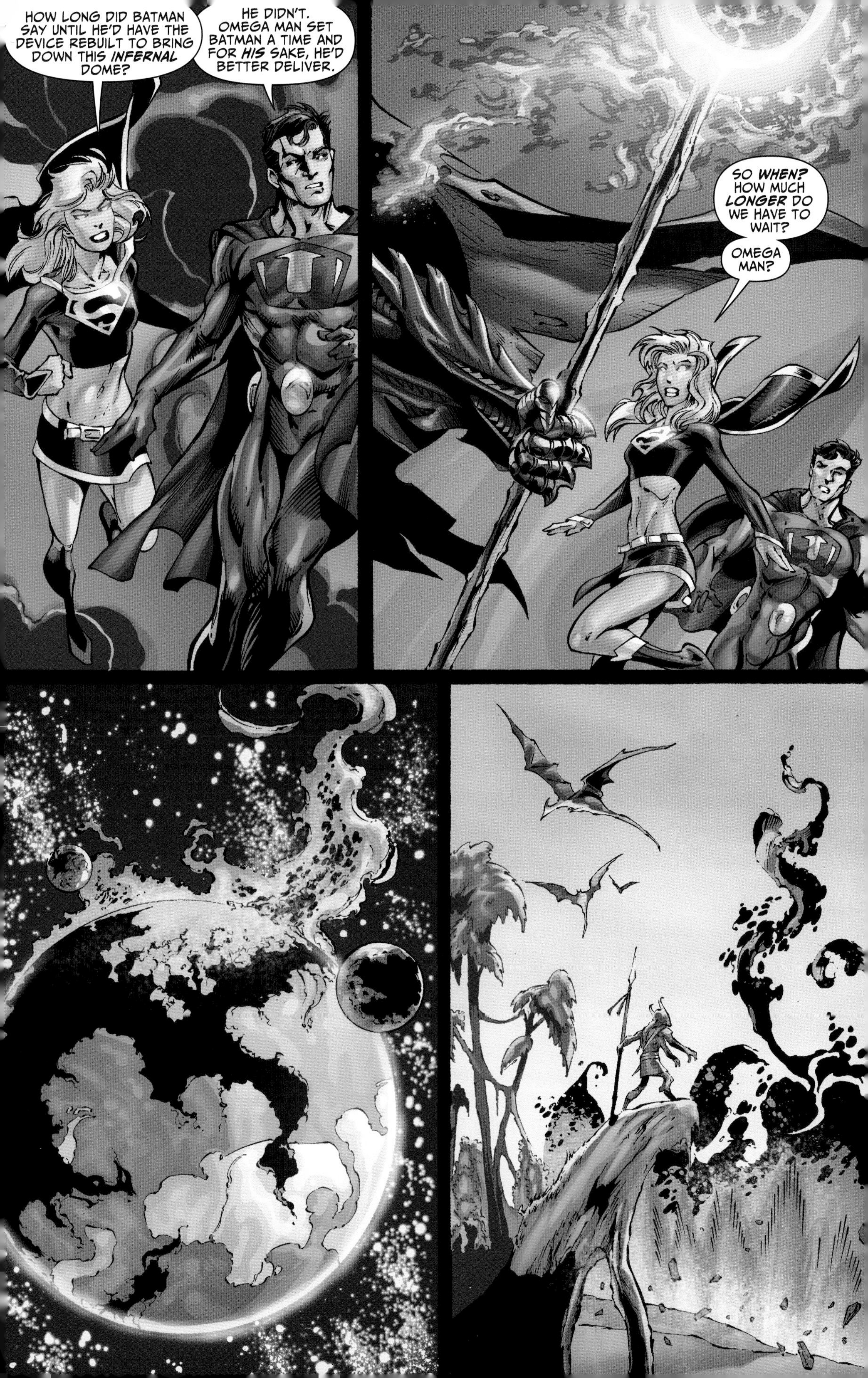
HOW LONG DID BATMAN SAY UNTIL HE'D HAVE THE DEVICE REBUILT TO BRING DOWN THIS *INFERNAL* DOME?
HE DIDN'T. OMEGA MAN SET BATMAN A TIME AND FOR *HIS* SAKE, HE'D BETTER DELIVER.
SO *WHEN?* HOW MUCH *LONGER* DO WE HAVE TO WAIT?
OMEGA MAN?

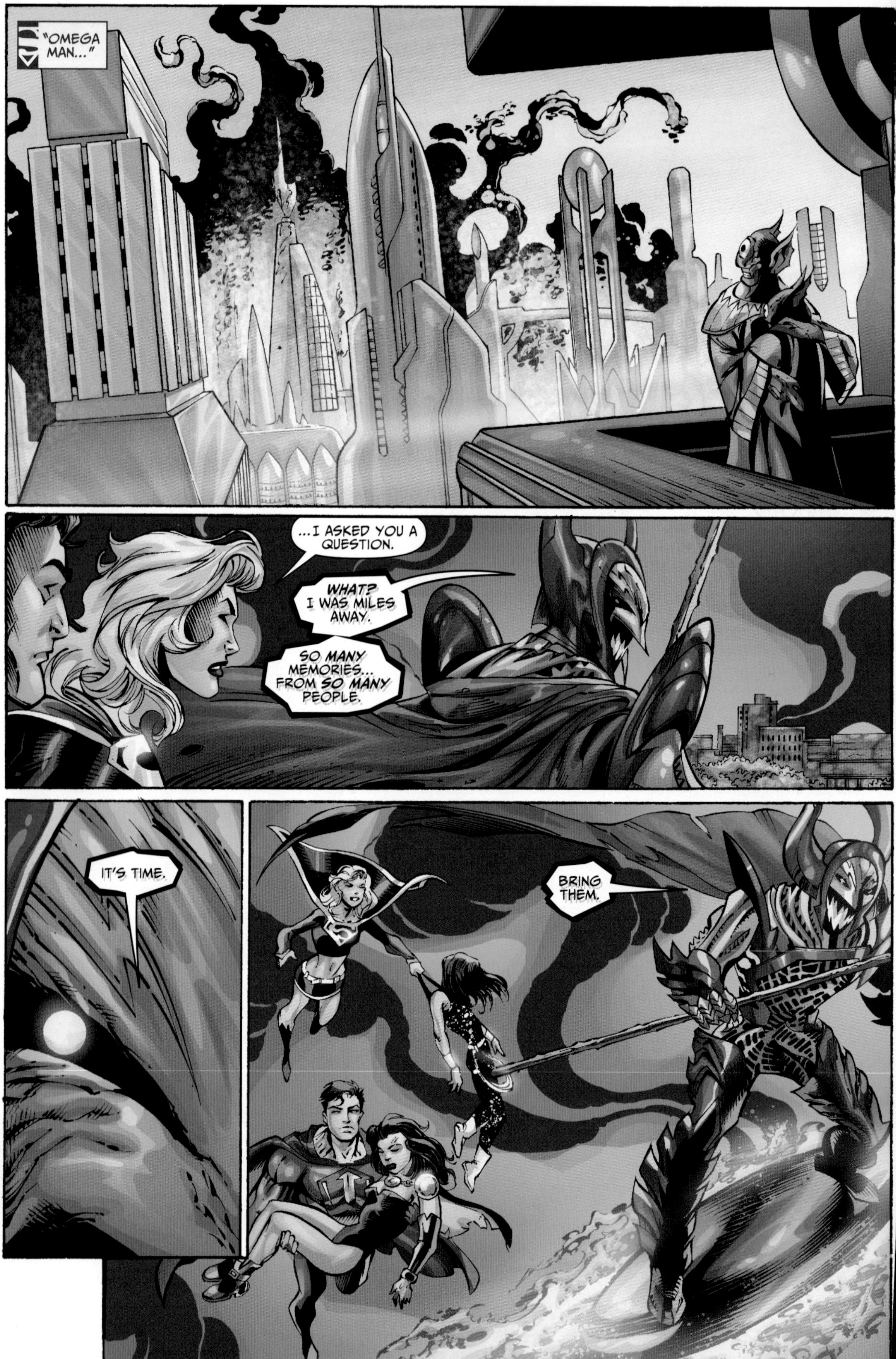
"OMEGA MAN..."
...I ASKED YOU A QUESTION.
WHAT? I WAS MILES AWAY.
SO MANY MEMORIES... FROM SO MANY PEOPLE.
IT'S TIME.
BRING THEM.

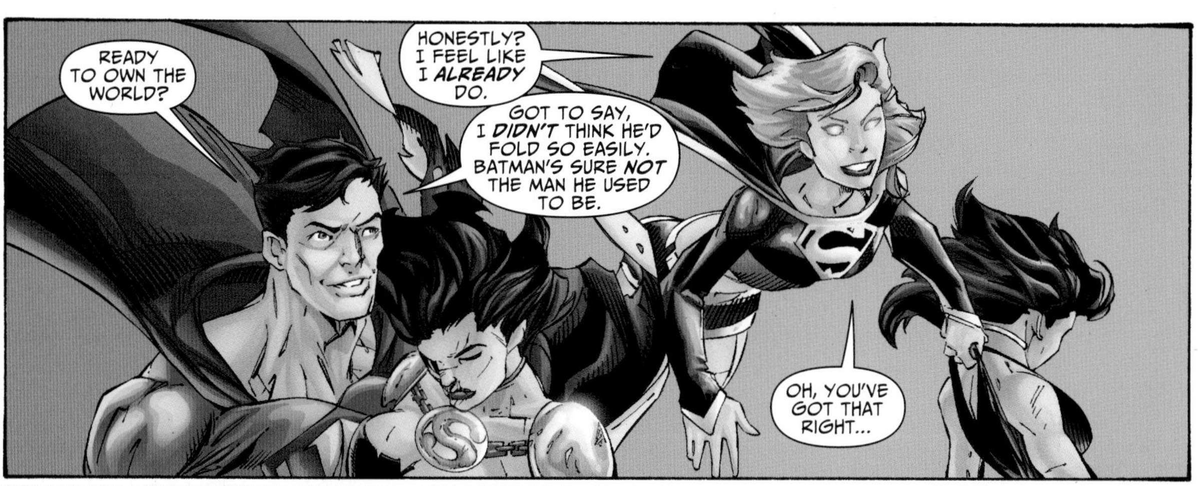
READY TO OWN THE WORLD?
HONESTLY? I FEEL LIKE I ALREADY DO.
GOT TO SAY, I DIDN'T THINK HE'D FOLD SO EASILY. BATMAN'S SURE NOT THE MAN HE USED TO BE.
OH, YOU'VE GOT THAT RIGHT...

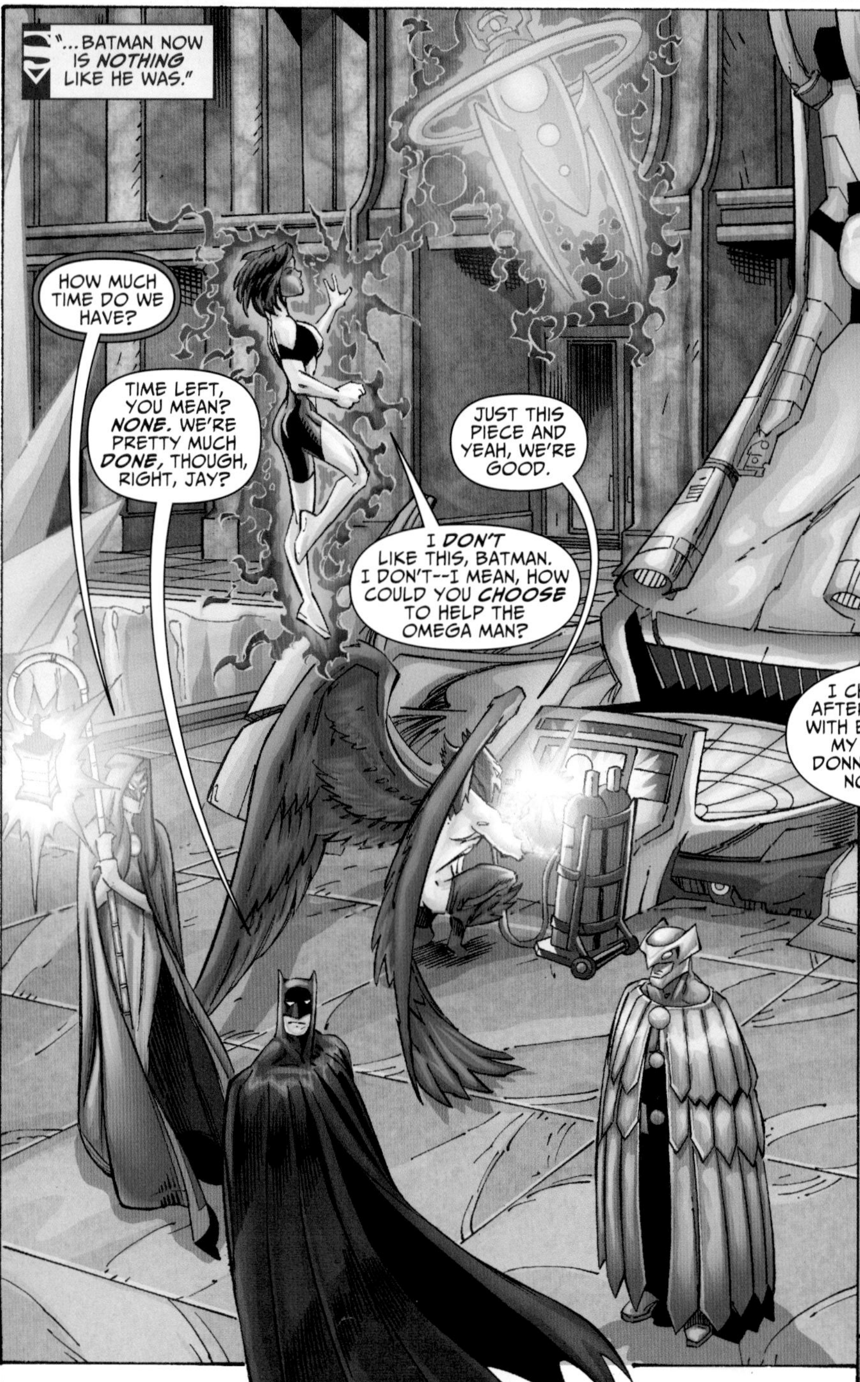
"...BATMAN NOW IS NOTHING LIKE HE WAS."
MY NAME IS JAY ABRAMS. BLUE JAY TO THE FEW OF YOU WHO KNOW OF ME OR CARE TO.
AND THIS IS MY LAST DAY ON EARTH.
HOW MUCH TIME DO WE HAVE?
TIME LEFT, YOU MEAN? NONE. WE'RE PRETTY MUCH DONE, THOUGH, RIGHT, JAY?
JUST THIS PIECE AND YEAH, WE'RE GOOD.
I DON'T LIKE THIS, BATMAN. I DON'T--I MEAN, HOW COULD YOU CHOOSE TO HELP THE OMEGA MAN?

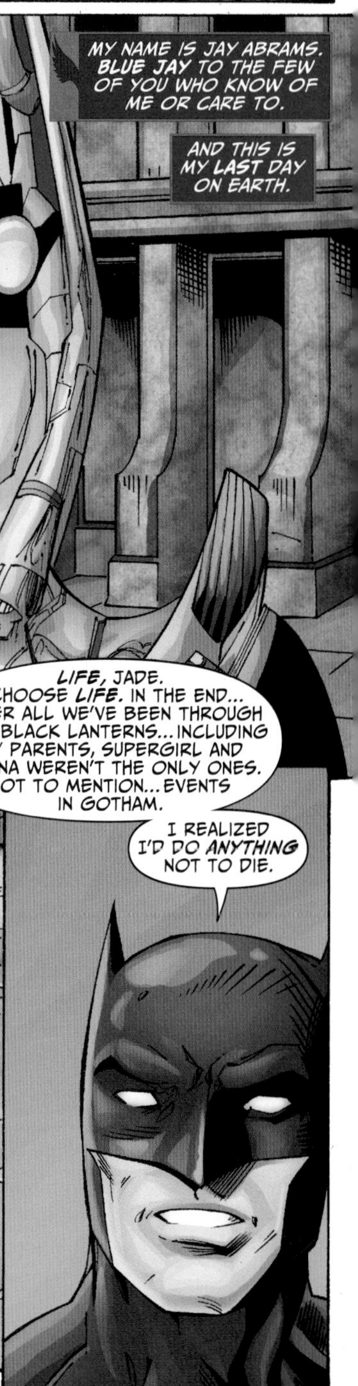
LIFE, JADE. I CHOOSE LIFE. IN THE END... AFTER ALL WE'VE BEEN THROUGH WITH BLACK LANTERNS...INCLUDING MY PARENTS, SUPERGIRL AND DONNA WEREN'T THE ONLY ONES. NOT TO MENTION...EVENTS IN GOTHAM.
I REALIZED I'D DO ANYTHING NOT TO DIE.

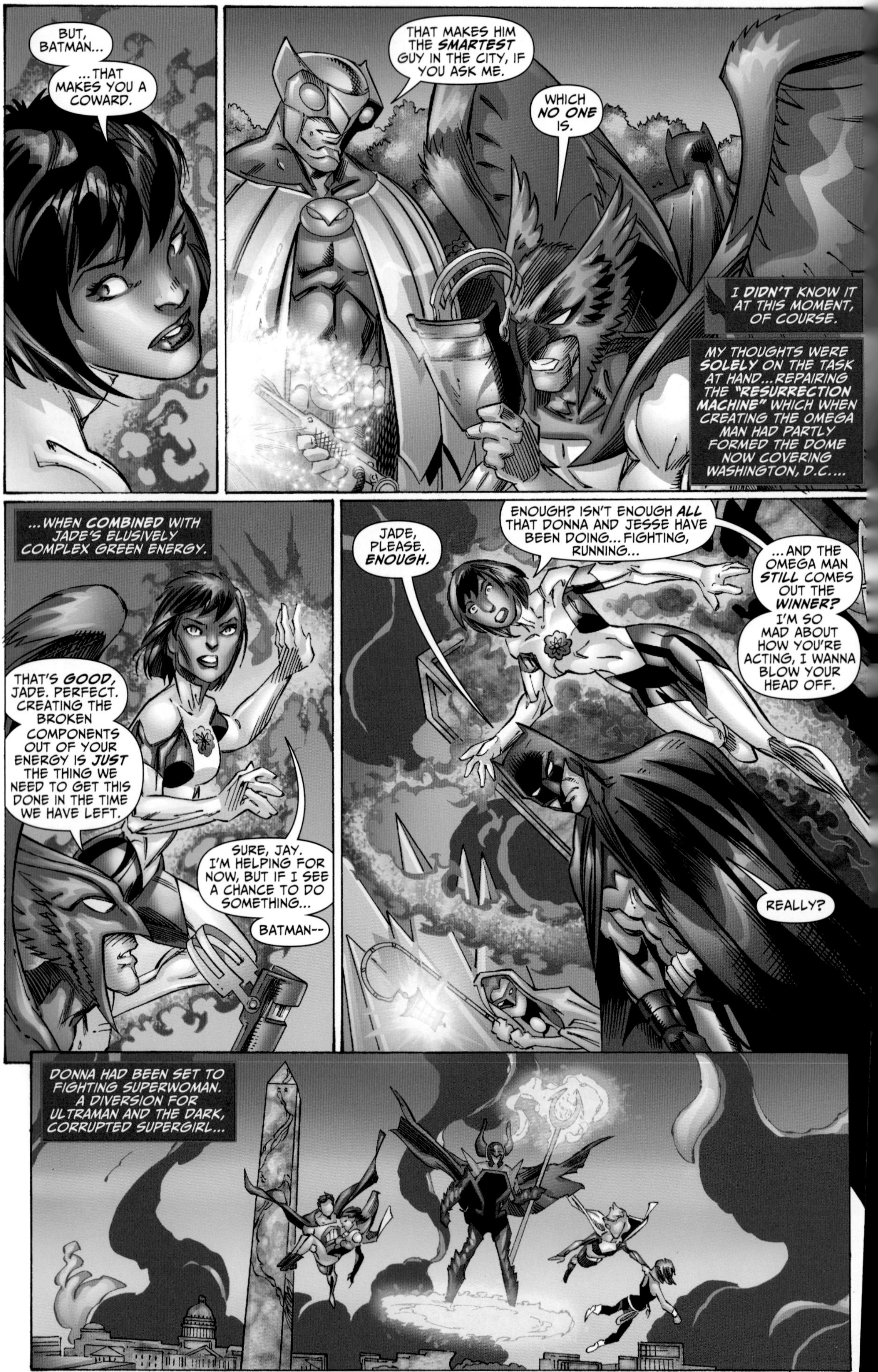

BUT, BATMAN...
...THAT MAKES YOU A COWARD.
THAT MAKES HIM THE SMARTEST GUY IN THE CITY, IF YOU ASK ME.
WHICH NO ONE IS.
I DIDN'T KNOW IT AT THIS MOMENT, OF COURSE.
MY THOUGHTS WERE SOLELY ON THE TASK AT HAND...REPAIRING THE "RESURRECTION MACHINE" WHICH WHEN CREATING THE OMEGA MAN HAD PARTLY FORMED THE DOME NOW COVERING WASHINGTON, D.C....
...WHEN COMBINED WITH JADE'S ELUSIVELY COMPLEX GREEN ENERGY.
THAT'S GOOD, JADE. PERFECT. CREATING THE BROKEN COMPONENTS OUT OF YOUR ENERGY IS JUST THE THING WE NEED TO GET THIS DONE IN THE TIME WE HAVE LEFT.
SURE, JAY. I'M HELPING FOR NOW, BUT IF I SEE A CHANCE TO DO SOMETHING...
BATMAN--
JADE, PLEASE. ENOUGH.
ENOUGH? ISN'T ENOUGH ALL THAT DONNA AND JESSE HAVE BEEN DOING...FIGHTING, RUNNING...
...AND THE OMEGA MAN STILL COMES OUT THE WINNER? I'M SO MAD ABOUT HOW YOU'RE ACTING, I WANNA BLOW YOUR HEAD OFF.
REALLY?
DONNA HAD BEEN SET TO FIGHTING SUPERWOMAN. A DIVERSION FOR ULTRAMAN AND THE DARK, CORRUPTED SUPERGIRL...

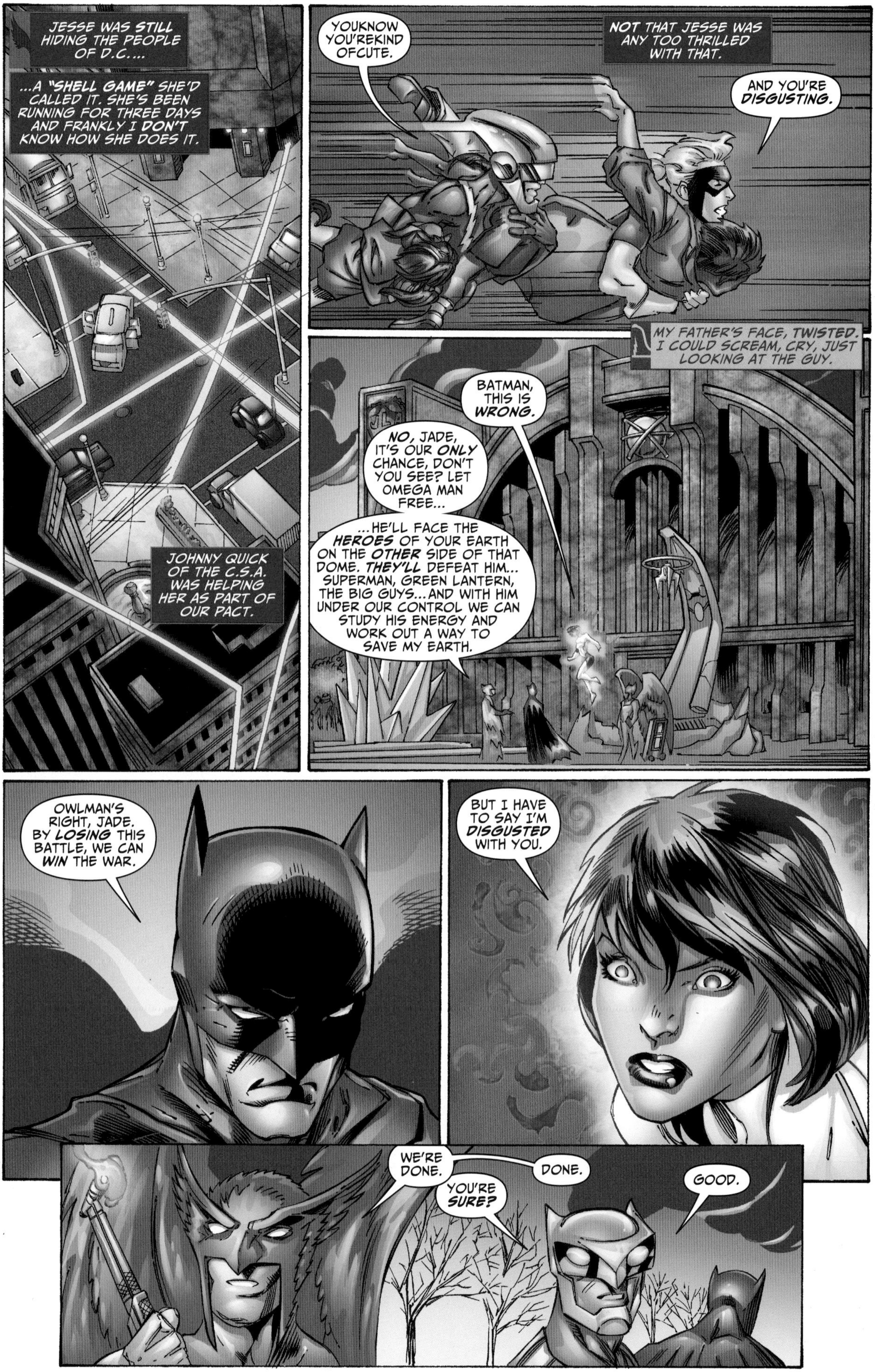
JESSE WAS STILL HIDING THE PEOPLE OF D.C....
...A "SHELL GAME" SHE'D CALLED IT. SHE'S BEEN RUNNING FOR THREE DAYS AND FRANKLY I DON'T KNOW HOW SHE DOES IT.
JOHNNY QUICK OF THE C.S.A. WAS HELPING HER AS PART OF OUR PACT.
YOUKNOW YOU'REKIND OFCUTE.
NOT THAT JESSE WAS ANY TOO THRILLED WITH THAT.
AND YOU'RE DISGUSTING.
MY FATHER'S FACE, TWISTED. I COULD SCREAM, CRY, JUST LOOKING AT THE GUY.
BATMAN, THIS IS WRONG.
NO, JADE, IT'S OUR ONLY CHANCE, DON'T YOU SEE? LET OMEGA MAN FREE...
...HE'LL FACE THE HEROES OF YOUR EARTH ON THE OTHER SIDE OF THAT DOME. THEY'LL DEFEAT HIM... SUPERMAN, GREEN LANTERN, THE BIG GUYS... AND WITH HIM UNDER OUR CONTROL WE CAN STUDY HIS ENERGY AND WORK OUT A WAY TO SAVE MY EARTH.
OWLMAN'S RIGHT, JADE. BY LOSING THIS BATTLE, WE CAN WIN THE WAR.
BUT I HAVE TO SAY I'M DISGUSTED WITH YOU.
WE'RE DONE.
YOU'RE SURE?
DONE.
GOOD.

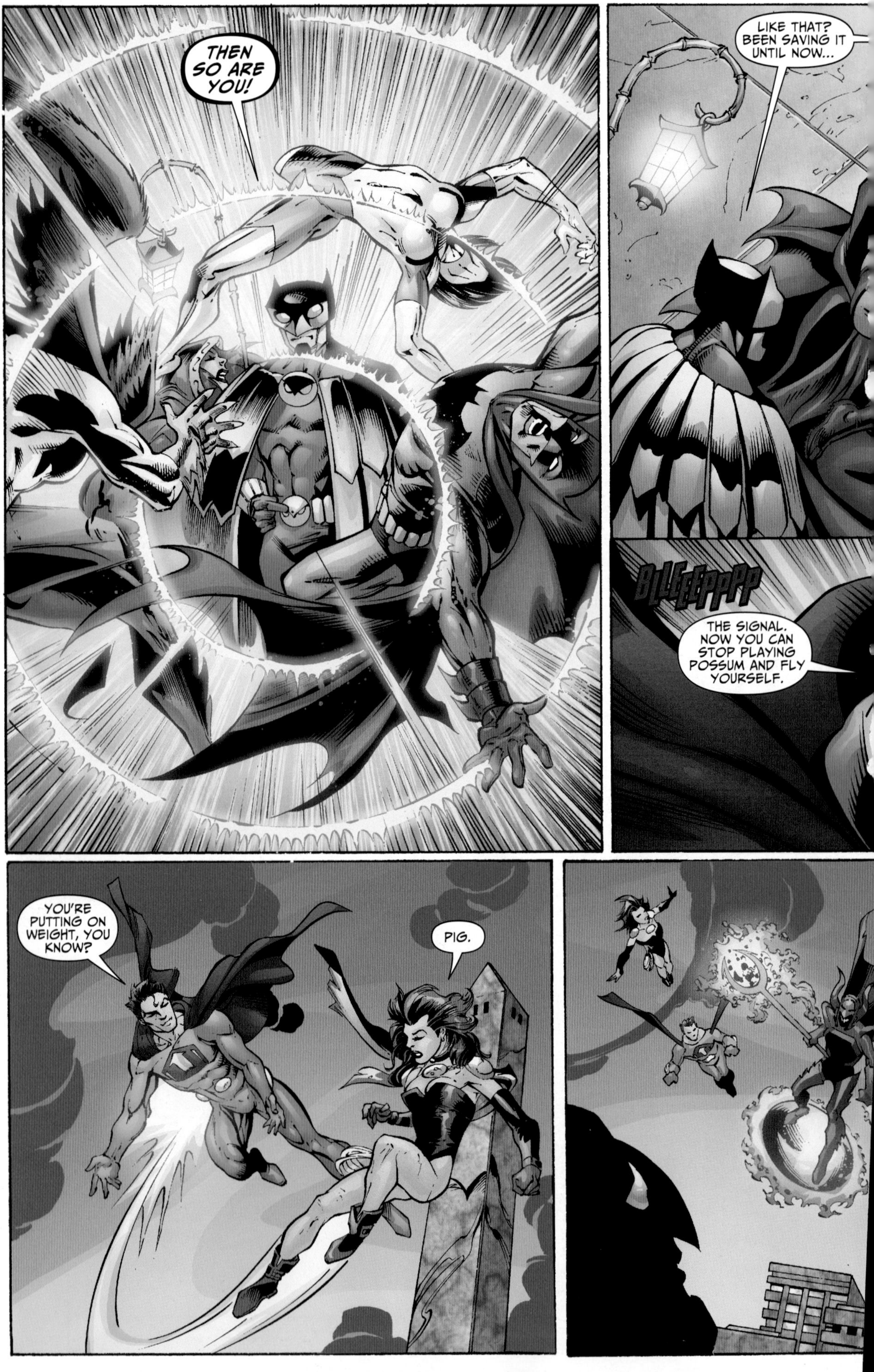
THEN SO ARE YOU!
LIKE THAT? BEEN SAVING IT UNTIL NOW...
BLLEEEEPPPP
THE SIGNAL. NOW YOU CAN STOP PLAYING POSSUM AND FLY YOURSELF.
YOU'RE PUTTING ON WEIGHT, YOU KNOW?
PIG.

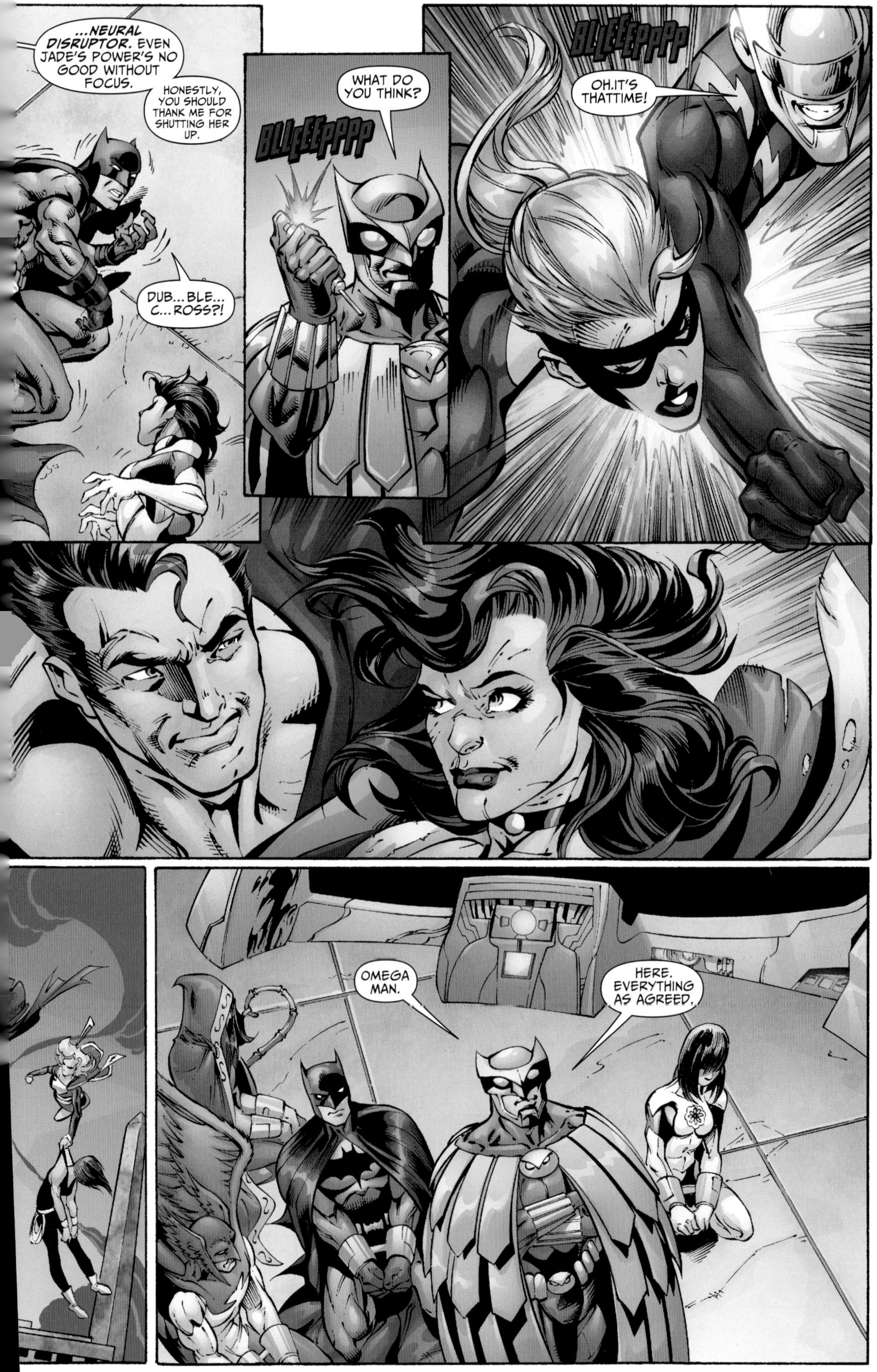
...NEURAL DISRUPTOR. EVEN JADE'S POWER'S NO GOOD WITHOUT FOCUS.
HONESTLY, YOU SHOULD THANK ME FOR SHUTTING HER UP.
DUB...BLE... C...ROSS?!
WHAT DO YOU THINK?
BLLEEEPPPP
BLLEEEPPPP
OH.IT'S THATTIME!
OMEGA MAN.
HERE. EVERYTHING AS AGREED.

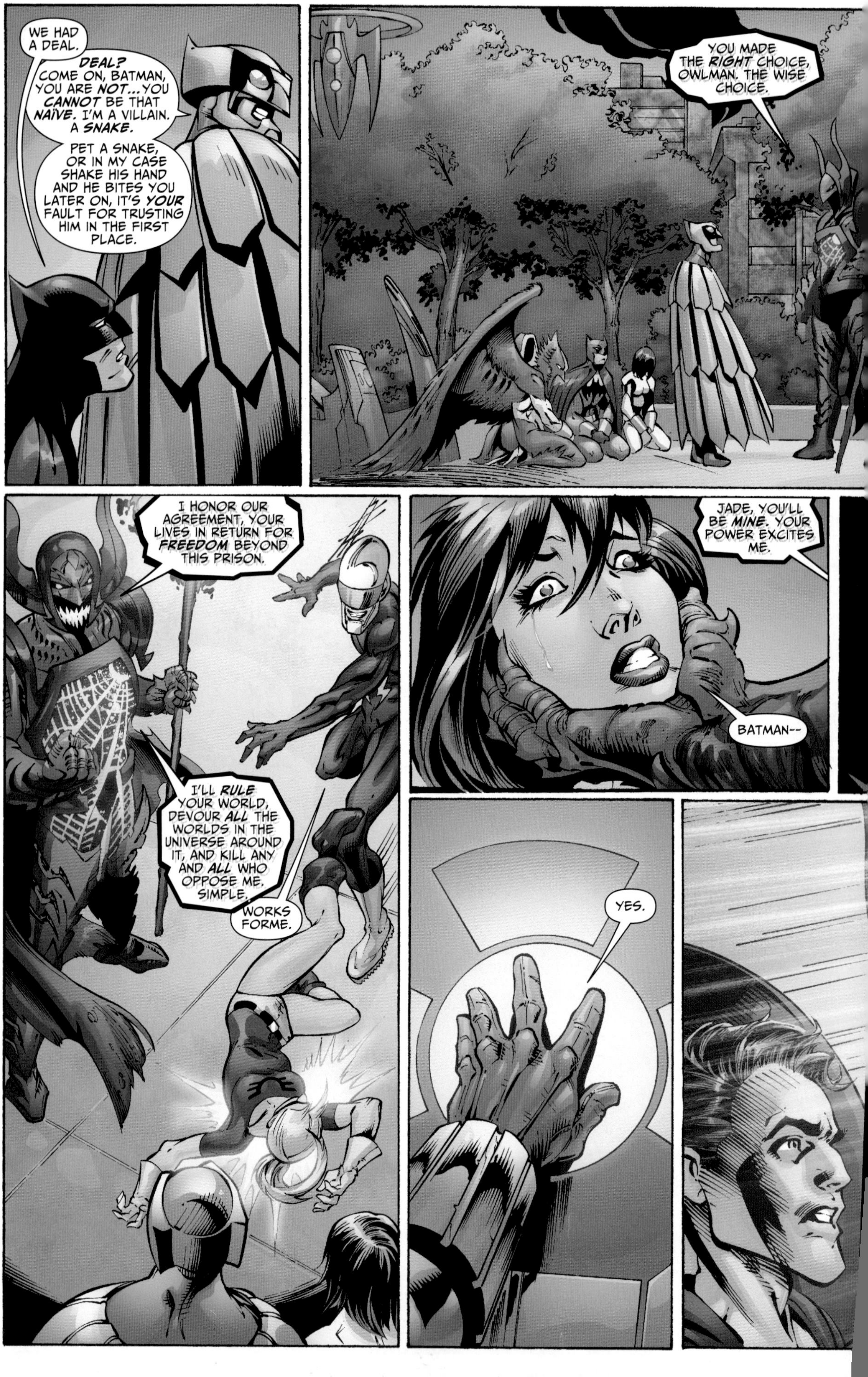
WE HAD A DEAL.
DEAL? COME ON, BATMAN, YOU ARE NOT...YOU CANNOT BE THAT NAÏVE. I'M A VILLAIN. A SNAKE.
PET A SNAKE, OR IN MY CASE SHAKE HIS HAND AND HE BITES YOU LATER ON, IT'S YOUR FAULT FOR TRUSTING HIM IN THE FIRST PLACE.
YOU MADE THE RIGHT CHOICE, OWLMAN. THE WISE CHOICE.
I HONOR OUR AGREEMENT, YOUR LIVES IN RETURN FOR FREEDOM BEYOND THIS PRISON.
I'LL RULE YOUR WORLD, DEVOUR ALL THE WORLDS IN THE UNIVERSE AROUND IT, AND KILL ANY AND ALL WHO OPPOSE ME. SIMPLE.
WORKS FORME.
JADE, YOU'LL BE MINE. YOUR POWER EXCITES ME.
BATMAN--
YES.

AND *WHAT* WAS THAT?

MY WORLD, THE CRIME SYNDICATE'S IS *GONE. DEAD.* TOOK ME A WHILE TO ACCEPT THAT, BUT I CAME AROUND. FOR *ONCE* ULTRAMAN HAD THE FORESIGHT I DIDN'T.

I'LL TAKE THAT AS A COMPLIMENT, I GUESS.

BETTER WE MAKE THIS WORLD *OURS,* WITH THE OMEGA MAN'S HELP. I'LL MAKE YOUR GOTHAM CITY *MINE...* LIKE MINE *WAS.*

I *CAN'T* BELIEVE I TRUSTED YOU.

YES, YOU REALLY WERE *OUTPLAYED.* THIS *WHOLE* TIME YOU'VE ALWAYS BEEN ONE STEP *BEHIND* ME. THE OMEGA MAN. EVERYTHING.

SO WHAT *NOW?*

I'M *SORRY,* JADE. I'VE--

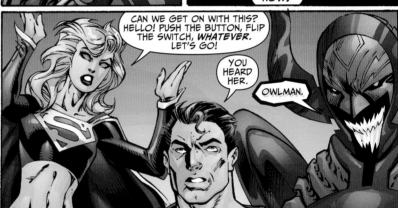

CAN WE GET ON WITH THIS? HELLO! PUSH THE BUTTON, FLIP THE SWITCH, *WHATEVER.* LET'S GO!

YOU HEARD HER.

OWLMAN.

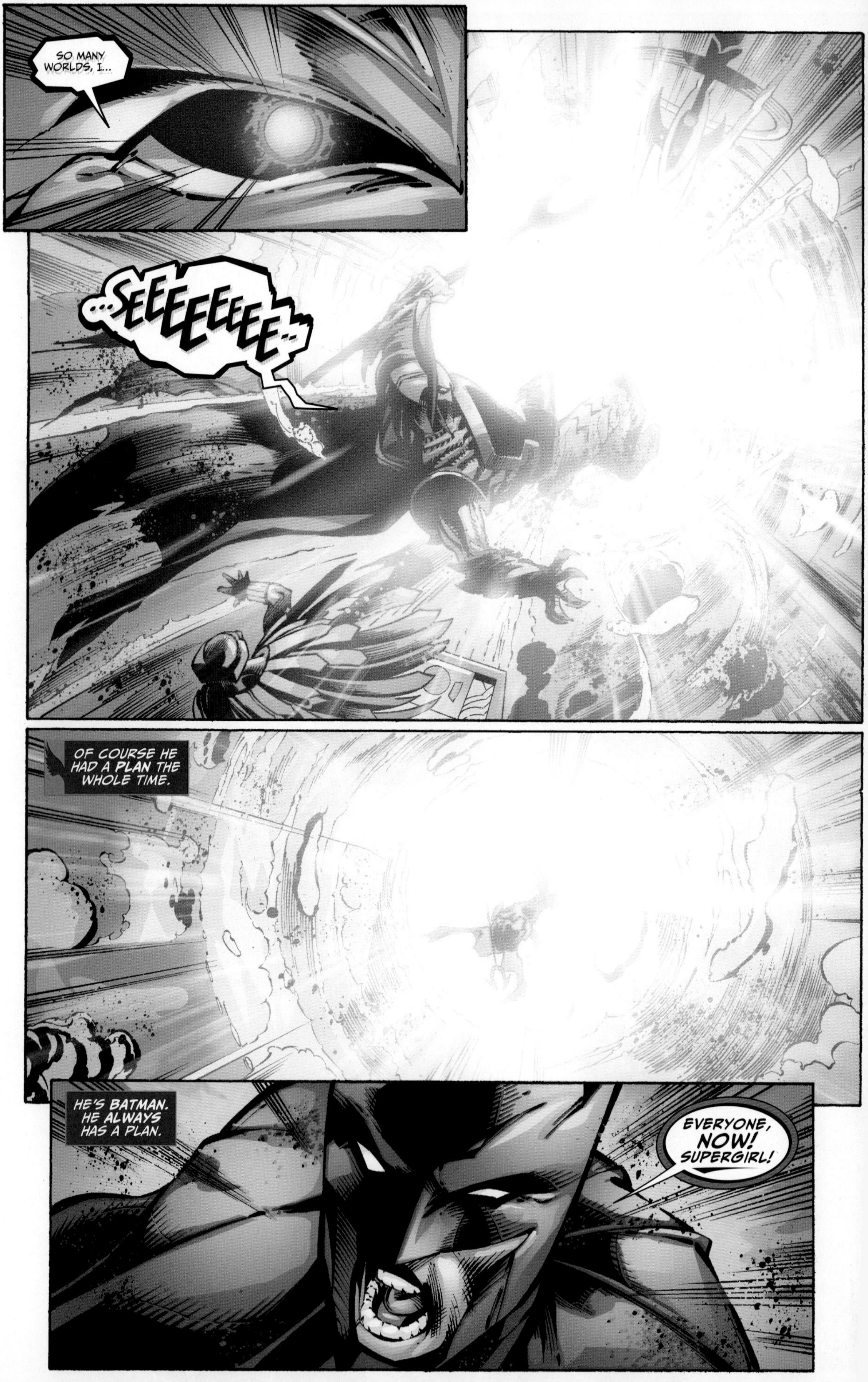
SO MANY WORLDS, I...
...SEEEEEEEE--
OF COURSE HE HAD A PLAN THE WHOLE TIME.
HE'S BATMAN. HE ALWAYS HAS A PLAN.
EVERYONE, NOW! SUPERGIRL!

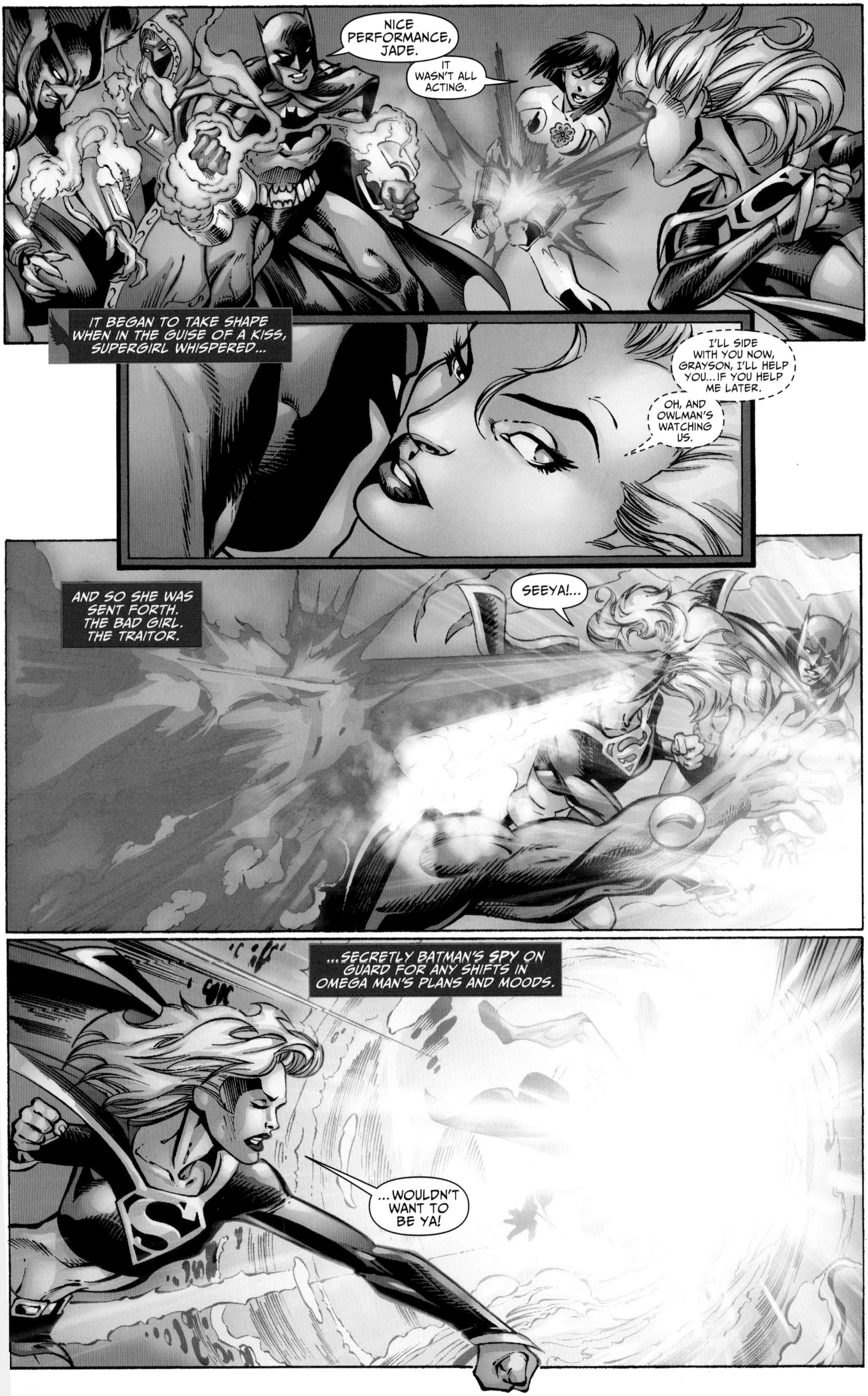
NICE PERFORMANCE, JADE.
IT WASN'T ALL ACTING.
IT BEGAN TO TAKE SHAPE WHEN IN THE GUISE OF A KISS, SUPERGIRL WHISPERED...
I'LL SIDE WITH YOU NOW, GRAYSON, I'LL HELP YOU...IF YOU HELP ME LATER.
OH, AND OWLMAN'S WATCHING US.
AND SO SHE WAS SENT FORTH. THE BAD GIRL. THE TRAITOR.
SEEYA!...
...SECRETLY BATMAN'S SPY ON GUARD FOR ANY SHIFTS IN OMEGA MAN'S PLANS AND MOODS.
...WOULDN'T WANT TO BE YA!

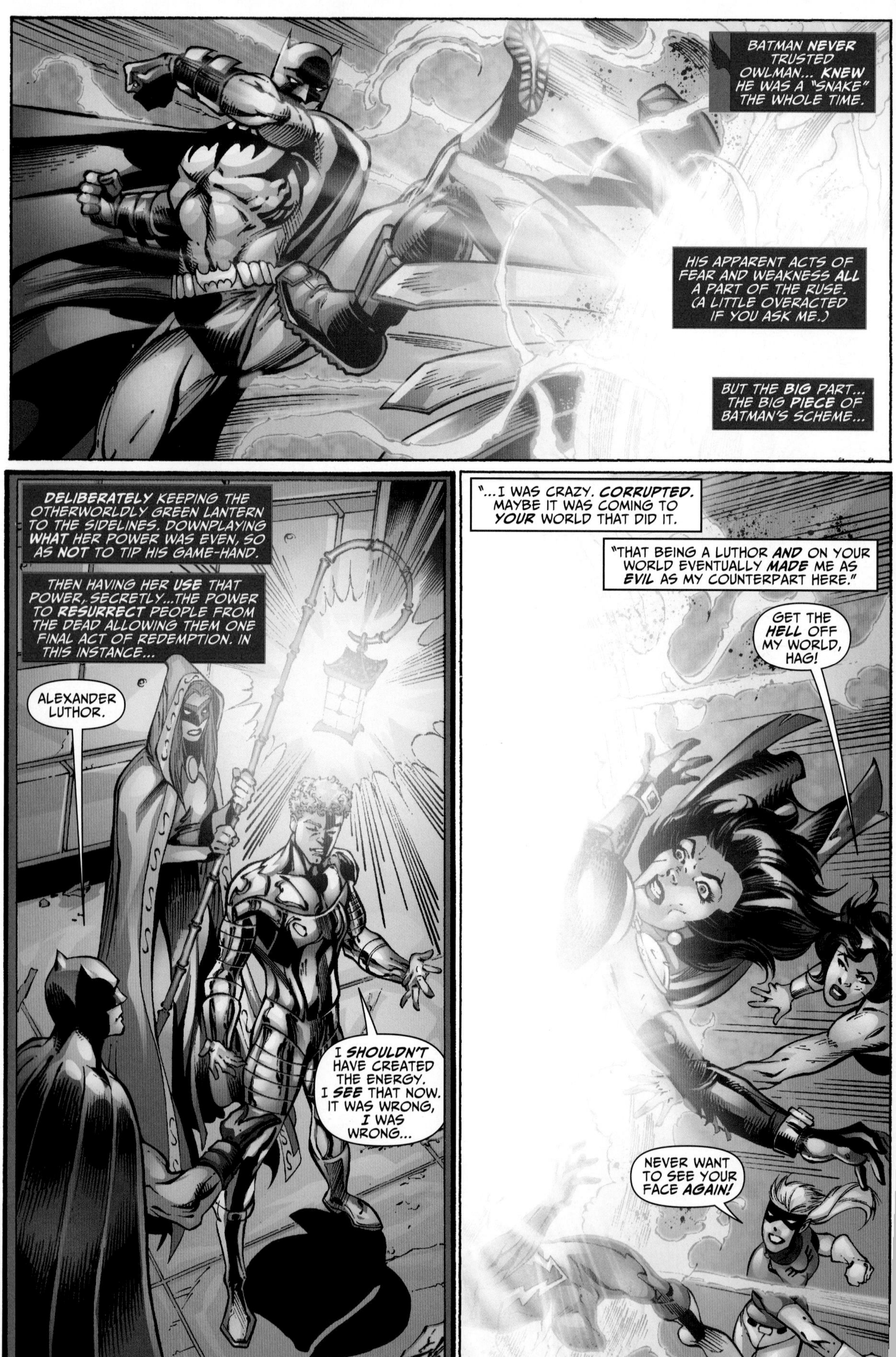

BATMAN NEVER TRUSTED OWLMAN... KNEW HE WAS A "SNAKE" THE WHOLE TIME.
HIS APPARENT ACTS OF FEAR AND WEAKNESS ALL A PART OF THE RUSE. (A LITTLE OVERACTED IF YOU ASK ME.)
BUT THE BIG PART... THE BIG PIECE OF BATMAN'S SCHEME...
DELIBERATELY KEEPING THE OTHERWORLDLY GREEN LANTERN TO THE SIDELINES. DOWNPLAYING WHAT HER POWER WAS EVEN, SO AS NOT TO TIP HIS GAME-HAND.
THEN HAVING HER USE THAT POWER, SECRETLY...THE POWER TO RESURRECT PEOPLE FROM THE DEAD ALLOWING THEM ONE FINAL ACT OF REDEMPTION. IN THIS INSTANCE...
ALEXANDER LUTHOR.
I SHOULDN'T HAVE CREATED THE ENERGY. I SEE THAT NOW. IT WAS WRONG, I WAS WRONG...
"...I WAS CRAZY. CORRUPTED. MAYBE IT WAS COMING TO YOUR WORLD THAT DID IT.
"THAT BEING A LUTHOR AND ON YOUR WORLD EVENTUALLY MADE ME AS EVIL AS MY COUNTERPART HERE."
GET THE HELL OFF MY WORLD, HAG!
NEVER WANT TO SEE YOUR FACE AGAIN!

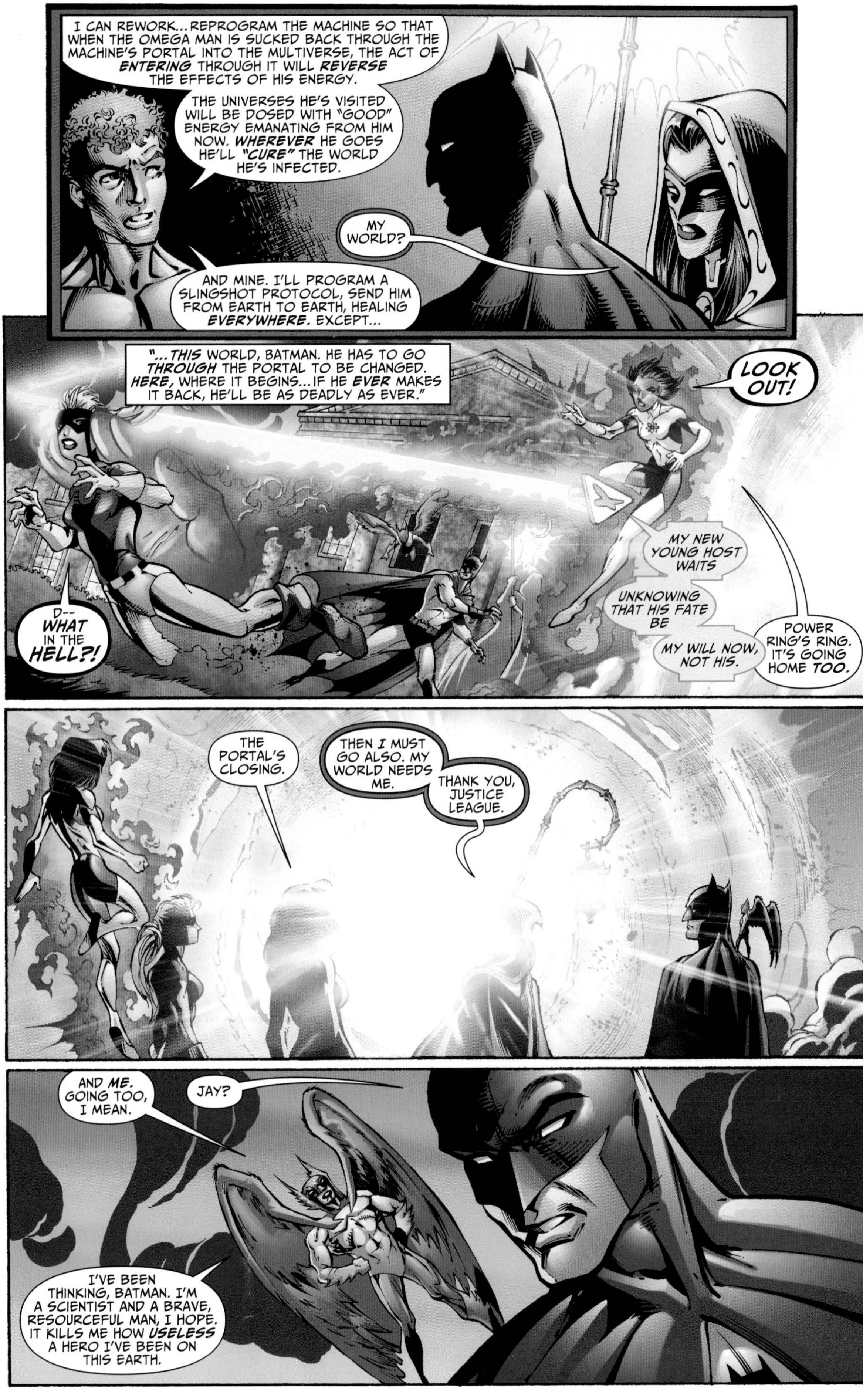
I CAN REWORK...REPROGRAM THE MACHINE SO THAT WHEN THE OMEGA MAN IS SUCKED BACK THROUGH THE MACHINE'S PORTAL INTO THE MULTIVERSE, THE ACT OF ENTERING THROUGH IT WILL REVERSE THE EFFECTS OF HIS ENERGY.
THE UNIVERSES HE'S VISITED WILL BE DOSED WITH "GOOD" ENERGY EMANATING FROM HIM NOW. WHEREVER HE GOES HE'LL "CURE" THE WORLD HE'S INFECTED.
MY WORLD?
AND MINE. I'LL PROGRAM A SLINGSHOT PROTOCOL, SEND HIM FROM EARTH TO EARTH, HEALING EVERYWHERE. EXCEPT...
"...THIS WORLD, BATMAN. HE HAS TO GO THROUGH THE PORTAL TO BE CHANGED. HERE, WHERE IT BEGINS...IF HE EVER MAKES IT BACK, HE'LL BE AS DEADLY AS EVER."
LOOK OUT!
D-- WHAT IN THE HELL?!
MY NEW YOUNG HOST WAITS
UNKNOWING THAT HIS FATE BE
MY WILL NOW, NOT HIS.
POWER RING'S RING. IT'S GOING HOME TOO.
THE PORTAL'S CLOSING.
THEN I MUST GO ALSO. MY WORLD NEEDS ME.
THANK YOU, JUSTICE LEAGUE.
AND ME. GOING TOO, I MEAN.
JAY?
I'VE BEEN THINKING, BATMAN. I'M A SCIENTIST AND A BRAVE, RESOURCEFUL MAN, I HOPE. IT KILLS ME HOW USELESS A HERO I'VE BEEN ON THIS EARTH.

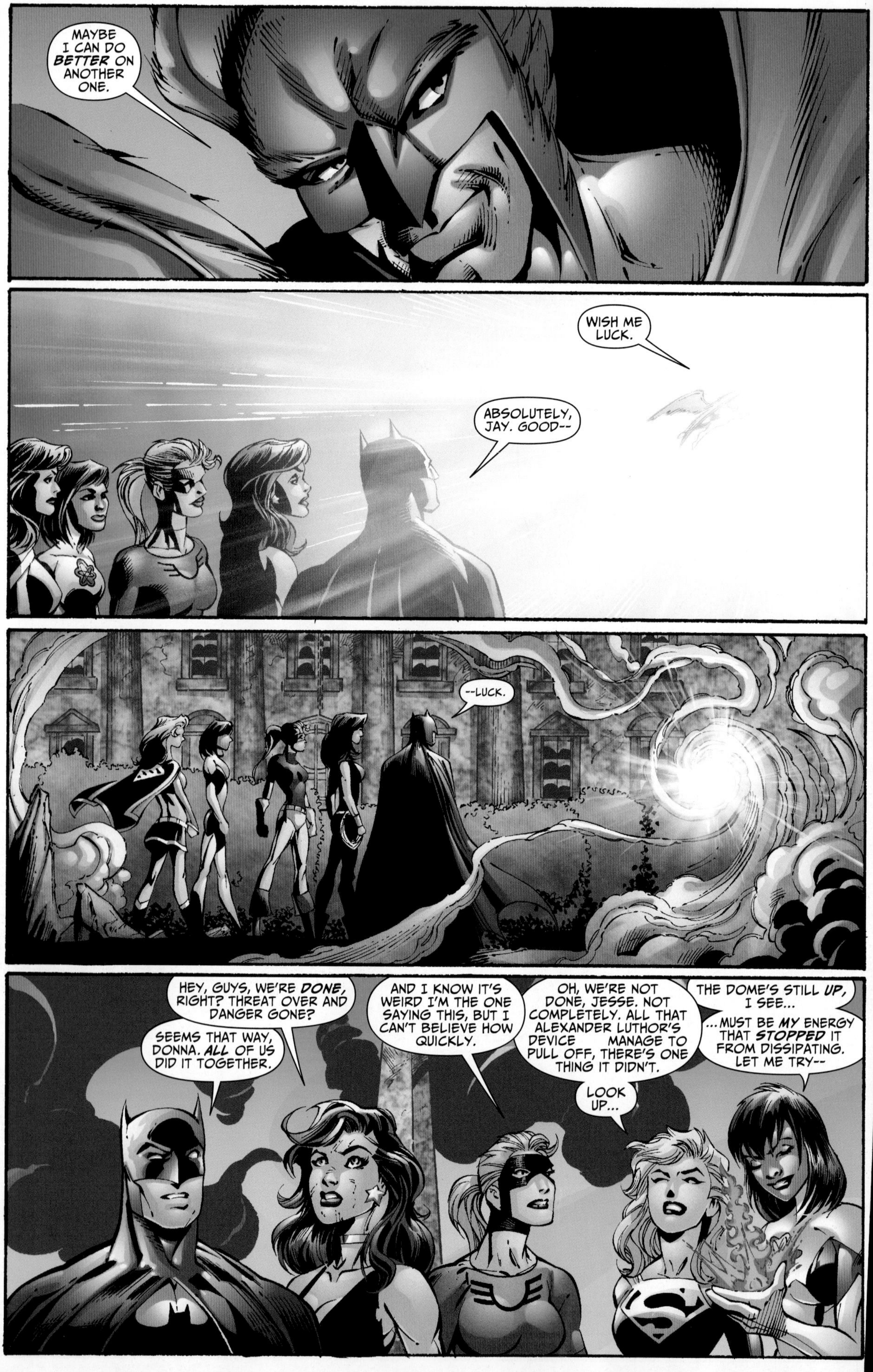
MAYBE I CAN DO *BETTER* ON ANOTHER ONE.
WISH ME LUCK.
ABSOLUTELY, JAY. GOOD--
--LUCK.
HEY, GUYS, WE'RE *DONE*, RIGHT? THREAT OVER AND DANGER GONE?
SEEMS THAT WAY, DONNA. *ALL* OF US DID IT TOGETHER.
AND I KNOW IT'S WEIRD I'M THE ONE SAYING THIS, BUT I CAN'T BELIEVE HOW QUICKLY.
OH, WE'RE NOT DONE, JESSE. NOT COMPLETELY. ALL THAT ALEXANDER LUTHOR'S DEVICE MANAGE TO PULL OFF, THERE'S ONE THING IT DIDN'T.
LOOK UP...
THE DOME'S STILL *UP*, I SEE...
...MUST BE *MY* ENERGY THAT *STOPPED* IT FROM DISSIPATING. LET ME TRY--

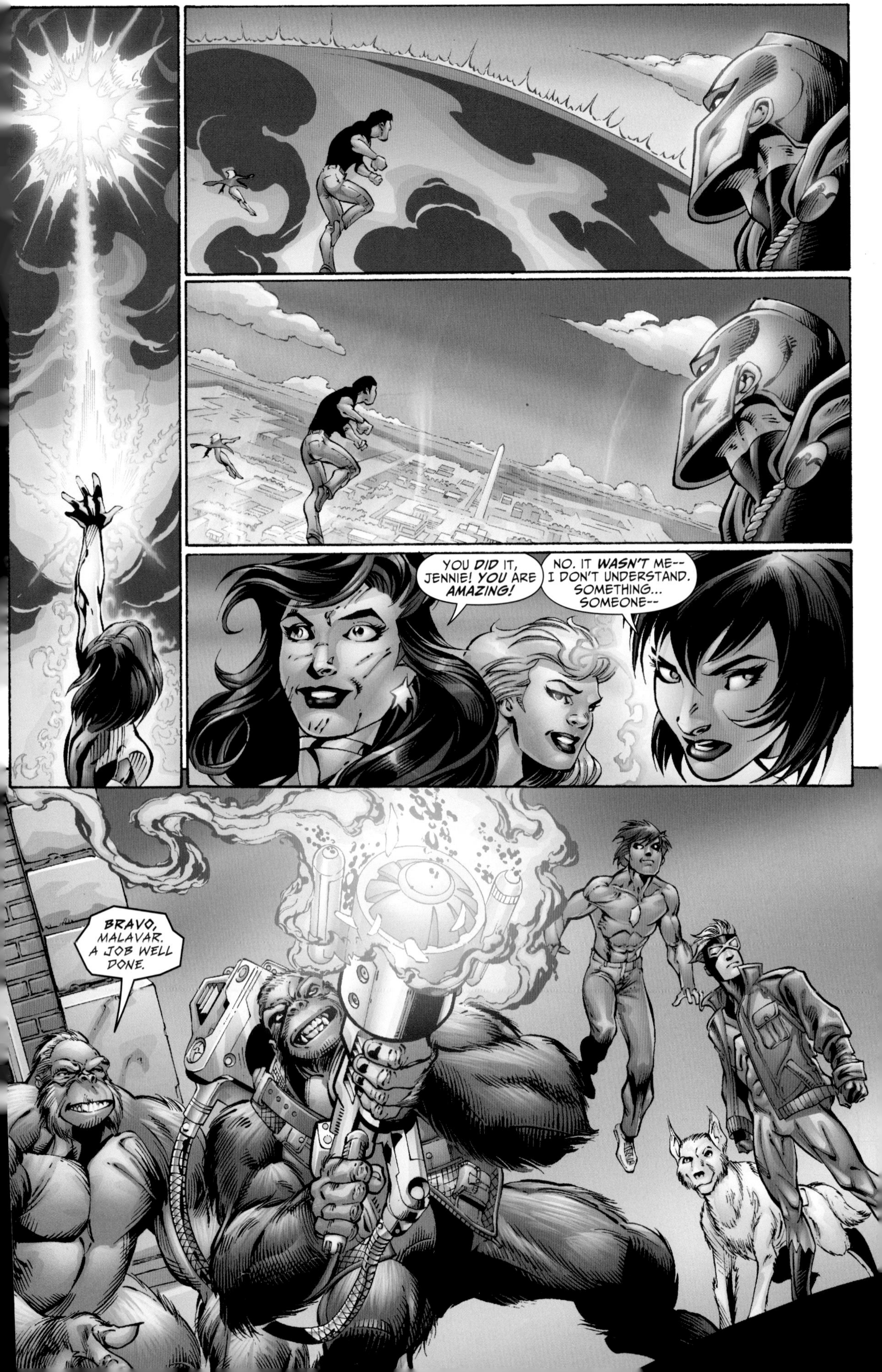
YOU *DID* IT, JENNIE! *YOU* ARE *AMAZING!*
NO. IT *WASN'T* ME-- I DON'T UNDERSTAND. SOMETHING... SOMEONE--
BRAVO, MALAVAR. A JOB WELL DONE.

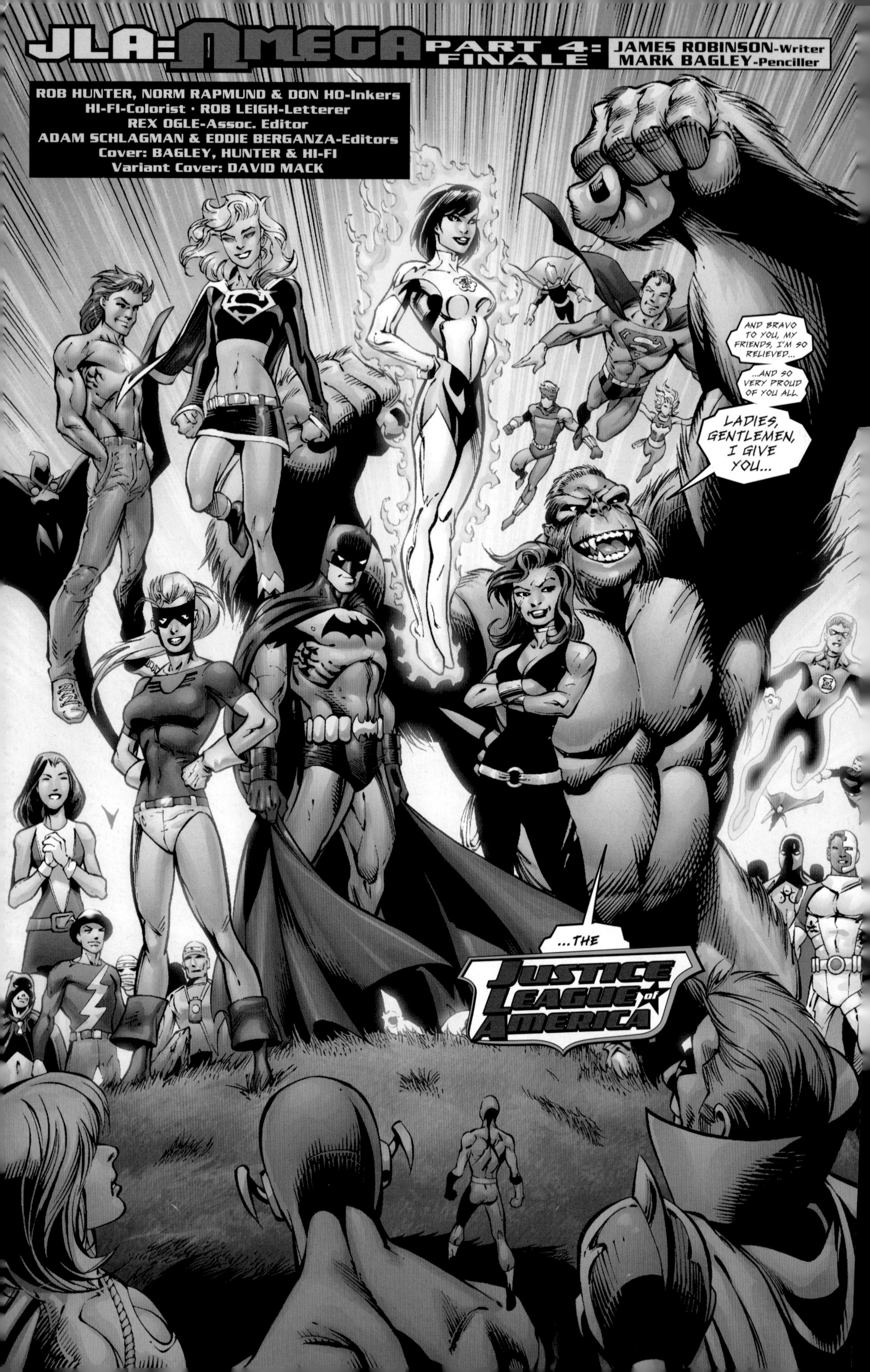
JLA: OMEGA PART 4: FINALE
JAMES ROBINSON-Writer
MARK BAGLEY-Penciller
ROB HUNTER, NORM RAPMUND & DON HO-Inkers
HI-FI-Colorist · ROB LEIGH-Letterer
REX OGLE-Assoc. Editor
ADAM SCHLAGMAN & EDDIE BERGANZA-Editors
Cover: BAGLEY, HUNTER & HI-FI
Variant Cover: DAVID MACK
AND BRAVO TO YOU, MY FRIENDS, I'M SO RELIEVED...
...AND SO VERY PROUD OF YOU ALL.
LADIES, GENTLEMEN, I GIVE YOU...
...THE
JUSTICE LEAGUE of AMERICA

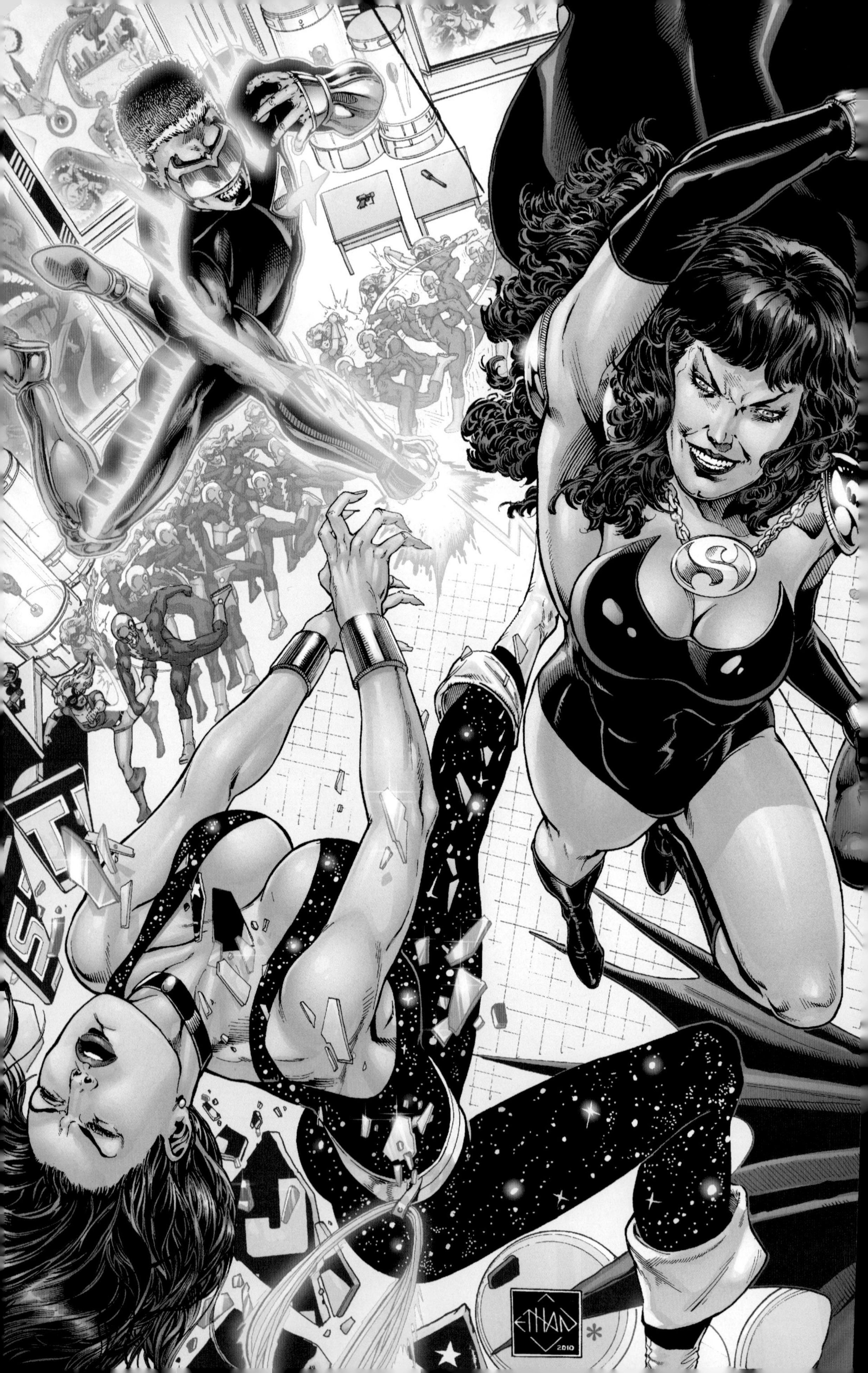

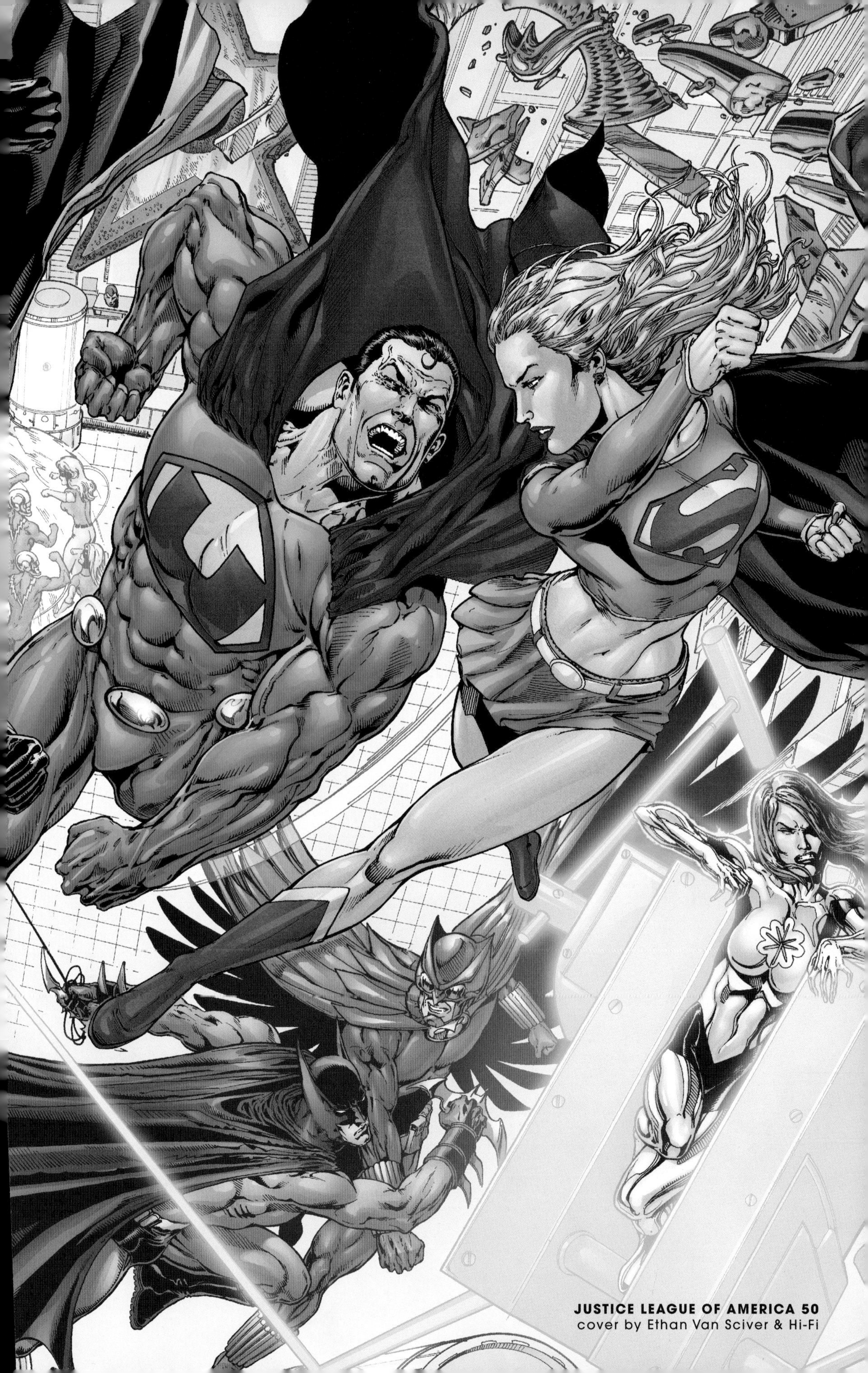

JUSTICE LEAGUE OF AMERICA 50
cover by Ethan Van Sciver & Hi-Fi

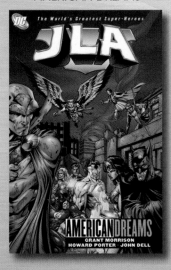

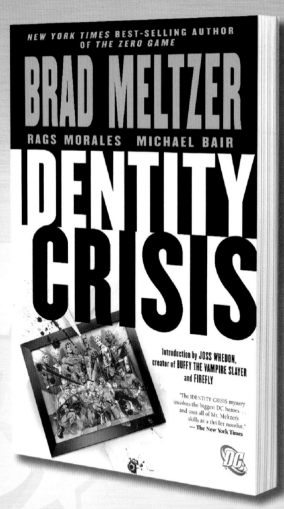